GLOBALIZATION IN LATIN AMERICA

The approach of Latin American countries to preferential trade agreements (PTAs) is a fascinating topic. There is a rich history of policymakers using PTAs to pursue different economic and political models of integration. What really stands out is the diversity of approaches and attitudes to the use of PTAs. While some countries have been rule-makers and have made innovative attempts to introduce new issues, others have been reluctant to use PTAs. In response to the growing interest in and politicization of PTAs in the wider public – including renewed consideration of 'with whom to trade' – this book brings together scholars from inside and outside Latin America to address the past, present and future challenges associated with PTAs. The contributions, from a variety of disciplinary backgrounds, offer new insights into issues related to the design, diffusion and impact of PTAs. This title is also available as open access on Cambridge Core.

Manfred Elsig is Professor at the World Trade Institute, University of Bern. His research focuses on international political economy and international institutions. He is a co-founder of the Design of Trade Agreement database (DESTA) and the co-editor of the journal *World Trade Review*. Recent publications include *The Concept Design of a Twenty-First Century Preferential Trade Agreement* (Cambridge University Press, 2024).

Rodrigo Polanco is Senior Lecturer, Researcher and Academic Coordinator at the World Trade Institute, University of Bern; Legal Adviser at the Swiss Institute of Comparative Law; and Visiting Professor at the University of Chile. He has published extensively on investment, trade, tax and environmental law with leading international academic publishers and journals.

Andrew Lugg is Assistant Professor at the University of Nevada, Las Vegas. His research focuses on international political economy and international organizations. His work has appeared in academic journals including *International Studies Quarterly*, *Review of International Organizations*, *Journal of Conflict Resolution* and *Journal of International Economic Law*.

Globalization in Latin America

THE LAW, POLITICS AND ECONOMICS OF PREFERENTIAL TRADE AGREEMENTS

Edited by

MANFRED ELSIG
University of Bern

RODRIGO POLANCO
University of Bern

ANDREW LUGG
University of Nevada, Las Vegas

CAMBRIDGE
UNIVERSITY PRESS

CAMBRIDGE
UNIVERSITY PRESS

Shaftesbury Road, Cambridge CB2 8EA, United Kingdom

One Liberty Plaza, 20th Floor, New York, NY 10006, USA

477 Williamstown Road, Port Melbourne, VIC 3207, Australia

314–321, 3rd Floor, Plot 3, Splendor Forum, Jasola District Centre, New Delhi – 110025, India

103 Penang Road, #05–06/07, Visioncrest Commercial, Singapore 238467

Cambridge University Press is part of Cambridge University Press & Assessment, a department of the University of Cambridge.

We share the University's mission to contribute to society through the pursuit of education, learning and research at the highest international levels of excellence.

www.cambridge.org
Information on this title: www.cambridge.org/9781009568081

DOI: 10.1017/9781009568067

When citing this work, please include a reference to the DOI 10.1017/9781009568067

First published 2025

A catalogue record for this publication is available from the British Library

A Cataloging-in-Publication data record for this book is available from the Library of Congress

ISBN 978-1-009-56808-1 Hardback

Contents

Figures

Tables

Contributors

Nicolás Albertoni is the Deputy Minister of Foreign Affairs of Uruguay. He is a Fulbright-Laspau Scholar and Professor at the Universidad Católica del Uruguay. He is an active researcher at the Uruguayan National System for Researchers (SNI-ANII). He received a PhD in political science and international relations from the University of Southern California (USC) and a PhD in business administration from the Catholic University of Argentina. He received a master's degree in economics, a master's degree in politics both from USC and a master's degree in Latin American studies from Georgetown University´s School of Foreign Service, and a BA in international business and integration from the Catholic University of Uruguay. He is the author of three books: *Uruguay como solución: Un análisis sobre su insercion interncional* (Penguin Press, 2019); *Instrucciones para inventar la rueda* (Penguin Press, 2014) and *Entre el barrio y el mundo ¿Mercosur o el modelo Chileno?* (Penguin Press, 2011). His opinion articles have been featured in the *New York Times*, *El País* (Spain), CNN and *El País* (Uruguay).

José Manuel Álvarez Zárate is Professor and Researcher at the Economic Law Department Director of the Universidad Externado de Colombia. His areas of interest are international trade and investment law, Andean Community law and, in general, international economic law. During his professional career, he has worked as an advisor on matters related to international commercial law, international arbitration, and Community law of the Andean Community of Nations, in the sectors of mining, port concessions and waste disposal, telecommunications and services. Also, he was an advisor to the private sector in the negotiations for the conformation of the Free Trade Area of the Americas and the Free Trade Agreement with the United States, and has collaborated in the drafting of laws and decrees related to international trade, arbitration and competition, among others. He has been a litigator before national and international courts, in disputes related to intellectual property, competition law, services, distribution and agency agreements, telecommunications and mining. He has almost thirty years of experience as a professor and lecturer on topics related to international law, and international economic and investment law. He has more than fifty publications in books and specialized magazines, and is the general editor of the *International Economic Law Collection* and the *Con-Texto Journal of the Economic Law Department* of Universidad Externado de Colombia Law School.

Amrita Bahri is an associate professor of international trade law at the Instituto Tecnológico Autónomo de México (ITAM) and Co-Chair Professor for the WTO Chair Program (Mexico). Dr Bahri has published in the areas of international trade law, WTO dispute settlement, capacity-building in emerging economies, trade and gender. Her work has been published in prestigious journals, including the *Journal of International Economic Law*, *World Trade Review*, *Journal of World Trade*, *Trade, Law & Development*, *Global Trade & Customs Journal*, and *Journal of International Trade Law & Policy*. Dr Bahri has been appointed by the European Commission to the pool of candidates to chair the Expert Panel Proceedings on Trade and Sustainable Development. She also serves as an Advisory Board Member of the Center on Inclusive Trade and Development at Georgetown University. Working with the International Trade Centre (ITC)'s team, she has designed the very first framework to measure the gender-responsiveness of free trade agreements. She explains this framework in ITC's policy paper titled 'Mainstreaming Gender in Free Trade Agreements'.

Diana María Beltrán Vargas is a lecturer in international economic law at Universidad Externado de Colombia. Her areas of interest are public international law and international economic law, particularly investment law. Professionally, she has worked in litigation and private counselling, in matters related to commercial arbitration and contracts. She is currently a lecturer in the undergraduate course of international litigation, and coordinates Universidad Externado de Colombia teams for the FDI Moot Court and the Philip C. Jessup International Law Moot Court Competition. She has co-authored chapters of books related to dispute resolution methods and international investment law, and has participated in conferences on the same topics. She holds an undergraduate degree in law and a postgraduate degree in contract law and legal business relations from the Universidad Externado de Colombia, and a master's degree (LLM) in international commercial law from the University of Leicester, United Kingdom.

Andrés Bórquez is an assistant professor at the Institute of International Studies, University of Chile (since 2019). He holds a doctorate in international politics from Fudan University, China; a master's degree in social policy from the University of Paris 1, France; a bachelor's degree in international negotiations from the University of Valparaíso, Chile; and a bachelor's degree in management from Montpellier Business School, France. He is the coordinator of the master's programme in Development and International Cooperation and of the Diploma Coordinator in

Asian Studies and Diploma Coordinator in Chinese Studies at the University of Chile. His awards and recognitions include the Recognition Medal for his contribution to bilateral relations between Chile and China, awarded by the Chilean Ministry of Foreign Affairs (2020), the Membership of the Civil Society Council of the Undersecretary of International Economic Relations (2022), and the Chile Scholarship for Postgraduate studies in 2015. He is the co-editor of the book *China's Trade Policy in Latin America* and *Relations between Chile and China: A Comprehensive Focus* (with Dorotea López, Felipe Muñoz and Guoyou Song, Springer, 2022). He is a principal researcher at the Millennium Nucleus on the Impacts of China in countries of Latin America and the Caribbean.

Javiera Cáceres is an instructor professor at the Institute of International Studies of the University of Chile, a legal research fellow at the Centre for International Sustainable Development Law (CISDL) and PhD fellow at the International Development department, London School of Economics and Political Science, United Kingdom. She holds a BA in English literature and linguistics from the Pontifical Catholic University of Chile and an MA in international strategy and trade policy from the University of Chile. She has been a consultant for the World Bank, Interamerican Development Bank, ECLAC, and the Chilean Under-Secretariat of International Economic Affairs on international trade and trade policy issues. Her main research interests are international development, intellectual property and artificial intelligence, trade policy, and gender and trade.

Julia Calvert is a senior lecturer in international political economy at the University of Edinburgh. Her research focuses on international political economy, domestic norms, Latin American politics, international investment law and international organizations. She is the author of *The Politics of Investment Treaties in Latin America* (2022, Oxford University Press), which examines the reform of international investment law in Ecuador, Peru, and Argentina. Her work has also appeared in the *Review of International Political Economy*, *New Political Economy*, the *Canadian Journal of Foreign Policy*, and edited volumes.

María Camila Camargo Moncayo is a legal advisor at the Instituto Geográfico Agustín Codazzi, supporting the implementation of the multipurpose cadastre policy established under Colombia's Peace Agreement. She holds a law degree and a master's degree in International Affairs from Universidad Externado de Colombia. She specializes in public law, and has experience as a legal advisor, researcher, and professor of constitutional and international law. Additionally, she has co-authored chapters in books on constitutional law, environmental governance, and trade agreements.

Daniela Campello is an associate professor of politics and international affairs at the Getúlio Vargas Foundation, in Brazil. Campello received her PhD in political science from UCLA and was formerly an assistant professor at Princeton University. She was also Oxford-CAF Visiting Fellow at Oxford University and a Resident

Fellow at the Wilson Center for International Scholars. Campello's research lies at the frontier of international and comparative political economy, with a particular focus on the consequences of globalization for domestic politics in emerging economies. Her work has been published in leading political science journals, and she is the author of *The Politics of Market Discipline in Latin America* (Cambridge University Press, 2015), and co-author of *The Volatility Curse* (with Cesar Zucco, Cambridge University Press, 2020).

Letícia Daibert is a PhD candidate at Facultad Latinoamericana de Ciencias Sociales –FLACSO-Argentina, and an associate manager at Accenture. She has a law degree and an MA in international law, both from Universidade Federal de Minas Gerais (Brazil), with a period of academic exchange at Universidad Nacional del Litoral (Argentina) and at Herder-Institut, Universität Leipzig (Germany). She also has an LLM in international relations from the Faculdades Integradas Milton Campos (Brazil). Her research focuses on WTO, the multilateral dispute settlement, sustainability and the new economy, always under the perspective of developing countries.

Valentina Delich is a professor and researcher at FLACSO-Argentina, where she currently holds the Executive Director position. Delich holds a PhD in international public law from the University of Buenos Aires. Her research focuses on international economic relations, multilateral and regional trade, intellectual property, and Latin American development. She is frequently called to work for governments and international organizations on trade-related matters.

Andreas Dür is a professor of international politics at the University of Salzburg, Austria. He holds a PhD from the European University Institute in Florence (2004). Dür has published several books and more than fifty peer-reviewed articles on trade policy, interest group politics and European integration. Since 2017, he has been the principal investigator of the TRADEPOWER project, which is financed by the European Research Council.

Manfred Elsig is Full Professor of International Relations and Deputy Managing Director of the World Trade Institute, University of Bern. He was the Director of the National Centre of Competence in Research (NCCR) on Trade Regulation (www.nccr-trade.org) from 2013 to 2017. He holds a PhD in political science from the University of Zurich. His research focuses on international political economy, international organizations, international courts, preferential trade agreements and European trade policy. He is the author of a large number of publications in journals such as *European Union Politics*, the *European Journal of International Relations*, *International Studies Quarterly*, *Review of International Political Economy*, and *World Trade Review*. He is the co-editor of *Governing the WTO: Past, Present and Beyond Doha* (Cambridge University Press, 2011), *Assessing the World Trade Organization: Fit for Purpose?* (Cambridge University Press, 2017), and *The Shifting Landscape of Global Trade Governance* (Cambridge University Press, 2019).

Kirthana Ganeson is a PhD student in political science at the World Trade Institute, under the supervision of Professor Dr. Manfred Elsig. Her PhD project explores the linkages and impacts of trade on democracy. Ganeson holds an MSc in international political economy from the Rajaratnam School of International Studies at Nanyang Technological University, and a BA with honours in political science from the National University of Singapore. Her research interests include politics of international trade, EU–Asia trade relations, the role of private actors in international trade, and non-trade issues in preferential trade agreements.

Robert A Huber is a lecturer in comparative politics at the University of Reading, UK. He holds a PhD from ETH Zurich (2018). Huber has published extensively on globalization-induced challenges to liberal democracy, such as populism, climate politics and trade policy.

Sebastian Klotz is a senior manager at PwC Switzerland, where is work focuses on trade, technology, and sustainability. He completed his doctorate at the World Trade Institute with a dissertation on the linkages between international standardization organizations and international trade agreements. During his doctoral studies, he was a Doc.Mobility Fellow (Swiss National Science Foundation) at the University of Oxford and a visiting researcher at the Technical University of Munich. He also received the International Organization Research Fellowship of the Swiss Network for International Studies and the Young Researcher Promotion Fund of the University of Bern.

Dorotea López is an economist from the Instituto Técnologico Autónomo de México (ITAM), with a Master of Philosophy in Economics from the University of Cambridge, United Kingdom, and a PhD in social sciences at the University of Chile. She worked at the Mexican Central Bank and Mexican Economic Ministry. In Chile, she worked at the Chilean Ministry of Foreign Affairs as an official trade negotiator in WTO and Free Trade Agreements in the area of Trade in Services and Investment. Currently Titular Professor and Director of the Institute of International Studies, University of Chile, and WTO Chair holder. He is a principal researcher at the Millennium Nucleus on the Impacts of China in countries of Latin America and the Caribbean. Her main areas of interest are trade policy and services.

Andrew Lugg is an assistant professor at the University of Nevada, Las Vegas, and a non-resident fellow at the World Trade Institute, University of Bern. Previously he was a lecturer at the University of Maryland, a postdoctoral scholar at the World Trade Institute, and an assistant professor and postdoctoral scholar at DePauw University. He holds a PhD in political science from the University of Maryland (2020). His research focuses broadly on international political economy and international organizations, including a focus on the proliferation and design of trade and investment treaties. His publications have appeared in journals including *The Journal of*

Conflict Resolution, The Journal of International Economic Law, Global Policy, and *Research & Politics.*

Felipe Muñoz is an associate professor at the Institute of International Studies of the University of Chile. He holds a BA in economics and an MA in international studies, both from the University of Chile, and is a PhD fellow at Maastricht University, The Netherlands. His main research areas are trade policy and international economics, with particular emphasis on Latin America. He has participated in various research projects, including the WTO Chair program and UNCTAD's Virtual Institute, and consulting for the World Bank, Interamerican Development Bank, ECLAC, JETRO and the Chilean Under-Secretariat of International Economic Affairs, amongst others. His main research interests are trade policy, international development and trade in services.

Juliana Peixoto is a professor and researcher at the FLACSO-Argentina's International Relations department and a researcher at the National Scientific and Technical Research Council of Argentina. She holds a PhD in international law from the University of Buenos Aires and a master's degree in international relations from the same university. Her research agenda focuses on multilateral trade governance, regional integration and sustainable development. Her two latest publications discuss the politics of the Aid for Trade agenda and the crisis, stagnation and survival of the World Trade Organization.

Rodrigo Polanco is a senior lecturer, researcher and academic coordinator of master's programmes at WTI - University of Bern, and a legal advisor for Spanish- and Portuguese-speaking jurisdictions at the Swiss Institute of Comparative Law. He is also a visiting professor at the University of Chile. He holds a bachelor's and a master's degree in law from Universidad de Chile, an LLM in international legal studies from New York University and a PhD in law from the University of Bern. Polanco has published extensively as an author and editor in leading international academic publishers and international journals on investment, trade, tax and environmental law. He is a co-founder of EDIT (Electronic Database of Investment Treaties) and of the board of Fiscalía del Medio Ambiente (FIMA), a Chilean NGO, serving on the editorial committee of their law journal (*Justicia Ambiental*).

Marine Roux is a PhD candidate at the World Trade Institute, University of Bern. She is investigating the impact of the design and implementation of trade agreements and conditions to accede to the WTO on democracy as part of the SNSF-funded project TRADEM. Prior to joining the WTI, Roux worked as an economist in the public sector on a diverse range of areas, including regulation, trade policy and data science. Roux holds a master's degree in public policy and development from the Toulouse School of Economics and a bachelor's degree in economics from the University Paris Nanterre.

Víctor Saco is a full-time associate professor of international economic law at Pontificia Universidad Católica del Perú (PUCP), where he teaches and researches trade and investment topics, and is Director of the master's programme on international economic law at PUCP. He holds a law degree from PUCP, an LLM in International and European Law from the Catholic University of Louvain (Belgium), and is a PhD candidate at the World Trade Institute, University of Bern (Switzerland). He is a visiting professor at the Universidad del Externado, Colombia; Collaborative Online International Learning (COIL) professor at the Universidad Católica de San Pablo (Bolivia); and has also been a lecturer at the University of Antwerp Belgium on technical barriers to trade (TBT) and sanitary and phytosanitary (SPS) topics. Prof. Saco has attended the Hague Academy on International Law (PIL), Institut René Cassin (Strasbourg), the WTI Summer Academy, and the International Law Seminar (International Law Commission, United Nations, Geneva).

Cristian Ugarte is a senior economic officer at the European Free Trade Association (EFTA) in Geneva, Switzerland, where his work focuses on the negotiation and the implementation of FTAs. Previously, he worked as a trade policy analyst at the Trade Policies Review Division of the World Trade Organization (WTO), and before joining the WTO, he served as an economist for other international agencies, including the International Trade Centre, United Nations Conference on Trade and Development, Organisation for Economic Cooperation and Development, and World Bank. He holds a PhD in economics from the University of Geneva. As a researcher, he contributed to several papers and publications dealing with trade and development issues, notably barriers to developing countries' exports and the impact of trade-related policies. At the WTO, he was involved in the preparation of several Trade Policy Reviews for WTO members (CEMAC, Viet Nam, OECS, the United States, Dominican Republic).

Francisco Urdínez is a 2022–23 Fellow at the Woodrow Wilson Center and Associate Professor at the Political Science Institute of the Pontifical Catholic University of Chile, where he is affiliated with the Center of International Studies and the Center of Asian Studies. He is the director of the multi-year project Millennium Nucleus of the Impacts of China in countries of Latin America and the Caribbean, funded by the Chilean National Agency for Research and Development. Urdínez has testified to the US-China Economic and Security Review Commission of the American Congress on China-Latin American relations. Urdínez has been a Fellow of the Chilean Fund for Scientific and Technological Development. He received his PhD joint-degree from the University of São Paulo and King's College London in the field of international relations.

Sofía Urrea Zuluaga is a legal advisor at Colombia's Ministry of Trade, Industry, and Tourism, where she supports the country's defense in international trade disputes and the negotiation of trade agreements. She holds a law degree and a graduate degree in International Economic Law from Universidad Externado de Colombia. She specializes in international economic law and has experience as a legal advisor, professor, and researcher. Additionally, she has co-authored publications on trade policy, investment law, and food security, and has represented Colombia in high-profile cases before the Andean Community and WTO.

Carol Wise is a professor of political science and international relations at the University of Southern California (USC). She has written widely on trade integration, exchange rate crises, institutional reform and the political economy of market restructuring in the Latin American region. Wise is author of *Dragonomics: How Latin America is Maximizing (or Missing Out) on China's International Development Strategy* (Yale University Press, 2020), which received USC's Phi Kappa Phi Faculty Recognition Award in 2021 and the Luciano Tomassini 2021 Award-Honorable Mention for the Best Book on International Relations from the Latin American Studies Association. She is co-editor of *Unexpected Outcomes: How the Emerging Economies Survived the 2008-09 Global Financial Crisis* (Brookings, 2016), and co-editor of *The Political Economy of China-Latin American Relations in the New Millennium* (Routledge, 2016). She has also authored the article 'Grand Development Strategy or Simply Grandiose? China's Diffusion of Its Belt & Road Initiative into Central Europe' (with Oldrich Krpec) in the journal *New Political Economy* (2021). Wise holds a PhD in political science from Colombia University.

Julieta Zelicovich is a professor in the Department of International Relations at the National University of Rosario, Argentina, and a researcher at the National Scientific and Technical Research Council of Argentina. She holds a PhD in international relations from the National University of Rosario. Her primary research interests are international trade, global governance, regional integration and Argentinean foreign policy. Her latest publications discuss the changes and crisis of the World Trade Organization and its effects on developing countries' trade policy.

Preface

Latin American countries' approach to PTAs is a fascinating topic. There is a rich history of how policymakers have used trade agreements to advocate different economic and political models of integration. What we observe is an important variation across time and space. What really stands out is the diversity of approaches and attitudes towards using PTAs. While some countries have been rule-makers and engaged in innovative attempts to introduce new topics, others have been reluctant to use reciprocal trade agreements. The landscape of trade agreements has been further affected by regional integration attempts in the Southern and Central American regions and the existing interests of outside trading partners, such as the US and Europe, not to mention China's non-traditional approach to trade cooperation. Finally, we have noticed an increasing interest and politicization in the wider public when it comes to different treaty projects and the question of 'with whom to trade'.

This project brings together scholars from within and outside the region to address some past, current and future challenges related to PTAs. The contributions offer, from various disciplinary backgrounds, new insights related to questions of the design, diffusion and effects of PTAs. Some of the contributions focus on single countries, on single issue areas; others take a more comparative approach. We thank everyone involved in this collaborative effort and hope that the partnerships developed throughout the process will generate many follow-up studies on the history and the future of trade relations in Latin America.

Our special thanks go to all participants of the World Trade Forum 2022, where early versions of the chapters were presented and discussed. We also thank Sophia Thompson for editorial support and Cambridge Law for supporting the Forum Series over the years.

We also acknowledge financial support from the University of St. Gallen and the Institute of Management in Latin America (GIMLA), which acts as a Leading House from the State Secretariat for Education, Research and Innovation (SERI), granting incentives and developing joint research cooperation projects with Latin America.

1

Introduction

Manfred Elsig, Andrew Lugg and Rodrigo Polanco

1.1 MOTIVATION

Important developments are currently affecting the global trading system. We witness increasing calls for protectionism and a surge in populism in some major economies, while other trading nations continue to liberalise trade, driven by the dynamics of global value chains (GVCs). Even committed trading nations have shown an increased willingness to use industrial policies and have elevated the pursuit of geopolitical concerns through trade. On top of this, calls have increased to tackle the climate crisis through trade policy instruments. In short, important shifts induced by politics and economics shape today's trade policies.

At the same time, we have also witnessed a shift away from multilateral trade negotiations through the World Trade Organization (WTO) in favour of regional and bilateral trade agreements, which often reflect the competing interests of major trading countries such as the United States (US), China and the European Union (EU). Preferential trade agreements (PTAs) have proliferated widely in recent years, attracting the attention of scholars and policymakers. Beginning in the 1990s, a new wave of 'regionalism' (Mansfield and Milner 1999) led to an expansion of increasingly ambitious PTAs around the globe and, more recently, the negotiation of so-called mega-regionals (e.g., CPTPP, CETA, RCEP) has expanded.[1] These new PTAs are deeper and broader in scope than any prior agreements, covering areas that go well beyond tariffs to include provisions on everything from labour, environment investment, technical barriers, intellectual property rights, services and digital commerce (Dür et al. 2014). Understanding variation in the design of trade agreements, as well as the impact of these design choices, has become a central task of research across multiple disciplines. Importantly, many newer agreements are no longer simply

[1] The Comprehensive and Progressive Transpacific Partnership (CPTPP), the Comprehensive Economic and Trade Agreement (CETA) and the Regional Comprehensive Economic Partnership (RCEP).

copy-pasted as important new models are being created (and contested) through treaty-making practice.

These developments in global economic rulemaking are accompanied by an increasing backlash against globalisation in the public sphere (Mansfield et al. 2021; Walter 2021). While a rising number of developing countries have embraced ideas of market integration and foreign investment protection in recent years, we have also been witnessing street protests and opposition to trade and investment agreements in many parts of the world. Moreover, successive US administrations have shifted to addressing trade imbalances, particularly trade deficits, and have targeted China, as well as other important trading partners, including Mexico, Canada, South Korea and the European Union. Economic nationalism is again on the rise (Arp and Polanco 2022).

What has received less attention in the literature is how the above-described shifts, ranging from geopolitics and protectionism to climate risks and increasing market integration through GVCs, are shaping the trade architecture in regions such as Latin America. Mapping these challenges and, in particular, understanding how they affect Latin America is the primary rationale behind this book. We were particularly interested in working on the research frontier that addresses variation in trade agreement design, the impact of trade agreements on economic, political and legal institutions, as well as how citizens are affected by and react to trade agreements. This is particularly important in times when economic globalisation is undergoing tremendous changes.

The project received initial funding from a 2019 Swiss National Science Association Seed Money Grant, which the State Secretariat for Education, Research and Innovation (SERI) commissioned to the University of St. Gallen through its Centro Latinoamericano-Suizo. It helped bring together four university institutions: the University of Bern; the Institute of International Studies of the Universidad de Chile in Santiago, Chile; the Facultad Latinoamericana de Ciencias Sociales (FLACSO), Argentina; and the Pontificia Universidad Católica del Perú (PUCP). The funding allowed us to first meet virtually during the COVID-19 pandemic, coordinate research activities across institutions and support the organisation of in-person events in the fall of 2022. The project then became an integral part of the World Trade Forum, an annual meeting organised by the World Trade Institute and the European University Institute. It brought together experts working on the political economy and law of trade relations, many of which are based in Latin American research institutions. It involves political scientists, legal scholars and economists working at universities and various international organisations passionate about understanding the rich and varying experiences of Latin American countries negotiating trade deals since the democratisation processes in the second half of the twentieth century. This book, then, represents a collective endeavour to better understand the political, economic and legal sources (and consequences) of trade agreements in Latin America as we move further into the twenty-first century.

1.2 OBJECTIVES AND LEADING QUESTIONS

Against the above-described backdrop of the increasing politicisation of trade agreements, one important objective was to address the different challenges and opportunities for trade policy in Latin America. Acknowledging a rich and fascinating history in trade policy and the existence of substantial variation in trade policy approaches (see Elsig, Ganeson, Lugg and Roux, Chapter 2), the objective of the book has been to advance our understanding of the different design choices witnessed in PTAs, as well as evaluate their evolution and impact. In addition, building on the microfoundations of trade policy, the book also focuses on citizens' perceptions and support for policies that liberalise or oppose trade. At the same time, we hope to further unpack differences across Latin America and provide glimpses here and there of the main political-economy forces in place. We started the project knowing we could not do justice to the full range of variation across all countries, time and context in the region. Still, we hoped to bring different scholars and perspectives together to build an interdisciplinary community focusing on the state-of-the-art in studying PTAs.

The contributions aim to tackle some of the key research questions in the political economy of PTAs. We see important questions centred around three major themes: (1) understanding PTA design choices, including both which topics are more or less likely to be included as well as with whom; (2) examining the economic, political and social effects of PTAs in the region; and (3) addressing the sources and consequences of increasing politicisation of trade within societies.

As to the design of PTAs, a set of chapters provides insights into the question of whether PTA templates exist in Latin America. On an aggregate level focusing on diffusion in treaty design, we find that there does not appear to be a dominant template or templates used exclusively by countries in the region, but that there is some substantial US imprint in some agreements (Elsig, Ganeson, Lugg and Roux, Chapter 2). We do, however, see that there is diffusion with respect to specific design provisions. For example, there is evidence that the inclusion of some provisions is driven by countries' interactions within PTAs, as well as through Committee work in international organisations (e.g., Saco, Chapter 10, on food labelling).

Also, with respect to design, a number of chapters focus on the inclusion of new topics that have become more salient in the LA trade community and, which have in some cases led to innovation in PTA design in the region. Contributions in the book pay particular attention to gender provisions (Bahri, Chapter 4), digital trade and environmental provisions (Klotz and Ugarte, Chapter 6) and flexibilities in the form of special and differential treatment (S&DT) provisions (Zelicovich, Peixoto,

Daibert and Delich, Chapter 5). Design also means redesign, and one of the chapters takes a closer look at how PTA's investment chapters are reformed as a result of the backlash against the existing investment regime (Calvert, Chapter 11).

When designing PTAs, it is also important to take into account public opinion. Three contributions deal with these important microfoundations. One contribution examines public and elite opinions towards different PTA partners across several countries in the region (Dür and Huber, Chapter 3), whereas other chapters analyse public opinion in Chile (López and Bórquez, Chapter 8) and Brazil (Campello and Urdínez, Chapter 13), providing important country-specific context. A common thread in these contributions is the critical role that ideology and politics play in trade policy choices. This helps explain why trade remains a highly salient topic in the region and often features more prominently in national election cycles relative to other parts of the world.

With respect to the effects of PTAs, the book covers a variety of areas. One chapter finds that digital trade provisions have had a small positive impact on exports, whereas environmental provisions seem to have a small negative impact (Klotz and Ugarte, Chapter 6). Another contribution demonstrates that services sector liberalisation has had a positive impact on female labour force participation in Chile (Muñoz and Cáceres, Chapter 9). A third chapter shows that even though states in the region have legal obligations through their WTO and PTA obligations, they still retain significant policy space, which in the case of Colombia has allowed them to implement ambitious domestic politics related to food security in the aftermath of the 2016 Peace Agreement with the main rebel group (Revolutionary Armed Forces of Colombia - FARC) (see Álvarez Zárate, Camargo Moncayo, Urrea Zuluaga and Beltrán Vargas, Chapter 7).

Finally, some evidence is also presented that PTAs in the region might lead to unintended or even contradictory consequences. One chapter shows that 'murky protectionism' has increased among the signatories of North American Free Trade Agreement (NAFTA) and Southern Cone Common Market (MERCOSUR) (Albertoni and Wise, Chapter 12).

In the next section, we summarise the chapters and the main takeaways.

1.3 BOOK OVERVIEW

The book consists of thirteen chapters. The first two chapters set the stage. After this introduction, the second chapter by Manfred Elsig, Kirthana Ganeson, Andrew Lugg and Marine Roux analyses the overall landscape of PTAs in the region, with a specific focus on understanding differences (and commonalities) in design. The authors address the varied motivations of Latin American countries to sign PTAs and then use the design of trade agreements (DESTA) database to empirically map patterns in the region (Dür et al. 2014). The chapter shows considerable variation in terms of PTA design both within the region and when Latin America is compared to other regions. Finally, the chapter uses quantitative text analysis to address whether common models or templates are observed in the region. The chapter presents some evidence that agreements involving the US have diffused within the region, yet it finds little evidence of a single template or templates that Latin American countries routinely adopt. In sum, the chapter shows that there is rich variation in the PTA landscape across Latin America.

Chapters 2 to 6 focus on current challenges and new agendas. They address four important challenges of today's trade policy landscape. First, do citizens and elites care about the question 'with whom do we trade?'. For many years, the trade policy literature was focused on the distributional consequences of trade and incorporated both pocketbook and sociotropic motivations for understanding support for trade agreements. More recent research suggests that trading partners matter as well. Citizens care about where trade and services originate and are exported. Chapter 3 by Andreas Dür and Robert Huber provides a comparative analysis that explains the support for different trading partners across several countries in Latin America, focusing on both voters and elites. They test whether economic interests, geopolitical concerns or political ideology drive support for different PTA partners. Using both elite and individual survey data, they find that political ideology is an important predictor of preferences for trading partners for both political elites and citizens. By contrast, economic considerations only matter for legislators' preferences and geopolitical considerations only for citizens' preferences.

A second contribution pays attention to the way trade affects women. In Chapter 4, Amrita Bahri focuses on gender provisions in Latin American trade agreements. The chapter emphasises that there is important variation across regions with respect to the inclusion of gender provisions and illustrates important examples of difference and overlap. The second part of this chapter shows that Latin America has emerged as a frontrunner in drafting trade agreements with gender commitments. This part examines the ways in which countries have drafted gender provisions, the roles of women these provisions have focused on and the strategies of mainstreaming which are unique to this region (such as the inclusion of standalone chapters and the creation of dedicated implementation mechanisms).

Third, Latin America has been a region at the forefront of advocating for S&DT in the international trade regime, and many countries have experimented with various forms of differentiated integration, protection of infant industries and other S&DT policies based on countries' level of development. Chapter 5 – by Julieta Zelicovich, Juliana Peixoto, Leticia Daibert and Valentina Delich – examines S&DT through the lens of PTAs. They discuss the current literature on S&DT in trade agreements and present a novel conceptualisation. This allows them to map differences in the way Latin American countries have opted for such provisions over time. With a novel conceptualisation at hand, they find that S&DT provisions are rarely located in dedicated chapters but are more frequently found scattered across various parts of the agreements; these may include a patchwork of exclusions, including exemptions, transition periods and safeguards.

Fourth, a variety of Latin American countries have also spearheaded how trade diplomacy can address new trade issues, such as the greening of the economy and digitalisation. Chapter 6, by Sebastian Klotz and Cristian Ugarte, takes a critical look at these two themes. The chapter examines the design and the effects of digital and environmental provisions of Latin American PTAs. The chapter compares domestic policies and then maps the design of these topics in treaty-making. The second part focuses on a preliminary empirical test of whether these provisions have an impact on trade flows. Interestingly, the results suggest that the presence of digital and environmental provisions in Latin American PTAs has no statistically significant impact on the volume and composition of imports. For exports, however, the analysis indicates that digital provisions in PTAs tend to increase flows, while the opposite is true for environmental provisions. Neither the inclusion of digital nor environmental provisions in PTAs are found to result in a statistically significant change in the composition, that is a 'greening' or 'digitalising', of exports.

Chapters 7 to 10 of the volume examine the effect of PTAs on countries in the region (single country focus), to better understand how these agreements affect important political and economic developments. These concern the impact on food security in Colombia, the effects of service liberalisation on the female workforce in Chile and how a set of countries pursue health-related societal goals in line with technical barriers to trade commitments in the Pacific Alliance. This part also takes a closer look at how in Chile, the perceptions of elites and citizens have evolved over time when it comes to signing trade agreements.

Chapter 7 – by José Manuel Álvarez Zárate, María Camila Camargo Moncayo, Sofía Urrea Zuluaga and Diana Beltrán Vargas – focuses on how the Peace Deal that ended years of civil war in Colombia has incorporated a set of trade-related measures to increase food security. The chapter assesses how existing trade obligations emanating from the WTO and the US-Colombian PTA have influenced the different programmes and highlights areas where clashes of commitments could arise now and in the future development of the implementation of the peace treaty. This chapter contributes, in particular, to the debate on how trade obligations can be designed to allow sufficient policy space for countries to pursue important societal goals.

This is followed by a closer look at the changing perspectives in Chile on the role of trade agreements. Chapter 8, by Dorotea López and Andrés Bórquez, uses a mixed-methods approach, relying on a survey, elite interviews and a media analysis to trace important changes and expectations about the role of trade policy in recent years. Whereas trade policy openness and active use of trade agreements were seen in a positive light and were strongly linked to democratisation policies in the past, recent developments provide evidence for a growing backlash to openness. This chapter discusses this increasing scepticism and provides a nuanced picture of the degree of politicisation discussing elite views, survey data and media coverage. The authors show that support for PTAs remains generally high but that there is more demand to address questions of inequality, environment and gender in these agreements.

The next chapter in this section by Javiera Cáceres and Felipe Muñoz carries out an impact assessment of services commitments in trade agreements on female workforce participation. Using the case of Chile, Chapter 9 assesses the impact of the inclusion of trade in service provisions on the participation of women in the labour force, particularly within the services sector. They argue that the inclusion of service provisions within PTAs can enhance the development of that sector, which should positively impact women's employment. For this reason, a more substantial impact of PTA on women's employment rather than on that of men should be encountered, which should help reduce the gender gaps in this sector. To test these hypotheses, the authors use a panel composed of data from Latin American economies from 1990 to 2021. A series of econometric specifications suggest that the inclusion of service provisions in Chilean PTAs positively impacted women's employment, particularly in the services sector. For men, the results showed a negative or non-significant effect. Finally, the chapter shows that these agreements can contribute to reducing the gender gap in the workforce.

The final contribution in this group by Víctor Saco takes a closer look at how food labelling regulations to pursue health objectives have diffused across Latin America and, in particular, across members of the Pacific Alliance. Saco shows in Chapter 10 how a specific label system developed in Chile was then adopted by other countries in the region (Peru and Mexico). The case nicely illustrates how the Pacific Alliance served as a platform for diffusion. It also shows that concerns about consistency with international trade law and criticism by some trading partners and businesses led to only minor adjustments but did not stop the diffusion of health policy labels in the region.

Chapters 11 to 13 focus on systemic challenges facing Latin America (other than trade-related issues and future challenges). It starts with a deep dive into the highly politicised field of investment arbitration and how trade agreements have started to incorporate investment regulation. Julia Calvert analyses the changing nature of investment provisions in PTAs. In Chapter 11, she finds that PTA investment chapters demonstrate an increasing variety of reforms over time. This variation is driven in part by the legitimacy crisis in international investment law. Arguably, this crisis has created more political space for South American preferences in investment treaty law-making. However, who dominates reform debates matters just as much to countries' reform preferences as their experience in investor–state arbitration. Regardless of reform preferences, the main outcome of PTA investment chapters has been further fragmentation in an already complex and incomplete area of international economic law. This fragmentation, if continued, may exacerbate the very challenges governments are seeking to address in promoting sustainable and inclusive development through their reform efforts.

Chapter 12, by Nicolás Albertoni and Carol Wise, addresses the rise of protectionism in the region through an examination of two of the largest economic powers in Latin America. They provide an insightful overview of both Mexico's and

Brazil's trade relationship with their neighbours through the NAFTA and MERCOSUR agreements, respectively. Looking at two reluctant globalisers, they particularly focus on how trade policy has evolved since the Global Financial Crisis of 2008. Their chapter shows that PTAs, long considered as key trade and investment-creating conduits, are also emerging as venues within which non-tariff measures (NTMs), a hidden form of protectionism, are simultaneously increasing. The good news is that membership in these PTAs has mitigated some intra-bloc protectionism, albeit against a backdrop of rising NTMs within these PTAs. The picture on protectionism would not be complete without accounting for the increasing influence of China in the region, which has strongly influenced the choices of domestic trade policies in Brazil and Mexico as well.

Chapter 13 nicely links to the preceding chapter and the role of China by focusing on how Brazilian citizens view China as a trading partner. China has become the most important trade partner for a number of Latin American countries, in particular Brazil. Daniela Campello and Francisco Urdínez address an interesting puzzle related to 'China-bashing'. They show through survey data that an import shock translates into negative perceptions in regions where Chinese imports have surged over the years. By contrast, they show that in regions that benefit from a boom in exports of agricultural products to China, no positive attitudes towards China are found. They argue that the negative effects on the import side are more visible relative to the positive effects of exports. However, overall attitudes may have been affected by the Bolsonaro government's vocal criticism of China during the Covid pandemic.

The above chapters provide in-depth analyses of various topics for different countries across different time dimensions. They show how salient trade policy and, in particular, PTA are and remain in Latin America. We hope that the collected work can act as a building ground for many more empirical investigations into the design and effects of the growing network of PTAs and their substantive obligations.

REFERENCES

Albertoni, N. and C. Wise 2025. "Trade Protectionism and Integration in Latin America the Cases of Brazil and Mexico," this volume.

Álvarez Zárate J. M., M. C. Camargo Moncayo, S.Urrea Zuluaga and D.Beltrán Vargas, 2025. "Trade Law Impact on Food Security in Latin America: Colombia's 2016 Peace Agreement Case," this volume.

Arp, B. and R. Polanco 2022. "International Arbitration in Times of Economic Nationalism", Kluwer Law International, Wolters Kluwer.

Bahri, A. 2025. "Making Trade Agreements Work for Women: What's Behind the South American Approach?," this volume.

Calvert, J. 2025. "The Political Economy of Investment Protection Reform in South American PTAs," this volume.

Campello, D. and F. Urdinez 2025. "Anti-China Sentiment and the Politics of Brazilian Agribusiness," this volume.
Dür, A. and R. Huber 2025. "Preferences for Trading Partners: Evidence from Citizens and Legislators in Latin America," this volume.
Dür, A., L. Baccini and M. Elsig 2014. "The Design of International Trade Agreements: Introducing a New Dataset," *The Review of International Organizations* 9(3): 353–375.
Elsig, M., K. Ganeson, A. Lugg and M. Roux 2025. "Mapping the PTA Universe in Latin America," this volume.
Klotz, S. and C. Ugarte 2025. "Digital and Environmental Provisions in Latin American Trade Agreements," this volume.
López, D. and A. Bórquez 2025. "How Preferential Trade Agreements are Perceived in Chile: From Love to Hate in a Single Step?," this volume.
Mansfield, E. and H. Milner 1999. "The New Wave of Regionalism," *International Organization* 53(3): 589–627.
Mansfield, E. D., H. V. Milner and N. Rudra 2021. "The Globalization Backlash: Exploring New Perspectives," *Comparative Political Studies* 54(13): 2267–2285.
Muñoz, F. and J. Cáceres 2025. "Chile's PTA Services Impact Assessment: Looking beyond Trade Flows: Women's Employment Participation," this volume.
Saco, V. 2025. "Food Labelling Regulation of the Pacific Alliance Members," this volume.
Walter, S. 2021. "The Backlash against Globalization," *Annual Review of Political Science* 24: 421–442.
Zelicovich, J., J. Peixoto, L. Daibert and V. Delich 2025. "Assessing Special and Differential Treatment in Latin American Trade Agreements," this volume.

2

Mapping the PTA Universe in Latin America

Manfred Elsig, Kirthana Ganeson, Andrew Lugg and Marine Roux

2.1 INTRODUCTION

In this chapter, we provide a general overview of Latin American (LA) countries' experience with and exposure to preferential trade agreements (PTAs), with a specific emphasis on empirically situating the current landscape. This is an important stock-taking exercise as it helps contextualize the more focused contributions contained in the subsequent chapters of this volume. Our primary goal in this chapter, therefore, is not to lay out a precise argument, which we then test empirically, but rather to uncover important patterns that can help serve as a starting point for additional theoretical and empirical work.

We turn our focus first to understanding the macro-level drivers underlying countries' motivations to negotiate and use PTAs in the region. We argue that currently there are three distinct clusters of countries with different underlying motivations behind their engagement with PTAs, which we label the *liberal globalists, reluctant globalists* and *anti-globalists*. The liberal globalists use PTAs as part of a broader commitment to a relatively open, liberal economic strategy, which entails signing deep PTAs with a variety of partners both within and outside the region that contain significant commitments to market liberalism. The reluctant globalists, in contrast, tend to pursue shallower PTAs aimed at furthering more statist developmental goals and are more oriented towards the region, whereas the anti-globalists either opt out of PTAs altogether or sign agreements that are more explicitly political in an effort to counter or prevent outside influence in the region.

After this theoretical stock-taking exercise, we turn to empirical examinations at the regional, PTA and country levels. First, we explore whether major differences exist when we compare LA to other world regions. Second, we seek to understand differences within the region in terms of how many PTAs countries sign as well as their design. We find that several economic and political factors help explain the content and ambition of PTAs. The results suggest that richer, more democratic countries not only sign more PTAs but that they also sign deeper PTAs, which typically include issues that go beyond just trade. Third, we employ text-as-data methods to explore whether there are models from which LA countries regularly adopt language when designing their PTAs. Our empirical analyses show some evidence that agreements involving the US have diffused within the region, but we fail to uncover strong evidence of a single template or templates that LA countries disproportionally emulate.

Overall, our results have important implications for understanding the design and diffusion of PTAs in LA. They paint a picture of a region where political and economic differences from country to country produce profound differences with respect to PTA signing patterns and PTA design. We conclude by pointing out how our mapping exercise helps contextualize the results in subsequent chapters of the book, as well as suggesting some promising avenues for future research.

2.2 LATIN AMERICAN PTAS TODAY

Currently, the underlying motivations for the use of PTAs in Latin America vary greatly from country to country. Nevertheless, in order to understand broad patterns of PTA signing in the region, we argue that it is useful to classify countries into three groups, which we label *liberal globalists*, *reluctant globalists* and *anti-globalists*.[1] Each group varies with respect to the underlying rationale – in terms of both economic and foreign policy goals – for why the country in question is motivated to sign PTAs. We acknowledge at the outset that these categories are broad, and hence likely conceal fine-grained differences between countries, but we nonetheless wager that these classifications can help us understand more nuanced differences in terms of both partner choice and treaty design.

Our first group we dub the *liberal globalists*, which is a group of countries that, by and large, use PTAs as a way to engage in relatively open trade with countries both within and outside Latin America.[2] These countries, which include Chile, Peru, Colombia, Mexico and most of the Central American countries, have signed PTAs that liberalize many sectors of the economy and typically include a variety of non-trade or trade-related provisions that aim to reform domestic economic and political systems (Sanahuja 2009; Quiliconi 2014; Carranza 2017; Laursen 2018; Bohigues and Rivas 2019). To varying degrees, this reflects a domestic political consensus in many of these countries that such agreements advance important interests in society, including generating economic growth and enhancing gains from trade, as long as

1 We base these groups upon a similar classification found in the excellent review by Bohigues and Rivas (2019).

2 Some countries, such as Chile, went even further by unilaterally liberalizing markets and cutting tariffs. The contribution by López and Bórquez (Chapter 8) shows, however, how recent politicization and change of government question Chile's past consensus on PTAs as a way to globally integrate. As to how Mexico has navigated both integration and protection, see Albertoni and Wise (Chapter 12).

they are designed to exclude and protect some important domestic economic actors, and are supported by strategic sectors and transnational firms (Hicks et al. 2014; Bohigues and Rivas 2019).[3] Moreover, several of these countries are thought to have used trade agreements as a vehicle to 'lock-in' domestic reforms that would be difficult to make in the absence of international legal commitments (see Fernandez and Portes 1998; Baccini and Urpelainen 2014). Many of these countries have signed PTAs with the US and EU, have participated in relatively open regional efforts such as the (aborted) Free Trade Area of the Americas (FTAA) and the Trans-Pacific Partnership/Comprehensive and Progressive Agreement for Trans-Pacific Partnership (TPP/CPTPP), and have signed bilateral and regional trade agreements with other liberal globalists in and outside the region.

In contrast, another group of countries, which we call the *reluctant globalists*, are still committed to engaging in international trade but have generally been more sceptical of a fully open or liberal model of doing so. Thus, these states have attempted to foster a more developmental or protection-based form of regionalism and have viewed PTAs with extra-regional partners as potentially costly in both economic and sovereignty terms. Argentina, Brazil, Paraguay and Uruguay fit this mould.[4] These countries still engage in considerable international trade but do so to promote statist industrial development goals more in line with 'new South American regionalism', which evolved after the switch away from import-substitution industrialization (ISI) strategies (Briceño-Ruiz 2013; Vieira 2014; Bohigues and Rivas 2019). These countries have sought to channel their cooperation through agreements such as the Southern Common Market (MERCOSUR) in an effort to consolidate regional integration along with developmental and social goals. Domestically, these countries have economies that contain significant, and politically influential, export-oriented sectors, but they often benefit from state industrial policy (Brooks and Kurtz 2012).[5] These countries also, on average, promote a larger role for the state in the economy than the liberal globalists.[6] At the same time, however, it should be noted

[3] We are agnostic as to whether support in these countries is primarily driven by factor endowments or sectoral concerns. At the same time, we are also sensitive to the fact that public opinion is not monolithic and can shift quickly. For example, the Central American Free Trade Agreement (CAFTA) was significantly politicized in Central America (particularly in Costa Rica), and the ratification of the Comprehensive and Progressive Agreement for Trans-Pacific Partnership (CPTPP) in Chile was highly contested.

[4] As to how Brazil has navigated both protectionism and integration, see the contribution by Albertoni and Wise (Chapter 12).

[5] In a simplistic sense, the legacy and institutions associated with ISI have been stronger in several of these countries, likely due to the fact that certain import-competing groups have, on average, been more successful at influencing state policy and/or have found themselves on the winning side of political debates (see Cardoso and Faletto 1979; Evans 1995).

[6] For example, in 2018 central government expenditures were 38.90, 38.49 and 33.21 per cent of GDP in Argentina, Brazil and Uruguay, respectively, compared to 25.67, 25.36 and 21.41 per cent in Mexico, Chile and Peru (www.oecd-ilibrary.org/sites/2eef1841-en/index.html?itemId=/content/component/2eef1841-en).

that these countries have often vacillated between elements of an open and closed economy depending on political developments (Briceño-Ruiz 2018). Regardless, the primary difference between this group and the liberal globalists is that, in general, the reluctant globalists are more sceptical of the benefits of across-the-board openness and seek to sign economic agreements that promote state developmental goals even if some of those come at the potential expense of economic growth and trade expansion.

Finally, there are the *anti-globalists*, which have generally sought to limit their exposure to trade and investment, especially if it is outside the region. Moreover, to the extent that these countries have engaged in regional and bilateral PTAs, they have tended to be oriented towards the pursuit of social goals such as group rights, redistribution and social inclusion, while also pushing back against agreements and policies that are perceived as neo-colonial or imperialist (Bohigues and Rivas 2019, p. 6). This group includes Venezuela, Cuba, Bolivia, Nicaragua and several Caribbean countries. When countries in the anti-globalist group sign PTAs, they are often less oriented towards trade and economic integration, instead pursuing political goals such as the need to counter perceived US or foreign dominance in the region. One of the most notable attempts here is the creation in 2002 by Venezuela and Cuba of the Bolivarian Alliance for the Peoples of Our America or ALBA agreement, which was conceived of as an alternative to the US-proposed FTAA (Serbin and Serbin Pont 2017). Since its creation, ALBA has added ten additional members – including Bolivia, Nicaragua, Dominica, Antigua and Barbuda, St. Vincent and the Grenadines, Saint Lucia, Grenada, and Saint Kitts and Nevis – but has seen the withdrawal of Honduras and Ecuador.

These groupings suggest several important observable implications that we address in the following sections. First, it suggests that we should see considerable variation at the country level in the region. In other words, we should expect that countries in the different groupings will sign notably different types of economic agreements. Thus, we should expect to see some degree of fragmentation across the PTA universe in the region. Moreover, and as we discuss further in the conclusion, changes in the domestic political dynamics within each country also affect the stability of country preferences over time. At this point it is unclear, however, which state-level factors are likely to systematically explain this variation. One possibility is that economic factors such as reliance on trade or market structures at the country level predict variation in PTA design. Another possibility is that political factors, such as type of government, left–right orientation or geopolitical interests, affect PTA design. Second, it suggests that we are likely to see competing models of agreements in the region. As noted above, we expect broadly that the liberal globalists will prefer deeper agreements and will be more willing to work across regional divides, whereas the members of the other groups are more likely to sign shallower agreements with regional partners who share similar interests.

To address these issues, we proceed in three steps. First, we compare LA to other regions to identify broad differences at the regional level. Second, we look at variation across several economic and political dimensions at the country and PTA levels. Third, we use quantitative text analysis to look for patterns of text diffusion in the region. Our aim here is to better understand whether there are clear PTA templates from which LA countries routinely draw.

2.3 COMPARING LATIN AMERICA TO OTHER WORLD REGIONS

As a first exercise, we compare Latin America to six other world regions. We rely on the World Bank's definition of region, which, for Latin America, includes forty-two countries spanning Central America, the Caribbean and South America.[7] We compare regions not only on their overall relationship to PTAs but also along relevant political and economic dimensions. Although this method of comparison is crude, masking considerable intra-regional variation, we view it as important to help establish if there are any unique regional patterns.

Table 2.1 compares Latin America to six other world regions with respect to the average number of PTA partners, PTA design and across several political and economic dimensions.[8] For our primary design variable, we include *depth* from the Design of Trade Agreements (DESTA) database, which measures the degree to which a PTA requires the state to undertake significant economic liberalization across areas including trade in goods, services, investment, standards, public procurement, competition and intellectual property rights (IPRs) (Dür et al. 2014). The variable is constructed as an additive index which varies from 0 (shallow) to 7 (deep). We also include the degree of democracy for each country as measured by the commonly used *Polity2* score which ranges from −10 to +10 (Marshall and Gurr 2020). Gross domestic product (GDP) per capita, as well as exports, mining, merchandise exports, and natural resources rents as a percentage of GDP are all from the World Bank's *World Development Indicators*.[9]

Several interesting trends stand out. First, column 2 shows that LA countries have the second-highest number of average PTAs signed of all regions at nearly twenty-three. At first glance, this might appear surprising as international trade is less important as a percentage of the economy in LA than in several other regions

[7] The World Bank region, Latin America and the Caribbean (data code LCN), consists of these forty-two countries: Antigua and Barbuda, Argentina, Aruba*, Bahamas, Barbados, Belize, Bolivia, Brazil, British Virgin Islands*, Cayman Islands*, Chile, Colombia, Costa Rica, Cuba, Curacao,* Dominica, Dominican Republic, Ecuador, El Salvador, Grenada, Guatemala, Guyana, Haiti, Honduras, Jamaica, Mexico, Nicaragua, Panama, Paraguay, Peru, Puerto Rico,* Sint Maarten (Dutch part)*, St. Kitts and Nevis, St. Lucia, St. Martin (French part),* St. Vincent and the Grenadines, Suriname, Trinidad and Tobago, Turks and Caicos Islands,* Uruguay, Venezuela, and Virgin Islands,* Please note that the countries with an asterisk (*) are excluded due to data coverage and consistency issues.

[8] The number of members of the other regions is as follows: ECA: 55; LA: 33, NA: 2; MENA: 21; SSA: 48: EAP: 31; SA: 8.

[9] https://datatopics.worldbank.org/world-development-indicators/

TABLE 2.1 *Comparing PTAs and political and economic characteristics of Latin America to other world regions.*

Region	Number of PTAs	PTA depth	Polity2 score	GDP per capita in 1,000$	Exports % of GDP	Mining as % of GDP	Merchandise exports as % of GDP
Europe & Central Asia (ECA)	42.69	3.99	8.45	27,101	45.55	4.74	66.32
Latin America & Caribbean (LA)	22.88	2.54	5.33	6,968	30.13	11.63	51.76
North America (NA)	21.5	4.91	9.88	46,465	20.41	5.43	34.17
Middle East & North Africa (MENA)	17	2.09	−5.32	12,657	48.23	7.53	62.04
Sub-Saharan Africa (SSA)	13.5	1.93	−2.46	1,781	27.47	13.23	50.24
East Asia & Pacific (EAP)	11.61	3.8	3.04	17,217	61.38	5.13	95.09
South Asia (SA)	8.62	1.26	3.11	1,251	19.46	3.84	36.22

Note: Data on PTAs taken from the DESTA database; Polity2 scores from Polity5 data; all additional variables from the World Bank's World Development Indicators. All indicators are averages computed over the years corresponding to the signature of PTAs.

(column 6), including East Asia and the Pacific, Europe and Central Asia, and the Middle East and North Africa (MENA). For example, exports comprise about 30 per cent of the average LA country economy compared to 61 per cent for East Asia. What also stands out is the relatively high importance of mining for many economies (column 7), providing a potential additional incentive for negotiating PTAs from the perspective of the export market.

One potential driver for the relatively high number of PTAs relative to other regions is that LA is, on average, much more democratic than other regions with similar economic profiles. Numerous studies have argued for a positive effect of democracy on PTA signing (Mansfield et al. 2000; Milner and Kubtoa 2005; Manger and Pickup 2016). Mansfield and Milner (2012) argue that democratic governments tend to sign more PTAs on average than other countries as this can help leaders communicate to domestic audiences that the government is a good steward of the economy. Column 4 shows that the average Polity2 score for the LA region is 2 points higher than East Asia and the Pacific and South Asia, and approximately 8 points and 10 points higher than sub-Saharan Africa and MENA, respectively.

Figure 2.1 visualizes the aggregate relationship between democracy and the total number of PTAs across the seven regions. This is an admittedly broad comparison, as there is significant intra-regional variation, which we explore below, but it is nonetheless illustrative. The graph shows that the general trend is for regions with more democracies to have more PTAs on average. Aside from Europe and Central Asia, which is an extreme outlier due to its high values on both variables, the LA region stands out. It is the region having signed on average the second-highest number of PTAs while scoring third in terms of level of democracy.[10] Thus, the fact that the average LA country has more PTA partners than sub-Saharan Africa, MENA, East Asia and the Pacific and South Asia might be related to higher levels of democracy. These data alone, however, do not tell us the full story of the relationship between PTAs and democracy, which may potentially be endogenous.

A second interesting trend illustrated by the regional comparisons concerns the design of PTAs, which we assess with the *depth* measure from DESTA. The data indicate that LA countries are clearly in the middle of the pack, with neither overly deep nor shallow PTAs. The average depth of LA PTAs is 2.54, which is well below regions such as Europe and Central Asia, North America, and East Asia and the Pacific, which have average depth values of 3.99, 4.91, 3.8, respectively, but higher than MENA, sub-Saharan Africa and South Asia with averages of 2.09, 1.93 and 1.26, respectively. One potential explanation for this middle position might be due to the fact that the region is comprised primarily of middle-income countries. Figure 2.2 shows that there is a strong relationship between GDP per capita across the different

[10] It may well be that the correlation between democracies and PTA signing has also weakened over time. We have been witnessing in recent years increased forms of trade integration by non-democratic countries using trade agreements (e.g., China, Vietnam).

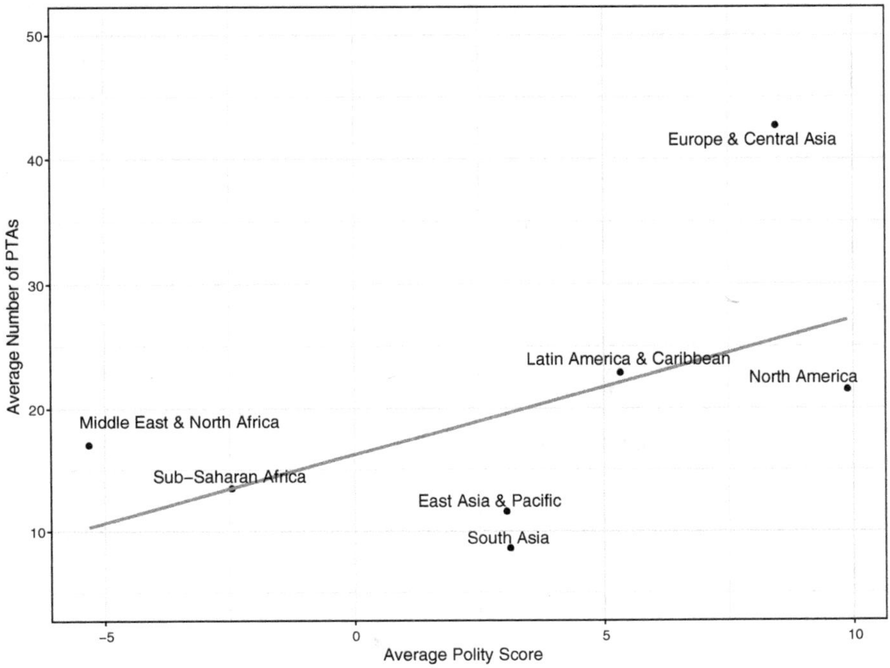

FIGURE 2.1 Average levels of democracy and the number of PTAs per country across seven regions.
Source: DESTA database.

regions and the average depth of PTAs. This relationship is explored at the country level later, but here it is useful because it shows that even though LA countries sign many PTAs, due to their relatively more democratic governments, on average, their PTAs tend to be less ambitious.

This also corroborates our country classification, as this middle position is also a function of the fact that there is considerable heterogeneity in the type of agreements pursued, with the liberal globalists preferring more open agreements relative to the reluctant globalists and anti-globalist groups. For example, the liberal globalists began signing more open agreements in the 1990s and continue to sign deep agreements today with a variety of countries inside and outside the region. Whereas the other groups have tended to sign shallower agreements, often with regional partners. Thus, the fact that the average depth of the region is lower than Europe, North America and East Asia but higher than regions such as Africa and South Asia makes sense, given the more varied agreements.[11]

[11] The standard deviation in the DESTA depth index is one of the highest in the LA region compared to all other regions: ECA: 2.34; LA: 2.42; NA: 2.43; MENA: 2.02; SSA: 1.39: EAP: 2.36; SA: 1.64.

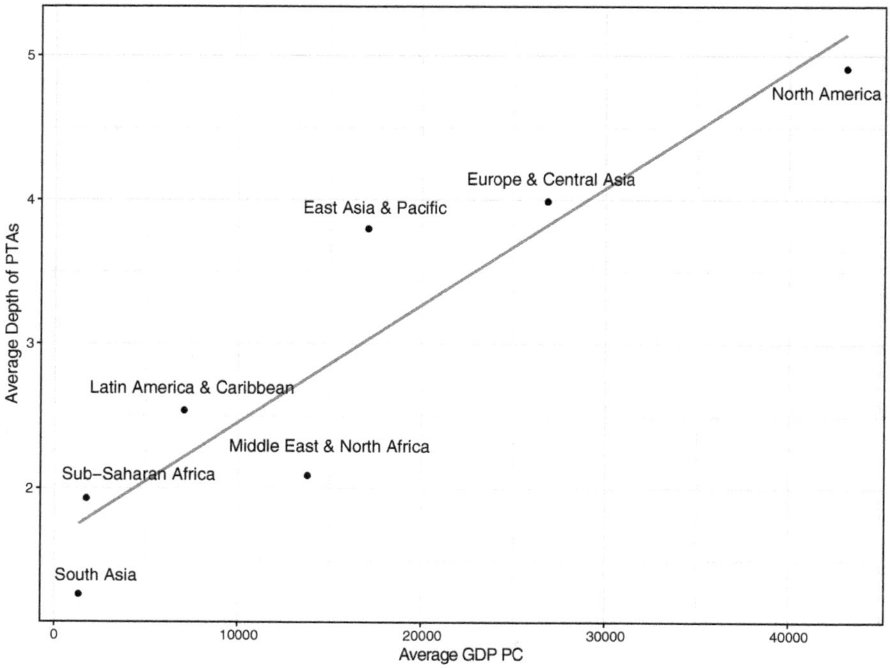

FIGURE 2.2 Average GDP per capita and the design of PTAs across seven regions. *Source*: DESTA database.

2.4 WITHIN LA REGION VARIATION

In this section, we examine variation in PTA design at the country and PTA levels. Our goal is both empirical and conceptual. Empirically, we hope to illustrate important differences between countries in the region with respect to the political and economic determinants of PTA design. Conceptually, we hope to better understand how these associations are related to the broad country groupings we laid out in the opening section. We also hope to improve our understanding of how country-specific factors lead to different treaty outcomes.

In Table 2.2, we summarize key descriptive statistics on the number of PTAs and their design, which we average at the country level. As above, we are particularly interested in the *depth* of PTAs, but we also include *flexibility*, also from DESTA, which measures the degree to which countries can opt out of core provisions, and *DSM strength*, which is the strength of dispute settlement provisions in each PTA (Allee and Elsig 2016).[12] The data show that seven countries have signed more than

[12] *Flexibility* is an additive index (0–4) capturing provisions enabling a party to temporarily breach the agreement in case of unforeseen circumstances. These can include general safeguard provisions, specific provisions in case of balance of payment problems, countervailing duties and anti-dumping duties. *DSM strength* is an additive index (0–9) capturing the strength of the PTA dispute settlement mechanism (DSM). The index components refer to the DSM set-up and rules (choice of panel, choice of venue, chairman, time limits, etc.).

TABLE 2.2 *Latin American countries and PTA design.*

Country	# PTAs	Depth	Flexibility	DS strength
Chile	46	4.21	3.1	5.97
Mexico	43	3.02	2.63	3.57
Argentina	40	1.31	2.1	2.24
Peru	37	4.09	2.94	5.48
Brazil	35	1.45	2.15	2.75
Uruguay	34	1.48	2.11	2.9
Colombia	33	3.00	2.83	4.03
Venezuela	27	0.88	2.14	1.61
Cuba	27	1.11	2.33	1.5
Guatemala	26	2.96	2.64	5.00
Costa Rica	25	4.18	3.05	5.95
El Salvador	25	2.91	2.55	5.18
Panama	25	3.27	2.59	5.14
Paraguay	24	1.71	2.33	3.74
Honduras	23	3.52	2.9	5.62
Guyana	21	1.84	2.47	2.53
Nicaragua	21	3.05	2.65	4.6
Ecuador	20	1.29	2.57	2.73
Trinidad & Tobago	20	2.00	2.63	3.05
Grenada	18	2.18	2.41	3.12
Antigua & Barbuda	17	2.38	2.62	2.81
Barbados	17	2.19	2.56	3.00
Dominica	17	2.31	2.44	3.00
St. Lucia	17	2.31	2.44	3.00
Jamaica	16	2.27	2.47	3.2
St. Kitts & Nevis	16	2.47	2.53	3.00
St. Vincent & Grenadines	16	2.47	2.53	3.00
Bahamas	14	2.38	2.38	3.31
Belize	14	2.69	2.62	3.69
Bolivia	13	2.33	2.67	2.89
Suriname	12	2.64	1.91	3.45
Dominican Republic	10	3.62	2.25	4.75
Haiti	6	2.40	2.20	3.20

Source: DESTA database.

thirty total PTAs, including Chile, Mexico, Argentina, Peru, Brazil, Uruguay and Colombia. Again, this suggests that many countries in the region, aside from the anti-globalists, have made PTAs central to their foreign economic policy. It is, however, striking to observe the considerable variation in design. Chilian and Peruvian PTAs have an average depth of over 4, which is much higher than the average depth of Argentinian, Brazilian and Uruguayan PTAs, which average between 1 and 1.5. Mexico and Colombia stand in the middle with an average depth of 3. This pattern is relatively similar when looking at other design aspects such as *flexibility* and *DSM strength*.

We know that deeper agreements tend to include on average more flexibility provisions (Baccini et al. 2015). Chile, Costa Rica and Peru demonstrate this tendency, as these countries sign PTAs characterized by a high average depth and flexibility. In contrast, Argentina, Brazil, Uruguay and Paraguay show an inverse pattern on average, signing shallower PTAs but with few flexibility provisions. This makes sense, given that shallower agreements have fewer commitments and thus less need for flexibility. This contrasts with countries such as Bolivia, and to some extent Ecuador, which have signed fewer agreements but have tended to sign shallower agreements with more flexible provisions.

Taken together, this illustrates that there are different logics that underlay the rationale for PTA design. The liberal and reluctant globalist groups both negotiate and sign many PTAs, but the design of their agreements is quite different. The liberal globalists sign newer generation PTAs that include extensive liberalization, cover a variety of new trade issues and include dispute settlement and flexibility provisions. In contrast, the reluctant globalists sign shallower agreements that lack the same level of ambition and, as a consequence, do not need the same degree of flexibility. For example, the average depth of PTAs signed by the liberal globalists is 3.46 compared to an average of 1.96 for the reluctant globalists.

Other examples of differences in design include Panama and Nicaragua who have signed on average much deeper and more comprehensive agreements relative to Paraguay and Ecuador, even though they have signed a similar number of agreements (20–25). Costa Rica and Venezuela also follow a similar pattern. Dominican Republic is another interesting case. Although the country has signed a relatively small number of agreements (10) compared to other LA countries, they seem to be very comprehensive with high scores across PTA design metrics.

We now focus on the degree to which PTAs in the region include provisions beyond trade in goods. Figure 2.3 summarizes the percentage of each country's PTAs that include provisions on trade-related issues (e.g., investment, services, IPR) and non-trade issues (NTIs) (e.g., environment and labour). These issues are among the most important issues that indicate the overall ambition of agreements. Three groups of countries emerge. The first group is composed of countries in the top one-third of the chart, from Chile to El Salvador, that tend to regularly include trade-related and NTIs in their agreements. The second group, roughly the middle third of the figure from Suriname through Bolivia, tend to include investment and services but do not regularly include IPR, environment and labour provisions. Finally, the last third, from Uruguay down, tend to only sparingly include provisions on investment, and nearly never include provisions on the other NTIs.

What this exercise demonstrates is that the liberal globalists, including Chile, Peru, Colombia and many of the Central American countries, tend to include a variety of trade-related and NTIs in their PTAs. This reinforces the patterns above, which

	Investment	Services	IPR	Environment	Labour
Chile	65	54	50	20	17
Costa Rica	64	48	52	18	18
Dominican Republic	60	50	40	25	25
Peru	62	46	41	22	22
Honduras	57	48	39	19	19
Nicaragua	52	38	43	20	20
Panama	44	44	36	23	23
Guatemala	54	42	38	12	12
Colombia	52	36	24	21	21
El Salvador	48	36	32	14	14
Suriname	58	50	17	9	9
Haiti	50	33	17	20	20
Belize	64	43	14	8	8
Mexico	42	42	40	6	6
Bahamas	50	43	14	8	8
St. Vincent & Grenadines	50	38	12	7	7
St. Kitts & Nevis	50	38	12	7	7
Jamaica	50	38	12	7	7
St. Lucia	47	35	12	6	6
Dominica	47	35	12	6	6
Barbados	47	35	12	6	6
Antigua & Barbuda	47	35	12	6	6
Trinidad & Tobago	40	40	10	5	5
Grenada	44	33	11	6	6
Guyana	38	29	10	5	5
Bolivia	46	8	8	0	0
Uruguay	24	9	6	4	4
Cuba	26	4	4	0	0
Paraguay	29	4	0	0	0
Brazil	23	6	3	0	0
Argentina	17	5	3	3	3
Ecuador	25	5	0	0	0
Venezuela	15	4	7	0	0

FIGURE 2.3 Percentage of agreements including trade-related and non-trade issues by LA.
Source: DESTA database.

demonstrate that this group also signs deeper agreements on average. In contrast, the reluctant globalists and anti-globalists often include investment and services but rarely include newer generation issues such as IPR, the environment and labour.

These broad comparisons demonstrate that the liberal globalists and reluctant globalists both sign many trade agreements on average but that there are major differences in design, with the liberal globalists signing deeper, more ambitious agreements on average. Moreover, they include more clauses related to the environment as well as investment, IPR and labour.[13] In contrast, the reluctant globalists are

[13] On environmental provisions, see Klotz and Ugarte (Chapter 6); on investment and particular approaches to reform, see Calvert (Chapter 11); on services and their impact on female labour participation in Chile, see Muñoz and Cáceres (Chapter 9).

also active signers of PTAs but sign agreements that are both shallower and narrower in scope. Finally, the anti-globalists sign fewer agreements on average, and those that are signed tend to be even shallower and narrower.

2.5 EMPIRICAL ANALYSIS – WHAT FACTORS DETERMINE PTA DESIGN?

The evidence suggests that our typology is helpful as a heuristic. Therefore, in this section, we engage in a more systematic empirical analysis of the determinants of PTA design in the region. We focus on three sets of explanations for PTA design. First, we look at the economic determinants of PTA design, including level of development and the export orientation of the parties. Second, we look at the political determinants of design, including regime type and government ideology. Finally, we examine whether design is impacted by partner choice.[14] We focus both on intra-LA PTAs (i.e., a PTA signed by LA countries only) and extra-LA PTA (i.e., a PTA signed by at least one LA country but that also includes members from a country or countries outside the region).

The three main dependent variables used in the analyses are PTA depth, flexibility and dispute settlement strength from the DESTA database.[15] We use the World Bank's *World Development Indicators* and the UN's *COMTRADE* data to measure the economic characteristics of the PTA members. We measure level of development with *Per Capita GDP*, which is members' average GDP per capita. *Exports* measure the members' average exports.[16] *Ceteris paribus*, we expect that countries with a higher GDP per capita as well as more reliance on exports should favour deeper agreements. We also expect this to go hand in hand with more flexible agreements, as these provide assurance against shocks as well as provide safeguards for groups who stand to lose from liberalization (Rosendorff and Milner 2001; Baccini et al., 2015). Finally, we do not have strong expectations about whether economic factors are directly related to the strength of dispute settlement as other research indicates that dispute settlement design is related most strongly to other design features, such as depth (Allee and Elsig 2016).

For political determinants, we use data from both the Polity Project and Global Leader Ideology (Herre 2023). *Polity* is the members' average Polity 2 score and has been rescaled to a 0–20 scale for regression purposes. *Ideology leader* captures the leaders' ideology of countries, classifying them as 'leftist', 'centrist' or 'rightist'. We recoded this variable as 1 (leftist), 2 (centrist) and 3 (rightist) and computed the average ideology at the PTA level across countries at the time of signing the

[14] As for perceptions of citizens vis-à-vis PTA partners and differences of attitudes between elites and individuals, see Dür and Huber (Chapter 3).

[15] For more information on these indices, please refer to the DESTA codebook (available on the DESTA website) and to Dür et al. (2014).

[16] Trade flows estimated in thousands USD.

agreement. Although this measurement is very crude, it still enables us to evaluate whether leader ideology matters for PTA design. Overall, we expect that more democratic countries will sign PTAs that are deeper as democratization has been associated with economic reform in LA (Murillo 2001; Weyland 2002) as well as globally (Milner and Mukherjee 2009; Baccini 2012). At the same time, we expect that democratic polities will demand more flexibility as they face on average domestically more veto players (Allee and Elsig 2017), while they tend to be more open to legalized dispute settlement, as democracies support the rule of law and implementation of commitments. We also expect that as the membership of a PTA becomes more rightist in orientation that PTA design should become deeper as rightist governments are more insulated from social groups and therefore able to make more widespread economic reforms, such as those entailed by deeper PTAs (O'Donnell 1978; Nelson 1990). Similarly, we expect that left-wing governments are more likely to include flexibility provisions due to the influence of social groups who fear losses; however, this is a weak expectation due to the fact that depth and flexibility are often empirically related (Baccini et al., 2015). We do not have clear expectations for the influence of leader ideology on the strength of dispute settlement.

The remaining three independent variables capture other aspects of PTA membership: *EU* is a dummy variable to identify whether the EU is part of the agreement; we include a similar dummy variable for the *US*. In both of these cases, we expect that the presence of the US or EU as a PTA partner should lead to deeper, more flexible and more legalized agreements.[17] Intra – LA is a dummy variable, where 1 identifies an agreement composed by only LA countries and 0 an agreement signed by at least one LA country but also includes members from outside the region. Initially, we are agnostic about the sign of this variable, as it is not a priori clear whether intra-regional agreements will be driven more by the preferences of the liberal globalists or one of the other groupings. PTAs signed among members from other regions are not included in this analysis.

Lastly, PTAs including more flexibility clauses also tend to be deeper, as adding such clauses can ease the negotiations of deeper provisions (Baccini et al. 2015). Similarly, stronger DSM are more likely to be included in deeper agreements (Allee and Elsig 2016). We therefore also include the PTA depth in our flexibility and DSM strength regressions as these design provisions are often substantially related.

As our dependent variables are all ordered indices, we use ordered logistic regression to estimate the relationship between political, economic and membership

[17] There are several possible mechanisms that could explain this. One is that the US and Europe have a preference for deeper agreements and will use their bargaining power to influence treaty outcomes (see Allee and Lugg 2016). At the same time, however, there may be a selection effect whereby some countries in the region have a preference for deeper agreements.

TABLE 2.3 *Determinants of PTA design signed by Latin American countries.*

	(1) Depth	(2) Flexibility	(3) DSM
Depth index		0.64***	0.78***
		(0.09)	(0.10)
Log mean GDPPC	1.05***	−0.53	−1.03***
	(0.28)	(0.32)	(0.34)
Log mean exports	0.23*	0.01	0.13
	(0.09)	(0.09)	(0.11)
Mean polity score	0.14**	0.01	0.22***
(0–20)	(0.04)	(0.04)	(0.06)
Mean ideology leader	0.27	0.07	−0.33
	(0.23)	(0.25)	(0.28)
Intra-LA	−1.08**	−1.20***	−1.92***
	(0.37)	(0.45)	(0.49)
EU	−0.05	−0.49	0.64
	(0.71)	(0.76)	(0.77)
US	0.26	−1.72**	3.28***
	(0.80)	(0.77)	(1.20)
Observations	181	168	171
McFadden R-squared	0.24	0.32	0.46

Note: As we estimate an ordered logistic regression, there are several intercepts for all the different intervals in the dependent variable. The full set of results are available by request from the authors. Significance levels are 0.01 (***), 0.05(**), 0.1(*).
Sources: DESTA database, World Development Indicators (WDI), Polity Project, Global Leader Ideology dataset.

patterns on PTA design.[18] Our sample includes all PTAs signed by at least one LA country and includes a total of 231 PTAs over the period from 1951 to 2021.[19]

2.5.1 *Discussion of Results*

The results of the regression in Table 2.3 highlight several important dynamics. First, as expected, PTA depth is a strong predictor of the level of flexibility and the strength of dispute settlement provisions in PTAs. Second, the average members' GDP per capita has a positive and statistically significant effect ($p < .01$) on *depth* but, surprisingly, a negative and significant effect on *DSM*. This contradictory effect

[18] To note, however, that this may affect the interpretability of the results on PTA flexibility as the index range (1–4) may be too small to provide a good estimation of the logistic regression. One last note of caution when interpreting our results; the results displayed in Table 2.3 are the direct estimations of the logistic regression (expressed in log odds).

[19] In our three sets of regressions, 181, 168 and 172 observations were estimated due to missing values for some of the independent variables. The years 2019 to 2021 are particularly affected due to lack of data availability for these years.

could be explained by the fact that countries with higher level of development are generally more economically powerful and might sign deep agreements to boost their economy but see less need to rely on a legalized dispute settlement system. Third, the average members' export level has a positive and significant effect on *depth* but neither on *flexibility* nor on *DSM strength*. These results are in line with the findings of Allee and Elsig (2016) on the determinants of dispute settlement provisions in PTAs. In particular, the authors find that trade volumes do not seem to have an important impact.

Turning to our political determinants, we find a positive and significant impact of the members' average polity score on two of the three design variables. The coefficients for depth and DSM are positive and significant at the 99 per cent level. The coefficient for flexibility is positive but not significant. This demonstrates that PTAs with more democratic members are deeper and contain stronger DSM provisions on average.[20] By contrast, we find no significant relationship between leader ideology and the main PTA design characteristics. There are several potential explanations for this. First, contained within the 'right', 'left' and 'centre' categories, there are potentially very different types of regimes (which would also have an effect as seen previously). Second, the variable we use only captures the ideology of the leader but does not account for the ideology of other parts of the government (parliament, ministers, etc) which may be different. Lastly, it is also possible that trade policy is less sensitive to changes in government than to overall regime type. Moreover, as has been shown recently, in many countries there is institutional inertia in the bureaucracy which can be reinforced by interest groups domestically. For example, Calvert and Tienhaara (2022) show that many bureaucrats and interest groups in Peru continued to support investment provisions in PTAs, even after Peru experienced costly arbitration, due to embedded ideas about the positives of liberal, market-based policies.

Lastly, we also uncover interesting patterns when it comes to PTA membership. An important finding is the negative and significant impact of intra-LA on all our dependent variables. Most importantly, PTAs signed among LA countries tend to be on average shallower than those signed by LA countries and partners outside the region. One interpretation is that this is the result of distributional concerns: LA countries are willing to engage in deeper liberalization with developed partners outside the region where there are likely to be significant gains from trade due to complementary factor endowments (capital-rich and labour-rich, respectively) but sign shallower agreements with countries with similar factor endowments. This result tracks with theoretical thrust of Rodrik's argument (1992) as well as the

[20] The coefficient for Polity2 is positive and significant in models where depth is omitted, indicating that democracies likely prefer more flexible agreements. This effect, however, is moderated significantly by the robust correlation between depth and flexibility.

empirical pattern shown in Baccini (2012). Moreover, this indicates that the design of intra-LA PTAs is driven by reluctant globalists.

Surprisingly, the EU and US variables are not systematically significant across our models, except for a negative impact of US membership on flexibility and a positive impact of US membership on DSM strength. These results may seem surprising as the EU and the US are known for being influential trade partners with strong preferences for deeper, more legalized agreements. Although the EU and US have signed deep agreements with countries from LA, they represent a relatively small share in comparison to the overall number of deep PTAs signed by at least one LA country.[21] The significant negative impact of US membership on flexibility is driven by the low representation of the US among the most flexible agreements.[22] By contrast, the US is a member of 40 per cent of the agreements, including the most far-reaching DSM provisions.[23] To test for the robustness of this result, we re-estimated the model adding the PTA overall depth as an independent variable, and we still find a strong correlation.[24] This seems to signal the US' willingness to include strong DSM in trade agreements.

Overall, the regression results reveal several important patterns. First, we see that the economic characteristics of countries help explain PTA design outcomes. There is strong evidence, for example, that richer countries and those who have more export-oriented economies have a preference for deeper PTAs. Second, we also see that political factors matter. Our analyses reveal that PTAs with more democratic memberships favour agreements that are deeper and have more legalized dispute settlement provisions. Third, we show that there appears to be stark differences with respect to geographic scope, and therefore partner selection logic of LA PTAs. Intra-regional PTAs tend to be much shallower on average. Surprisingly, however, we did not find that these design differences are overwhelmingly influenced by economically powerful partners from outside LA. The results did not show, for example, that PTAs signed with the US or EU were deeper or more flexible than agreements signed with other outside the region partners. We did, however, find that the agreements with the US tended to have more legalized dispute settlement. Taken together we interpret this as evidence that the liberal globalists sign deeper agreements with a wide range of countries outside of LA, whereas agreements within the region tend to be driven by preferences of reluctant globalists or anti-globalist states (or at least reconciled with their interests).

2.6 TEXT ANALYSIS OF LA PTAS

In this section, we look at the text of negotiated PTAs to determine whether there are distinct models or templates around which LA PTAs converge. There exist several

[21] We refer here to deep PTAs, as those scoring 6 or more with respect to the depth index.

[22] We refer here to most flexible agreements as PTAs having a flexibility index equal to 4.

[23] We refer here to most far-reaching DSM agreements, as PTAs having a DSM strength index equal to 9.

[24] Results available on request.

different theoretical perspectives for why states may choose to reuse language in PTAs. Allee and Elsig (2019) show that many countries directly copy PTA text from earlier agreements. This phenomenon is driven by several dynamics. First, states with low bureaucratic capacity may rely on copy-pasting as a way to bypass their lower capacity. Second, powerful states may strategically reuse language in order to push their preferences (see Allee and Lugg 2016), which they can deploy via strategic sequencing (Castle 2023). Moreover, states may choose to adopt language from different agreements, including from other forums such as the World Trade Organization (WTO) or bilateral investment treaties (BITs) in order to incorporate their preferred language (see Allee et al., 2017; Chaisse et al., 2022). Third, Peacock et al. (2019) posit that copy-pasting creates consistency that can benefit firms, consumers and the economy by promoting innovation, reducing costs and increasing competition. Fourth, recent research suggests that countries may reuse language in order to enhance the legitimacy of cooperation (Clark and Pratt 2024). In contrast, Kim (2015) finds that commonalities in text among PTAs is low on average, which suggests the existence of different templates. Given the current debate (and potential mechanisms), we conduct text analyses on PTAs signed by LA countries to discern what determines levels of similarity, if they do exist. The main question we are interested in is whether there are distinct clusters or models around which countries' PTA practices converge.

To determine similarity between PTAs, we use automated text analysis to examine the text of 185 trade agreements signed by at least one LA country.[25] To facilitate analysis, we employed basic pre-processing on the text by removing numbers and transforming all text to lower case, while still retaining word order. To identify identical text, we require that the text between two agreements matches word-for-word (with no deviations) in sequences of five words or more. We then compute *Jaccard* scores, which tell us the total number of words shared between two documents (Alschner and Skougarevskiy 2016).[26] The resulting numbers range from 0 to 1, with higher numbers indicating greater similarity between two PTAs.

Text analysis of 185 PTAs in our corpus of texts does not indicate that there are distinct clusters or models that dominate in the region. At the same time, however, there is evidence that some of the countries do copy-paste on occasion. Below we present four heatmaps to show country networks. Darker cells indicate areas of increased overlap. For illustrative purposes we chose Chile, Mexico, Brazil and Venezuela as these countries represent the different groupings of liberal globalists, reluctant globalists and anti-globalists. What the results suggest is that similarity is not uniformly distributed throughout each country's network. In other words, we do

25 The list of PTAs used in this text analysis is found in the Appendix.

26 Given two documents, represented as n-grams, Jaccard similarity is calculated as the size of the intersection of the sets divided by the size of the union of the sets. The final similarity measure provides a quantitative indication of the similarity between the two documents, based on common words they share.

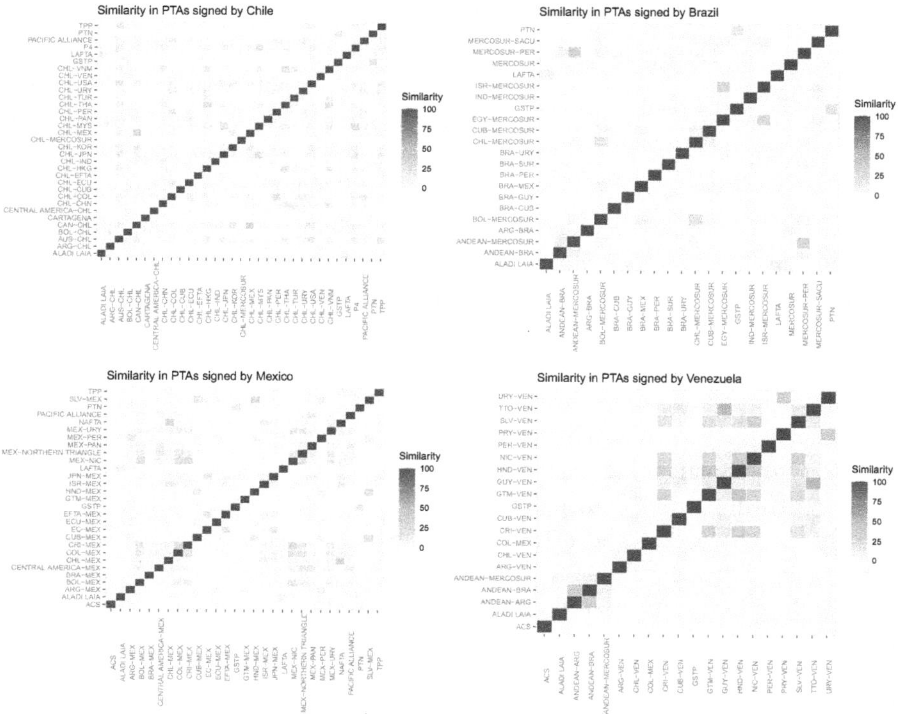

FIGURE 2.4 Country-level heatmaps of PTA similarity.
Source: DESTA database.

not observe countries adopting a single unique model which they then use repeatedly or expand upon. Instead, they seem to opportunistically reuse language from one treaty to the next, which is likely influenced by the preferences and power of the other country or countries involved (Figure 2.4).

This variation poses a unique possibility: perhaps there are specific agreements that are copy-pasted regularly, even if there is no evidence that countries are engaging in widespread copy-pasting in their own networks. Is there evidence that LA countries draw much of their language from their treaties with outside countries, or if they do so primarily within the region? For example, do we observe an overwhelming influence of US or EU-led PTAs, or do LA countries draw from within the region, or, perhaps, from their own networks? To investigate this, we took four distinctive PTAs of the different models we are interested in, namely MERCOSUR for an intra-regional template, Chile-EC for the EU template, and both Central American Free Trade Agreement (CAFTA) and Peru-US for a US template. We then compared the similarity scores between these agreements and all other agreements signed by at least one LA country.

These PTA templates were chosen for a number of reasons. First, there has been a considerable time span since they were signed (MERCOSUR in 1999, EC Chile in

2002, CAFTA in 2004 and Peru-US in 2006) which increases the possibility that they might be used as model templates for later agreements. We then looked at the characteristics of the most important PTAs signed to date and found that Chile-EC, CAFTA and Peru-US all have comparable features, such as depth and average polity scores of member countries.[27] MERCOSUR was chosen as the Latin America PTA template since it was created with the intention of regional integration and the establishment of a Southern Common Market (Manzetti 1993). Therefore, despite the characteristics of MERCOSUR being different to the other PTA templates, it still stands out as the most relevant treaty template for an intra-regional model (Table 2.4).

The results suggest the US PTAs have had an impact in the region, albeit not as extensive as one might expect. The highest similarity percentage across all four PTAs is between Peru-US and Colombia-US, with an overlap of 75 per cent. Moreover, there is some evidence that language included in both CAFTA and Peru-US has diffused to PTAs where the US is not a partner, such as Nicaragua-Taiwan, Australia-Chile and Australia-Peru. That said, there is not extensive evidence that these models have been adopted broadly in the region. Similarly, there is some evidence suggesting that European agreements, both EC and EFTA, have been copied, especially when the EC is a common partner. However, these percentages are typically around or below 20 per cent of the total language re-used, indicating, as in the case of US agreements, that there are limits to their diffusion. In contrast, we find little evidence that text from MERCOSUR has widely diffused in the region.

Overall, there does not appear to be a model or models that LA countries copy text from exclusively, either within or outside the region. There is some evidence that countries draw text from US and European PTAs, but the degree to which this is occurring is not as high as one might initially suspect. Our intuition is that this is due to the fact that countries within the liberal globalist group sign many deep agreements but, given the nature of their treaty networks, tend to draw language from a variety of sources or craft new provision on an ad hoc basis. Thus, the most likely story is that LA countries – principally the liberal globalists – tend to draw from their own past treaty practice but that the actual content is likely to be an amalgam of several of their different past treaties which can be with a diverse slate of countries geographically and politically. We see this in the treaty networks of countries such as Chile, which have signed relatively liberalizing agreements with partners across the Pacific Rim and elsewhere, including the US, Singapore, Australia, Indonesia, Vietnam, Malaysia, Japan, the UK and Turkey.

[27] The average polity scores of Chile-EC, CAFTA and Peru-US are 19.9, 18.3 and 19.5, respectively, on a 20-point scale. The depth index (a 7-point depth score from the DESTA database) of these three agreements is also comparable – with both Chile-EC and CAFTA at 7, CAFTA at 6.

TABLE 2.4 *PTA models in Latin America.*

MERCOSUR (1999)		Chile-EC (2002)		CAFTA (2004)		Peru-US (2006)	
Argentina Brazil	6%	Chile EFTA	28%	CAFTA-DR	72%	Colombia-US	75%
Mexico Nicaragua	5%	CARIFORUM EC EPA	21%	Nicaragua-Taiwan	30%	Panama US	63%
Mexico Panama	5%	EFTA Mexico	18%	Panama US	27%	Nicaragua-Taiwan	12%
El Salvador Mexico	5%	Central America EC	12%	Peru-US	23%	Transpacific Partnership (TPP)	12%
Ecuador Paraguay	5%	EC Mexico	12%	Colombia-US	20%	Australia-Peru	12%
Trinidad and Tobago Venezuela	4%	Colombia EC Peru	11%	Australia-Chile	16%	Colombia Korea	11%
Latin American Free Trade Area (LAFTA)	4%	Chile Thailand	11%	Transpacific Partnership (TPP)	14%	Korea Peru	11%
Guyana Venezuela	4%	Central America EFTA	8%	Panama Singapore	13%	Canada Colombia	10%
Cuba Mexico	4%	Colombia EFTA	8%	Canada Peru	12%	Canada Peru	10%
Honduras Mexico	4%	Chile Japan	8%	Canada Honduras	12%	Australia-Chile	9%

Source: DESTA database.

2.7 CONCLUSIONS

The analyses in this chapter paint a picture of a heterogeneous region with respect to exposure to, experience with and preferences towards PTAs. One central conclusion, which is borne out strongly by the analyses, is that governments in the region sign different types of agreements, with different partners, depending on their underlying preferences with respect to economic development. The economically liberal states in the region, principally Chile, Peru, Colombia, Mexico, Costa Rica and Panama, have tended to seek out partners both within and outside Latin America with whom they can negotiate relatively deep PTAs. Importantly, these deep PTAs contain provisions that go beyond trade liberalization, to include investment and non-tariff barriers as well as a variety of other NTIs, including environmental standards, and labour provisions.

In contrast, the reluctant globalists – including Brazil, Argentina, Paraguay and Uruguay – sign shallower agreements which skew towards other, like-minded countries in the region. There are notable exceptions to this pattern, of course, but in general these countries' scepticism of liberalization and the political obstacles towards the dismantling of a strong developmental state, mean that their agreements tend to be shallower and narrower in design.

Finally, the anti-globalist states – including Venezuela, Cuba and Bolivia – have a distinct pattern of PTA signing altogether. They have, on average, signed fewer agreements than the other groups and signed much shallower agreements on average, which often have underlying geopolitical motivations such as the ALBA initiative. As such, these countries have not been exposed to market forces or international trade and investment flows to the same degree as the countries in the other groups. Instead, PTAs, to the extent that they are pursued at all, often reflect the more idiosyncratic priorities of individual regimes.

Interestingly, however, these divergent underlying preferences towards PTAs have not led to a coalescing of treaty practice whereby countries anchor their PTA design around one of several distinct PTA templates. For the liberal globalists, major US-influenced initiatives in the region such as CAFTA and Peru-US have clearly had some impact on design choices. Moreover, we see that several of the more ambitious countries in this group have tended to sign deep agreements by seeking out like-minded states both within and outside the region. But, that said, there was no clear single template around which these states engaged with, indicating that their own idiosyncratic preferences are embedded in their treaty practice and that the final provisions are influenced in part by negotiating dynamics in any given case.

Ultimately, it is useful to highlight here several important larger dynamics which help contextualize the chapters to come and should help serve as a guide for future research. First, many LA countries clearly have domestic political incentives to sign PTAs, and most countries have heeded this call. The aggregate data suggest that this may be a function of LA's high level of democracy relative to other regions, as current research suggests that leaders in democratic countries are incentivized to sign PTAs (Mansfield and Milner 2012). Moreover, this is borne out by looking within the region; the countries with weaker democratic elements have tended to sign fewer agreements on average, and their design often reflects the idiosyncratic preferences of their leaders or important domestic actors. There are important differences within the democratic societies of the region, however. Rather than signing similar PTAs, countries in the region have chosen to sign qualitatively different PTAs, likely in response to divergent domestic political factors unique to each country.

This core dynamic is taken up in important ways in several of the other chapters in this volume. Dür and Huber (Chapter 3), for example, show that preferences for PTA partners are driven by relevant domestic political cleavages, including citizen and legislator political ideology. Moreover, the chapter by Calvert (Chapter 11) shows how preferences for reform of investment provisions in PTAs hinge on the influence of various domestic political actors. Similarly, how popular PTAs are, and hence the ability of governments to sign future agreements, also depends greatly on domestic politics, as highlighted by Campello and Urdínez (Chapter 13) and López and Bórquez (Chapter 8). Future studies should continue to probe this important research vein to better understand how democratic politics within LA – and variation in the nature of democratic institutions and societal preferences across LA countries – affects the supply and demand for PTAs. Importantly, these factors, by impacting PTA partner selection and design, are likely to condition the economic impact of a given PTA.

Second, we see that the legacy of the development state and ongoing domestic political debates about how to reconcile a developmental state with the exigencies of an increasingly globalized world clearly influence treaty design, which may have important downstream effects. The less statist, more liberal states in the region have tended to be the most ambitious in signing deep PTAs. Whereas countries with a more statist legacy have tended to sign shallower agreements that favour protecting important domestic economic and political interests. This may show up under the auspices of special and differential treatment, as shown by Zelicovich et al. (Chapter 5), but also likely impacts partner selection and design through multiple channels. How this has impacted countries' political economy is unclear, however. For example, we see that per capita wealth and treaty practice are correlated in the region – with richer countries signing more and deeper PTAs on average – but it is unclear whether PTAs are a consequence of greater levels of development or, potentially, a cause. Future studies should aim to unravel this relationship in more detail. Moreover, the developmental state and backlash against globalization in places like Brazil and Mexico can also lead to 'murky protectionism', as highlighted by Albertoni and Wise (Chapter 12). This is something that we also observe in formerly liberal globalist states where public opinion is shifting as shown in the case of Chile by Lopez and Borquez (Chapter 8).

Third, we see LA is also a fertile ground for experimentation in the design of PTAs, which may also explain the high degree of heterogeneity in terms of design outcomes (see, e.g., the chapter on gender provisions by Bahri (Chapter 4), as well as on digital provisions by Klotz and Ugarte (Chapter 6)). The analyses in this chapter do not yield determinative predictions with respect to when policy experimentation will occur, but they do strongly suggest that the dynamics of democratic politics in the region as well as the fact that LA countries are more than willing to sign agreements with a variety of countries both within and outside the region likely plays a role. This experimentation may lead to inconsistency in countries' PTA networks, which can complicate the rules required for domestic economic actors and provide openings for disguised protectionism, but it also indicates a certain level or responsivity of PTA design to citizen concerns. Moreover, as is the case with the gendered economic impact of service provisions in Chilean PTAs, as shown by Munoz and Caceres (Chapter 9), experimentation may be particularly important as an avenue for countries to help foster sustainable development in line with local preferences. Importantly, as is shown in the chapter by Álvarez Zarate et al. (Chapter 7), while bound in many cases by legal obligations at the WTO and in PTAs, countries often still retain policy space to seek domestic goals. Finally, the contribution by Saco (Chapter 10) shows how public policies 'travel' across Latin America and how some PTAs can act as catalysts of policy diffusion, a role the past research has not sufficiently accounted for.

REFERENCES

Allee, T. and M. Elsig 2016. "Why Do Some International Institutions Contain Strong Dispute Settlement Provisions? New Evidence from Preferential Trade Agreements," *The Review of International Organizations* 11: 89–120.

2017. "Veto Players and the Design of Preferential Trade Agreements," *Review of International Political Economy* 24(3): 538–567.

2019. "Are the Contents of International Treaties Copied and Pasted? Evidence from Preferential Trade Agreements," *International Studies Quarterly* 63(3): 603–613.

Allee, T. and A. Lugg 2016. "Who Wrote the Rules for the Trans-Pacific Partnership?" *Research & Politics* 3(3): 1–9, 2053168016658919.

Allee, T., M. Elsig and A. Lugg 2017. "The Ties between the World Trade Organization and Preferential Trade Agreements: A Textual Analysis," *Journal of International Economic Law* 20(2): 333–363.

Alschner, W. and D. Skougarevskiy 2016. "Mapping the Universe of International Investment Agreements," *Journal of International Economic Law* 19(3): 561–588.

Baccini, L. 2012. "Democratization and Trade Policy: An Empirical Analysis of Developing Countries," *European Journal of International Relations* 18(3): 455–479.

Baccini, L. and J. Urpelainen 2014. "International Institutions and Domestic Politics: Can Preferential Trading Agreements Help Leaders Promote Economic Reform?" *The Journal of Politics* 76(1): 195–214.

Baccini L., A. Dür and M. Elsig 2015. "The Politics of Trade Agreement Design: Revisiting the Depth-Flexibility Nexus," *International Studies Quarterly* 59(4): 765–775.

Bohigues, A. and J. M. Rivas 2019. "Free Trade Agreements and Regional Alliances: Support from Latin American Legislators," *Revista brasileira de política internacional* 62(1), e001.

Briceño-Ruiz, J. 2013. "Ejes y modelos en la etapa actual de la integración económica regional en América Latina," *Estudios Internactionales* 45(175): 9–39.

2018. "Times of Change in Latin American Regionalism," *Contexto Internacional* 40: 573–594.

Brooks, S. M. and M. J. Kurtz 2012. "Paths to Financial Policy Diffusion: Statist Legacies In Latin America's Globalization," *International Organization* 66(1): 95–128.

Calvert, J. and K. Tienhaara 2023. "Beyond Once BITten Twice Shy: Defending the Legitimacy of Investor-State Dispute Settlement in Peru and Australia," *Review of International Political Economy* 30(5): 1799–1823.

Cardoso, F. H. and E. Faletto 1979. *Dependency and Development in Latin America*. Berkeley: University of California Press.

Carranza, M. E. 2017. "Resilient or Declining?: Mercosur and the Future of Post-neoliberal Regionalism in Latin America." In J. Briceño-Ruiz and I. Morales (Eds.), *Post-Hegemonic Regionalism in the Americas*. Abingdon: Routledge, pp. 125–140.

Castle, M. A. 2023. "How Do Global Trade Rules Evolve? Strategic Sequencing in International Economic Law," *Review of International Political Economy* 30(4): 1387–1412.

Chaisse, J., M. Elsig, S. Jusoh and A. Lugg, 2022. "Drafting Investment Law: Patterns of Influence in the Regional Comprehensive Economic Partnership (RCEP)," *Journal of International Economic Law* 25(1): 110–128.

Clark, R. and T. Pratt 2024. "The Art of Imitation: IO Legitimacy and Strategic Treaty Design," *Political Economy of International Organizations Conference 2024*. https://www.peio.me/wp-content/uploads/PEIO16/submission_163.pdf

Dür, A. and R. Huber 2025. "Preferences for Trading Partners: Evidence from Citizens and Legislators in Latin America," this volume.

Dür, A., L. Baccini and M. Elsig 2014. "The Design of International Trade Agreements: Introducing a New Dataset." *The Review of International Organizations* 9(3): 353–375.

Evans, P. B. 1995. *Embedded Autonomy: States and Industrial Transformation*. Princeton: Princeton University Press.

Fernandez, R. and J. Portes 1998. "Returns to Regionalism: An Analysis of Non-traditional Gains from Regional Trade Agreements," *The World Bank Economic Review* 12(2): 197–220.

Herre, B. 2023. "Identifying Ideologues: A Global Dataset on Political Leaders, 1945–2020," *British Journal of Political Science* 53(2): 740–748.

Hicks, R., H. V. Milner and D. Tingley 2014. "Trade Policy, Economic Interests, and Party Politics in a Developing Country: The Political Economy of CAFTA-DR," *International Studies Quarterly* 58(1): 106–117.

Kim, S. Y. 2015. "The Language of Institutional Design: Text Similarity in Preferential Trade Agreements," *Political Economy of International Organizations Conference 2015*. www.peio.me/wp-content/uploads/PEIO9/102_80_1443623786996_SYKim30Sept2015.pdf

Klotz, S. and C. Ugarte 2025. "Digital and Environmental Provisions in Latin American Trade Agreements," this volume.

Laursen, F. 2018. *Comparative Regional Integration: Theoretical Perspectives*. Abingdon: Routledge.

López, D. and A. Bórquez 2025. "How Preferential Trade Agreements Are Perceived in Chile: From Love to Hate in a Single Step?," this volume.

Mansfield, E. D., H. V. Milner and B. P. Rosendorff 2000. "Free to Trade: Democracies, Autocracies, and International Trade," *American Political Science Review* 94(2): 305–321.

Mansfield, E. D. and H. V. Milner 2012. *Votes, Vetoes, and the Political Economy of International Trade Agreements*. Princeton: Princeton University Press.

Manzetti, L. 1993. "The Political Economy of Mercosur," *Journal of Interamerican Studies and World Affairs* 35(4): 101–141.

Marshall M. G. and T. R. Gurr. 2020. *Polity5: Political Regime Characteristics and Transitions, 1800–2018*. Vienna: Center for Systemic Peace, 2.

Milner, H. V. and K. Kubota 2005. "Why the Move to Free Trade? Democracy and Trade Policy in the Developing Countries," *International Organization* 59(1): 107–143.

Milner, H. V. and B. Mukherjee 2009. "Democratization and Economic Globalization," *Annual Review of Political Science* 12(1): 163–181.

Muñoz, F. and J. Cáceres 2025. "Chile's PTA Services Impact Assessment: Looking beyond Trade Flows: Women's Employment Participation," this volume.

Murillo, M. V. 2001. *Labor Unions, Partisan Coalitions, and Market Reforms in Latin America*. Cambridge: Cambridge University Press.

Nelson, J. M. 1990. *Economic Crisis and Policy Choice: The Politics of Adjustment in the Third World*. Princeton: Princeton University Press.

O'Donnell, G. 1978. "Reflections on the Patterns of Change in the Bureaucratic-Authoritarian State," *Latin American Research Review* 13(1): 3–38.

Peacock, C. K., K. Milewicz and D. Snidal 2019. "Boilerplate in International Trade Agreements," *International Studies Quarterly* 63)4): 923–937.

Quiliconi, C. 2014. "Competitive Diffusion of Trade Agreements in Latin America," *International Studies Review* 16(2): 240–251.

Rodrik, D. 1992. "The Rush to Free Trade in the Developing World: Why So Late? Why Now? Will it Last? NBER Working Paper Series No. 3947.

Rosendorff, B. P. and H. V. Milner 2001. "The Optimal Design of International Trade Institutions: Uncertainty and Escape," *International Organization* 55(4): 829–857.

Saco, V. 2025. "Food Labelling Regulation of the Pacific Alliance Members," this volume.

Sanahuja, J. A. 2009. "Del "regionalismo abierto" al regionalismo post-liberal," In: Alfonso, L. L. Peña. and M. Vazquez (Eds.), *Anuario de la integración regional de América Latina y el Gran Caribe*. Buenos Aires: Coordinadora Regional de Investigaciones Económicas y Sociales, pp. 11–55.

Serbin, A. and A. Serbin Pont 2017. "The Foreign Policy of the Bolivarian Republic of Venezuela: The Role and Legacy of Hugo Chávez," *Latin American Policy* 8(2): 232–248.

Vieira, V. R. 2014. "Invisible Legacies: Brazil's and South Korea's Shift from ISI towards Export Strategies under Authoritarian Rule," *Journal of International Relations and Development* 17: 157–190.

Weyland, K. 2002 *The Politics of Market Reform in Fragile Democracies: Argentina, Brazil, Peru, and Venezuela*. Princeton: Princeton University Press.

World Bank n.d. *World Development Indicators*. Washington: The World Bank. https://databank.worldbank.org/home

Zelicovich, J., J. Peixoto, L. Daibert and V. Delich 2025. "Assessing Special and Differential Treatment in Latin American Trade Agreements", this volume.

3

Preferences for Trading Partners

Evidence from Citizens and Legislators in Latin America

Andreas Dür and Robert A. Huber

3.1 INTRODUCTION

Public opinion surveys consistently demonstrate that international trade is viewed favourably by most citizens. However, when people are asked about trade with specific countries, differences emerge as people are more supportive of trade with some countries than with others. This suggests that they have preferences for certain trading partners. While citizens have only an indirect influence on a country's trade policy, political elites such as legislators have a direct say in these policies. Similar to citizens, political elites also may have preferences for certain trading partners over others. In light of these observations, this contribution poses two questions. First, what factors explain attitudes towards trade with different countries? Second, do the factors that determine trading partner preferences differ between citizens and political elites?

We address these questions for the case of Latin American countries. Data from the Design of Trade Agreements (DESTA) project (Dür et al. 2014) show that these countries have been particularly active in forging trade agreements. Importantly, countries in Latin America have reached out to Western partners, such as the United States (US) and the European Union (EU), but also to non-Western countries, in particular China. Which of these entities becomes the major trading partner has important implications, as China, the EU, and the US put forward substantially different models of trade liberalization.

In answering these questions, we present three broad explanations for trading partner preferences, all of which are applicable to both citizens and political elites. For one, economic interests may matter. While trade is generally welfare-enhancing, specific groups within a country may nonetheless lose from an increase in trade with a particular trading partner. In a Latin American country, for example,

We are grateful to Andrew Lugg and participants at the 2022 World Trade Forum in Bern for comments on earlier versions of this chapter. This research received funding from the ERC under the EU's Horizon 2020 research and innovation programme (grant agreement No 724107).

a person working in the textile sector may welcome more trade with the US (whose textile industry generally is not competitive internationally, see e.g. Huber et al. 2023) but loathe more trade with China (which has an internationally highly competitive textile industry). Second, geopolitical concerns may influence preferences for trading partners. Trade can cause dependencies that one side may use to exert power over the other (Hirschman 1945). At the same time, trade may cement alliances (Jackson and Nei 2015). People consider the potential effects of trade on security; therefore, they can be expected to have a preference for allies as trading partners (Carnegie and Gaikwad 2022). Finally, the choice of preferred trading partner could be a function of political ideology. For ideological reasons, people may have a greater affinity to some countries than to others. For example, preferential trade agreements with the US most clearly follow the idea of market liberalization and open trade. Thus, right-wing individuals could prefer trading with the US (e.g., vis-à-vis agreements with China) because the underlying ideational orientation of the trading partner fits their view on the economy.

Empirically, we scrutinize these theoretical propositions by investigating two core actors in the formulation of trade policy in Latin America: citizens and members of parliament. First, we use public opinion data from the Latinobarómetro that asked respondents about their evaluation of trade with the US and China. We take the differences between the assessments of these two trading partners as our dependent variable, which is the support for the US relative to China. Second, we use the Latin American Elites Database, which contains data from surveys of members of parliament in a series of Latin American countries since 1994. Among other questions, the legislators were asked to evaluate free trade agreements with the US and the EU, and the Pacific Alliance and the Bolivarian Alliance for the Peoples of Our America. We calculate the differences between the assessment of a free trade agreement with the US and the other assessments to arrive at our dependent variables.

The results indicate that political ideology is an important predictor of preferences for trading partners for both political elites and citizens. By contrast, the findings only offer partial support for the other two explanations. Specifically, economic considerations only matter for legislators' preferences and geopolitical considerations only for citizens' preferences.

In two ways, our study contributes to a better understanding of the political economy of trade, especially for the case of Latin America. On the one hand, whereas a large literature analyses trade attitudes in general (Kuo and Naoi 2015; Stiller et al. 2022), so far only a few studies have looked at the question of whether and how trade attitudes vary across trading partners. (For some exceptions, see Chiang et al. 2013; Spilker et al. 2016; Jungherr et al. 2018; Kim et al. 2023.) Our study shows that trade support is multifaceted, and understanding trade attitudes requires going beyond questions on whether someone favours trade in the abstract. Such generic questions fall short of capturing attitudes towards trade, given that there is considerable variation across trading partners in terms of trade support. As done here, this variation across trading partners can help disentangle different explanations that shape attitudes towards trade. On the other hand, we compare the trade attitudes of political elites and citizens. We detect some differences, but also important parallels across these two actor types. In fact, our key takeaway in this respect is that legislator and citizen attitudes towards trade are more similar than different. This finding is good news for democratic representation in an increasingly politicized policy area and has important implications for the responsiveness of political elites to citizens' views on trade as well as the emerging literature on the elite-citizen gap (Dellmuth et al. 2022).

3.2 ARGUMENT

Three major factors can shape actors' preferences with respect to the choice of trading partner: economic considerations, geopolitical considerations, and ideology. In the following, we discuss these three factors and how they might influence the preferences for trading partners of citizens and legislators.

3.2.1 *Economic Considerations*

Let's start with economic considerations, a person's economic fortunes may differ across potential trading partners. Following the Stolper-Samuelson theorem, high-skilled workers should benefit more from an agreement with a country at a lower level of development (Alt and Gilligan 1994). This is so because trade liberalization with such a country should increase (relative) domestic demand for high-skilled workers and hence their wages and job opportunities. By contrast, the trade liberalization entailed by an agreement with a more highly developed country should reduce demand for high-skilled workers and hence their wages. For low-skilled workers, the expectation is just the opposite. Chiang et al. (2013) found support for these expectations in Taiwan. In their study, high-skilled workers showed greater support for a trade agreement with both China and the US, but the difference to low-skilled workers was higher for the former than for the latter, which they interpret as support for the Stolper-Samuelson theorem.

The Stolper-Samuelson theorem is not the only attempt at explaining the distributional effects of trade. 'New new' trade theory starts from the observation that only a small number of 'superstar' firms engage in trade (Osgood et al. 2017). These firms hire the most productive workers, many of whom can be expected to be highly skilled. The expectation hence is for international trade to generally benefit high-skilled workers (Burstein and Vogel 2017). Still, even following this newer reasoning, it can be argued that high-skilled citizens should be *relatively* more supportive of trade with less advanced economies. As before, this is so because exports to such countries should generally consist of relatively more capital-intensive goods and services, which require relatively more input from high-skilled workers.

Two objections can be raised against the economic-considerations argument. For one, citizens may have very little understanding of the distributional consequences of trade (Rho and Tomz 2017). While this is plausible, it can be argued that whenever people directly experience the distributional effects of trade, they can correctly attribute them. For example, American voters have been shown to change their electoral behaviour in response to rising trade exposure (Baccini and Weymouth 2021). Moreover, citizens may receive cues from better-informed actors, such as trade unions or political parties, remedying their relative lack of knowledge.

The second objection concerns the fact that only a minority of citizens directly experience the wage- or job-related consequences of trade. This is so because a significant proportion of a society at any time does not participate in the labour market (e.g., because they are retired, in long-term unemployment) or produces nontradable services (for the role of employment status and trade attitudes, see also Stiller et al. 2022). In addition, sociotropic, rather than self-interested considerations, could drive attitudes towards trade. Hence, the effect of economic considerations may only be indirect (Schaffer and Spilker 2019). The elite cues referred to above, however, may also be available to citizens not directly affected by trade. Citizens who previously participated in the labour market may also have had direct experiences with the effects of trade in the past. To the extent that this objection is still valid, our estimates below will underestimate the role of skill level on trading partner preferences.

For legislators, the economic argument needs to be adapted in two ways. On the one hand, the problem of lack of information should be less pertinent for them. They can be expected to have sufficient knowledge to understand the consequences of trade with different trading partners. On the other hand, trade does not really affect demand for and the wages of legislators. Their economic considerations thus most likely relate less to the effects of trade directly for them, and more to the effects of trade for the economic well-being of the citizens that they represent (Dür et al. 2023). On average, an increase in trade is expected to enhance economic growth in all countries. In practice, at least in the short term, an increase in import competition can produce economic losses in some parts of a country. To the extent that economic considerations are important for them, legislators hence should favour trading partners that maximize the economic opportunities for the citizens they represent while minimizing the economic disruption created by trade. Following the discussion above, this is a function of the share of high-skilled workers in a district: the greater the share of high-skilled citizens in a district, the greater the preference for an economically less developed trading partner should be. Two hypotheses summarize this reasoning concerning economic considerations:

H1a: High-skilled citizens prefer relatively less economically developed trading partners.

H1b: The higher the average skill level of the workers legislators represent, the more they prefer relatively less economically developed trading partners.

3.2.2 *Geopolitical Considerations*

Preferences for partner countries may also be shaped by geopolitical considerations. To the extent that geopolitics is important, both citizens and legislators can be expected to prefer allies rather than adversaries as trading partners. This is so because trade with other countries tends to have security externalities (Gowa and Mansfield 1993), which imply that trade with allies positively influences a country's national security whereas trade with adversaries negatively affects a country's security. Following this line of argument, Bailey (2003) concluded that geopolitical concerns made the American public support early Cold War US trade policy. Similarly, the findings by Jungherr et al. (2018) indicate a role for geopolitics in individual-level preferences for trading partners. Concretely, they find that German citizens who are highly supportive of US leadership in foreign policy were more supportive of the planned Transatlantic Trade and Investment Partnership (TTIP). DiGiuseppe and Kleinberg (2019) found that security considerations play a large role in shaping individual trade preferences in the US. Finally, Carnegie and Gaikwad (2022) show that citizens prefer trade with allies but increase support for trade with enemies if they are told that trade can promote peace.

While it is likely that the importance of geopolitics for citizens varies over time and across countries, partly as a function of what happens in the world, at least broad notions of whether a country is friendly or not can serve as a heuristic for citizens to judge the consequences of a trade agreement with that country. In fact, they may rather have a general view of a country as a friend or a foe than understand the exact economic consequences of a trade agreement with that country. Alternatively, citizens may see trade as a means to advance peace and hence prefer trade with hostile countries (Bulman 2022). We do not deem this likely, however, as we expect citizens to lack the political sophistication to make this link between trade and peace (unless explicitly told about this link, as was done by Carnegie and Gaikwad 2022).

For legislators, geopolitical concerns should be of even greater importance on average, as they have a better understanding of the security externalities of trade. They may care about geopolitics for intrinsic reasons. Alternatively, re-election concerns may make them pay attention to geopolitics. The latter applies if citizens take geopolitical considerations seriously and hold politicians accountable that do not share this preference. Two hypotheses result from this argument:

H2a: Citizens prefer countries as trading partners that are (perceived as) geopolitical allies.

H2b: Legislators prefer countries as trading partners that are (perceived as) geopolitical allies.

3.2.3 *Ideological Considerations*

Finally, political ideology may play a role in trade partner preferences. Some countries may be seen as ideologically closer than others. In support of this line of reasoning, Spilker et al. (2016) found that citizens prefer partner countries in trade agreements that are culturally similar. Steiner (2018) stresses the role of postmaterialist concerns in creating opposition to TTIP. The best overall approximation of a person's political ideology, however, remains the left-right dimension (Jost et al. 2009). On this dimension, the political right can be defined as conservative and accepting of inequality, whereas the political left is associated with change and equality. The ideological position on the left–right dimension also should matter for people's economic views. A person towards the right tends to support capitalism with (relatively) little state intervention. By contrast, a person towards the left tends to favour state intervention in markets and redistributive policies. This can (such as for a considerable number of citizens in some Latin American countries) but does not need to include rejection of capitalism as a form of organizing the economy.

There is much debate about the extent to which people really ascribe to a consistent political ideology (Zaller 1992; Jost et al. 2009; Carmines and D'Amico 2015). It seems plausible enough, however, that people have at least broad notions of their own ideological leanings and also of what kind of ideology at least a select number of prominent countries represent. For example, the US stands representative of a relatively free-market, capitalist country. China, by contrast, represents a country with a much stronger state involvement in the economy. Following this reasoning, right-wing citizens might show a greater preference for the US as a trading partner than left-wing citizens. Note that this is a relative argument: even citizens on the left may prefer the US as a trading partner (e.g., because of concern about human rights abuses in China), but this preference may be weaker than in the case of citizens on the right.

Whereas the relevance of political ideology for citizens' attitudes can be disputed, for legislators it seems clear that they possess sufficient political sophistication to adopt ideologically consistent political attitudes. Their leaning on the left–right dimension can thus also be expected to matter for their preferences with respect to trade agreement partners. In fact, Bohigues and Rivas (2019) have already shown that among Latin American legislators, those further to the right are more supportive of trade agreements with the US and the EU than those further to the left. We again derive two hypotheses from this reasoning:

H3a: Greater alignment by a country with a citizen's leaning on the left–right dimension leads to greater support by this citizen for this country as trading partner.

H3b: Greater alignment by a country with a legislator's leaning on the left–right dimension leads to greater support by this legislator for this country as trading partner.

3.2.4 *Summary*

In Table 3.1, we summarize the various arguments presented. In the following two sections, we test these expectations using data for citizens and legislators in the case of Latin America. While we formulated the argument generically, there are some specificities to Latin America that are useful when testing the argument. For one, the US plays a strong role as a geopolitical ally for some countries and as a geopolitical adversary for others. This facilitates testing the geopolitical considerations argument. Moreover, the left–right dimension is very strong in Latin America, with a large number of citizens placed on either end of the spectrum.

TABLE 3.1 *Preferences for trading partners*

	Citizens	Legislators
Economic considerations	High-skilled individuals: greater support for labour-abundant trading partners and vice versa	Greater share of high-skilled workers among constituents: more support for labour-abundant trading partners and vice versa
Geopolitical considerations	Greater support for allies as trading partners	Greater support for allies as trading partners
Ideology	Greater support for trading partners that are seen as ideologically aligned	Greater support for trading partners that are seen as ideologically aligned

3.3 CITIZENS' TRADING PARTNER PREFERENCES

In order to test the three hypotheses concerning citizens' attitudes, we rely on the 2020 Latinobarometro survey.[1] This public opinion project conducts annual surveys with a representative sample of Latin American citizens. Specifically, it collects data for about 1,000 citizens each from eighteen Latin American countries.[2] The 2020 wave of the survey includes a question with respect to two potential trading partners that reads: 'What is your opinion on trade between [USA/China] and (country)? Is it very favorable (1), somewhat favorable (2), somewhat unfavorable (3), or very unfavorable (4) for the economic development of the country?' In this chapter, we thus use this question for all 20,204 respondents in the eighteen countries outlined above.

We propose two ways of operationalizing preferences for one trading partner over the other. First, we reverse the scale (so higher values indicate more positive perceptions of the US and China) and subtract the perceptions regarding China from those regarding the US. Thereby we create a variable that can theoretically range from −3 to 3, with higher values indicating relatively better perceptions of trade with the US. The mean for this variable (0.089) indicates a slight preference for the US as a trading partner, but this varies strongly across countries in Latin America, as shown in Figure 3.1. For example, citizens in Venezuela have a strong preference for China, while citizens in several other countries show a clear preference for the US. Second, we recode this variable into a categorical variable, which indicates whether the respondent prefers the US to China, China to the US, or is indifferent (with the last functioning as the reference category). In Venezuela, 39.6 per cent of respondents favour China, whereas only 21.3 per cent depict a clear preference for the USA. In contrast, 33.1 per cent of Colombian respondents prefer the USA, while only

[1] www.latinobarometro.org.

[2] These countries are Argentina, Bolivia, Brazil, Chile, Colombia, Costa Rica, the Dominican Republic, Ecuador, El Salvador, Guatemala, Honduras, Mexico, Nicaragua, Panama, Paraguay, Peru, Uruguay, and Venezuela.

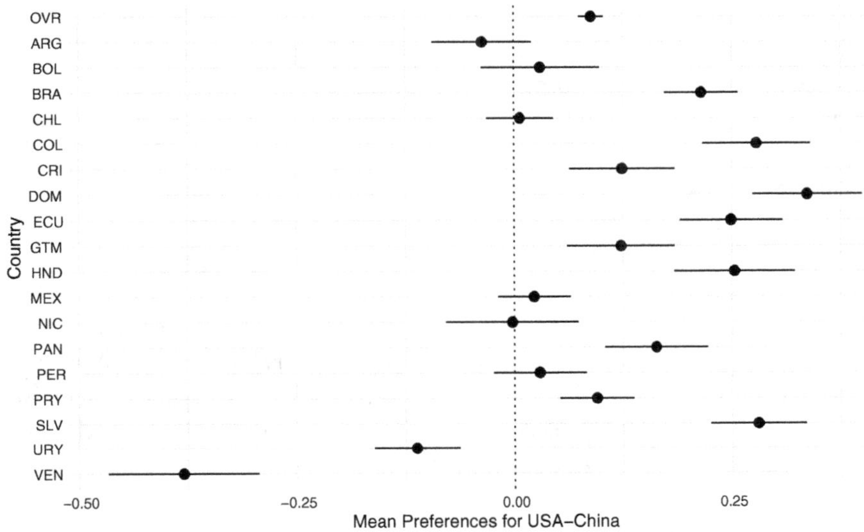

FIGURE 3.1 Mean preferences for trade partners among Latin American citizens.
Note: The first line (indicated by the label OVR) shows the attitudes of all citizens in our sample.
Source: Authors' own elaboration.

13.5 per cent prefer China. The former variable functions as our main dependent variable and the latter as a robustness check.

Following much of the literature on the topic, we operationalize skill levels based on formal education (see, e.g.,Scheve and Slaughter 2001: Menéndez González et al. 2023). The survey asked respondents about their age when they finished their formal education. We dichotomize this variable and label those who were older than eighteen years when they finished their education as highly skilled (*Education high*). When used to explain general trade attitudes, education has the disadvantage that it can proxy for a series of broader attitudes that people have. For example, more highly educated people tend to be more cosmopolitan, which may affect people's views of trade. In our case, this is less of a concern, as we try to explain relative preferences for different trading partners. Still, years of schooling may not fully capture what we are interested in. We thus include information on respondents' type of employment as a second measure for skill levels in our models. Concretely, we classify respondents who indicated that they are working as professionals, business owners, or in management as high-skilled (*High-skilled employment*).[3] The correlation between the two proxies for skill levels is relatively low (r = 0.2), making it possible for us to include both in the same model. As the US is economically more highly developed than China, Hypothesis 1a lets us expect negative coefficients for these two variables.

[3] The respective other categories 'Farmer/fisherman', 'Self-employed, informal', and 'Other' are coded as *Low-skilled employment*.

To capture geopolitical orientation, we utilize two questions that ask respondents about their perceptions concerning their country's relationship with the US and China, respectively.[4] Similar to our dependent variable, we subtract the score for China from the one for the US and obtain a variable ranging from −3 to 3, with higher values indicating a better-perceived relationship with the US (*Perception relationship*). These two questions allow us to capture a subjective notion of alliance: not all people within a country need to have the same perception of which country is an ally. At the country level, moreover, we include disagreement between the country and the US in United Nations General Assembly (UNGA) voting in the model (*US Disagreement in UNGA voting*). Data for this variable comes from Bailey et al. (2017) and captures the distance in ideal points based on UNGA voting. Specifically, we take the absolute distance between a country and the US and use a three-year moving average to account for minor fluctuations in individual years. Lower values indicate that the country and the US pursue a more similar foreign policy, which – while not equivalent to – seems at least a precondition for the status as allies. Whereas *Perception relationship* captures a subjective perception of allies, this variable tries to capture objective aspects of alliances. Following Hypothesis 2a, the coefficients for *Perception relationship* should be positive, whereas for *US Disagreement in UNGA voting* it should be negative.

Finally, we capture political ideology using a standard item asking respondents to self-place themselves on a scale from 0 (left) to 10 (right) (*Political ideology*). As discussed before, we expect left-wing respondents to have a relatively worse perception of the US than China. A positive coefficient on *Political ideology* would hence support Hypothesis 3a.

In the models below, we control for a series of variables at the individual and country levels. Specifically, this concerns respondents' age and gender, generic trade support, and satisfaction with democracy and the economy. At the country level, moreover, we include the relative strength of trade ties between the country and the US and China as a control variable.[5] Given the numerical character of our dependent variable, we use linear mixed effects models. A mixed effects model allows us to use random intercepts at the country level to control for country-level factors while also including a country-level measure of relative trade ties.[6]

Table 3.2 summarizes the findings. In Model 1, we use the dependent variable that results from subtracting the rating of trade with China from the rating of trade with the US. In this model, we do not find support for the economic explanation (Hypothesis 1a). Neither of the two variables capturing high-skilled workers is statistically significant, although the one for *High-skilled employment* has the right sign (negative) and nearly reaches statistical significance. By contrast, the coefficient

[4] The precise question wording was: 'And how would you rate the relations between (COUNTRY) and the United States [China]? Would you say they are very good/fairly good/ fairly poor/very poor?'

[5] In form of an equation, $\log\left(\frac{\text{Trade with US}}{\text{Trade with China}}\right)$.

[6] Replication files are deposited in the Harvard Dataverse. https://doi.org/10.7910/DVN/5AMIA7.

TABLE 3.2 *Explaining citizens' trade partner preferences*

	Model 1	Model 2	
		(Pro-USA)	**(Pro-CN)**
Education high	0.00	0.03	-0.04
	(0.02)	(0.06)	(0.07)
High-skilled employment	−0.04	−0.06	0.15*
	(0.02)	(0.06)	(0.07)
Perception relationship	0.30***	0.51***	−0.40***
	(0.01)	(0.03)	(0.03)
US Disagreement in UNGA voting	0.07*	−0.06	−0.07
	(0.03)	(0.04)	(0.04)
Political ideology	0.04***	0.05***	−0.08***
	(0.00)	(0.01)	(0.01)
Age	0.00	0.01**	0.00
	(0.00)	(0.00)	(0.00)
Gender (female)	0.02	0.02	−0.13*
	(0.02)	(0.06)	(0.06)
Trade support	0.03	−0.04	−0.15***
	(0.01)	(0.04)	(0.05)
Satisfaction with democracy	−0.05***	−0.04	0.05
	(0.01)	(0.04)	(0.04)
Satisfaction with the economy	−0.03*	−0.09*	0.05
	(0.01)	(0.04)	(0.05)
Relative trade ties	0.03*	−0.05*	−0.10***
	(0.01)	(0.02)	(0.02)
Intercept	−0.32*	−0.50*	0.21
	(0.12)	(0.21)	(0.20)
AIC	22370.20	14801.52	
BIC	22468.79	15181.76	
Log likelihood	−11171.10	−7346.76	
Num. Obs.	8447	8447	
Num. Groups: country_short	18		
Var: country_short (Intercept)	0.00		
Var: Residual	0.82		
Deviance		14,693.52	
K		3	

Source: Own calculations. * $p < 0.05$, ** $p < 0.01$, ***, $p < 0.001$.

for *Education high* even has the wrong sign. In short, the evidence is at variance with Hypothesis 1a.

However, the results lend some support to the geopolitical explanation (Hypothesis 2a). The coefficients for both *Perception relationship* and *US Disagreement in UNGA voting* are positive and statistically significant. Respondents that rate their countries' relationship with the US relatively better favour the US as a trading partner. At the same time, contrary to the geopolitical considerations expectation, respondents from countries with a foreign policy broadly aligned with the US are less likely to favour the US as a trading partner. The effect of the *Perception relationship* variable is large. Moving this predictor by one step on the scale from −3 (best relationship with China, worst with the US) to 3 (excellent relationship with the US but very poor relationship with China) increases the preference in favour of the US as a trading partner by 0.3 points on the scale from −3 to 3. In contrast, the effect for *US Disagreement in UNGA voting*, which runs counter to the geopolitical considerations expectation, is substantially smaller. One step in dissimilarity increases support for the US by 0.07, on a scale that runs from 1.6 to 4.2. Hence, we consider this broadly supportive for H2a.

Finally, the model hints at an effect of political ideology (Hypothesis 3a). A positioning towards the right goes hand in hand with a preference for the US as a trading partner. Again, the effect is of substantive relevance, although much smaller than the one for *Perception relationship*. Concretely, the model predicts a shift of preferences in favour of the US by 0.4 on the seven-point scale when an individual moves from being far-left to far-right.

With respect to the control variables, citizens who are satisfied with the state of democracy and the economy are less supportive of trade with the US. The positive and statistically significant coefficient for the relative trade ties variable indicates that more trade with the US (relative to China) improves respondents' views of the US as a trading partner. This may hint at economic reasoning, but it is also possible that this reflects geopolitical considerations, as trade and geopolitical alliances often go together.

Model 2 in Table 3.2 reports results from a multinomial regression model that relies on the categorical version of our dependent variable. This model includes country-fixed effects rather than random effects. The results are similar to those reported before. In terms of Hypothesis 1a, the coefficient for *High-skilled employment* now is positive and statistically significant in the equation with pro-China attitudes as the dependent variable. This is in line with the economic considerations explanation as the higher skilled should benefit from trade with a country that mostly relies on low-skilled workers. The coefficients for *Education high*, however, are not statistically significant and even have the wrong signs. Support for the economic considerations explanations hence remains tenuous. The positive and strongly statistically significant coefficients for *Perception relationship* continue to support Hypothesis 2a. In the pro-USA equation of the model, the second variable that we use to measure geopolitical allies (*US Disagreement in UNGA voting*) now has the expected sign (negative) but still fails to reach statistical significance. *Political ideology*, finally, works as expected in Hypothesis 3a.

Overall, for citizens we have found most support for the ideology argument and some support for the geopolitical considerations expectation. Economic considerations, at least as operationalized here, do not seem to play a major role in shaping preferences over trading partners.

The Latinobarometro also includes two questions that ask people to indicate why they perceive trade with China as good or bad. These two questions allow us to

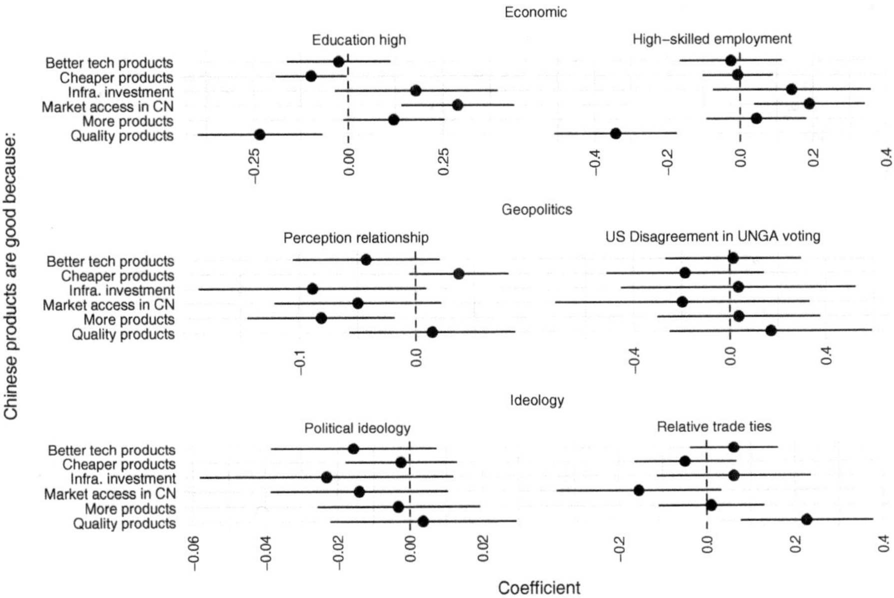

FIGURE 3.2 Reasons why trade with China is good.

Note: Figure 3.2 depicts the unstandardized regression coefficients from various mixed effects logistic regression models, which estimate whether an individual selected the respective label (e.g., 'Better tech products') or all reasons as a response to a question on the benefits of trade with China (see footnote 7 on the precise wording). Both economic variables are dummies. The perception of the relationship ranges from −3 to +3, with higher values expressing more sympathy for the US vis-à-vis China. US Disagreement in the UNGA is a numeric variable with a range of 3. Political ideology is captured on a seven-point range, and relative trade ties range from −0.47 to +6.23. See replication files for individual models.

Source: Authors' own elaboration.

probe a bit deeper into people's reasoning when thinking about China as a trading partner. Individuals were asked to pick from a list or indicate 'none' or 'all'.[7] In analysing the responses, we use a multilevel logistic regression with the same covariates as before. Figures 3.2 and 3.3 present the results. On the *x*-axis, they present the respective reason, whereas the *y*-axis shows the regression coefficient,

[7] Specifically, the question asked respondents to report their opinions on two questions. First, they were asked to indicate their response to the following question (authors translation): '[Even if, overall, trade with China is not beneficial] What would you say is the main advantage of trading with China?' with the following response categories: 1) Cheaper products, 2) Good-quality products, 3) Assess to more products, 4) Rapid improvement in tech products, 5) A large market for us to sell to, 6) Investment in infrastructure projects, 7) Other, 8) All, 9) None. In addition, respondents were asked to indicate the main disadvantages of trade (authors translation): '[Even if, overall, trade with China is not disadvantageous] What would you say is the main disadvantage of trading with China?'. Responses are 1) Low-quality products, 2) Human rights problems in their country, 3) Low safety standards for products and food, 4) Low environmental standards, 5) Their workers take our jobs because they work for less, 6) Increase in debt to Chinese government or business interest, 7) Other, 8) All, 9) None.

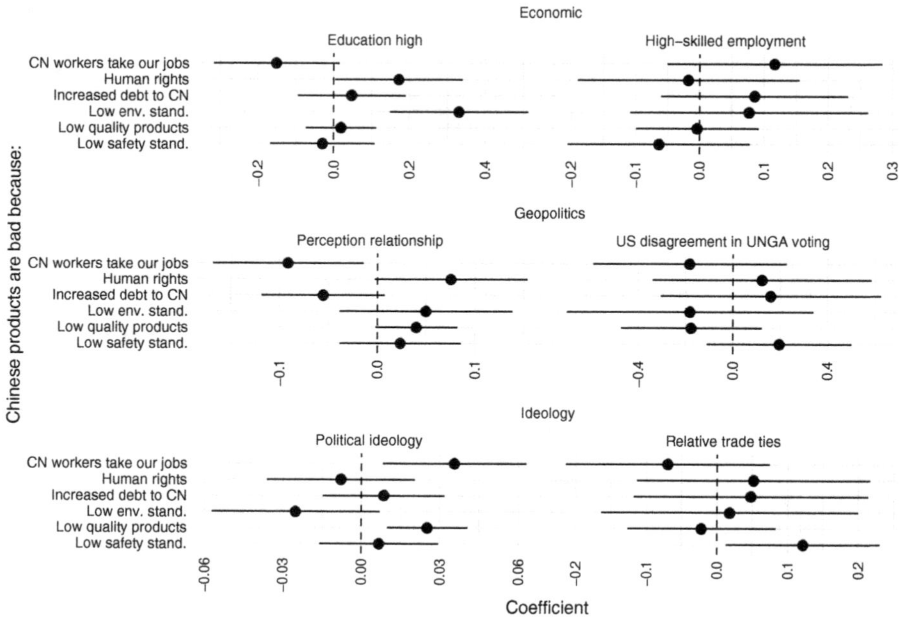

FIGURE 3.3 Reasons why trade with China is bad.

Note: Figure 3.3 depicts the unstandardized regression coefficients from various mixed effects logistic regression models, which estimate whether an individual selected the respective label (e.g., 'Chinese workers take our jobs') or all reasons as a response to a question on the disadvantages of trade with China (see footnote 7 on the precise wording). Both economic variables are dummies. The perception of the relationship ranges from −3 to +3, with higher values expressing more sympathy for the US vis-à-vis China. US Disagreement in the UNGA is a numeric variable with a range of 3. Political ideology is captured on a seven-point range, and relative trade ties range from −0.47 to +6.23. See replication files for individual models.

Source: Authors' own elaboration.

and the individual panels correspond to the predictors. Ranges represent 95 per cent confidence intervals.

Figure 3.2 provides important additional information to assess the three theoretical arguments. Individuals with high education and high skills perceive market access to China as a core benefit of trading with China. This is perfectly in line with the economic considerations argument. They are also less likely to perceive the (high) quality of Chinese products, potentially also in line with their awareness of their comparative advantage. In contrast, we do not find meaningful variation with regard to the two other sets of arguments. This is additional evidence in favour of the economic considerations argument.

Figure 3.3 investigates the related question on the negative consequences of trade with China. We find that highly educated individuals are somewhat less concerned with job loss due to Chinese trade (significant at the 10 per cent level) and worry about human rights and environmental standards. The latter two are potential indicators that education also captures cosmopolitanism. Individuals perceiving a more positive relationship with the US are less concerned about jobs but more concerned with human rights standards in China. Finally, right-wing individuals are more concerned about job losses. Overall, these findings provide some additional support for the economic consideration argumentation but also indicate that political ideology plays a role.

3.4 LEGISLATORS' TRADING PARTNER PREFERENCES

To estimate political elites' attitudes towards trading partners, we use data from the Parliamentary Elites of Latin America project (Alcántara 2019). This project has conducted several surveys with legislators in national parliaments from across Latin America. Between 2005 and 2019, the questionnaire also contained questions concerning the preferences of legislators with respect to a series of partners in trade agreements. Concretely, the question reads: 'On a scale from 1 to 10, where "1" means very negative and "10" means very positive, how do you evaluate [a free trade agreement with the US/a free trade agreement with the EU/the Bolivarian Alliance/ the Pacific Alliance]?' In this chapter, we use data for up to 1,753 legislators, who give answers with respect to at least two partners in trade agreements.

Similar to what we did for citizens above, we calculate the dependent variables for legislators as the difference between a legislator's evaluation of a free trade agreement with the US and their other three evaluations. For example, we subtract the evaluation of the EU as a trading partner from the evaluation of the US as a trading partner. The resulting three variables can range from −9 to 9. ALBA implies increasing the importance of countries such as Venezuela, Cuba, Nicaragua, and Bolivia as trading partners. The Pacific Alliance has Chile, Colombia, Mexico, and Peru as members. We always keep the US as a reference point to make this analysis as similar to the one for citizens as possible.

Figure 3.4 describes these variables. On average (as indicated by the estimate across all legislators, labelled 'OVR'), legislators have a slight preference (0.69) for the EU vis-à-vis the US, no real preference for the US vis-à-vis the Pacific Alliance (the Pacific Alliance is slightly preferred by 0.13, but this is indistinguishable from zero), and a strong preference for trade with the US, compared to ALBA (0.98). At the country level, we find more interesting variation. Uruguay and Ecuador are particularly fond of the EU as a trade partner vis-à-vis the US. Legislators from Ecuador are on average 2.14 points more in favour of the EU. Interestingly, there is not a single country in which the legislators, on average, prefer the US to the EU. The picture is more diverse when it comes to the Pacific Alliance. The US is the preferred partner for legislators in Chile, the Dominican Republic, Honduras, Panama, and El Salvador, whereas legislators from Bolivia, Ecuador, and Uruguay strongly prefer the Pacific Alliance. Finally, only Ecuadorian legislators prefer ALBA as a partner compared to the US. Legislators from all other countries are either

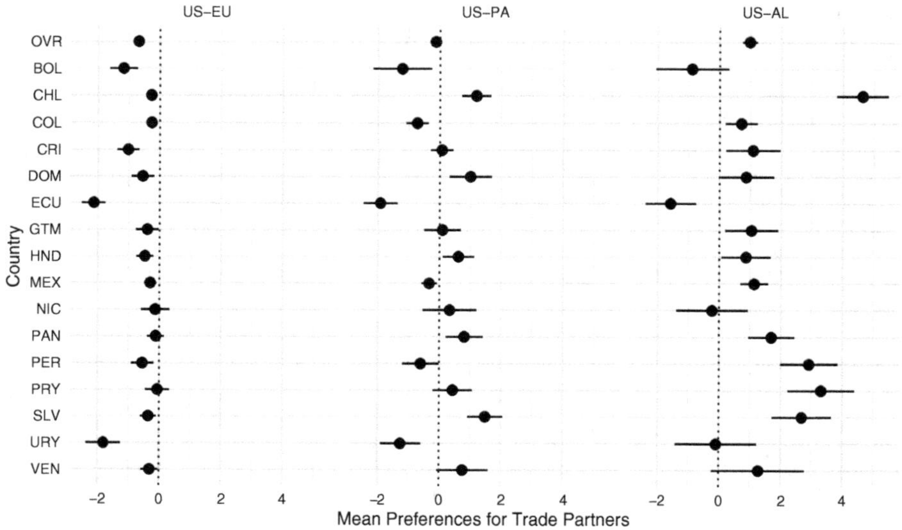

FIGURE 3.4 Mean preferences for trade partners among Latin American legislators.
Source: Authors' own elaboration.

indifferent (Bolivia, Nicaragua, Uruguay, and Venezuela) or (strongly) prefer the US. For example, the average rating of the US is 4.64 points higher than the rating of ALBA among Chilean legislators.

We operationalize the average skill level of the workers that legislators represent (Hypothesis 1b) with the mean year of schooling of people in the legislator's district (*Average skill level*). The data for this variable comes from Smits and Permanyer (2019). Moreover, we rely on the district's gross national income per capita to operationalize the idea underlying Hypothesis 1b (*GNIpc (region, log)*). This data also stems from Smits and Permanyer (2019). Richer districts, on average, should contain a larger number of high-skilled workers. Given the argument that forms the basis for Hypothesis 1b, the expectation is for these two variables to have little explanatory power in the model comparing the US and the EU as trading partners (because both trading partners are at approximately the same level of development). By contrast, the coefficients for these variables should be negative in the models comparing the US to ALBA and the Pacific Alliance, as these entities consist of countries at lower levels of economic development than the US. To capture geopolitical allies or foes, we again rely on voting data from the United Nations General Assembly (*Agreement in UNGA voting*). Finally, for ideology, we use legislators' placement on the left–right dimension (*Political ideology*). We expect more right-wing respondents to always prefer the US in the comparisons that we focus on, although this effect should be weakest for the Pacific Alliance, which is an explicitly right-wing alternative to ALBA.

In terms of control variables, we include legislators' age, gender, education, and income in the models. Moreover, we control for whether legislators are members of parties in the government. Finally, we also include the relative importance of the US and the other countries as trading partners in the model, following the equation provided in footnote 2 (*Relative share partners*).

In Table 3.3, we report results from the three models. We find no support for either the economic or geopolitical considerations explanations. With respect to the former (H1b), the coefficients for the *GNIpc (region, log)* variable have the expected signs, but they never reach statistical significance. The coefficients for *Mean years of schooling* even have the wrong signs. In none of the models does *US disagreement in UNGA voting* reach statistical significance, and only in one has it the expected sign (H2b). By contrast, *Political ideology* has considerable explanatory power. Across all three models, the respective coefficient is positive, meaning that respondents further to the right consistently prefer the US as a trading partner. This preference is weakest for the EU and strongest for ALBA. Especially the latter effect is not surprising as ALBA is generally considered a left-wing alternative to other trade agreements. This evidence thus is in line with Hypothesis 3b.

3.5 DISCUSSION AND CONCLUSION

This chapter contributes to a better understanding of citizens' and legislators' trade partner preferences. Utilizing high-quality survey data with citizens and legislators, our findings suggest important commonalities and minor differences between the two sets of actors. Overall, ideology is the most consistent predictor of which trade partner citizens and legislators prefer. Right-wing citizens and legislators are more supportive of the US as a trading partner than of other partners such as China, the EU, or smaller regional organizations. While legislators' preferences seem to be entirely driven by ideological considerations, the picture is more diverse among citizens. Citizens' attitudes also indicate some influence of geopolitical and economic considerations.

These differences should not come as too much of a surprise. For one, given their level of political sophistication, legislators can easily apply their ideological leaning to the specific case of trade agreements. Geopolitical considerations, in contrast, may show up in citizens' trade partner preferences because they reflect citizens' generic notions of specific countries. In that sense, we may not so much capture geopolitics in these answers as broader positive or negative views of countries. Geopolitics may show up to a lesser extent in legislators' attitudes as they have better individual resources to form opinions on trade partners and do not rely on generic notions of countries. Finally, economic considerations are harder to measure for legislators than for citizens. Legislators in multimember districts may follow differential strategies when representing low- or high-skilled workers. That is, while some

TABLE 3.3 *Explaining legislators' trade partner preferences*

	Model 3 (US–EU)	Model 4 (US–PA)	Model 5 (US–ALBA)
Mean years of schooling	0.08	−0.03	−0.03
	(0.06)	(0.10)	(0.12)
GNIpc (region, log)	−0.34	0.12	0.43
	(0.22)	(0.40)	(0.50)
US disagreement in UNGA voting	0.01	−0.01	0.47
	(0.15)	(0.33)	(0.39)
Political ideology	0.21***	0.45***	1.20***
	(0.02)	(0.03)	(0.04)
Relative trade ties	0.22*	0.13	−0.02
	(0.09)	(0.16)	(0.14)
Age	0.00	0.01	0.02*
	(0.00)	(0.01)	(0.01)
Primary education	1.25	−1.83	-0.00
	(1.69)	(2.60)	(3.46)
Secondary education	1.72	−1.61	−1.15
	(1.65)	(2.51)	(3.36)
Tertiary education	1.88	−0.48	0.32
	(1.64)	(2.49)	(3.34)
Income (1,000–4,000 USD)	−0.22	−0.10	0.99
	(0.39)	(0.64)	(0.85)
Income (4,000–7,000 USD)	−0.02	−0.04	1.35
	(0.40)	(0.66)	(0.87)
Income (7,000–10,000 USD)	0.06	0.34	2.13*
	(0.42)	(0.70)	(0.91)
Income > 10,000 USD)	0.19	0.34	2.34**
	(0.42)	(0.70)	(0.91)
Government	−0.32***	−0.58***	−0.92***
	(0.09)	(0.16)	(0.19)
Intercept	−1.23	−2.82	−11.94*
	(2.48)	(4.28)	(5.49)
AIC	6100.93	5762.60	8404.97
BIC	6202.77	5859.64	8507.00
Log likelihood	−3031.46	−2862.30	−4183.49
Num. obs.	1572	1221	1587
Num. groups: district	378	323	372
Num. groups: country_year	30	23	30
Var: district (Intercept)	0.00	0.02	0.03
Var: country_year (Intercept)	0.19	0.72	1.42
Var: Residual	2.65	6.09	10.95

Source: Own calculations. * $p < 0.05$, ** $p < 0.01$, ***, $p < 0.001$.

legislators in one district may represent high-skilled citizens, others represent citizens with lower skills. In contrast, their skill level has substantially more direct consequences for individuals, meaning that they should react more directly to this variable when forming attitudes towards trade partners.

These findings have important implications. First, the findings provide a more comprehensive picture of trade attitudes. Ideology seems to be an important driver of preferences regarding trading partners. As a result, at least in Latin America right-wing individuals and legislators are particularly keen on trade with the US, whereas left-leaning individuals and legislators are potentially more open to other partners. At the same time, while economic interests do not have much explanatory power regarding trade partner preferences, this does not render economic interests irrelevant. Rather, economic considerations may be more important in forming attitudes on trade in general. Additionally, the more fine-grained analysis of citizens' perceptions of trade with China provides important insights into which dimensions of trade are perceived as good or bad. Economic considerations, particularly as captured by high education, behave as expected and suggest that individuals with higher education are aware of the comparative advantage they enjoy vis-à-vis a trade partner focused on low-skilled workers.

Second, the findings suggest a certain degree of responsiveness of political elites. The elite-citizen gap is rather small, as ideology is a core driver among both groups. Potentially, voting for right-wing candidates would allow right-wing individuals to see their views on trade partners realized. At the same time, there are differences with regard to geopolitical and economic considerations. These differences may be rooted in variation in the levels of sophistication across legislators and citizens. While citizens may need to rely on country cues to form their opinions, a better understanding of the matter may allow legislators not to depend on geopolitical cues. Economic considerations are less pronounced among legislators. This could be because citizens experience the consequences of trade depending on their skills more directly, whereas legislators may follow different electoral strategies.

Future research could extend the analysis to more partners and compare them more systematically. At the moment, we rely on secondary data that provides trade partner preferences for the US and China among citizens, and the US, EU, PELA, and ALBA for legislators. Thus, the comparison between legislators and citizens is imperfect. The more detailed perceptions of positives and negatives regarding trade with China in the Latinobarometro provide interesting additional evidence. At the same time, it hints at a more nuanced picture potentially in line with the economic argument. This may speak to slight differences in the underlying concepts. Stiller et al. (2022) have similarly suggested that general trade attitudes may be less discriminatory, whereas concrete perceptions of trade consequences show a substantially more nuanced pattern. Hence, some of our arguments may speak more to the general sympathy towards specific trade partners, whereas economic considerations are particularly prevalent when evaluating the concrete (economic) consequences of trade with specific partners. Ideally, future research would compare both general partner preferences as well as concrete perceptions of trade with different partners.

REFERENCES

Alcántara, M. 2019. *Proyecto Elites Latinoamericanas (PELA-USAL)*. Universidad de Salamanca (1994–2018).

Alt, J. E. and M. Gilligan 1994. "Survey Article: The Political Economy of Trading States: Factor Specificity, Collective Action Problems and Domestic Political Institutions," *The Journal of Political Philosophy* 2(2): 165–192.

Baccini, L. and S. Weymouth 2021. "Gone For Good: Deindustrialization, White Voter Backlash, and US Presidential Voting," *American Political Science Review* 115(2): 550–567.

Bailey, M. 2003. "The Politics of the Difficult: Congress, Public Opinion, and Early Cold War Aid and Trade Policy," *Legislative Studies Quarterly* 28(2): 147–177.

Bailey, M, A., A. Strezhnev and E. Voeten 2017. "Estimating Dynamic State Preferences from United Nations Voting Data," *Journal of Conflict Resolution* 61(2): 430–456.

Bohigues, A. and J. M. Rivas 2019. "Free Trade Agreements and Regional Alliances: Support from Latin American Legislators," *Revista Brasileira de Política Internacional* 62(1): 1–22.

Bulman, D. 2022. "Instinctive Commercial Peace Theorists? Interpreting American Views of the US–China Trade War," *Business and Politics*. www.cambridge.org/core/journals/business-and-politics/article/instinctive-commercial-peace-theorists-interpreting-american-views-of-the-uschina-trade-war/E1BE56E8C5EDC56EA6E69ECC6FDE5EB4 (accessed on 8 November 2022).

Burstein, A. and J. Vogel 2017. "International Trade, Technology, and the Skill Premium," *Journal of Political Economy* 125(5): 1356–1412.

Carmines, E. G. and N. J. D'Amico 2015. "The New Look in Political Ideology Research," *Annual Review of Political Science* 18: 205–216.

Carnegie, A. and N. Gaikwad 2022. "Public Opinion on Geopolitics and Trade: Theory and Evidence," *World Politics* 74(2): 167–204.

Chiang, C., J. Liu and T. Wen 2013. "Individual Preferences for Trade Partners in Taiwan," *Economics & Politics* 25(1): 91–109.

Dellmuth, L., J. A. Scholte, J. Tallberg and S. Verhaegen 2022. *Citizens, Elites, and the Legitimacy of Global Governance*. Oxford: Oxford University Press.

DiGiuseppe, M. and K. B. Kleinberg 2019. "Economics, Security, and Individual-Level Preferences for Trade Agreements," *International Interactions* 45(2): 289–315.

Dür, A., L. Baccini and M. Elsig 2014. "The Design of International Trade Agreements: Introducing a New Dataset," *Review of International Organizations* 9(3): 353–375.

Dür, A., R. A. Huber and Y. Stiller 2023. "Trade Competitiveness, Constituency Interests, and Legislators' Attitudes Towards Trade Agreements," *Legislative Studies Quarterly*, first view (first published, 7 June).

Gowa, J. and E. D. Mansfield 1993. "Power Politics and International Trade," *American Political Science Review* 87(2): 408–420.

Hirschman, A. O. 1945. *National Power and the Structure of Foreign Trade*. Berkeley: University of California Press.

Huber, R. A., Y. Stiller and A. Dür 2023. "Measuring Subnational Trade Competitiveness," *Scientific Data* 10(331): 1–13.

Jackson, M. O. and S. Nei. 2015. "Networks of Military Alliances, Wars, and International Trade," *Proceedings of the National Academy of Sciences* 112(50): 15277–15284.

Jost, J. T., C. M. Federico and J. L. Napier 2009. "Political Ideology: Its Structure, Functions, and Elective Affinities," *Annual Review of Psychology* 60(1): 307–337.

Jungherr, A., M. Mader, H. Schoen and A. Wuttke 2018. "Context-Driven Attitude Formation: The Difference between Supporting Free Trade in the Abstract and Supporting Specific Trade Agreements," *Review of International Political Economy* 25(2): 215–242.

Kim, S. E., J. H. Park, I. Rhee and J. Yang 2023. "Target, Information, and Trade Preferences: Evidence from a Survey Experiment in East Asia," *American Journal of Political Science* 67(4): 898–914.

Kuo, J. and M. Naoi 2015. "Individual Attitudes." In: L. Martin (Eds.), *The Oxford Handbook of the Political Economy of International Trade*. Oxford: Oxford University Press, pp. 99–118.

Menéndez González, I., E. Owen and S. Walter 2023. "Low Skill Products by High Skill Workers: The Distributive Effects of Trade in Emerging and Developing Countries," *Comparative Political Studies* 56(11): 1724–1759.

Osgood, I. et al. 2017. "The Charmed Life of Superstar Exporters: Survey Evidence on Firms and Trade Policy," *Journal of Politics* 79(1): 133–152.

Rho, S. and M. Tomz 2017. "Why Don't Trade Preferences Reflect Economic Self–Interest?," *International Organization* 71(S1): S85–S108.

Schaffer, L. M. and G. Spilker 2019. "Self-Interest Versus Sociotropic Considerations: An Information-Based Perspective to Understanding Individuals' Trade Preferences," *Review of International Political Economy* 26(6): 1266–1292.

Scheve, K. and M. Slaughter 2001. "What Determines Individual Trade-Policy Preferences?," *Journal of International Economics* 54(2): 267–292.

Smits, J. and I. Permanyer 2019. "The Subnational Human Development Database," *Scientific Data* 6(1): 190038.

Spilker, G., T. Bernauer and V. Umaña 2016. "Selecting Partner Countries for Preferential Trade Agreements: Experimental Evidence From Costa Rica, Nicaragua, and Vietnam," *International Studies Quarterly* 60(4): 706–718.

Steiner, N. D. 2018. "Attitudes towards the Transatlantic Trade and Investment Partnership in the European Union: The Treaty Partner Heuristic and Issue Attention," *European Union Politics* 19(2): 255–277.

Stiller, Y., A. Dür and R. A. Huber 2022. "Education and Trade Attitudes: Revisiting the Role of Economic Interest," *World Trade Review* 21(4): 497–4511.

Zaller, J. 1992. *The Nature and Origins of Mass Opinion*. New York: Cambridge University Press.

4

Making Trade Agreements Work for Women:

What's Behind the South American Approach?

Amrita Bahri

4.1 INTRODUCTION

Trade agreements create both 'losers' and 'winners', with the ability to benefit some and leave others without benefits or with negative ramifications. This is mainly because women and men play different roles and have varied access to opportunities in society, markets and the economy (Elson and Fontana 2018). It is therefore important that these trade policy instruments are negotiated with a gender lens to ensure that they can be used as a tool to minimize the negative impact and maximize the positive impact of international trade on women.[1]

Various international organizations, think tanks and countries are now turning their focus on developing a better understanding of the trade and gender equality nexus and how gender equality can be integrated into countries' trade policies. In 2017, 115 Members and Observers of the World Trade Organization (WTO) agreed to a joint declaration on enhancing women empowerment in international trade.[2] This was a landmark initiative by WTO Members in which they acknowledged the high degree of interconnectedness between trade and gender, and the need to have inclusive trade policies that are geared towards women empowerment. This development sits well with the objectives of the WTO, as the Marrakesh Agreement has pertinently included the objective of achieving sustainable development in its preamble (WTO 1994). The Addis Ababa Agenda of Action (Finance for Development 2015) also builds a clear network between international trade and

[1] Gender relates to constructed social identities and has a wider scope than cisgender identities. However, this chapter uses the term 'gender' only with respect to cisgender identities. Gender equality refers to a state of being in which access to rights and opportunities is not affected by gender. Discriminatory social and gender norms, violence against women and girls, and notions of masculinity and social exclusion all undermine gender equality. Elimination of these factors would support greater gender equality.

[2] By 2020, 127 WTO member countries had signed the Buenos Aires Declaration; 'Buenos Aires Joint Declaration on Trade and Women's Economic Empowerment' 2017.

gender equality as it reads as follows: 'Recognizing the critical role of women as producers and traders, we will address their specific challenges in order to facilitate women's equal and active participation in domestic, regional and international trade (UN 2015a).'

The UN General Assembly has called upon the WTO, the World Bank Group (WBG) and other international and regional bodies to support governmental initiatives and develop complementary programmes to help countries achieve full implementation of the Beijing Declaration and Platform for Action to protect women's rights (UN Women 2020). Moreover, the 2030 UN Agenda for Sustainable Development recognizes international trade as an engine for inclusive and sustainable economic growth, and an important means to achieve the UN's 2030 Sustainable Development Goals (SDGs) (UN 2015b). These developments are aligned with and complement the other international legal instruments such as the UN Convention on the Elimination of all Forms of Discrimination against Women (CEDAW) 1979.[3]

Many existing trade agreements already contain provisions relating to gender equality that could provide a basis for translating into national trade policies to support women (Monteiro 2018). Some of these provisions directly deal with empowering women as social actors or mothers such as ones on access to health care and maternity services and elimination of violence and discrimination based on sex (Hasham et al. 2022). Similarly, and in parallel, trade agreements, notably the Eurasian Economic Union Agreement (EAEU) and the EU-Central America Free Trade Agreements (FTAs), contain various provisions that seek to mitigate purely market-oriented and economic barriers that women face such as access to employment and finance, and access to information and to trade-related capacity-building programmes (Bahri 2021). These examples show that there are already several potential solutions included in the existing trade policy instruments that can help in ensuring that the opportunities offered by trade agreements are enjoyed equally by all including women.

As per the WTO's database on gender provisions in preferential trade agreements (PTAs),[4] there are more than 300 provisions included in about 100 PTAs that are explicitly vocal about women's interests or gender equality. This represents almost a third of PTAs currently in force and notified to the WTO by its members (WTO Gender Database 2022). Moreover, recent years have witnessed a sharp increase in the number of PTAs, mainly in the new-generation trade agreements, leading to the mainstreaming of concerns relating to women's empowerment. These recent developments pose a challenge to the long-standing assumption that trade and gender are

3 Convention on the Elimination of All Forms of Discrimination against Women, Adopted and opened for signature, ratification and accession by United Nations General Assembly (resolution 34/180) (New York, 18 December 1979).

4 The word 'PTA' (preferential trade agreement) has been used interchangeably with RTA and FTA.

not interconnected, and on the contrary, they reflect that gender mainstreaming in trade agreements is here to stay. However, it is interesting to note that trade agreements have included these provisions in various different ways. Moreover, some countries have led the inclusion of these provisions in their trade agreements, and many others are yet to take their very first step in this direction. This chapter looks at variation in the degree to which countries have included gender provisions in their trade agreements, and with a special focus on the case of South America as various countries in this region have employed a number of innovative approaches to apply gender lens to their trade agreements.[5]

The chapter's first part looks at different approaches with which gender-related commitments are included by different regions in their trade agreements, through some interesting practice examples to show various differences and overlaps within the regions. The second part of this chapter zooms into one of these regions, that is, South America, as it has emerged as a frontrunner in drafting trade agreements with various different kinds of gender commitments and mainstreaming approaches. This segment provides reflection on the ways in which countries in South America have drafted gender provisions, the roles of women these provisions have focused on and the strategies of mainstreaming which are unique to this region (such as the inclusion of stand-alone chapters and the creation of dedicated implementation mechanisms).

4.2 GENDER MAINSTREAMING IN TRADE AGREEMENTS: A REGIONAL COMPARISON

The focus areas covered by gender-related provisions in present-day trade agreements vary from one region to the other, ranging from an economic- and market-oriented focus, education and training, representation of women in decision-making roles, women's employment status and labour conditions, female entrepreneurship, to purely social, maternity-related and healthcare concerns. Yet, there is some overlap. The following illustration underlines the most-commonly-used trends and focus areas in trade agreements negotiated by five different regions: North and South America, the European Union, Asia Pacific and Africa. These five regions are discussed in this chapter because, as seen in Figure 4.1 (Bahri 2021), these are the five major regions where countries have made some efforts in respect of negotiating

[5] Gender lens in the context of trade agreements can be applied during negotiation and/or implementation of trade agreements. The findings in this chapter are only limited to the negotiation and drafting stage of the agreements. Gender mainstreaming or application of gender lens is a means to achieve gender equality. In the context of trade agreements, it is a process by which parties seek to include a gender perspective in trade liberalization efforts and policies. Mainstreaming affirms a country's commitment, understanding and political will to reduce gender inequalities through trade policies and agreements.

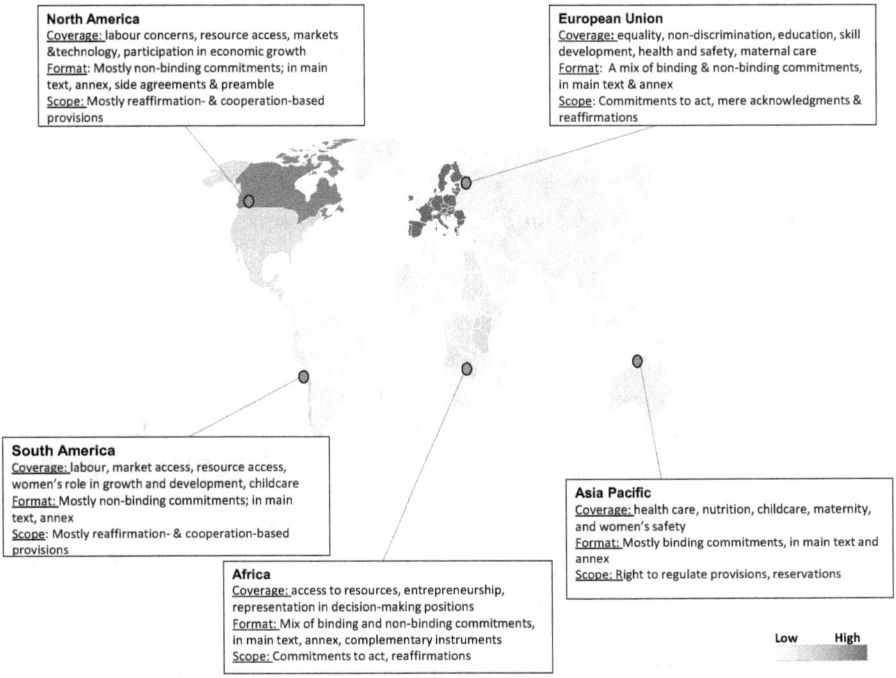

FIGURE 4.1 Gender provisions in trade agreements: regional trends.
Notes: *The colour code reflects the aggregation of the number of times gender-explicit words are used in all existing FTAs signed by each country. The darker it is, the higher the frequency of gender-explicit words included in FTAs signed by that country; ** Only FTAs with explicit gender provisions were considered for the illustration. Some FTAs are included in the assessment of more than one country, depending upon the countries that are party to those agreements; *** Gender-explicit words used for listing products or entities are not included in this assessment; **** Only trade agreements notified to WTO and currently in force (as of 15 April 2022) are included in this assessment.
Source: Bahri (2021).

their trade agreements with explicit gender commitments, and hence these regions have a story to be told.

The illustration identifies countries that have led the inclusion of gender-explicit commitments in their trade agreements. The author is of the view that the content of gender provisions is much more relevant than the number of times gender-related words are mentioned in a specific agreement and a look at the number of times gender-explicit words are mentioned does not reveal the scope of commitments. Nevertheless, a mere look at the number of relevant words included in an agreement can provide an initial indication of whether a given trade agreement includes gender concerns and the extent to which these concerns are included. The underlying assumption is that the higher the usage of gender-explicit words, the higher is the number of legal provisions focused on gender concerns in a given agreement (Bahri 2021).

As seen in this illustration, gender mainstreaming in current trade agreements is quite heterogeneous as its approach differs from one region to the other. In the case of North America, the trade agreements signed by Canada, United States and Mexico (USMCA) have treated gender-related concerns from an economic and a market access perspective. A similar approach is observed in the Comprehensive and Progressive Agreement for Trans-Pacific Partnership (CPTPP) under Article 23.4. These provisions mainly focus on labour standards, women's access to productive resources, markets and technology, skill development and their participation in economic growth. A leading recent example from this region is from the USMCA, whereby parties commit to enhancing trade and investment opportunities for small businesses, including those owned by women, as mentioned under Article 25.2 titled 'Cooperation to increase trade and investment opportunities for SMEs', and the agreement also includes improvement of labour standards such as elimination of discrimination, occupational safety, health and other workplace practices; the prevention of occupational injuries and illnesses; and the prevention of gender-based workplace violence and harassment listed under Article 23.12.2 (v).

The EU's mainstreaming approach in some agreements such as the EU-Central America PTA and the EU-Albania PTA includes the above-mentioned issues, but this approach is more geared towards a wider range of concerns that deal with issues such as non-discrimination (pursuant to Article 24 in EU-Central America FTA), labour standards (under Article 13 in EU-Central America FTA), education and skill development (under Article 43 in EU-Central America FTA and Article 100 of EU-Albania PTA, respectively), health and safety (under Article 42 in EU-Central America FTA and Article 99 in EU-Albania PTA), and maternal care (under Article 44 of EU-Central America FTA). However, it is important to note that most of these agreements negotiated by the EU, strictly speaking, are broader than mere trade agreements as they are drafted as 'Association Agreements' (AAs), Economic Partnership Agreements (EPAs) or Strategic Partnership Agreements (SPAs). These broader agreements include several pillars that go beyond the trade regime and into areas such as politics, cooperation, immigration, social development, poverty and environment. Gender-relevant provisions in these agreements are generally included in the non-trade pillars such as the ones on cooperation and social development. Hence, there remains a question as to whether such inclusions can be seen 'strictly speaking' as gender mainstreaming efforts in trade policy context (Villup 2015).

The EU has also taken the lead in respect of including gender-explicit provisions in its chapters or provisions on sustainable development in multiple PTAs. For example, chapter 9 in subsection IV in the EU-Armenia partnership agreements is titled 'Trade and Sustainable Development'. It contains several provisions where parties seek to cooperate on activities to enhance sustainable development. The parties in this chapter in Article 272 'reaffirm their commitment to promote the development of international trade in such a way as to contribute to the objective of sustainable development, for the welfare of present and future generations'. The EU-Georgia Association Agreement has a stand-alone chapter 13 on trade and sustainable development. Parties in this chapter seek cooperation on various aspects, including labour, environment, human resource development and conservation of exhaustible resources such as forests and fisheries. The benefit of this approach is that it allows the parties to embrace various elements of sustainable development which may (or may not) include gender concerns and undertake commitment to work on different activities focused on environment, climate change, labour standards, poverty reduction and fight against corruption. The fundamental problem though with this approach is that because such chapters include a range of issues such as labour, child labour, environment, climate change, deforestation and human resource development, the focus on gender equality is included as 'one' of the concerns amongst many others. Often, such chapters therefore leave no room for inclusion of concrete commitments, activities and implementation machineries to achieve these varied goals.

Another contrast in gender mainstreaming approach can be seen in the topic areas covered by countries in the Asia Pacific. The PTAs' gender provisions in this region mostly relate to women's personal welfare concerns. Many of the inclusions in this region are drafted as 'right to regulate' provisions, wherein member countries reserve the policy space to regulate specific areas that may impact women's health and maternal concerns, such as healthcare, nutrition, childcare and women's personal safety (as seen in Australia New Zealand Closer Economic Agreement (ANZCERTA) under Annex II and Chile-South Korea Free Trade Agreement under Article 10.2). ANZCERTA, Annex II, for example, contains a reservation wherein New Zealand reserves the right to regulate certain social services including childcare. Childcare challenges pose a significant barrier to work, especially for mothers, who disproportionately take on unpaid responsibilities when they cannot find affordable childcare (Barnes 2015; Parker 2015). Provision of affordable childcare facilities is therefore vital, as their absence limits women´s employment opportunities and educational aspirations.

Another example is the ASEAN-South Korea PTA, which focuses on women's physical safety. Singapore (an ASEAN member state) reserves the right to regulate certain types of social services, including statutory supervision services related to the provision of accommodation for women and girls detained in a place of safety under Section 160 of the Singapore's Women's Charter (CPC 93312). In the New Zealand-South Korea FTA, parties reserve the right to regulate certain health and social services that relate to female professionals and women's health interests. In its Annex II on Services and Investment, the parties reserve the right to adopt or maintain any measure with respect to maternity deliveries and related services, including services provided by midwives, and with respect to childcare. In the Korea-Singapore Free Trade Agreement (KSFTA), chapter 9 on cross-border trade-in services does not apply to subsidies or grants (including government-supported loans, guarantees and insurance) or social services provided in conjunction with childcare under Article 9.2.3 (d). Also, in chapter 10 on investment, parties reserve the right to regulate foreign investment in respect of childcare services under Article 10.2.5. This 'right to regulate' type of reservation helps to strike a balance between the protection of investment or trade liberalization on the one hand and the state's policy space to regulate on issues such as national security, public health, environment and gender equality, among others (Gaukrodger 2017).

The gender-explicit provisions found in PTAs signed by African countries seek primarily to integrate women into the region's development process by enhancing women's access to resources, promoting female entrepreneurship and increasing women's representation and participation in political and decision-making positions. This can be seen in the Revised Treaty of *Economic Community of West African States (ECOWAS)* under Articles 3 and 63, and Common Market for Eastern and Southern Africa (COMESA) under Articles 154 and 155. In the COMESA, for example, parties have assumed various commitments relating to gender equality. In chapter 24 of this agreement which focuses on women in development and business, the parties affirm that 'women make significant contribution towards the process of socio-economic transformation and sustainable growth and that it is impossible to implement effective programmes for rural transformation and improvements in the informal sector without the full participation of women'. Through legislation and other measures, parties pledge to increase women's participation in decision-making, eliminate regulations and customs that are discriminatory against women entrepreneurs and inhibit their access to resources, promote their education and awareness and adopt technology to support the professional progress of women. Similar commitments are seen in chapter 22 of the EAC, wherein countries seek to enhance women's representation in socio-economic development, including their role in political bodies such as the East African Parliament listed under Article 121.

It is interesting to see that most of the gender-explicit provisions in the agreements negotiated by African countries, mainly East African countries, are drafted with affirmative and binding expressions (Laperele-Forget 2022). Moreover, some gender-related provisions are included in the ambit of the agreements' dispute settlement mechanisms and are therefore enforceable and legally binding in nature. One such example is the Agreement on Trade Development and Cooperation between the EU and the Republic of South Africa. This is an interesting and unique best practice example, which differs from gender-related provisions drafted in best-endeavour language as is mostly visible in the case of PTAs negotiated by other regions as previously discussed.[6]

6 For example, see Articles 54 and 86 of the Agreement, as parties in these provisions assume commitments relating to women-owned small- and medium-sized enterprises (SMEs) and reducing social problems such as violence against women, discrimination and gender inequality, and these provisions are drafted with somewhat binding expressions.

Finally, there is another aspect of the South American approach that resembles that of North America but with some differentiating elements. Gender-related provisions negotiated by countries in that region focus on labour concerns, market and resource access, and women's role in growth and development; though the agreements that South American countries have signed with Asian and Central American countries also include women's personal welfare concerns (see, e.g., in the Chile-South Korea FTA, Article 10.2.4). Moreover, like in the case of North America, the provisions included in the agreements in this region are mostly drafted as best-endeavour cooperation-based provisions, without the use of any binding or enforceability-related expressions. Yet, this region stands apart due to certain features of its gender mainstreaming approach that distinguish this region from the others. One such feature includes reliance on stand-alone trade and gender chapters and the other could be its implementation-focused approach. The following section zooms into these distinguishing features and the overall gender mainstreaming approach employed by South American countries mainly in the new-generation trade agreements.

4.3 ZOOMING INTO THE SOUTH AMERICAN APPROACH

The South American countries have employed a number of mainstreaming trends for the negotiation and drafting of their trade agreements. This section will provide reflections on the four most distinguishing features of this approach. These features are explained in the following categories: (i) inclusion of stand-alone chapters on trade and gender; (ii) economic- and market-oriented focus areas, drafted in the spirit of cooperation; (iii) implementation-focused approach; and (iv) the language and location of relevant provisions (Bahri 2021) (Figure 4.2).

4.3.1 *Inclusion of Stand-Alone Chapters on Trade and Gender*

A best practice example that emerges from this region is the addition of a stand-alone trade and gender chapter. So far, out of nine countries that have signed PTAs with stand-alone chapters on trade and gender (i.e., Chile, Canada, Uruguay, Argentina, Brazil, Ecuador, Japan, the UK and Israel), five are from South America.[7] Chile has taken the lead and has included a stand-alone chapter on gender and trade in multiple PTAs (i.e., with Uruguay, Canada, Argentina, Brazil and Ecuador). Chile is also negotiating a gender chapter with Paraguay, and together with Colombia, Mexico and Peru, it is considering the inclusion of a gender chapter in the Agreement between the Pacific Alliance and Associates (Canada, New Zealand and Singapore).[8]

7 This includes several FTAs not yet notified to WTO (as of 12 June 2022).

8 Interview with trade negotiator [12 October 2022, details withheld, on record with author]

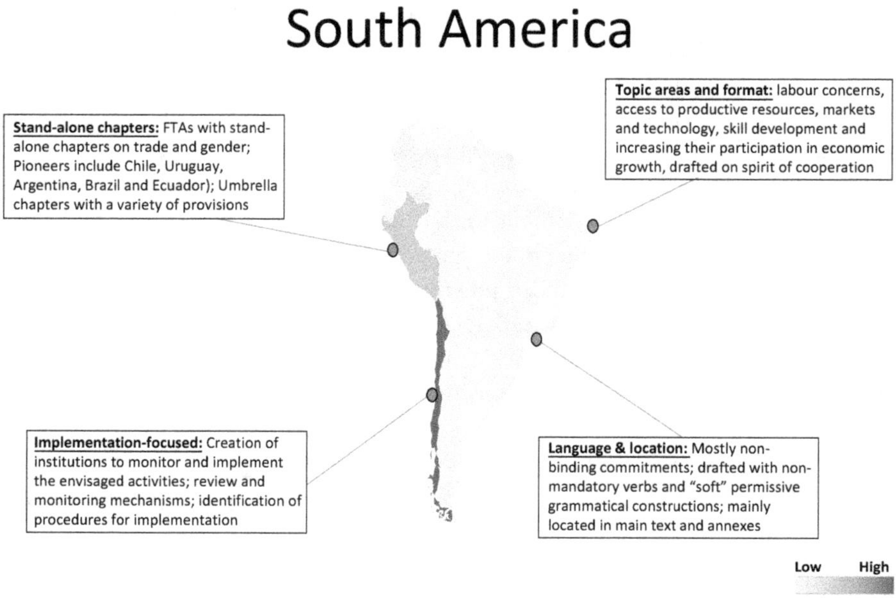

FIGURE 4.2 Zooming into the South American approach.
Notes: *The colour code reflects the aggregation of the number of times gender-explicit words are used in all existing PTAs signed by each country. The darker it is, the higher the frequency of gender-explicit words included in FTAs signed by that country; ** Only PTAs with explicit gender provisions were considered for the illustration. Some PTAs are included in the assessment of more than one country, depending upon the countries that are party to those agreements; *** Gender-explicit words used for listing products or entities are not included in this assessment; **** Only trade agreements notified to WTO and currently in force (as of 15 April 2022) are included in this assessment; *****The countries included in the South American region for the purposes of this assessment are Argentina, Bolivia, Brazil, Chile, Colombia, Ecuador, Guyana, Paraguay, Peru, Suriname, Uruguay and Venezuela.
Source: Bahri (2021).

An interesting recent development in this respect is the amended Chile-Ecuador trade agreement, which contains a new, dedicated chapter on trade and gender. Chapter 18 of this Agreement is quite comprehensive; as in other gender chapters negotiated by Chile, as it includes various affirmations, cooperation-based commitments and reaffirmations. However, it is the first of its kind as the parties to the agreement have created a detailed and dedicated bilateral consultation procedure to solve differences that may arise from the provisions included in this chapter. It is also the very first agreement that requires its parties to set up a national consultative committee that is responsible for gathering views from the public (including representatives from women's organizations and business entities) on matters covered in the stand-alone gender chapter.

The EU and Chile are also negotiating a gender chapter for the modernized EU-Chile Association Agreement, wherein both countries have tabled their own draft chapter. If the EU's proposed draft is included in the agreement, it will probably emerge as one of the most comprehensive chapters on trade and gender negotiated so far. Its scope is vast. Parties in this chapter reaffirm their commitment to gender-specific international conventions, such as CEDAW and International Labour Organization (ILO) Conventions. As a substantive obligation, they commit not to promote trade or investment opportunities by weakening or reducing the protection provided in domestic law and regulation relating to gender equality. They also commit to progressively eliminating discrimination against women in employment (Article 3.4 (b)); they also seek to work on various cooperation activities to enhance capacity and conditions of women not merely as employees but also as business leaders (Article 4.2); the agreement also allows parties to identify specific activities to work on connecting more women to the formal economy that includes work to increase women's access to digital skills and online tools, decent quality jobs through trade, safety and health at work, flexible work conditions, affordable child-care, preparing girls for science, technology, engineering and mathematics (STEM) careers and joint collection of sex-disaggregated data (Article 4.3). The text also contains a detailed bilateral consultation procedure to solve differences that may arise from the provisions included in this chapter (Article 6.3). Hence, this chapter goes beyond an attempt to merely insulate women from the possible negative impacts of trade liberalization or trade agreements; it seems more proactive as it can possibly increase women's access to more trade opportunities and resources.

Inclusion of a dedicated chapter is a possible way forward to mainstream gender concerns in trade agreements as such a chapter can serve as an umbrella chapter for all kinds of provisions on gender, including cooperation activities, legal standards, affirmations and reaffirmations (Hughes 2019). This is comparatively a newer approach of gender mainstreaming; most of the existing agreements with such chapters were negotiated in the last six to seven years. However, it is important to mention that some earlier agreements (negotiated as regional integration agreements) by countries in Africa had started to include stand-alone chapters on women empowerment as early as the 1990s; in the year 1993, the 1993 treaty establishing the COMESA was negotiated as the first agreement in the world to feature that featured a stand-alone chapter on women in its main text (i.e., chapter 24, titled 'Women in Development and Business'). Thereafter, it was replicated in 1999 as the treaty for the establishment of the East Africa Community (EAC), wherein countries also included a chapter on women in the year 1999 (i.e., chapter 22, titled 'Enhancing the Role of Women in Socio-Economic Development').

This approach does translate into something specific as it has four clear benefits: visibility, room for exploration, implementation machinery and capacity building. *First*, such chapters raise the profile of gender equality concerns in trade discourse and the visibility of gender considerations in trade policy instruments. Giving higher visibility to the 'problem' gender commitments can solve means trade negotiators and policymakers will have incentives to gain more awareness in this respect. It also helps negotiators justify the time and resources they spend on bilaterally negotiating these commitments with their counterparts.[9] *Second*, they justify the creation of institutions and mobilization of funds for putting gender commitments into action.[10] In the existing PTAs that have included a stand-alone chapter on gender and trade, parties have gone ahead to create a specialized committee or unit that will be responsible for implementing or overseeing the implementation of commitments contained in this umbrella chapter. As seen from the Canada-Chile FTA (CCFTA), Article N bis-04 titled 'Trade and gender committee' specifically details dedicated committees overseeing the work, providing advice and preparing reports, forming concrete action plans, and eventually tracking the progress of efforts and activities in respective countries. The Gender Committee created by Canada-Chile, for instance, has created a detailed workplace for implementation, with ten action items. For each action item, parties identify the objectives, implementation plan, expected results and action leads. These action items correspond to and mirror the provisions included in the gender chapter. Moreover, with a whole chapter to work on, the experts can likely engage in bilateral negotiations with dedicated counterparts on these issues, and this separate branch of negotiation can provide them legitimacy to mobilize funds for their meetings and activities.

The *third* benefit is that it gives parties much more room to include different, concrete commitments and also outline precise activities and procedures the specialized committees might work on and can employ to implement the commitments. It gives room to put in writing various 'nuts and bolts' including: what is the purpose of empowering women? What activities to engage in? Why can these activities help women? How exactly can the commitments be implemented or financed? And who might be responsible for their implementation or monitoring of implementation? The space for including different categories of provisions a chapter provides allows agreements to address these pertinent questions. These chapters may not resolve the deeply engrained social, cultural and legal barriers, but they can comprise provisions that may touch upon the barriers that impede women from accessing foreign trade opportunities and stimulate dialogue for their removal.[11] The *fourth* benefit is that such chapters can strengthen capacity building, especially when one of the countries is still in its early phases of understanding the interrelation between trade and gender. A specific chapter on gender will require (or at least motivate) countries negotiating that chapter to appoint dedicated negotiators with understanding of these issues to engage with their counterparts. This incentivizes countries to develop the capacity in this respect. A gender chapter can encourage appointment of expert officials for negotiation of gender and trade issues. Negotiators responsible for this chapter can have their own table to discuss, share

9 Interview with a trade negotiator [15 September 2022, details withheld].

10 Interview with a trade negotiator [2 March 2022, details withheld].

11 Interview with a trade negotiator [18 November 2021, details withheld].

their experiences, exchange best practices and understand better each other's domestic conditions in this respect.[12]

These benefits to some extent can also be realized with the inclusion of specific provisions on trade and gender, for example, in the case of CPTPP. Article 23.4 in CPTPP is a provision titled 'Women and Economic Growth'. In this provision, parties 'recognise that enhancing opportunities in their territories for women, including workers and business owners, to participate in the domestic and global economy contributes to economic development'. Parties under Article 19.10 and Article 21.2 also 'consider undertaking cooperative activities aimed at enhancing the ability of women, including workers and business owners, to fully access and benefit from the opportunities created by this Agreement'. These activities touch upon and address the barriers discussed in chapter 1, but this approach does not allow the same room for exploring the inclusion of different kinds of provisions as a chapter would. It may also not have the similar kinds of capacity-building benefits discussed before.

4.3.2 *Economic- and Market-Oriented Focus Areas, Drafted in the Spirit of Cooperation*

The trade agreements signed by South American countries, mainly the new generation agreements, treat gender-related concerns primarily through an economic and market access perspective. The provisions in these agreements cover areas relating to women's access to productive resources, markets and technology, skill development and increasing women's participation in economic growth.

The modernized CCFTA trade accord presents an interesting example in this respect. This agreement has included a number of cooperation activities under Article N bis-03; these activities envision women as entrepreneurs, leaders, decision-makers and scientists. The activities envisaged by parties include focus on improving educational or skills development opportunities that can translate to high-paid job opportunities for women (such as STEM and information and communication technology (ICT)). This agreement is exceptional in this respect, as most trade pacts only consider cooperation focused on fields that have traditionally been reserved for women (such as farming, handicraft, textile and fisheries). Other activity areas it includes are promoting financial inclusion for women, including financial training, access to finance, and financial assistance; advancing women's leadership and developing women's networks in business and trade; fostering women's representation in decision-making and positions of authority in the public and private sectors, including on corporate boards; promoting female entrepreneurship and women's participation in international trade; conducting gender-based analysis; and sharing methods and procedures for the collection of sex-disaggregated data, the use of indicators and the analysis of gender-focused statistics related to trade. These new

[12] Interview with a trade negotiator [2 March 2022, details withheld].

areas can enhance women's access to productive resources and markets and enable women to move away from the traditional stereotypical jobs that the societies have imposed on them such as farming, nursing or household responsibilities.

Parties in the Chile-Uruguay Economic Agreement seek to focus on women as workers as well as entrepreneurs through its chapter 14 on trade and gender; they seek to also promote the development of skills and competencies of women in labour and business; to improve women's access to technology, science and innovation; to promote financial women's access to technology, science and innovation; to develop women's leadership networks; to further the participation of women in decision-making positions in the public and private sectors and promote female entrepreneurship, and others as listed under Article 14.3. However, most of these cooperation-based commitments are drafted in best-endeavour language, and, hence, are not binding on the parties. Such best endeavours drafted with permissive expressions are also found in other trade agreements wherein South American countries have negotiated gender provisions such as in the Chile-Ecuador and Chile-Argentina trade agreements. Nevertheless, the value of aspirational provisions cannot be underrated, as these provisions can still change the normative environment of trade negotiations and can act as a starting point in negotiating gender-related commitments for countries with less developed appetite or understanding on these matters.

The countries in such cooperation-based provisions assume soft commitments, and they often contain a list of activities that parties seek to work on and also provide a list of affirmative statements recognising the problem. Countries in these provisions have also reaffirmed in such provisions their commitments under other international instruments, including the United Nations 2030 Agenda and Sustainable Development Goals; the Convention on the Elimination of All Forms of Discrimination Against Women (CEDAW) 1979; the Universal Declaration of Human Rights; the International Covenant on Civil and Political Rights; the International Covenant on Economic, Social, and Cultural Rights; the Beijing Declaration of 1995 and Platform for Action, as well as the ILO conventions that refer to women's labour rights and the ILO Declaration on Fundamental Principles and Rights at Work. Even though these reaffirmations can send an important signal to the international community about the priorities of these countries, they are nevertheless reaffirmations where parties merely recall their already assumed commitments; these provisions do not identify or provide space for parties to undertake a specific positive action in respect of women empowerment.

One final observation to note in this regard is that the focus of gender provisions has changed when South American countries have negotiated agreements with Asian countries. The gender provisions in many of those agreements are drafted as binding right to regulate reservations upholding women's role as mothers. For example, Article 10.2 of the Chile-South Korea FTA contains a right to regulate childcare services. A similar reservation can be found in the Annex II of the Peru-

South Korea FTA. These reservations are drafted with binding expressions and language, making them legally enforceable in nature. They are worded as the right to regulate provisions, wherein countries reserve policy space to regulate specific areas that may affect women's health and maternal concerns, such as health care, nutrition, childcare and women's personal safety.

4.3.3 *Implementation-Focused Approach*

Despite the proliferation of gender-related provisions and chapters in the existing trade agreements, current approaches merely scratch the surface of what they can achieve in respect of empowering women. This is due to many reasons, but one of the major reasons is that the current gender provisions often fall short of providing a mechanism to implement and oversee the implementation of such commitments. Almost no PTA so far contemplates how gender-related commitments could be put into action. As of today, most of the PTAs that incorporate gender equality concerns do not clarify procedures for implementation, nor do they identify channels to finance these activities.[13] Countries have gone ahead to assume commitments, often without a single mention of which stakeholder or institution in their countries would be responsible for the implementation of the best-endeavour promises they load their gender-specific provisions or chapters with. Without such an implementation mechanism, it is difficult to see how gender-related commitments will translate into concrete actions. However, some countries in South America have carved out an exception to this rule in their agreements.

Some recent agreements have established specialized committees to oversee and monitor the implementation of gender-focused provisions and gender impact of trade. One example is the Chile-Uruguay FTA, which provides for the creation of a gender committee under Article 14.4. It provides that this committee is to be composed of representatives from the government institutions responsible for relevant gender and trade matters from each concerned party, but it falls short of prescribing its functions and operation requirements. The CCFTA raises the bar higher as it provides for some operational requirements and functions of the trade and gender committee under Article N bis-04. This Committee under both agreements is supposed to meet at least once a year, and it should review the implementation of the chapter after two years. The Agreements also provide for a mechanism for parties to engage in consultations to resolve disputes, as there are provisions under CCFTA Article N bis-05 and Chile-Uruguay FTA Article 14.5 that state that the contracting parties will make all necessary efforts to solve any issues that may arise regarding chapter's application and interpretation, through consultations and

[13] As per authors' calculations, using ITC maturity toolkit: ITC, 'Mainstreaming Gender in Free Trade Agreements' (8 July 2020). https://intracen.org/es/media/2411 (accessed 25 January 2021).

dialogue. Similar provisions are also found in Chile-Argentina FTA (Article 15.5), Chile-Brazil FTA (Article 18.6) and Chile-Ecuador PTA (Article 18.8).

These attempts at creating institutions and procedures are worth applauding, but resources are needed to carry out these functions, and the required provisions often fall short of clarifying how these functions or activities or committee meetings might be financed. Moreover, in most of the attempts where countries have identified institutions and procedures for implementation, the agreements have fallen short of specifying various other aspects required for effective implementation of such provisions. This is because the existing provisions often do not clarify precise functions of such committees, the way the activities and meetings of these committees will be financed, the procedures they might employ in performing their functions, the timelines and action plans.

Overcoming this barrier to some extent, the Chile-Ecuador PTA not only defines contact points and their responsibilities, but it also provides for a dedicated bilateral consultation mechanism to solve differences that may arise from the provisions included in Article 18.7 in the stand-alone trade and gender. This process is based on a mutually acceptable resolution and is guided by established timelines for each step of the process. First, the affected party is required to present a request through contact points to solve the matter; if it is not solved, the request is then transferred to the specialized committee; and in case there is no resolution by this stage, it can be sent to the related government ministers. At any stage of this process, parties can use the good offices, and if an agreement is reached, the final report is to be publicly made available.

In line with these recent developments, it is important that future PTAs contemplate and clearly outline the functions of the committees, milestones and objectives it is expected to achieve, and a timeline by which it is expected to achieve these milestones. There should be clear provisions on how committee's work will be monitored, and who will comprise these committees. The most important in this regard is providing for funding arrangements to finance the activities and functioning of such committees if we genuinely intend these committees to function. However, such an institutionalization may likely become quite burdensome for developing countries that may not have the required resources to provide for the same for every trade agreement they sign.

4.3.4 *Language and Location of Relevant Provisions*

With very few exceptions, most of the gender-related concerns included in the regions' existing agreements are drafted with non-mandatory verbs and 'soft' grammatical constructions (Bhala and Wood 2019). This soft nature of these provisions implies that compliance with them is completely voluntary, and non-compliance does not attract any consequence. The provisions on cooperation have another problem: most of these provisions in South American PTAs have left their implementation to the willingness and available resources that the concerned parties may have. For example, CCFTA Article N bis-03.6 explicitly states that the 'priorities for cooperation activities shall be decided by the parties based on their interests and available resources'. The countries have generally left the implementation of these activities to their available resources and willingness, because they are probably not ready to undertake these commitments as binding and enforceable.

This is not unique to this region only, as even in other areas with very few exceptions, gender mainstreaming approach so far has been rooted in the spirit of cooperation wherein parties seek to use cooperation as a route to start this dialogue with others, as seen in the EU-Central America Agreement (Article 24.1). Moreover, such provisions list their benefits, as the value of aspirational and/or vague provisions cannot be underrated. These provisions can still change the normative environment of trade negotiations and serve as a starting point in negotiating gender-related commitments for countries with less developed appetites or understanding on how trade and gender relate to each other. This is mainly because countries sometimes need some flexibility in assuming commitments that they do not entirely understand the implications for and before using trade agreements to protect women when they do not know how the agreements will affect the women in their jurisdictions. To better establish this nexus between trade and gender and have evidence for policymakers, more gender-disaggregated data is required on this subject (UNECE 2021 and Peltola and MacFeely 2019).

In terms of the location of these provisions in trade agreements signed by South American countries, gender-related provisions have mostly appeared in the agreements' main text. Only occasionally, they are added in a side agreement or in an annex as seen in Peru-South Korea FTA. In the main text, the gender-explicit provisions have most commonly been loaded in agreement's provisions on cooperation or development. For instance, the Chile-Vietnam FTA proposes gender as one of the spheres of cooperation under Article 9.3 within its cooperation chapter, and the Peru-Australia FTA (PAFTA) refers to women and economic growth under Article 22.4 within its development chapter. In this provision titled 'Women and Economic Growth', the contracting parties have recognized the importance of enhancing opportunities for women so as to contribute to economic development, for which it promotes cooperation activities that aim at enhancing the ability of women to fully access and benefit from the opportunities created by the agreement.

Another recent development of this nature is the Global Trade and Gender Arrangement, signed in August 2020 between Canada, Chile and New Zealand (and Mexico in 2021). This is an independent instrument not annexed to any particular agreement. Through this, parties impose commitments on their respective governments as well as on the business stakeholders. In trade-in services under Section 4, the parties undertake to ensure that no sex-based discrimination is made in measures relating to licensing requirements and procedures, qualification requirements and procedures, or technical standards relating to authorization for the supply of a service. In this Arrangement, each party encourages 'enterprises operating within its territory or subject to its jurisdiction to voluntarily incorporate into their internal policies those internationally recognised standards, guidelines and principles that address gender equality that have been endorsed or are supported' by that member state under Section 5. Parties also identify a wide range of cooperation activities to enhance the 'ability of women, including workers, entrepreneurs, businesswomen and business owners, to fully access and benefit from the opportunities created by this Arrangement' under Section 8(b). However, what is not clear is the kind of opportunities the parties are referring to here, as the Arrangement is neither an understanding on trade agreement nor attached to any other trade agreement that may be seen as creating trade opportunities for women in these economies.

4.4 FINAL THOUGHTS

Through gender mainstreaming, FTAs can help reduce the formidable barriers that impede women's participation in the economy. Using such inclusions, countries can bind themselves to certain minimum legal standards for improving the employment conditions for women or prohibiting sex-based discrimination. Countries can also endeavour to increase women's access to health services, education and skill development. They can also create encouraging conditions for women businesses to flourish, for example by the creation of business networks and improved infrastructure in relevant sectors and industries. Countries in PTAs could also commit to increasing the representation of women in decision-making and policy-making roles. Moreover, trade-in services being an important area for women in a number of South American countries such as Chile, PTAs should go beyond their current scope to include provisions on enhancing women's participation in services sectors of these countries. The baseline is thus: countries can use trade agreements as laboratories where they can experiment with different legal provisions and commitments regarding gender equality. However, there is a half-opened door in PTAs that countries need to push upon further by finding different ways of implementing or enforcing their gender-related commitments.

Some recent agreements signed by South American countries have taken the next step to push open this door further, but more needs to be done in this respect. Almost no PTA in the region so far contemplates how gender-related commitments could be legally enforced, and most of the gender equality considerations included in the existing agreements are drafted with non-mandatory verbs and 'soft' permissive grammatical constructions.[14] As of today, even the most advanced PTAs in respect of

[14] *Note*: It is pointed that most gender-related commitments in USMCA and CPTPP are aspirational and non-binding, and hence non-enforceable, and that they are sometimes drafted with vagueness and ambiguity, and so they are susceptible to myriad interpretations.

gender equality concerns have not identified channels to finance these much-promised actions. To ensure that trade agreements and policies work to create an inclusive trading environment, they need to be drafted with a gender-responsive approach; a gender-responsive approach calls for the inclusion of gender-related provisions that are not merely best-endeavour promises but are also enforceable, implementable and effective in nature.

It is expected that the ongoing trade negotiations on several PTAs in the region (which include Canada-Mercosur, Pacific Alliance, Chile-European Union and Chile-Paraguay) will take a step further and include trade and gender issues in a more concrete and unambiguous manner. As these negotiations are still in process, it is not possible to make an assumption about the ways in which they will include commitments on gender issues, but empirical research shows that the negotiators of these policy instruments are considering various options for making these instruments work for everyone, including women. The discussions in this chapter have shown that there is clearly a strong political will and expertise in the region in the area of trade and gender, yet the question remains as to whether we will see these future trade agreements take the next step in this direction.

A significant part of future trade policy-making in this respect would also depend upon the trade partners these countries engage with, as countries in this region may be able to assume more proactive commitments if they negotiate with countries that are also willing to accept gender-related commitments, are like minded or are similarly situated in terms of gender development levels (which for example could be measured by gender development index) (Monteiro 2021). Having trade partners with similar domestic conditions minimizes the fears of associated fears and provides a larger zone of confidence to deal with domestic yet culturally sensitive matters such as this. Moreover, some countries may not have the required capacity to understand the inter-relationship between trade, investment and gender; gather concrete gender-disaggregated data to disentangle the impact of trade and investment on gender roles; and negotiate such provisions with their trade partners, while others may have a more nuanced approach and experience of negotiating such provisions.[15]

REFERENCES

Bahri, A. 2021. "Gender Mainstreaming in Free Trade Agreements: A Regional Analysis and Good Practice Example," Gender, Social Inclusion and Trade Knowledge Product Series, www.genderandtrade.com/_files/ugd/86d8f7_ea7e603922c54ff7a9e1f81e594a5d9f.pdf

Bahri, A. and D. Boklan 2022. "Not Just Sea Turtles, Let's Protect Women Too: Invoking Public Morality Exception or Negotiating a New Gender Exception in Trade Agreements?," *European Journal of International Law* 33(1)237–270.

[15] 'Mainstreaming Gender in Free Trade Agreements (2020) ITC Geneva, https://intracen.org/media/file/2411 (accessed 10 November 2022).

Barnes, M. 2015. "Gender Differentiation in Paid and Unpaid Work during the Transition to Parenthood," *Sociology Compass* 9(5).

Bhala, R. and C. Wood 2019. "Two Dimensional Hard-Soft Law Theory and the Advancement of Women's and LGBTQ+ Rights Through Free Trade Agreements," *Georgia Journal of International and Comparative Law* 47(2): 299–306.

Elson, D. and M. Fontana 2018. "When It Comes to Gender Analysis, Modern Trade Agreements Are Lacking." CIGI Online. 4 April, www.cigionline.org/articles/when-it-comes-gender-analysis-modern-trade-agreements-are-lacking/

Financing for Development 2015. "A DESA Briefing Note on the Addis Ababa Action Agenda: Financing Sustainable Development and Developing Sustainable Finance". www.un.org/esa/ffd/ffd3/wp-content/uploads/sites/2/2015/07/DESA-Briefing-Note-Addis-Action-Agenda.pdf.

Gaukrodger, D. 2017. "The Balance between Investor Protection and the Right to Regulate in Investment Treaties: A Scoping Paper," *OECD Working Papers on International Investment, 2017/02, OECD Publishing, Paris,* 2017/02: http://dx.doi.org/10.1787/82786801-en.

Hasham, N., L. Naliaka, A. Bahri, L. Pettinotti and M. Mendez Parra 2022. "Making the AfCFTA Work for Women: The Nuts and Bolts," UNECA and ODI Report, December 3. www.undp.org/africa/publications/futures-report-making-afcfta-work-women-and-youth.

Hughes, V. 2019. "Gender Chapters in Trade Agreements: Nice Rhetoric or Sound Policy." CIGI Series: Mainstreaming Gender in Trade Agreements, 9 October www.cigionline.org/articles/gender-chapters-trade-agreements-nice-rhetoric-or-sound-policy/.

Laperele-Forget, L. 2022. "Gender Provisions in African Trade Agreements: What Commitments Are There for Reconciling Gender Equality and Trade." Working Papers Tralac, 25 March. www.tralac.org/publications/article/15567-gender-provisions-in-african-trade-agreements-what-commitments-are-there-for-reconciling-gender-equality-and-trade.html.

Medora, B. 2015. "Gender Differentiation in Paid and Unpaid Work during the Transition to Parenthood," Sociology. *John Caroll University Caroll Collected*, 24: 350–364.

Monteiro, J. 2018. "Gender-related Provisions in Regional Trade Agreements," *WTO Staff Working Papers ERSD-2018-15*, Economic Research and Statistics Division.

2021. "The Evolution of Gender-related Provisions in Regional Trade Agreements," WTO Working Papers, ERSD-2021-8. https://www.wto.org/english/res_e/reser_e/ersd202108_e.htm

Parker, P. 2015. "Women More Than Men Adjust Their Careers for Family Life," Pew Research Center, October 1, 2015. www.pewresearch.org/fact-tank/2015/10/01/women-morethan-men-adjust-their-careers-for-family-life/.

Peltola, A. and S. MacFeely 2019. "Towards a Conceptual Framework for Measuring Gender-in-Trade in Official Statistics," United Nations Economic Commission for Europe Conference of European Statisticians 15–17 May https://unece.org/fileadmin/DAM/stats/documents/ece/ces/ge.30/2019/mtg1/WP25_Peltola_ENG.

UN 2015a. "Addis Ababa Action Agenda of the Third International Conference on Financing for Development" (Addis Ababa Action Agenda), A/RES/69/313, (adopted 27 July 2015), p. 90. www.un.org/ga/search/view_doc.asp?symbol = A/RES/69/313&Lang = E.

2015b. "UN General Assembly: Transforming our World: The 2030 Agenda for Sustainable Development," 21 October 2015, A/RES/70/1. www.refworld.org/docid/57b6e3e44.html (accessed 13 November 2020).

UN Women 2020. "On the Twenty-fifth Anniversary of Landmark Beijing Declaration on Women's Rights, UN Women Calls for Accelerating Its Unfinished Business."

www.unwomen.org/en/news/stories/2020/9/press-release-25th-anniversary-of-the-beijing-declaration-on-womens-rights.

UNECE. 2021. "UNECE Policy for Gender Equality and the Empowerment of Women: Accelerating the Attainment of SDGs with a Gender Lens in the UNECE Region 2021–2025." https://unece.org/sites/default/files/2021-07/ECE_INF_2021_2_ECE%20Policy%20on%20GEEW_1.pdf.

Villup, E. 2015. "The EU's Trade Policy: From Gender Blind to Gender Sensitive." Directorate-General for External Policies Policy Department, July. www.europarl.europa.eu/RegData/etudes/IDAN/2015/549058/EXPO_IDA(2015)549058_EN.pdf.

WTO 1994. Agreement: Marrakesh Agreement Establishing the World Trade Organization, April 15, 1994, 1867 U.N.T.S. 154, 33 I.L.M. 1144.

WTO Gender Database 2022. Database on Gender Provisions in RTAs. www.wto.org/english/tratop_e/womenandtrade_e/gender_responsive_trade_agreement_db_e.htm.

Appendix

LIST OF TRADE AGREEMENTS

Abbreviation	Full Agreement Name
ANZCERTA	Australia-New Zealand Closer Economic Relations Trade Agreement (signed (G) 14 December 1982, (S) 18 August 1988; enforced (G) 1 January 1983, (S) 1 January 1989)
Argentina-Chile	Argentina-Chile Free Trade Agreement (signed 2 November 2017; enforced 2 May 2019)
AKFTA	ASEAN-Korea Free Trade Agreement (signed (G) 24 August 2006, (S) 21 November 2008; enforced (G) 1 January 2010, (S) 1 May 2009)
Canada-Chile	Canada-Chile Free Trade Agreement (signed 5 December 1996; enforced, 5 July 1997)
Chile-Brazil	Chile-Brazil Acuerdo de Complementación Económica (signed 21 November 2018; enforced 25 January 2022)
Chile-Ecuador	Chile-Ecuador Acuerdo de Complementación Económica (signed 13 August 2020; not yet enforced)
Chile-Uruguay	Chile-Uruguay Acuerdo de Complementación Económica (signed 4 October 2016; enforced 13 December 2018)
Chile-South Korea	Free Trade Agreement between the Republic of Korea and the Republic of Chile (signed 15 February 2004; enforced 1 April 2004)
Chile-Vietnam	Chile-Vietnam Free Trade Agreement (signed 11 November 2011; enforced 1 January 2014)
COMESA	Common Market for Eastern and South Africa Treaty (signed 5 November 1993; enforced 8 December 1994)
CPTPP	Comprehensive and Progressive Agreement for Trans-Pacific Partnership (signed 8 March 2018; effective 30 December 2018)

Abbreviation	Full Agreement Name
EAC	The Treaty for the Establishment of the East African Community (signed 30 November 1999; enforced (G) 7 July 2000, (S) 1 July 2010)
EAEU	Eurasian Economic Union Agreement (signed 29 May 2014; enforced 1 January 2015)
ECOWAS	Revised Treaty of the Economic Community of West African States (signed 24 July 1993; enforced 23 August 1995)
European Community-South Africa	Agreement on Trade, Development and Cooperation between the European Community and Its Member States, of the One Part, and The Republic of South Africa, of the Other Part (signed 11 October, enforced 1 January 2000)
EU-Albania	Stabilisation and Association Agreement between the European Communities and Their Member States of the One Part and the Republic of Albania of the Other Part (signed 12 June 2006; enforced (G): 1 December 2006, (S) 1 April 2009)
EU-Central America (EU-CAAA)	Agreement Establishing an Association between the European Union and Its Member States, on the One Hand, and Central America on the Other (EU-Central America FTA (signed 29 June 2012; enforced, 1 August 2013).
EU-Chile	Modernisation of EU-Chile Association Agreement, (negotiations launched again: November 2017; originally enforced, (G): 1 February 2003, (S): 1 March 2005)) Draft provision on Trade and Gender Equality. https://trade.ec.europa.eu/doclib/docs/2018/june/tradoc_156962.pdf
EU-Georgia	Association Agreement between the European Union and the European Atomic Energy Community and Their Member States, of the One Part, and Georgia, of the Other Part (signed 27 June 2014, enforced, 1 July 2016)
GTAGA	Global Trade and Gender Arrangement (signed 4 August 2020; amended 25 May 2022). www.sice.oas.org/TPD/GTGA/ITAG_GTGA_Text_e.pdf
KSFTA	Republic of Korea-Singapore Free Trade Agreement (signed 02 February 2006; enforced 2 March 2006)
Korea-New Zealand FTA	Korea-New Zealand Free Trade Agreement (signed 23 March 2015, enforced 20 December 2015)
PAFTA	Peru-Australia Free Trade Agreement (signed 12 February 2018; enforced 11 February 2020)
KPFTA	Peru-Korea Free Trade Agreement (signed 21 March 2011, enforced 1 August 2011)
USMCA	United States-Mexico-Canada Agreement (signed 30 November 2018; enforced 1 July 2020)

OTHER INTERNATIONAL INSTRUMENTS

Abbreviations	Agreements
Beijing Declaration	United Nations, & World Conference on Women (1996), The Beijing Declaration and the Platform for Action: Fourth World Conference on Women, Beijing, China, 4–15 September 1995. New York: Dept. of Public Information, United Nations (contain a progressive blueprint for advancing women's empowerment).
CEDAW	The Convention on the Elimination of All Forms of Discrimination Against Women (CEDAW), G.A Res34/180, United Nations, Treaty Series vol 1249, p. 13 (December 18, 1979)
ICCPR	International Covenant on Civil and Political Rights, G.A. Res. 2200 (XXI), art. 3, U.N. GAOR, 21st Sess., Supp. No. 16, U.N. Doc. A16316 (December. 16, 1966) (mentions women's right to equality)
ICESCR	International Covenant on Economic, Social and Cultural Rights, arts. 3, 7, G.A. Res. 2200 (XXI), U.N. GAOR, 21st Sess., Supp. No. 16, U.N. Doc. A/6316 (Dec. 16, 1966) (mentions women's right to equality and women's right to a fair wage)
ILO	ILO conventions that refer to women's labor rights [ILO gender equality conventions are the Equal Remuneration Convention (No. 100), Discrimination (Employment and Occupation) Convention (No. 111), Workers with Family Responsibilities Convention (No. 156) and Maternity Protection Convention (No. 183). Resolution concerning Gender Equality at the Heart of Decent Work adopted in June 2009; and the Resolution concerning the Promotion of Gender Equality, Pay Equity and Maternity Protection adopted in June 2004. Attention to gender equality in all aspects of the ILO's technical cooperation is mandated by the Governing Body's March 2005 Decision on Gender Mainstreaming in Technical Cooperation] International Labour Organization (ILO), The ILO Declaration on Fundamental Principles and Rights at Work, adopted 86th Session, Geneva (June 1998), amended 2022. www.ilo.org/wcmsp5/groups/public/—ed_norm/—declaration/documents/normativeinstrument/wcms_716594.pdf
Women's Charter 1961	Singapore's Women's Charter (CPC 93312). https://sso.agc.gov.sg/Act/WC1961?ProvIds = P1I-#pr2
UDHR	Universal Declaration of Human Rights, G.A. Res. 217A (III), at 71, U.N. GAOR, 3d Sess., 1st plen. mtg., U.N. Doc. A/180, (Dec. 10, 1948) [hereinafter UDHR] (points to the importance of equal rights of men and women, women's right to marry, and equal rights as to its dissolution)
UN SDG 2030	United Nations, 2015. Transforming Our World: The 2030 Agenda for Sustainable Development. New York: UN Publishing

5

Assessing Special and Differential Treatment in Latin American Trade Agreements

Julieta Zelicovich, Juliana Peixoto, Leticia Daibert, and Valentina Delich

5.1 INTRODUCTION

Special and differential treatment (S&DT) has a long history in multilateral trade negotiations, dating back to the General Agreement on Tariffs and Trade (GATT) of 1947. Born as a response to the development gap among members, S&DT has evolved into a framework of rules – both substantive and procedural – intended to grant developing countries more extensive permissions and longer implementation periods than originally outlined in the GATT rules. Scholars agree that Latin American countries have played a pivotal role in shaping these rules, redefining the policy space for developing nations in the realm of trade governance (Tussie and Glover 1993; Peixoto 2010). By "policy space" we mean "the combination of both the de jure policy sovereignty and de facto national policy autonomy" that each country possesses (Mayer 2009, p. 376).

How these rules manifest in preferential trade agreements (PTAs) has remained overlooked in international relations and international law studies, which have tended to focus on S&DT in multilateral agreements. This chapter aims to fill this gap by exploring how Latin American PTAs – signed among countries in the region and signed with extra-regional trade partners – have included S&DT principles and operative clauses.[1] In doing so, one of the main contributions of our study is to explore the S&DT dimension in the PTAs, tracing its reach across the different commitments and chapters. In addition, we describe the evolution of the development-related policy space notion in trade agreements recently signed by Latin American countries and the differences concerning the legal S&DT architecture across PTAs.

Our main argument is that S&DT clauses in Latin American PTAs are a diverse set of provisions dependent on the composition of negotiating parties, the purpose of

[1] Operative clauses are policies established under an agreement. They delineate a course of action intended by the parties.

the agreement, and the historical context. We find that S&DT clauses are rarely placed in ad-hoc chapters but are more frequently presented in various parts of the agreements relying on general criteria or across-the-board S&DT instruments. Our sample of PTAs shows that S&DT provisions often appear as a patchwork of exclusions, including exemptions, transition periods, and safeguards. S&DT may be found in connection with specific trade topics, considered "sensitive" to local development strategies, and thus often constitute red lines for negotiation purposes.

Among those often included are tariff exclusions, albeit with limited scope, as well as special provisions in chapters dealing with rules of origin, reliance on longer transition periods for implementing sanitary and phytosanitary regulations, the use of exemptions in services' commitments, and, more recently, the inclusion of specific chapters devoted to capacity building. In some agreements, S&DT is reflected by the absence of a specific trade topic upon a developing country's request. In other cases, S&DT includes clauses of best endeavor, reducing the level of ambition required in the commitments to provide for greater flexibility. Finally, in some cases, Latin American countries must accept a "less favorable" treatment under an Agreement than their developed countries' counterparts.

The chapter is organized as follows: First, we look back at the evolution of the development dimension in the international trade system. This is followed by a discussion of our analytical framework. Third, we characterize and classify S&DT in Latin American PTAs using our framework. Lastly, we discuss findings and propose a new typology for understanding S&DT approaches in Latin American PTAs.

5.2 THE DEVELOPMENT DIMENSION IN INTERNATIONAL TRADE AGREEMENTS – EARLY STAGES[2]

Development asymmetries have been part and parcel of the international trade discussions in the negotiations leading up to GATT in 1947. In fact, of the original twenty-three Contracting Parties, ten were developing countries, including Brazil, Chile, and Cuba from Latin America.

Until then, S&DT was not considered in trade agreements (Bacchus and Manak 2021). The GATT/1947 initially had only a few mechanisms to deal with and eventually to reduce the impact of asymmetries among countries. However, GATT provisions allowed many mechanisms for countries to manage their integration into world markets through some form of flexibility. For instance, signatory parties could apply antidumping measures, safeguards, and compensatory duties

[2] We do not work with a specific definition of the term "development". We consider it a broad and multifaceted concept that has changed over time. We use the term "development" to indicate a certain level of growth, education, and health, which in turn defines countries' needs and the degree of policy space.

without having to follow strict and detailed procedures. Countries facing severe distress in their balance of payment could apply import restrictions.

Interestingly, no attempt was made to categorize any types of countries with differing obligations in the GATT/47. This absence of formal distinctive treatment for developed and developing countries in the original treaty could be explained by the dominating idea that concessions should, in principle, be reciprocal among trade partners. However, Contracting Parties faced different development needs. The United States was emerging as the leading economic power after the end of the Second World War; European Countries and Japan were undergoing recovery from the economic, social, and political effects of the war; and other countries, including some in Latin America, were following an economic policy characterized by industrialization objectives and reliance on import substitution instruments.

Based on prior experience from early GATT rounds, developing countries quickly identified that many rules of the multilateral system did not satisfactorily address the developmental asymmetries among countries. They began to question, for example, the appropriateness of applying the most-favored-nation (MFN) principle indiscriminately/or without clear differentiation between developed and developing countries (Irwin et al. 2008).

However, it was not developing countries' criticism but concerns from the US and other like-minded countries that led to some changes. The US pointed to the existence of trade distortions caused by European protectionist policies in agriculture and, therefore, elevated this topic to the center of negotiations. As a result, GATT's Contracting Parties called for the establishment of a special group to study the topic (Ingco and Nash 2014). The final report of this special group, known as the Haberler Report (1958), concluded that the regulatory framework for trade liberalization generated different effects for developed and developing countries. As a result of the discussions that followed, in 1961, the Declaration on the Promotion of Trade in Least Developed Countries was agreed upon (De Vylder 2007). Several of the conclusions contained in the Haberler Report were included in this legal document.

Following the Haberler Report, in 1963, trade ministers agreed to initiate negotiations to amend GATT to address trade and development concerns more explicitly. What stands out is the inclusion of Part IV in the GATT. Although recognizing the effects of asymmetries in trade, this reform imposed few, if any, concrete obligations (Jackson 2006). In the following years, the tensions between upholding reciprocity and addressing development needs, both in terms of gradualness and diversity, increased. Poorer countries advocated trade rules that favored the promotion of development-friendly policies, which would be potentially hampered by the direct application of the MFN principle (Hoekman 2005). This was coupled with the perception that the reduction of tariff barriers was insufficient to ensure freer trade, since governments had developed other behind-the-border mechanisms that limited the potential gains from import liberalization.

As a result, the Tokyo Round (1973–1979), in addition to promoting tariff reductions, was the first trade round to address non-tariff barriers. The Tokyo Round negotiations also included the adoption of the "Understanding on Differential and More Favorable Treatment, Reciprocity and Broader Participation of Developing Countries", known as the Enabling Clause. This clause allowed parties in the GATT to negotiate a more favorable treatment for developing countries without applying such treatment to other contracting parties. It encouraged preferential tariff schemes in favor of developing countries as well as possibilities to negotiate more flexible regional arrangements among less developed contracting parties. Lamp (2015) suggests that these S&DT provisions were more the result of developed countries' preferences rather than those of developing countries. The Tokyo Round was thus marked by tension among the so-called transatlantic powers (USA and European Community-EC) and developing countries, members of the so-called Informal Group of Developing Countries (Peixoto 2010).

The Uruguay Round began in a context where many developing countries were somewhat empowered by S&DT flexibilities. However, the Marrakech package was markedly uneven in favor of developed countries and dealt a hard blow to the S&DT (Steinberg 2007). There was no consensus among developing countries for the adoption of a general "umbrella" framework for S&DT provisions, although there were not many chances of fighting for that either. Developing countries were at a crossroads – would they accept all the rules and obligations resulting from the negotiation, or would they remain outside the organization? In fact, the single undertaking resulted in causing developing countries and developed countries to assume very similar undertakings based on rules commonly biased in favor of developed countries. The concept of S&DT was changed, and its scope was restricted; it was a reflection of the unwillingness of developed countries to continue granting special treatment, particularly to middle-income countries (Whalley 1999; Fukusaku 2000; Tempone 2007).

5.3 SPECIAL AND DIFFERENTIAL TREATMENT IN A NUTSHELL

As noted earlier, trade agreements tend to reflect developed countries' needs, priorities, and preferences. This holds true in both multilateral and PTA negotiations. Larger countries are more likely to be "rule-makers" and set the patterns that shape PTAs. In turn, this has been proven to have a distinctly positive effect on their exports – to the detriment of poorer countries – (Seiermann 2018). As a result, everything that differs from the "template" of PTA texts built by the larger economies is likely to be considered as an S&DT demand. These demands, which result from developing countries' industry needs, advocate for a set of protection and assistance tools in the form of special clauses (Hoekman 2005; Chang 2006).

According to Weinhardt and Schöfer (2021, p. 5), S&DT can be defined as

> "an ordering principle that (a) differentiates between groups of states that are understood to be in a more advantageous position than the members of the other group; and (b) stipulates that those perceived to be in a less advantageous position are given more extensive rights, and/or those perceived to be in a more advantageous position were given more extensive obligations."

Other scholars refer to S&DT provisions in the context of providing sufficient policy space, which is often reconfigured after signing a trade agreement, owing to disparities in development among parties (Mayer 2009; Di Caprio 2010).

There are at least two broad discussions on S&DT provisions. The first debate is about exactly which Members can use these provisions. Weinhardt and Schöfer (2021) identify three approaches by which S&DT is assigned in trade agreements: a definition of certain criteria that countries need to accomplish to access these provisions, a list with specific countries, and auto-election.[3] The second debate concerns the scope and types of S&DT provisions. Different proposals exist on how to define and categorize such provisions.

The WTO Secretariat suggests a typology of six different types of S&DT provisions. These include:

> "1. Provisions aied at increasing developing countries' trade opportunities; 2. Provisions under which WTO Members should safeguard the interests of developing country Members; 3. Flexibility of commitments, of action, and use of policy instruments; 4. Transitional time periods; 5. Technical assistance; 6. Provisions relating to LDC Members" (World Trade Organization 2021).

Scholars such as Matsushita et al. (2015), for their part, posit that most WTO agreements contain some forms of exceptions, longer phase-in periods, or special provisions for developing countries. They argue that these provisions were designed to improve the situation of developing countries by granting lighter disciplines or increasing their "embedded expertise" on WTO-related issues. Vineet and Wouters (2021), by comparison, classify S&DT provisions in six categories "1) right to exemptions; 2) right to reduced commitments; 3) right of temporary derogation; 4) right to delayed application; 5) right of presumption; 6) duty on developed Members to refrain from litigation (Vineet and Wouters 2021, p. 19)." These categories can be extended by two additional criteria "1) the duration for which the differential treatment is provided; 2) the extent to which reciprocity is exempted, i.e., whether it is a complete exemption or a partial one (Vineet and Wouters 2021, p. 20)."

3 The definition approach applies a benchmark or a set of definitions to determine who counts as a developing country (e.g., using a per capita income level); the list approach names specific countries that, regardless a determined criterion, are included in a developing status category (e.g., the WTO's approach vis-à-vis LDCs); finally, the auto-election approach allows countries to decide for themselves what category they wish to belong to (Weinhardt and Schöfer 2021).

A special debate has also emerged around the multilateral regime's assessment of Special and Differential Treatment (S&DT) regulation within free trade zones or custom unions. According to General Agreement on Tariffs and Trade (GATT) Article XXIV, Preferential Trade Agreement (PTA)s are subject to rules regarding the scope, ambition, and time schedule of tariff reductions.[4] While considered exceptions to the Most-Favoured Nation (MFN) principle, these regulations do not relate explicitly to special treatment for developing countries. In fact, only the Enabling Clause of 1979 introduced a more flexible set of conditions for south-south agreements. These differences in attention to S&DT provisions depending on the PTA composition are viewed differently by scholars and experts. For some scholars, Article XXIV limits the negotiation of nonreciprocal North-South PTAs, which excludes the use of S&DT clauses (Yanai 2009). Other scholars share a broader interpretation of Article XXIV, allowing more extensive use of S&DT provisions through preferential frameworks (Brusick and Clarke 2005; Gallagher 2010; Kuhlmann 2021). The approach taken in this chapter follows this second understanding. We also would point out that most PTAs containing different types of S&DT clauses and/or flexibilities have been notified to the WTO and have not triggered a noteworthy controversy.

While uniform S&DT clauses could be expected in multilateral negotiations, negotiating parties in PTAs do not follow a consistent approach. This allows the design of more targeted provisions that account for levels of development and power. Developing countries have displayed different strategies and instruments, leading to more heterogeneity in terms of S&DT across PTAs.

Previous research on S&DT and policy space in PTAs has focused on a variety of instruments across PTA chapters to preserve policy space: the inclusion of safeguards, nonautomatic import licenses, exports' duty drawbacks, production subsidies, patent restriction in specific sectors, state-owned enterprises, movement of individuals, subsidized credit, local labor requirements, domestic content requirements, as well as technology transfer requirements and exceptional conditions under which some unilateral tariff increases could be allowed (Di Caprio 2010; Thrasher and Gallagher 2010). When policy space is granted in a discriminatory manner, considering the special needs of the less developed signing parties, S&DT comes to the forefront.

Brusick and Clarke, tracing S&DT through regional trade agreements, have pointed to instruments such as "provisions safeguarding the interests of less developed partners; exceptions and exemptions; transitional time periods; technical assistance (2005, p. 167)." Kuhlman (2021), for her part, has emphasized the role of flexibility as a component of S&DT in PTAs. In a recent publication, she observes that PTAs include broader development concerns both in preambular language

[4] The General Agreement on Trade and Services establishes a similar set of rules for PTAs liberalizing trade in services. According to Article V, Parties can enter a PTA provided that such an agreement has a substantial sectoral coverage and provides for the absence or elimination of substantially all discrimination. Notably, GATS' Article V, in paragraph 3, acknowledges the need for additional flexibilities for developing countries signing PTAs.

and/or through operative provisions (i.e., criteria for different treatment among countries according to their needs, transitional time periods, technical assistance and capacity building, and sustainable development).

In brief, existing literature agrees on the necessity to adapt the legal texts of PTAs to accommodate the varying development levels of signatories parties. A diverse array of instruments is employed to achieve this objective, spanning the preamble section and various chapters. There is no single template to refer to S&DT.

5.4 CONCEPTUALIZATION, METHODS, AND SAMPLING

Drawing upon these developments on the scope of S&DT, our analytical framework includes traditional "at-the-border" policy space measures (tariff exclusions, transitional periods, rules of origin), as well as capacity-building provisions and any other horizontal or specific measures that imply a nonreciprocal treatment due to development differences.

To map S&DT provisions in PTAs, we propose the following types:

- provisions recognizing the relevance of S&DT treatment or provisions recognizing development-based differences among parties;
- longer transition periods for tariff reduction and for implementing commitments, available only to developing countries;
- provisions granting exceptions, special flexibilities,[5] and/or special considerations in rules of origin, available only to developing countries;
- provisions providing exemptions to liberalization, such as tariff reduction exclusions, available only for developing countries;
- capacity-building mechanisms and technical cooperation for developing countries or countries with development needs;
- other provisions with nonreciprocal commitments benefiting less developed countries.

Our research follows a qualitative methodology based on manual content analysis. For each agreement, we traced and coded all S&DT provisions along the

[5] Baccini et al. (2015a, p. 3) define flexibility as "devices included in an agreement that allow states to anticipate and respond to domestic contingencies or to adjust their policies for other purposes without violating the terms of an agreement." They consider a "long-term flexibility variable" formed by "provisions allowing for the suspension of tariff cuts in case of balance of payments problems, a general safeguard provision, a provision allowing for the imposition of countervailing duties, and a provision allowing for the imposition of anti-dumping duties." They have included a "short-term flexibility" variable by considering the maximum number of years that countries are allowed to achieve tariff elimination envisaged in the agreement. These variables overlap with the flexibility variables considered in our analysis of S&DT. However, in our assessment, these flexibility provisions are considered part of the S&DT only when they are reserved for the developing member(s) in the case of a north-south agreement and for the less developed member(s) in the case of a south-south trade agreement.

preambulatory sections, chapters, and annexes. We considered whether the agreements acknowledge development asymmetries among parties and when and how the agreements' legal texts could be mapped onto one of our categories.

We have paid particular attention to who the beneficiaries are and how binding and legal commitments result (e.g., clauses of best endeavor, soft vs. deep commitments). In some cases, S&DT provisions are found in the body text, while in other cases, S&DT commitments are listed in footnotes or are phrased implicitly and fall into our broader "flexibilities" category. In tariff schedules, the S&DT dimension results from the interpretation of the level of ambition embraced by each party. Some examples of how legal texts are matched with our typology can be found in Table 5.1.[6]

TABLE 5.1 *Examples of S&DT provisions.*

Types of provisions	Text in the agreements
Provisions recognizing the relevance of S&DT treatment or provisions recognizing development-based differences among parties	**Mercosur-Egypt. Art 3.** The Parties and Signatory Parties to this Agreement, in accordance with Article XXIV of GATT 1994 and the Decision on Differential and More Favorable Treatment, Reciprocity and Greater Participation of Developing Countries of 1979, hereby establish a zone of free trade.
Provisions recognizing the relevance of S&DT treatment or provisions recognizing development-based differences among parties Provisions establishing longer transition periods for tariff reduction, and other commitments Provisions with capacity-building mechanisms and technical cooperation	**EU-Mercosur. Sanitary and Phytosanitary Measures. Art 19.**[7] "In application of article 10 of the SPS Agreement, when Paraguay has identified difficulties with a proposed measure notified by the EU Party, Paraguay may request, in its comments submitted to the EU, pursuant to Annex B to the SPS Agreement referred to in Article 7 of the SPS Agreement, an opportunity to discuss the issue. The EU Party and Paraguay shall enter into consultation in order to agree on: a) alternative import conditions to be applied by the importing Party according to Article 7 (alternative measures); or b) technical assistance according to Article 18 cooperation and technical assistance; or c) a transitional period of 6 months for proposed measures to apply to goods from Paraguay, which could be exceptionally extended for another period of no longer than 6 months."

[6] For the sake of space, this table doesn't include examples showing S&DT in tariff schedules.

[7] This provision is replicated in EU-Colombia & Peru FTA. Sanitary and Phytosanitary Measures. Art 100.

Types of provisions	Text in the agreements
Provisions with capacity-building mechanisms and technical cooperation	**EU-Colombia & Peru.**Chapter 5. **Transfer of Technology. Art 255.5.** "The EU Party shall facilitate and promote the use of incentives granted to institutions and enterprises in its territory for the transfer of technology to institutions and enterprises from the signatory Andean Countries in order to enable them to establish a viable technological base."
Provisions determining exemptions to liberalizing commitments, such as tariff reduction exclusions	**EU-Andean Countries.**Chapter 4. **Temporary presence of natural persons for business purposes. Art 124. footnote 35.** The entry and temporary stay of key personnel and graduate trainees shall be for a period of up to three years (35) for intra-corporate transferees. For Colombia, the maximum length of stay for intra-corporate transferees is two years, renewable for an additional year. For Peru, the work contract may be up to three years. However, the length of stay for intra-corporate transferees is up to one year, renewable provided that the conditions which motivated its granting are maintained.
Provisions with exceptions, special rules with flexibilities and/or special considerations in Rules of Origin	**EU-Andean Countries. Article 3. Accumulation of Origin. parr. 3.** Notwithstanding paragraphs 1 and 2, materials originating in Costa Rica, El Salvador, Guatemala, Honduras, Nicaragua, Panama, Venezuela or in a Member Country of the Andean Community which is not a Party to this Agreement shall be considered as materials originating in a signatory Andean Country when further processed or incorporated into a product obtained there.
Other provisions with non-reciprocal commitments	**Mercosur UE. Article X.35 Scope of Protection for Geographical Indications.** 4. Nothing shall prevent the use by a Party, with respect to any product, of a customary name of a plant variety or an animal breed, existing in the territory of that Party as of the date of entry into force of this Agreement. 5. Nothing shall prevent the use by a Party of an individual component of a multi-component term that is protected as a geographical indication in the territory of that Party if such individual component is a term customary in the common language as the common name for the associated good.

Source: Authors' coding.

We designed our sampling strategy to capture various theoretical expectations on the variety of S&DT configurations. First, we selected treaties that vary along the symmetry-asymmetry axes. Therefore, it includes both PTAs with members that are roughly similar in market size and PTAs where parties have significant differences

TABLE 5.2 *Selected Latin American PTAs.*

PTA	Year	Depth index (DESTA)	Notified in WTO as
EU-Mexico	2000	4	GATT Art. XXIV & GATS Art. V
Chile-China	2005	5	Art XXIV GATT & Art V GATS
MERCOSUR-Peru	2005	3	Enabling clause (ALADI)
MERCOSUR-Egypt	2010	3	Art XXVI
EU-Colombia & Peru	2012	7	GATT Art. XXIV & GATS Art. V
CPTPP	2018	7	GATT Art. XXIV & GATS Art. V
EU-MERCOSUR	2019 (agreement in principle)	5 (own calculation)	Not informed

Source: WTO Regional Trade Agreements database and DESTA database (www.designoftradeagreements.org).

regarding economic indicators and development status. Second, our sample further encompasses treaties that mirror the different waves in the evolving design of PTAs in Latin America, including the "open-type" agreements of the 1990s (Fuentes 1994), the beyond-the-border agreements characteristic of "twenty-first-century regionalism" (Baldwin 2021), and those identified as part of a "hybrid" regionalism[8] (Peixoto and Perrotta 2018). Third, we know from past literature (Gallagher 2010; Baccini et al. 2015b) that US-led, EU-led, and south-south agreements tend to have different legal structures and regulatory philosophies (and therefore, different models). To take this into account, the sample includes PTAs with the US, and the EU as partners as well as south-south agreements. Fourth, we consider variation in terms of the overall PTA ambition measured by the concept of depth (Dür et al. 2014), and we allow for potential differences driven by the time dimension by selecting treaties negotiated between 2000 and 2019.

Based on the above selection criteria, we study the following agreements: MERCOSUR[9]-EU, Comprehensive and Progressive Agreement for Trans-Pacific Partnership (CPTPP), EU-Colombia and Peru, MERCOSUR-Egypt, MERCOSUR-Peru, México-EU, and Chile-China FTA (see Table 5.2). We cover nine Latin American countries, individually or grouped in regional integration processes; additionally, we account for both traditional and nontraditional trading partners.

This selection covers the so-called two "waves of regionalism" within the region. In effect, during the 1990s and early 2000s, Latin American countries entered several asymmetrical PTAs, following an "open regionalism" model, that is, making

[8] This category integrates economic liberalization with cooperation in social and political matters.

[9] Argentina, Brazil, Paraguay, and Uruguay.

agreements with developed countries and abandoning import substitution policies (ECLAC 1994). The EU-Mexico agreement is part of this first group of treaties. The Chile-China FTA, MERCOSUR-Peru FTA, and MERCOSUR-Egypt FTA belong to a different type of agreement. They are part of the south-south agreements wave, a trend observed during the first decade of the 2000s: agreements among developing countries and, in the case of China, including rising emerging powers. The agreements with China and Egypt illustrate FTAs with nontraditional extra-regional partners.

In those same years of the first decade of the 2000s, "twenty-first-century regionalism" gained awareness among trade policymakers in the region. Some countries moved forward into asymmetrical trade agreements that involved beyond-the-border and WTO-plus regulations with extra-regional partners, reflecting the dynamics of global value chains (Baldwin 2021). Examples include the EU-Andean countries agreement and, more recently, the CPTPP (in which Chile, Mexico, and Peru are involved). The MERCOSUR-EU agreement is considered a case of an asymmetrical trade agreement with an extra-regional partner that includes WTO-plus clauses; however, the fact that it does not include deep commitments in areas such as investment or intellectual property rights has led to its classification as a "hybrid case" (Caetano 2022). Table 5.2 summarizes the characteristics of the selected agreements.

5.5 WHERE AND HOW IS S&DT INCLUDED IN LATIN AMERICAN PTAS?

Latin American countries have a long-standing tradition of promoting S&DT at the multilateral level. When it comes to PTAs, our analysis shows interesting patterns of variation. As a first observation, it is noteworthy that all seven agreements analyzed include some form of S&DT provisions.[10] In the following, we discuss how the six types of S&DT provisions identified in our analytical framework are present in these PTAs, differentiating between asymmetrical and symmetrical (south-south) agreements. Table 5.3 summarizes our findings.

5.5.1 *S&DT in South-South Agreements*

5.5.1.1 Chile-China PTA

Signed in November 2005, the Chile–China FTA was China's first PTA with a Latin American country. At that time, China had almost no PTAs negotiated and signed, and, therefore, for some observers, one of the reasons behind this agreement was the Chinese government's objective to gain negotiating experience (DIRECON

[10] It is important to note that none of the agreements analyzed include a definition for "development," or "asymmetry".

TABLE 5.3 *Special and differential treatment provisions in Latin American PTAs.*

	Recognition of S&DT or development-based differences	Longer transition periods for developing countries	Exemptions and special considerations in Rules of Origin for developing countries	Exemptions to liberalizing commitments for developing countries	Capacity-building mechanisms	Other provisions with non-reciprocal commitments
MERCOSUR–EU	Yes	Yes	Yes	Yes	Yes	Yes
CPTPP	No	Yes (not exclusively)	No	Yes	Yes	No
EU–Colombia & Peru	Yes	No	Yes	Yes	Yes	Yes
EU–Mexico	No	No	No	Yes	Yes	Yes
MERCOSUR–Peru	Yes	Yes	No	Yes	No	No
MERCOSUR–Egypt	Yes	Yes	Yes	Yes	No	No
Chile–China	No	No	No	Yes (temporal)	No	No

Source: Authors' coding.

2009). Negotiations were short, and although China's economy was notably larger than Chile's, they were carried out without any specific consideration regarding leveling the playing field. The first agreement was followed by a supplementary agreement on trade in services in 2010 and by an extended Protocol in 2019.

According to the feasibility study carried out in 2004, this PTA was expected to have a positive impact on bilateral trade and economic welfare, especially in trade in goods and investments (Chilean High Level Study Group 2004). Both parties' specialization patterns were considered potentially beneficial and complementary for each economy. Therefore, there was no perception of threats to merit the inclusion of asymmetrical in the treaty. Furthermore, from the Chilean perspective, it was expected that "the subscription of an FTA with China would contribute to minimizing trade deviations induced by agreements that Chile has negotiated with the European Union, the United States, and Korea" (Chilean High Level Study Group 2004, p. cxii). Considerations on S&DT were not a priority.

The agreement does not mention S&DT explicitly. Regarding flexibilities, it includes safeguard measures in the trade remedies chapter, and a special exception applies in case of "serious balance of payments and external financial difficulties or threats of thereof" (Art. 102). The treaty foresees cooperation in many areas, such as sanitary and phytosanitary measures, technical barriers to trade, transparency, and small and medium-sized enterprises. The 2019 Protocol added new areas with a cooperation-type clause, for example, e-commerce, competition, environment and trade, and economic and technical cooperation.

Commitments on tariff liberalization are similar for both parties. At the time of entry into force, Chile made 74.1 percent of tariff lines duty-free, representing 50.7 percent of Chile's total imports from China. In a ten-year transition period, 98.1 percent of tariff lines were reduced to 0, reaching 96.9 percent of Chile's total imports from China. For China, its initial commitments were smaller, with 28.5 percent tariff lines duty-free, representing 50.9 percent of China's total imports from Chile. After the transition period, liberalization reached 97.2 percent of total lines in China's tariff schedule, affecting 99.1 percent of Chile's exports during 2003–2005.

Within the agreement, there is only one provision in Chapter 1 that introduces a distinct treatment between parties. This provision pertains to an exemption of the interim duty outlined in the "Regulation on Import and Export Tariff of the People's Republic of China." According to this provision, "If a Party reduces its applied most favored nation import custom duty rate … after the entry into force of this Agreement and before the end of the tariff elimination period, the tariff elimination schedule (Schedule) of that Party shall apply to the reduced rate." However, it is essential to note that this obligation does not apply if the reduced rate is stipulated in the aforementioned interim duty (Article 8, Paragraph 3).[11]

[11] The exemption is listed again in the 2019 Protocol.

5.5.1.2 MERCOSUR-Peru PTA

MERCOSUR and Peru began negotiations for a PTA in the context of the Framework Agreement between the Andean Community and MERCOSUR, since Peru is a member of the Andean Community. Negotiations concluded on 25 August 2005 when parties signed the Economic Complementary Agreement No 58, which entered into force on 6 February 2006.[12]

The agreement's legal framework is strongly influenced by WTO and the 1980 Montevideo Treaty (ALADI). In fact, information on custom duties modifications among national authorities should be notified to the ALADI General Secretariat (Art. 9). GATT/94 sets a common legal basis for National Treatment (Art. III), disciplines such as antidumping, countervailing measures (Art. 14), custom valuation (Art. 21), intellectual property rights (Art. 32), technical procedures (Annex VIII), sanitary and phytosanitary measures (annex IX). GATT and ALADI also provide exceptions applicable in MERCOSUR–Peru such as the one contained in Article 50 of Montevideo Treaty and Articles XX and XXI of GATT/94 (Art. 10).[13]

As any agreement legally framed within ALADI, it is open to accession by other ALADI members, and there is an obligation to notify in case of negotiations with extra ALADI partners (Art. 40). This agreement has commitments on trade in goods while trade-in services and investments contain best endeavor clauses (Art. 28 to 31). Agricultural and industrial export subsidies are forbidden according to Article 18.

At the request of Peru, the intellectual property chapter recognizes the WTO TRIPs Agreement as the applicable legal framework as well as the Convention on Biological Diversity (CBD). Also, Parties agree to develop norms and disciplines to protect traditional knowledge.

There is only one explicit (though not direct) reference to S&DT in the Agreement: Article 1 establishes, as part of its objective to achieve harmonious development in the region, to consider the asymmetries derived from the different levels of economic development. In addition, S&DT is found in the liberalization schedule, where there are more flexible deadlines for Peru in the trade liberalization schedule regarding new products and the so-called ALADI historical heritage (namely, liberalization commitments taken before the agreement).

Beyond that, there is no special flexibility for less developed partners other than specific protection built through rules of origin. However, this underestimates the true extent of S&DT because each signatory party has its own rules of origin profile to protect sectors, including Argentina and Brazil, which are the more developed countries in this trade agreement. In fact, specific transformations, national or

[12] Source: www.sice.oas.org

[13] Exceptions include protection of public morality; regulation of imports or exports of arms; protection of life and health of people, animals, and plants; protection of the national patrimony of artistic, historical, or archaeological value; export, use and consumption of nuclear materials, radioactive products, among others.

regional content, are needed for trading dairy and agricultural products, textiles, multifiber and shoes, machinery and mechanical appliances, electrical equipment, sound recorders and reproducers, televisions, rail transport, automotive sector, and musical instruments among Argentina, Brazil, and Peru. Between Paraguay and Peru, specific transformation and/or requirements are needed for vegetable oil, original yarn for textiles and multifiber, shoes, and metal industrial products. Specific requirements are also needed for trading textiles, multifiber, and shoes between Uruguay and Peru.

5.5.1.3 MERCOSUR-Egypt PTA

MERCOSUR and Egypt started negotiating a PTA after talks held during the G-20 Meeting in November 2003. A PTA was not signed until 2 August 2010, within the framework of the XXXIX Meeting of the Council of the Common Market and the Summit of Heads of State of Mercosur and Associated States. The MERCOSUR-Egypt PTA entered into force seven years after its signature, on 1 September 2017, after the parties completed their internal procedures to ratify the agreement.[14]

The Agreement is legally framed within the multilateral trade rules. It relies on the WTO to define concepts such as tariffs, countervailing measures, antidumping, and safeguards (Arts. 2, 3, and 4), and to regulate disciplines such as quantitative restrictions, national treatment, sanitary and phytosanitary measures, technical barriers to trade, restrictions to safeguard the balance of payments, customs valuation, among others (Arts. 12 to 21). The agreement has the main objective of establishing a PTA following Article XXIV of the GATT and the Decision on Differential and More Favorable Treatment, Reciprocity and Fuller Participation of Developing Countries, known as the Enabling Clause (Art. 3).

Tariff-reduction schedules proceed according to five categories, following two deadlines. The first deadline is the date the agreement enters into force. The second deadline is one year after the agreement enters into force. There is one category for which tariff-cutting does not follow any deadline and depends on the decision of the joint committee. Trade in services is a future goal for negotiations and will proceed within the General Agreement on Trade in Services (GATS) framework.

Apart from the explicit reference in Article 3, S&DT is noticeable in two other sections: trade liberalization schedules and rules of origin. The trade liberalization schedule has a special column for S&DT for Paraguay but is reserved only for two tariff lines related to animal parts products.

Regarding rules of origin, the agreement establishes a different percentage for imported inputs in the case of Paraguay (up to 55% instead of 45% for the rest of the signatory parties). This flexibility reflects the recognition of Paraguay as the least developed country in the MERCOSUR. In addition, for trade between Uruguay

[14] Source: www.sice.oas.org.

and Egypt and between Paraguay and Egypt, the agreement establishes a change in tariff classification if imported inputs do not exceed 10 percent (except for textiles). It is important to note that textiles are quite a protected sector globally and do not usually include S&DT clauses. This is particularly true for Egypt, as a developing country with a long-standing tradition in the textile sector.

5.5.2 *S&DT in Asymmetrical PTAs*

5.5.2.1 EU-MERCOSUR PTA

The EU-MERCOSUR PTA has a long negotiating history. The Framework Agreement for the negotiation process was established in 1995 but negotiations were not launched before 1999. By June 2019, after twenty years, both parties reached an "agreement in principle" in the so-called trade pillar. Asymmetries between Europe and MERCOSUR are easily noticeable. While MERCOSUR represents barely 2 percent of EU exports, for MERCOSUR countries, the EU is one of their largest trading partners, accounting for more than 16 percent of the total export of goods from the block.

Trade patterns show that EU exports to MERCOSUR are mainly machinery and transport equipment, chemicals, and manufactured goods sectors. In contrast, MERCOSUR's export basket is concentrated around commodities and low-value-added goods. In addition, whereas the EU is deemed as one of the largest rule makers ("Brussels Effect"), having signed around fifty trade agreements (many of which have strong or deep commitments), this was the first deep agreement for MERCOSUR.

For many years, including S&DT commitments has been a precondition to reaching an agreement strongly advocated by MERCOSUR negotiators. The resulting "agreement in principle" suggests some success in this goal since the legal text contains both substantive and procedural S&DT clauses. Although there is no specific chapter on S&DT, many chapters include some kind of provision where the parties undertake different commitments, agree on differentiated transition periods, allocate exceptions only for MERCOSUR's members, and/or agree on capacity-building commitments. For some clauses, these considerations apply to all MERCOSUR countries, while in others, they are limited to Paraguay. Nevertheless, differential treatment is given to the EU in one case.[15]

The chapter on sanitary and phytosanitary measures is the sole chapter in the whole agreement that explicitly recognizes "special and differential treatment" (Art. 19). It also includes extended transition periods for implementing sanitary

[15] The EU has retained special provisions for itself, for example, regarding safeguard measures under the Current Payment and Capital Movements Chapter (Art 4 "Temporary safeguard measures" in "Current Payments and Capital Movements").

and phytosanitary (SPS) provisions in the case of Paraguay. The chapter also incorporates capacity-building provisions and explicitly acknowledges the different levels reached by regional integration processes within MERCOSUR and the EU. From that standpoint, it recognizes the necessity for more flexible regulation within MERCOSUR, urging it to "make its best efforts to gradually adopt, if applicable," some rules under the agreement.

Longer transition periods are considered in trade in goods provisions, tariff elimination schedules, rules of origin, custom and trade facilitation, and the already mentioned chapter on sanitary and phytosanitary measures.

Tariff commitments reflect each party's sensibilities: 14.1 percent of MERCOSUR custom duties are eliminated immediately, in contrast with a larger initial commitment of the EU of 74 percent of goods duty-free at the entry into force of the agreement.[16] After ten years, MERCOSUR reaches 72 percent of liberalization, whereas an additional 18.7 percent of custom duties are reduced in fifteen years, arriving at 90.7 percent of liberalized trade. Only 0.2 percent of goods are subject to quotas, and 9.1 percent of goods are excluded. The EU reaches a 92 percent liberalization in a ten-year transition process and retains partial access to 7.8 percent of goods – including 7.1 percent quotas – whereas 0.3 percent custom duties are excluded.

Notable is the chapter on intellectual property rights, which includes references to the multilateral standards. Although not specifically an S&DT clause, it merits special consideration for developing countries' IP interests and agenda by preserving multilateral flexibility instead of moving toward a TRIPS-plus agreement. The only TRIPS-plus inclusion in the MERCOSUR-EU Agreement pertains to geographical indications, where a list of European and MERCOSUR products benefit from special protection (the EU has listed 350 and MERCOSUR 220). At the same time, it is noticeable that some capacity-building provisions have been included in this chapter.

Special provisions have been provided only to Paraguay as a less developed treaty partner in the trade defense measures chapter and in the rules of origin provisions. The protocol on Rules of Origin restricts S&DT to specific conditions provided in Annex II (Product Specific Rule of Origin). These are restricted to Paraguay, to a limited set of goods, and with a temporal period not exceeding four years. Finally, there are exceptions or specific regulations for MERCOSUR countries in areas such as government procurement, state-owned enterprises, and export duties.

5.5.2.2 EU-Colombia and Peru PTA

The European Union-Colombia and Peru comprehensive trade agreement was signed in June 2012 (entry into force in 2013). Negotiations were launched in

[16] It has to be noticed that, according to WTO Trade Profiles, in 2020 60.3 percent of European Union imports were duty-free (www.wto.org/english/res_e/statis_e/daily_update_e/tariff_profiles/CE_E.pdf) whereas only an average of 13 percent of imported goods had a similar treatment in Mercosur.

February 2009 and concluded in 2010; later, in 2017, Ecuador joined the agreement.[17] It is worth noting that signing these PTAs implied the removal of Peru and Colombia from the European Generalized Scheme of Preferences Plus (GSP +) provisions. Ecuador was excluded from the programme after reaching the income requirements established by the GSP scheme (Borchert et al. 2021).

The trade-in goods chapter has a few S&DT provisions. The agreement authorizes Colombia and Peru to apply their price band system in agricultural goods as a special flexibility. Regarding the tariff schedule, S&DT provisions are limited. Before the agreement's entry into force, 25.2 percent of the EU's tariff lines were duty-free in contrast to 3.5 percent of Colombia's tariff lines and 55 percent of Peru's. As a result of the agreement, in the case of the European Union, additional 6,714 tariff lines (69.1% of the EU's tariff) have been liberalized for Colombian imports and 6,766 tariff lines (69.65%) for Peruvian imports. After ten years, 95.8 percent of the tariff lines are duty-free for products originating in Colombia, and 94.8 percent for Peru. Nevertheless, 4.2 percent of EU tariffs, representing 12.2 percent of imports from Colombia, remain subject to duties. Regarding EU commitments for Peru, 3 percent remain subject to duties, representing 2.8 percent of imports from Peru.

For the Andean countries, immediate tariff reductions were barely larger. After the agreement's entry into force 61.1 percent of Colombia's tariffs became duty-free, reaching 7,143 tariff lines liberalized over a ten-year schedule. 3.9 percent of Colombia's tariffs remain dutiable, representing 0.6 percent of Colombia's imports from the EU. In the case of Peru, the initial liberalization was 77.9 percent (55% MFN duty-free plus an additional 22.9%). After ten years, 98 percent of total lines in Peru's tariff schedule have become duty-free; therefore, 151 tariff lines remain subject to duties (1.5% of Peru's imports from the EU).

This unbalanced outcome of the tariff reduction commitments was brought up by Malaysia during the presentation of the agreement at the Committee on Regional Trade Agreements of the WTO. However, Colombia and Peru considered the outcome "satisfactory and comprehensive in terms of trade coverage and export and import interests and sensitivities" (World Trade Organization 2015, p. 2).

In regard to the rules of origin, a notable provision is the one that establishes that goods originating in Costa Rica, El Salvador, Guatemala, Honduras, Nicaragua, Panama, Venezuela, or in any member country of the Andean Community which is not a Party to the Agreement shall be considered as materials originating in a signatory Andean country when further processed or incorporated into a product obtained there. There is no comparable reciprocal clause for the EU.

The S&DT principle is formally included and explicitly recognized in the Sanitary and Phytosanitary chapter. Furthermore, this chapter provides an additional six-month transition period as well as technical assistance with specific measures for trade capacity building.

[17] Although the present analysis is based in the EU-Peru and Colombia FTA agreement text.

In the trade in services chapter, two provisions recognize a different treatment related to the temporary presence of natural persons for business purposes. In the first one, Colombia and Peru have different maximum lengths of stay for intra-corporate employers' transferees. In the second one, included in a footnote, both Peru and Colombia limit the application of commitments to major suppliers.

In the chapter covering current payments and movement of capital, a S&DT provision has been introduced as part of the safeguard measures. In addition, in the government procurement provisions, parties included a capacity-building commitment: The EU shall provide assistance to potential tenders from the Andean Community in the EU procurement process.

There are some S&DT provisions included in the intellectual property chapter. These include a differentiated approach to international agreements and their commitments based on the different conditions parties had before the agreements. For instance, whereas the EU "shall make all reasonable effort to comply" with the Patent Law Treaty, the Andean Countries "shall make all reasonable efforts" to accede to it. With regard to patents, the agreement recognizes different level commitments: for Colombia and the EU, data protection for biological and biotechnology products is included, while for Peru, the protection of the undisclosed information of such products shall be limited to TRIPS provisions, with a more restricted scope than for its counterparts. Lastly, the chapter considers a capacity-building commitment regarding the transfer of technology, according to which the EU shall facilitate and promote the use of incentives specific to institutions and enterprises for transferring technology to institutions and enterprises in the Andean Countries.

5.5.2.3 EU-Mexico PTA

The European Union and Mexico reached an Economic Partnership, Political Coordination and Cooperation Agreement in 1997, known as the Global Agreement or EUMFTA, mostly comprising trade in goods liberalization. The Global Agreement was the first transatlantic treaty negotiated by the European Union. Negotiations were concluded following a tight timeframe of less than a year. Both the European Council and the Mexican parliament approved it on March 20, 2000, so the treaty entered into force in July of the same year.[18]

The Global Agreement covers over 95 percent of trade in goods and services. It also provides for government procurement liberalization and for rules on competition, investment, and intellectual property. Mexico agreed to commitments similar to those granted to the United States and Canada under North American Free Trade Agreement (NAFTA), deregulating about 90 percent of cross-border trade.

[18] In 2001, the parties agreed to expand the agreement to rules on trade in services.

There are only a few provisions that provide for different treatment in favor of Mexico, with no chapter dedicated to special and differentiated treatment as such. The Global Agreement established a transition period of ten years for all liberalization commitments. In those areas where the Agreement provided for a complete liberalization, the EU had a nine-year transition period, whereas Mexico could use up to ten years (Arts. 8 and 10). It should be highlighted, however, that both countries have excluded significant products from the liberalization schedule.

It is notable that the EUMFTA incorporates a set of social clauses governing areas as human, labor, and environmental rights demanded by the EU, potentially limiting Mexico's internal policy space. The Global Agreement is comprehensive overall and has improved trade among its parties over the years (Zabludovsky and Lora 2005, p. 27). However, the agreement's text only superficially reflects the existing asymmetries between its members.

5.5.2.4 Comprehensive and Progressive Agreement for Trans-Pacific Partnership

Three Latin American countries are part of the CPTPP: Chile, Mexico, and Peru. This agreement was finalized in 2018 after the US left the original treaty known as Trans-Pacific Partnership (TPP). The CPTPP adopts the TPP text but suspends the application of some clauses that were of great importance to the US. This mega-regional agreement is considered a "new generation" PTA type of agreement due to its economic relevance (regarding its partners' economic power) and its ambitious commitments. However, on the S&DT dimension, the CPTPP is highly limited. There is no explicit mention of S&DT, and those relevant few are scattered across the treaty parts.

The CPTPP text does not have a distinct set of provisions applicable to developing countries. However, countries such as Brunei, Malaysia, Mexico, and Vietnam have longer phase-in periods before their commitments take full effect. However, the same applies to Japan. Mexico stands out with different liberalization categories for a limited number of tariff lines – those subject to country-specific tariff-rate quotas (TRQs). Furthermore, Mexico's liberalization schedule applicable to Vietnam is delayed by one year compared to other Parties.

Focusing on services, liberalization proceeds according to negative lists. Mexico and Chile have included some nonconforming measures excluding certain sectors, industries, and practices. For instance, in the case of Chile, the aviation and maritime sectors are exempted from MFN treatment. Aviation, fishing, and maritime services will proceed according to other international treaties. Chile further exempted services related to arts and cultural industries, including audiovisual cooperation.

Concerning state-owned enterprises, the chapter provides a list of nonconforming measures. For instance, in the case of Chile, it retains the ability for national television stations to provide preferential treatment to Chilean content and receive noncommercial assistance; and in the case of Mexico, it retains the ability for the national petroleum company to make purchases on a preferential basis from national firms in its exploration and production activities.

From an S&DT perspective, there are two noteworthy chapters related to development, chapter 21 "cooperation and capacity building" and chapter 23 "development". The chapter devoted to cooperation and capacity-building set the basis for providing financial or in-kind resources for cooperation and capacity-building activities. In our sample, this is the only agreement that includes financial support for cooperation as part of S&DT provisions. The development chapter also acknowledges the importance of implementing development policies but does not include specific commitments. It is noticeable how this provision does not create any differentiated rights for developing countries.

5.6 CONCLUSIONS

Our analysis has shown how S&DT is present in a sample of Latin American PTAs, although through different instruments. The PTA with the most S&DT provisions is the MERCOSUR-EU PTA, whereas the CPTPP and the Chile-China PTAs have the fewest provisions.

First, in relation to the broader literature on PTA design and on S&DT, our research has contributed to highlighting the idea that S&DT does not follow a single template and remains an elusive concept. Latin American countries have resorted to different ways of framing S&DT case-by-case. S&DT, regarding the traditional set of trade policy tools, has focused on excluding certain goods or services in the liberalizing commitments, agreeing on longer transition periods for tariff liberalization or for the implementation of sanitary and phytosanitary provisions. In chapters dealing with "behind the border" regulations, Latin American PTAs show some creativity in how countries sought to preserve their policy space by creating exemptions and carve-outs to regulatory commitments, such is the case in the MERCOSUR-EU PTA. In addition, Latin American cases confirm some of the expectations found in the literature (Di Caprio and Amdsen 2004; Peixoto 2010), according to which S&DT in PTAs often focus on chapters such as rules of origin. Our work shows that, at least in the Latin American PTAs we analyzed, this approach is aimed at preserving policy space for particular industrial products or regional value chains. Furthermore, we found that capacity-building mechanisms and technical assistance are a type of S&DT that takes place in asymmetrical trade agreements involving developed and developing countries but not in south-south trade initiatives.

Second, our analysis illustrates that the inclusion of S&DT clauses depends on at least two key factors: whether or not development was framed as an important issue during the negotiating process, and the level of asymmetry among parties. S&DT appears more prominently in cases where development-related concerns are part of the negotiations. Alternatively, when the parties do not frame the agreement as involving asymmetries and/or do not include development-related concerns, S&DT provisions are largely absent. It is striking to note that agreements involving developing countries appear not to take into account south-south asymmetries as much as expected.

Third, regarding who benefits from S&DT, we found that PTAs in Latin America follow a "list approach" to grant access to these provisions. S&DT was attributed to particular countries that were identified as beneficiaries in the exceptions, flexibilities, or carve-outs contained in the different chapters. S&DT did not follow a "pre-defined criteria approach". This is a practice even in south-south agreements where S&DT applied relatively more to less developed members such as Paraguay or Peru. This way of attributing S&DT departs from multilateral S&DT definitions and other PTAs, such as the Regional Comprehensive Economic Partnership (RCEP).[19]

Overall, S&DT remains an elusive concept. The actual practice of S&DT in PTAs looks more like a patchwork of clauses, exclusions, and text interpretations rather than a systematic, regular, consistent, and cohesive set of principles and clauses. There are no specific chapters that group these provisions together. The challenge is how to conceptualize and recognize them to allow for a proper assessment of their extent and importance. The analytical framework presented in this chapter is a first step in this direction. Our analysis can also inspire the development of automatized content analysis strategies. The next steps would be to look beyond Latin America to explore whether there are important regional differences and to evaluate the impact of S&DT clauses. We know very little about how these provisions are used and their effectiveness. Are principles more consequential than individual commitments? For instance, does the decision not to extend the duration of patent protection have a larger impact than a cooperation principle? These and other questions remain to be tackled to understand better how trade liberalization and S&DT can go hand in hand to support development.

REFERENCES

Bacchus, J. and I. Manak 2021. *The Development Dimension: Special and Differential Treatment in Trade*. London: Routledge.

Baccini, L., A. Dür and M. Elsig 2015a. "The Politics of Trade Agreement Design: Revisiting the Depth-Flexibility Nexus," *International Studies Quarterly* 59(4): 765–775.

Baccini, L., A. Dür and Y. Haftel 2015b. "Imitation and Innovation in International Governance: The Diffusion of Trade Agreement Design." In A. Dür and M. Elsig

[19] RCEP appeals to "least developing countries" as defining criteria, for example, in Article 8.23: Increasing Participation of Least Developed Country Parties which are Member States of ASEAN.

(Eds.), *Trade Cooperation: The Purpose, Design and Effects of Preferential Trade Agreements*. Cambridge: Cambridge University Press, pp. 167–194.

Baldwin, R. 2021. "Twenty-first Century Regionalism: Filling the Gap Between 21st Century Trade and 20th Century Trade Rules," World Trade Organization Economic Research and Statistics Division, n. ERSD2011-08.

Borchert, I., P. Conconi, M. Di Ubaldo and C. Herghelegiu 2021. "The Pursuit of Non-Trade Policy Objectives in EU Trade Policy," *World Trade Review* 20(5): 623–647.

Brusick, P. and J. Clarke 2005. "Operationalizing Special and Differential Treatment in Cooperation Agreements on Competition Law and Policy." In P. Brusick, A. M. Alvarez and L. Cernat (Eds.), *Competition Provisions in Regional Trade Agreements: How to Assure Development Gains*. Geneva: UNCTAD, pp. 161–188.

Caetano, G. 2022. "Análisis y prospectiva del Acuerdo de Asociación Unión Europea-Mercosur." Fundación Carolina. Documentos de Trabajo. N° Especial FC/EU-LAC (4)ES. www.fundacioncarolina.es.

Chang, H. J. 2006. "Policy Space in Historical Perspective with Special Reference to Trade and Industrial Policies," *Economic and Political Weekly* 41(7): 627–633.

Chilean High Level Study Group 2004. "Joint Feasibility Study on a Free Trade Agreements between Chile and China. Chilean Draft". www.sice.oas.org/TPD/CHL_CHN/Negotiations/Feasibility_e.pdf , accessed on 12 April 2023.

De Vylder. 2007. *The Least Developed Countries and World Trade.*Stockholm: Sida Studies.

Di Caprio, A. and A. Amsden 2004. "Does the New International Trade Regime Leave Room for Industrialization Policies in the Middle-Income Countries?," International Labour Office Working Paper No. 22. www.papers.ssrn.com.

DiCaprio, A. 2010. "US Free Trade Agreements and Policy Flexibility: Will New Rules Hinder Industrialisation?," *Development Policy Review* 28(4): 387–410.

DIRECON. 2009. *Chile. Veinte años de negociaciones comerciales*. Dirección General de Relaciones Económicas Internacionales, Ministerio de Relaciones Exteriores. www.subrei.gob.cl/docs/default-source/default-document-library/chile-20-anios-de-negociaciones-comerciales1.pdf?sfvrsn = a22683c9_0.

Dür, A., L. Baccini and M. Elsig. 2014. "The Design of International Trade Agreements: Introducing a New Dataset," *The Review of International Organizations* 9(3): 353–375.

Fuentes, J. A. 1994. "El regionalismo abierto y la integración económica," *Revista de la CEPAL* 53: 81–89.

Fukusaku, K. 2000. "Special and Differential Treatment for Developing Countries. Does it Help Those Who Help Themselves?" Working Paper n. 197. Brugge: World Institute for Development Economic Research, The United Nations University.

Gallagher, K. (Ed.) 2010. *Handbook on Trade and the Environment*. Northampton: Edward Elgar Publishing.

Hoekman, B. 2005. "Operationalizing the Concept of Policy Space in the WTO: Beyond Special and Differential Treatment," *Journal of International Economic Law* 8(2): 405–424.

Ingco, M. D. and J. D. Nash (Eds.). 2004. *Agriculture and the WTO: Creating a Trading System for Development*. Washington, DC: The World Bank.

Irwin, D., P. C. Mavroidis and A. O. Sykes 2008. *The Genesis of GATT*. New York: Cambridge University Press.

Jackson, J. H. 2006. *Sovereignty, the WTO and Changing Fundamentals of International Law*. New York: Cambridge University Press.

Kuhlman, K. 2021. *Handbook on Provisions and Options for Trade in Times of Crisis and Pandemic*. New York: United Nation Publications.

Lamp, N. 2015. "How Some Countries Became "Special": Developing Countries and the Construction of Difference in Multilateral Trade Lawmaking," *Journal of International Economic Law* 18: 743–771.

Matsushita, M., T. Shoernaum, P. C. Mavroidis and M. Hann 2015. *The World Trade Organization. Law, Practice and Policy*. Oxford: Oxford University Press.

Mayer, J. 2009. "Policy Space: What, for What, and Where?," *Development Policy Review* 27(4): 373–395.

Peixoto, J. 2010. "Flexibilities for Developing Countries in the Doha Round as Á La Carte Special and Differential Treatment: Retracing Uruguay Steps?," *Brazilian Journal of Latin American Studies* 9(1): 164–191.

Peixoto, J. and D. Perrotta. 2018. "El MERCOSUR en el nuevo escenario político regional: Más allá de la coyuntura," *Revista Desafios* 30(1): 91–134.

Seiermann, J. 2018. "Only Words? How Power in Trade Agreement Texts Affects International Trade Flows," UNCTAD Research Paper No. 26. https://unctad.org/system/files/official-document/ser-rp-2018d8_en.pdf?Repec

Steinberg, F. 2007. *Cooperación y conflicto. Comercio internacional en la era de la globalización*. Madrid: Akal.

Tempone, R. E. 2007. "Los dilemas institucionales de la OMC: Comentarios sobre el 'Informe Sutherland'," *Agenda Internacional* XIV(25): 181–199.

Thrasher, R. and K. Gallagher 2010. "Twenty-first Century Trade Agreements: Implications for Long-Run Development Policy," *Denver Journal of International Law & Policy* 38(2): 313–350.

Tussie, D. and D. Glover. 1993. *Developing Countries in World Trade: Policies and Bargaining Strategies*. Ottawa: IDRC.

Vineet, H. and J. Wouters 2021. "Special and Differential Treatment under the World Trade Organization: A Legal Typology." Leuven Centre for Global Studies. Working paper n. 227, November.

Weinhardt, C. and T. Schöfer 2021. "Differential Treatment for Developing Countries in the WTO: The Unmaking of the North–South Distinction in a Multipolar World," *Third World Quarterly* 43(1): 74–93.

Whalley, J 1999. "Special and Differential Treatment in the Millenium Round". Working Paper n. 30/99, CSGR.

WTO 2015. "Trade Agreement between the European Union and its member states, of the one part and Colombia and Peru, of the other (goods and services). Question and Replies." WT/REG333/2.

WTO 2021. "Special and Differential Treatment Provisions in WTO Agreements and Decisions. Note by the Secretariat." WT/COMTD/W/258.

Yanai, A. 2009. "Normative Influences of Special and Differential Treatment on North-South RTAs." IDE Discussion Papers, n. 197, Institute of Developing Economies, Japan External Trade Organization (JETRO). www.ideas.repec.org, accessed on 20 July.

Zabludovsky, G. and S. G. Lora 2005. "Principales retos de la negociación de un tratado de libre comercio con Estados Unidos: Disciplinas en materia de inversión". INTAL Working Papers 2826, Inter-American Development Bank, INTAL.

6

Digital and Environmental Provisions in Latin American Trade Agreements

Sebastian Klotz and Cristian Ugarte

6.1 INTRODUCTION

Is digitalisation the key to a sustainable future? At the World Economic Forum's 2022 meeting in Davos, Switzerland, this question was answered by industry representatives with a clear *Yes, it is!* (WEF 2022). And indeed, digitalisation and sustainability are increasingly regarded as closely intertwined complements. In the area of international trade governance, for instance, the World Trade Organisation (WTO) recently joined forces with the United Nations (UN) and other stakeholders to explore how '*[u]sing data and digital technologies [can] advance sustainable trade and environmental transparency*' (WTO 2021).

One popular example of the link between digitalisation and environmental sustainability[1] in the area of international trade governance is cross-border paperless trade. This term was first coined in a 2016 UN report, defining cross-border paperless trade as '*trade in goods, including their import, export, transit and related services, taking place on the basis of electronic communications, including exchange of trade-related data and documents in electronic form*' (UN 2016, p. 4). The idea is that paperless trade fosters sustainability through at least two channels: first, the eliminated use of paper in trade procedures reduces the amount of resources required for the production of paper and the greenhouse gas emissions associated with it; second, paperless digital trade procedures are expected to create broader process efficiency gains that further reduce resource intensity. While these effects might be partially offset by the resources used for electricity to power servers and computers, empirical studies indicate that the positive effect of paperless trade on the reduction of emissions dominates (see, e.g., UN 2021).

The views and opinions expressed in this chapter are those of the authors and do not necessarily reflect the views or positions of any entities they represent.

[1] The authors acknowledge that the term 'sustainability' covers a broad range of environmental, economic, and social topics. In this chapter, the term 'sustainability' is primarily used as short for environmental sustainability.

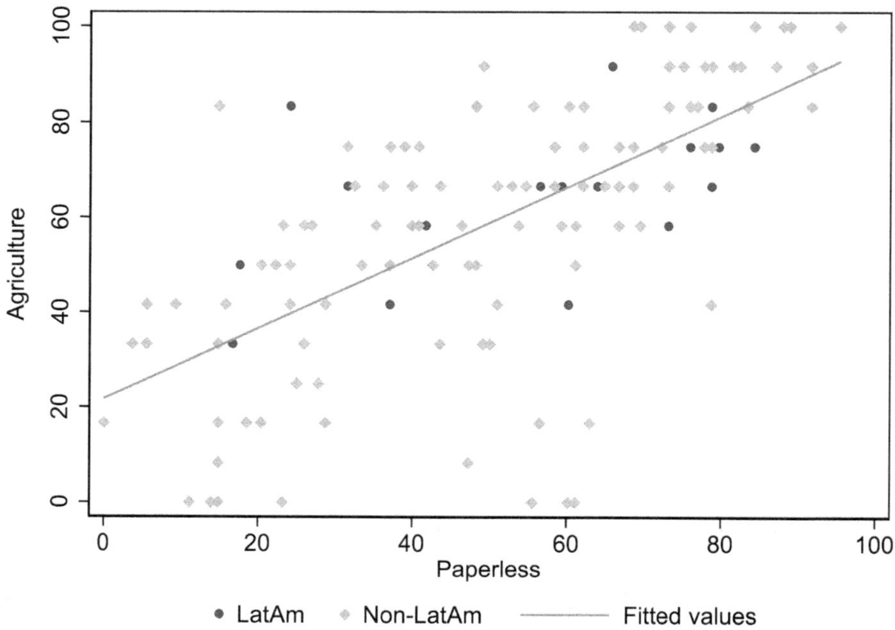

FIGURE 6.1 Paperless and agricultural trade facilitation.
Source: Authors' illustration based on UN (2022).

A more specific example which illustrates the increasingly close link between digitalisation and sustainability is the electronic processing of food trade-related documentation. Most importing countries around the world require sanitary and phytosanitary (SPS) certificates issued by the exporting country to certify that products have been inspected and are free from pests and diseases. The (analogue) application and issuance of such SPS certificates are used to complicate and prolong cross-border processes for food products. Recently, however, there has been a big push for digitalisation in this area. In 2017, only twelve countries worldwide had partially or fully implemented the electronic application and issuance of SPS certificates. By 2021, this number had already increased to sixty-four. To a large extent, these electronic SPS certificates are now directly electronically exchanged between exporters and importers (WCO 2021; UN 2022).

Given the link between digitalisation and sustainability, one would expect that governments coordinate their policies in these areas. In the area of trade facilitation at least, this appears to be the case indeed. A recent UN (UN 2022) on the digital and sustainable trade facilitation measures of 144 countries indicates a positive correlation between paperless trade and agricultural trade facilitation measures (Figure 6.1). Countries which put in place digital trade-facilitating measures are also likely to put in place sustainable trade-facilitating measures in the field of agriculture, and vice versa.

This chapter explores the link between digitalisation and sustainability in international trade governance further. The focus lies, more precisely, on digital and environmental provisions in preferential trade agreements (PTAs)[2]. The first substantial digital trade-related provisions in PTAs were introduced in Jordan–US (2000), while the first environmental provisions date back to the early 1990s and the establishments of the European Economic Area (1992) and the North American Free Trade Agreement (NAFTA) (1993). To provide a comparative account of digital and environmental provisions in PTAs, this chapter focuses primarily on PTAs signed between 2000 and 2019. In line with this book's overarching theme, we focus on PTAs signed by Latin American countries and consider their impact on trade values and on trade composition.

This chapter is organised as follows. The first part begins by briefly outlining some of the most relevant and recent literature on the design of digital and environmental provisions in PTAs. While it is not the purpose of this chapter to explain in detail how digital and environmental policies at the domestic and international levels may be related, the following section does provide an overview of the domestic policy landscape in Latin America. Following this, the next section explores the design patterns both between PTAs and within PTAs – thus between PTAs' digital and environmental trade provisions. Finally, the first part of this chapter addresses the question as to whether Latin American countries are rule-makers or rule-takers in the area of digital and environmental trade governance in PTAs. Having outlined the design features of Latin American PTAs in this section, the second part of this chapter explores these design features as the principal explanatory variables to assess the impact of PTA design on the quantity and composition of international trade flows. The final section of this chapter summarises the findings, discusses limitations, and offers pathways for future research.

6.2 DIGITAL AND ENVIRONMENTAL TRADE GOVERNANCE

Digital trade and environmental trade topics have been part of the multilateral trade policy regime, administrated by the WTO, and the plurilateral trade policy regime, represented by PTAs, for some time now. As previously mentioned, digital trade-related topics were first addressed in PTAs in the early 2000s while environmental topics were already featured in PTAs signed in the early 1990s. Similarly, the WTO became active in the area of digital trade when the Information Technology Agreement (ITA) was reached in 1996 and the Work Programme on Electronic Commerce was established in 1998. While the interest and progress in this topic was limited during the following years (Elsig and Klotz 2021), digital trade discussions were revived with the Joint Initiative on E-Commerce in 2019, which by now counts eighty-eight participating WTO members. In the area of environmental trade, a

[2] In this chapter, we use the terms 'green' and 'sustainability' interchangeably.

group of fourteen WTO members launched negotiations for an Environmental Goods Agreement (EGA) in 2014, which by now counts forty-six participating WTO members.

The study of how environmental considerations are covered in PTAs advanced considerably over the past years. The publication of the TRade & ENvironment Database (TREND; Morin et al. 2018; updated in 2022) was an important driver as researchers gained access to information on nearly 300 different types of environment provisions in 775 PTAs. Subsequent work analysed why countries include such provisions in PTAs (Blümer et al. 2020), how such provisions diffuse between PTAs (Morin et al. 2019; Hollway et al. 2020; Jinnah and Morin 2020), how such provisions relate to other development policies (Brandi et al. 2022), and how such provisions impact trade flows (Berger et al. 2020; Brandi et al. 2020).

In the area of digital trade governance, it was the publication of the Trade Agreements Provisions on Electronic-commerce and Data dataset (TAPED; Burri and Polanco 2020) which provided researchers access to detailed information on around 100 provisions in more than 340 PTAs. Using TAPED, subsequent work analysed how digital trade-related provisions diffuse through PTAs (Elsig and Klotz 2022) and how digital trade governance in PTAs is related to ongoing work in the WTO (Elsig and Klotz 2021). Other influential work focused on the growing digital divide between the US, the European Union, and China (Aaronson and Leblond 2018; Gao 2018; Azmeh et al. 2020). Polanco (2021) provides a detailed analysis of the regulatory convergence of data rules in Latin American PTAs, which goes far deeper and beyond the scope of this chapter.[3]

The contributions by Morin et al. (2018; TREND) and Burri and Polanco (2020; TAPED) are closely related to the Design of Trade Agreements database (DESTA; Dür et al. 2014). All three databases serve as sources for the descriptive and empirical analyses conducted in the first and second part of this chapter, respectively.

6.3 DOMESTIC DIGITAL AND ENVIRONMENTAL POLICIES IN LATIN AMERICA

Before discussing the design of Latin American PTAs and their impact on international trade flows, this section briefly outlines the domestic landscape of digital and environmental sustainability policy. The focus lies on the countries that are signatories to the PTAs assessed in the subsequent sections[4].

[3] For another recent study on Latin American countries, see López et al. (2020) and Thorstensen and Delich (2020).

[4] Antigua and Barbuda, Argentina, Bahamas, Barbados, Belize, Chile, Colombia, Costa Rica, Dominica, Dominican Republic, Ecuador, El Salvador, Grenada, Guatemala, Guyana, Haiti, Honduras, Jamaica, Mexico, Nicaragua, Panama, Paraguay, Peru, St. Kitts and Nevis, St. Lucia, St. Vincent and Grenadines, Suriname, Trinidad and Tobago, and Uruguay.

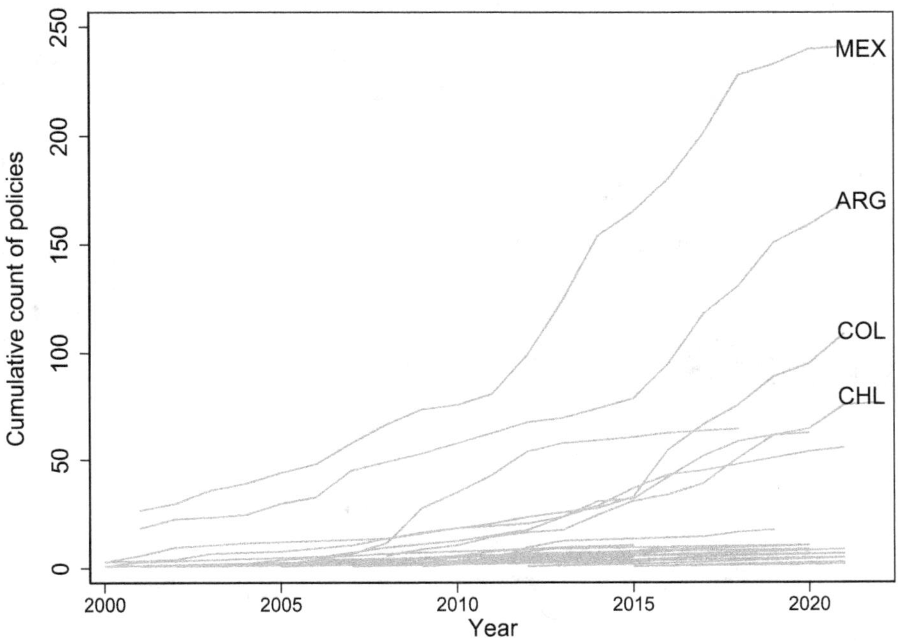

FIGURE 6.2 Climate policies in Latin America, 2000–2021.
Source: Authors' illustration based on the Climate Policy Database (2023).

While it is not the purpose to explicitly assess the link between domestic and international trade policy here, existing research does point to a strong correlation in both directions. In the area of digital policy, for example, Elsig and Klotz (2022) find that countries with more domestic digital policies are more ambitious in the digital trade-related provisions of their PTAs. In the area of environmental policy, Brandi et al. (2020) find that the design of environmental provisions in PTAs promotes green transformations at the domestic level.

In the area of sustainability and climate-related policies, Latin American countries have become increasingly more active since the early 2000s. In 2000, the region counted eight climate policies, up to ninety in 2005, and 250 in 2010. By 2021, the cumulative count of climate policies in Latin America is around 700. Mexico, Argentina, Colombia, and Chile are the main drivers of this development (Figure 6.2).

A closer look at these four countries illustrates some of the different climate policy foci. In all four countries, electricity is the primary target sector. Mexico and Argentina focused around 30 per cent of their climate policies on this sector, Colombia and Chile around 25 per cent and 35 per cent, respectively. After this, however, policy foci diverge. Mexico targeted around 25 per cent of its climate-related policies on the buildings sector, whereas Argentina focused an equal share

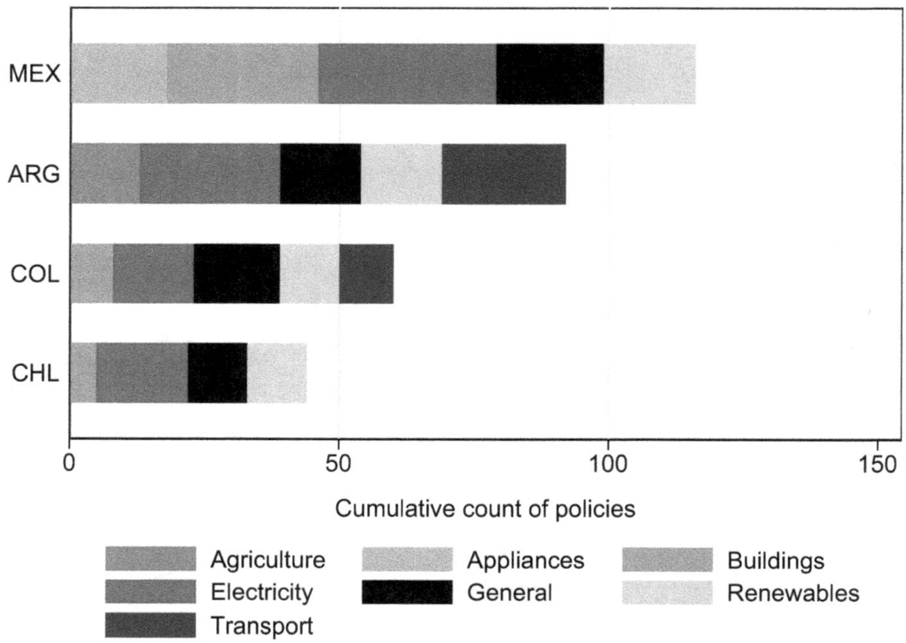

FIGURE 6.3 Climate policies in Latin America by policy area, 2000–2021.
Source: Authors' illustration based on the Climate Policy Database (2023).

on transport. Chile targeted around 23 per cent of its climate-related policies on renewables, whereas Colombia's policies were more general. Within this four-country group, Mexico is the only country to have focused any climate-related policies on appliances, and Argentina is the only country with such policies in the agriculture sector (Figure 6.3).

In the area of digital policies, there appears less of a gap between leading and lagging countries. Argentina is leading in this group with just under forty policies. Almost half of these policies focus on online sales and transactions and quantitative trade restrictions for information and consumer technology (ICT) goods, products, and online services. Ecuador focuses the largest share of its digital policies (21 per cent) on telecommunication infrastructure and competition. For Colombia, quantitative trade restrictions for ICT were also the primary policy focus (18 per cent), followed by public procurement of ICT goods and online services (12 per cent) (Figure 6.4).

For this group of countries overall, around half of the digital policies are targeted at online sales and transactions (15 per cent), telecommunication infrastructure and competition (15 per cent), and the public procurement of ICT goods and online services (Figure 6.5).

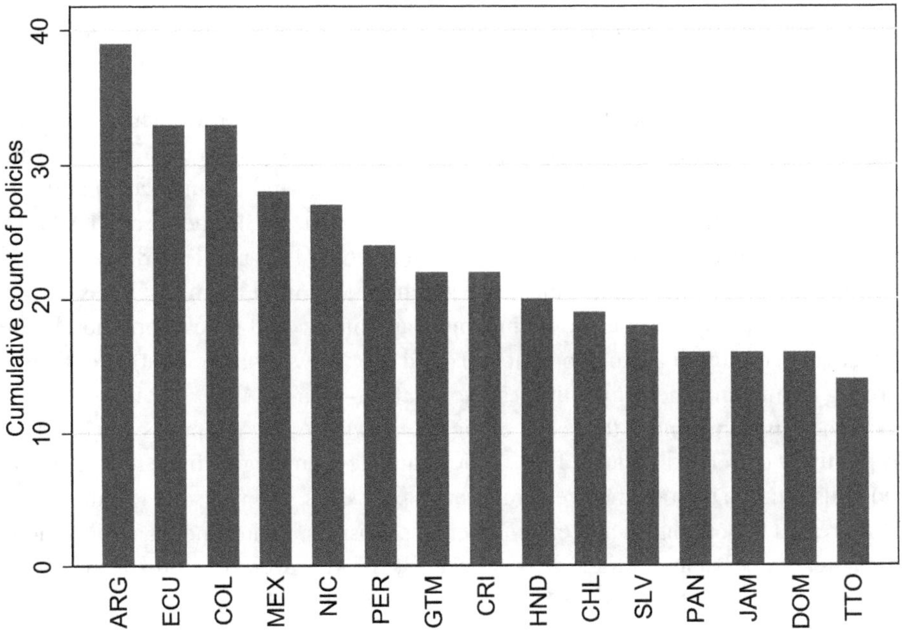

FIGURE 6.4 Digital policies in Latin America.
Source: Authors' illustration based on the Digital Trade Integration Database (2022).

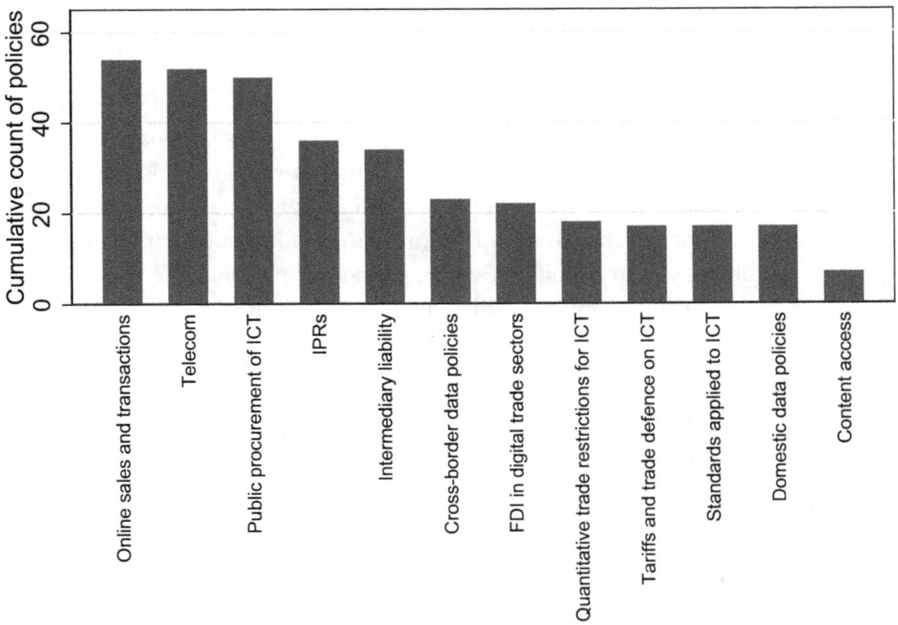

FIGURE 6.5 Digital policies in Latin America by policy area.
Source: Authors' illustration based on the Digital Trade Integration Database (2022).

6.4 DIGITAL AND ENVIRONMENTAL TRADE GOVERNANCE IN LATIN AMERICA

This section explores the design of Latin American PTAs with a specific focus on digital and environmental provisions collected by the Trade Agreements Provisions on Electronic-commerce and Data (TAPED) dataset (Burri and Polanco 2020) and the Trade and Environment Database (TREND, Morin et al. 2018). The set of PTAs used for the descriptive analysis of this section includes 168 PTAs, 14 PTAs (8 per cent) of which are signed among Latin American countries[5] (LatAm–LatAm), 35 PTAs (21 per cent) are signed by at least one Latin American country and at least one non-Latin American country (LatAm–Non-LatAm), and 119 PTAs (71 per cent) are signed among non-Latin American countries (Non-LatAm–Non-LatAm).[6]

Perhaps unsurprisingly, the scope of digital and environmental provisions in PTAs is positively correlated. Indeed, PTAs which include many digital trade-related provisions also tend to include many environmental provisions, and *vice versa* (Figure 6.6).[7] With regard to both digital and environmental provisions, Latin American PTAs show a higher scope[8] than non-Latin American PTAs. On average, non-LatAm PTAs include fifteen digital trade-related provisions, while LatAm–LatAm and LatAm–Non-LatAm PTAs include an average of twenty-eight provisions. Similarly, non-LatAm PTAs include an average of eleven environmental trade-related provisions, while LatAm–LatAm and LatAm–Non-LatAm PTAs include a respective average of fifteen and twenty such provisions.

Zooming into the PTAs further suggests that Central America–Dominican Republic–United States Free Trade Agreement (CAFTA-DR) (2004) is the LatAm PTA with the largest number of digital (50) and environmental provisions (88) (Figure 6.7). Central America–Panama (2002) and Mexico–Uruguay (2004), by contrast, are the LatAm PTAs with the smallest number of digital (2) and environmental (22) provisions. Overall, Central America–Panama (2002), Costa Rica–Peru (2011), Panama–Peru (2011) , Guatemala–Peru (2011), and Mexico–Uruguay (2004) appear to be relatively more ambitious with regard to the inclusion of environmental provisions than digital provisions, while the opposite is true for the other, the

5 The Latin American countries covered by these PTAs include Antigua and Barbuda, Argentina, Bahamas, Barbados, Belize, Chile, Colombia, Costa Rica, Dominica, Dominican Republic, Ecuador, El Salvador, Grenada, Guatemala, Guyana, Haiti, Honduras, Jamaica, Mexico, Nicaragua, Panama, Paraguay, Peru, St. Kitts and Nevis, St. Lucia, St. Vincent and the Grenadines, Suriname, Trinidad and Tobago, and Uruguay.

6 Note that PTAs signed by at least one Latin American country are used in the empirical analysis in the next section.

7 To facilitate the comparison, the elative share of provisions rather than the absolute number of provisions is used. Since the TAPED dataset includes 100 provisions, a PTA with 20 digital trade-related provisions has a relative scope of 20% (20/100 * 100 = 20%). Since the TREND dataset includes 295 provisions, a PTA with 20 green trade-related provisions has a relative scope of 7% (20/295 * 100 = 7%).

8 We use the term 'scope' to refer to the number of relevant provisions included in a PTA.

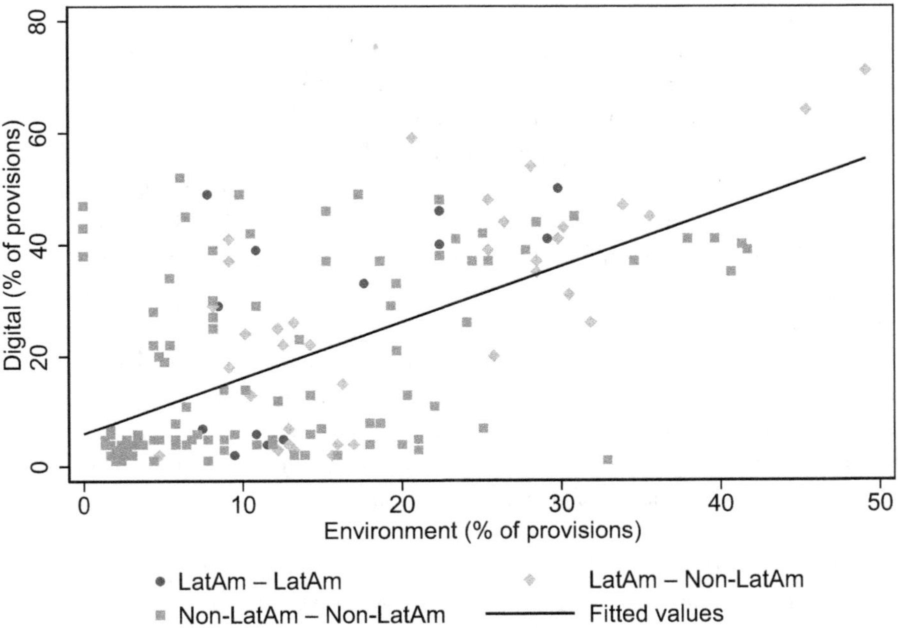

FIGURE 6.6 Digital and environmental provisions in PTAs.
Source: Authors' illustration based on TAPED and TREND.

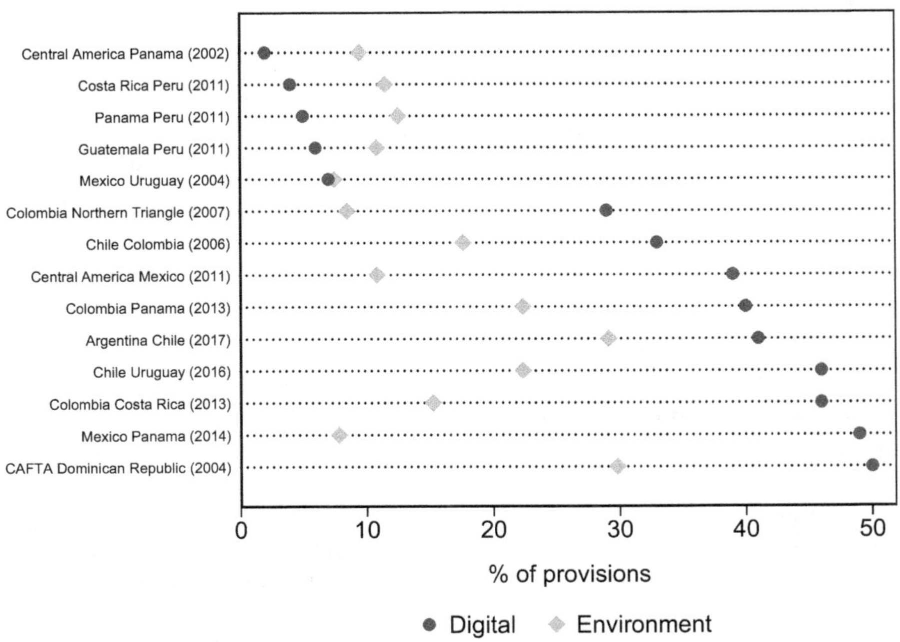

FIGURE 6.7 Digital and environmental provisions in PTAs among Latin American countries.
Source: Authors' illustration based on TAPED and TREND.

majority of, LatAm PTAs in the sample. Mexico–Panama (2014) stands out in particular; with forty-nine provisions, it presents the second most ambitious LatAm PTA in digital content. With only twenty-three environmental provisions, however, it presents the second-least ambitious LatAm PTA in this field.

The LatAm–Non-LatAm PTA with both the largest number of digital (71) and environmental (145) provisions is the United States–Mexico–Canada Agreement (USMCA) (2018) (Figure 6.8). Guatemala–Taiwan (2005) and Chile–Japan (2007), by contrast, present with only two digital and two environmental provisions the least ambitious PTAs in this group. Similar to the LatAm–LatAm PTAs, the majority of LatAm–Non-LatAm PTAs are relatively more ambitious with regard to digital than environmental provisions. A number of PTAs – including Chile–Japan (2007), Guatemala–Taiwan (2005), Chile–Korea (2003), Chile–Turkey (2009), China–Costa Rica (2010), China–Peru (2009), Panama–Taiwan (2003), Japan–Peru (2011), Canada–Costa Rica (2011), Central America–European Free Trade Association (EFTA) (2013), and Canada–Panama (2009) – are relatively more ambitious in the governance of environmental trade than digital trade. This gap is most notable in Australia–Peru (2018), which has a relatively large number of digital provisions (59) but a relatively small number of environmental provisions (61).

To put the previously outlined observations into context; the non-LatAm–non-LatAm PTA with the highest number of digital provisions (52) is Australia–Japan (2014), while EC–Vietnam (2019) is the non-LatAm–non-LatAm PTA with the highest number of environmental provisions (123).

6.5 LATIN AMERICAN PTAS: RULE-MAKERS OR RULE-TAKERS?

Out of the 100 digital provisions covered in TAPED, only one provision (1 per cent) was first introduced by a LatAm–LatAm PTA: CAFTA–DR (2004) was the first PTA to include a provision on the customs value of carrier mediums. Over the following years, this provision also diffused through the PTA network. Indeed, this provision is now included in another twenty PTAs: four of those LatAm–LatAm PTAs, five LatAm–Non-LatAm PTAs, and eleven Non-LatAm–Non-LatAm PTAs.

Another twenty-seven digital provisions (27 per cent) were first introduced by LatAm–Non-LatAm PTAs, including Canada–Costa Rica (2001), Chile–EC (2001), Chile–US (2003), Chile–China (2005), Nicaragua–Taiwan (2006), CARIFORUM–EC (2008), Canada–Colombia (2008), Colombia–EC–Peru (2012), Chile–Thailand (2013), Trans-Pacific Partnership (TPP) (2016), and USMCA (2018) (Annex).

Out of the 295 environmental provisions included in TREND, nineteen provisions (6 per cent) were first included by LatAm–LatAm PTAs. Central America–Panama (2002) introduced eight such provisions, CAFTA–DR (2004) introduced seven, Mexico–Uruguay (2004) two, and Panama–Peru (2011) and Colombia–Panama (2013) each introduced one such provision. Some of these provisions diffused considerably through the PTA network. For instance, the provision on

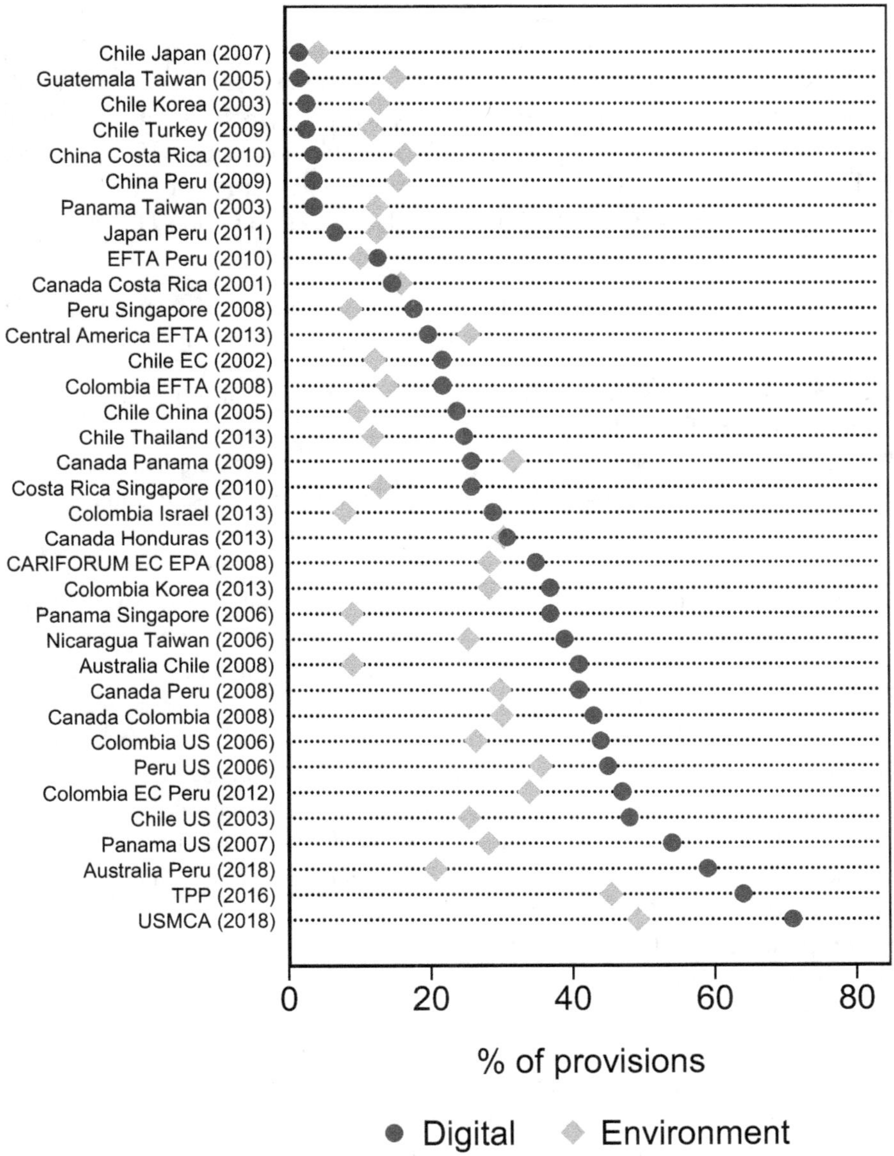

FIGURE 6.8 Digital and environmental provisions in PTAs between Latin American and non-Latin American countries.
Source: Authors' illustration based on TAPED and TREND.

the inappropriateness of encouraging investment by relaxing environmental measures, first introduced in Central America–Panama (2002), was subsequently included in eighty-three other PTAs; eleven of those LatAm–LatAm PTAs, twenty-three LatAm–Not-LatAm PTAs, and forty-nine Non-LatAm–Non-LatAm PTAs.

Another 114 environmental provisions (38 per cent) were first introduced by LatAm–Non-LatAm PTAs, including Canada–Costa Rica (2001), Chile–EC (2001), Chile–Korea (2003), Chile–US (2003), Panama–Taiwan (2003), Colombia–US (2006), Nicaragua–Taiwan (2006), Panama–Singapore (2006), Peru–US (2006), CARIFORUM–EC (2008), Canada–Colombia (2008), Canada–Peru (2008), Colombia–EFTA (2008), Canada–Panama (2009), China–Peru (2009), China–Costa Rica (2010), Colombia–EC–Peru (2012), Colombia–Korea (2013), and TPP (2016).

6.6 EFFECTS ON TRADE VALUES AND COMPOSITION OF DIGITAL AND ENVIRONMENTAL PROVISIONS IN LATIN AMERICAN PTAS

To assess the economic impact of digital and environmental provisions in Latin American PTAs, the analysis presented here follows the framework proposed by Berger et al. (2020). Given this book's specific focus on Latin American countries, the analysis is conducted separately for exports and imports because the analysis also concerns trade flows with extra-regional partners and regional partners not included in the TREND and TAPED datasets. The robustness of the empirical results presented below is tested through different settings with the aim of unveiling any alternative factors or characteristics that may drive the results. This approach is complemented by testing the possible changes to the composition of trade as suggested by Brandi et al. (2020).

The main dependent variable is constructed based on bilateral country-pair trade flows of merchandise trade as reported in the UN Comtrade dataset. The values present the total volume of exports (or imports) in manufacturing, mining, and agricultural products from (to) a Latin American country to (from) other countries around the world in million USD. In line with the literature, the natural log of trade values is used as the dependent variable (*Trade value*).

The resulting panel of more than 65,000 observations is unbalanced in trade relationships as countries may report only one side of trade in any given year. Other countries in the region may only report trade flows for a subset of the period, while their 'missing' observations are reported by their regional partners. For seventeen of the twenty-three Latin American countries reporting trade figures, the coverage extends to at least seventeen years between 2000 and 2021. At the aggregate level, import flows account for almost half of the sample (48.7 per cent).

To construct the explanatory variables, the maximum number of digital and environmental provisions in PTAs for each Latin American country-partner pair is used. Since two partners may be part of more than one unique PTA, the maximum number of provisions is used to signal a strengthened commitment. However, the de facto possibility for cumulation of commitments across PTAs is excluded. These two variables are denoted as DIG_{PROV} and ENV_{PROV} in the equation below. It is important to note that, given the inclusion of dummy variables capturing the existence of one (or more) PTA(s) between two countries, these counts of maximum numbers of provisions aim at identifying the additional impact of these provisions across PTAs. The basic econometric specification is the following:

$$Trade\ value_{ijt} = \beta PTA_{ijt} + \gamma DIG_{PROV_{ijt}} + \delta ENV_{PROV_{ijt}} + \alpha_{ij} + \alpha_{jt} + \alpha_{it} + \varepsilon_{ijt},$$

where i is the index for the Latin American country in the sample, j for the partner country, and t for the respective year. Note that all variables described above vary by bilateral dyad and time, and all regressions include a demanding set of three fixed effects: country-partner, country-year, and partner-year. In total, more than 6,000 fixed effects are estimated in every regression, controlling for specific nation-wide shocks or specificities (such as endowments, GDP levels, and unilateral openness or liberalisation to trade) in the countries of interest and their partners as well as for particularities such as geography, connectivity, and historical elements, which may explain closer or not trade relationships between dyads. Finally, ε_{ijt} denotes the error term, which is also clustered by dyads, implying that bilateral errors can be correlated over time. As usual, values for estimates are to be interpreted as additional percentages of exports or imports for the existence of a PTA or for an additional digital or environmental provision.

6.6.1 Results

Table 6.1 presents the results of this specification on the aggregate level of imports and exports where the number of each type of provision in the PTA has been

TABLE 6.1 *PTA and specific provisions on traded values.*

	Whole sample		Whole sample	
	Imports		Exports	
PTA dummy	−0.0507	−0.000203	0.105*	0.305***
	(0.0415)	(0.0914)	(0.0536)	(0.0882)
# of digital provisions		−0.00356		0.00760*
		(0.00655)		(0.00418)
# of environ. provisions		0.00103		−0.00659***
		(0.00349)		(0.00217)
Country-Year FE	Yes	Yes	Yes	Yes
Partner-Year FE	Yes	Yes	Yes	Yes
Country-Partner FE	Yes	Yes	Yes	Yes
Error-clust. ctry-partn.	Yes	Yes	Yes	Yes
Observations	33,694	33,694	32,045	32,045
R-squared	0.939	0.939	0.923	0.923

Robust standard errors in parentheses. *** $p < 0.01$, ** $p < 0.05$, * $p < 0.1$.

introduced after estimating the aggregate effect for PTAs in place. One, perhaps surprising, result is that the existence of a PTA does not have a statistically significant impact on imports by Latin American countries from their partners (first column) while an existing PTA can be associated with an increase of 10 per cent of exports (third column). This result highlights that negotiations tend to improve market access conditions for Latin American exports while for imports either improvements are not strongly perceived, or negotiations do not lead to improved market access. Eventually, integrating here the type and number of digital and environmental provisions will allow a better understanding of the absent impact for imports.

Columns 2 and 4 of Table 6.1 show the results after including the maximum number of provisions included in PTAs for Latin American countries. The absence of a statistically significant impact persists for imports while the results for exports deserve a closer analysis. Allowing for this heterogeneity increases the impact of the existence of a PTA with no digital and environmental provisions almost threefold. This observation is confirmed by the negative coefficient for the number of environmental provisions, which in this context seems to act as a deterrent for Latin American exports. On the contrary, the positive coefficient of digital provisions indicates that these provisions act as facilitators of trade as each additional digital provision increases exports by 0.7 per cent. Interestingly, the estimate for environmental provisions is of the same magnitude but of the opposite sign, indicating that an additional environmental provision cancels the positive outcome by an additional digital provision.

The following analysis explores in more detail the heterogeneity of these, rather puzzling, results. The first two columns of Table 6.2 aim to understand whether imposing a linear impact for the number of provisions may be a reason for the lack of statistical significance. For this, the square of the numbers of provisions is included, allowing sufficient flexibility to capture increasing or decreasing returns for additional provisions but also a change in sign at the extreme. Despite showing statistical significance at the individual level for some of those squared terms, the full derivative of the outcome with respect to the number of provisions is statistically significant neither for digital nor for environmental provisions. Consequently, this form of heterogeneity can be discarded. Although not reported here, an interaction term to capture potential synergies between digital and environmental provisions was also tested and yielded no statistically significant results.

The four columns on the right of Table 6.2 explore another dimension of heterogeneity by disentangling between trade flows with regional and non-regional partners. Results for imports remain statistically not significant while this splitting adds an interesting perspective to the previous observations. Regional exports take a boost out of the existence of one or several PTAs with the importing partner in the region, while this positive impact vanishes for exports towards extra-regional partners. On the other hand, the impact of provisions is mostly absorbed by PTAs with extra-regional partners. One potential explanation for this may be the limited

TABLE 6.2 *Exploring heterogeneity in marginal impact of provisions and partners.*

	Whole sample		Regionally		Extra-regionally	
	Imports	Exports	Imports	Exports	Imports	Exports
PTA dummy	0.254	−0.306	0.0352	0.304*	0.196	0.0931
	(0.270)	(0.284)	(0.118)	(0.158)	(0.130)	(0.117)
# of digital provisions	0.0176*	0.00301	0.00470	0.000216	−0.000493	0.0115**
	(0.00912)	(0.0122)	(0.00454)	(0.00877)	(0.00965)	(0.00493)
Sq. # of digital provisions	−0.000422**	0.000107				
	(0.000194)	(0.000239)				
# of environ. provisions	−0.0177*	0.0203	−0.00269	−0.00327	−0.00460	−0.00744**
	(0.00981)	(0.0124)	(0.00265)	(0.00392)	(0.00542)	(0.00316)
Sq. # of environ. provisions	0.000159**	−0.000221**				
	(7.30e-05)	(0.000102)				
Country-Year FE	Yes	Yes	Yes	Yes	Yes	Yes
Partner-Year FE	Yes	Yes	Yes	Yes	Yes	Yes
Country-Partner FE	Yes	Yes	Yes	Yes	Yes	Yes
Error-clust. ctry-partn.	Yes	Yes	Yes	Yes	Yes	Yes
Observations	33,694	32,045	26,132	25,048	7,562	6,997
R-squared	0.939	0.923	0.939	0.917	0.937	0.951

Robust standard errors in parentheses. *** $p < 0.01$, ** $p < 0.05$, * $p < 0.1$.

number of PTAs among Latin American countries including these types of provisions.

As a next step, the analysis incorporates the World Bank classification of (non-) high-income countries for partners of Latin American countries. The use of a fixed classification facilitates the interpretation of results and avoids introducing a potential bias to the previously outlined observations. More precisely, the analysis now explores the difference in results around two points in time: at the beginning of the period (classification in 2000) and at the end of the period (classification in 2020). These results are presented in Table 6.3 for non-high-income and high-income countries, denoted as Non-HIC and HIC respectively.

The splitting between more and less advanced countries in the year 2000 indicates that all trade impacts observed for Latin American countries are concentrated in exports to 2000 non-high-income countries. The structure of these results is qualitatively identical to the one observed in Table 6.2. In the last four columns of Table 6.3, however, a different pattern can be detected. Latin American imports from non-high-income countries in 2020 benefit from PTAs, although not specifically from the inclusion of environmental provisions in them. Imports from 2020 high-income countries are negatively affected by the presence of PTAs, although this may be related to a reorientation of previous imports to new destinations with more attractive or closer markets. The PTA impact on the export side is positive when exports are shipped to 2020 high-income countries, while the positive impact of digital provisions remains mainly with 2020 non-high-income countries. These changes between the left and right sides of Table 6.3 are due to the status changes of a limited number of countries: twenty-six partners shifted from non-high-income-country to high-income-country status over the period. These countries include nine European countries, four Latin American countries (Chile, Panama, Uruguay, and Trinidad and Tobago), and Korea, as well as several small island states. The enlargement of the European Union and the economic development of regional partners have been key to turning PTAs into drivers of exports. Digital provisions and likely the digitalisation of procedures have been a successful trigger for higher exports to less developed partners.

At this point, it seems necessary to consider whether an aggregate impact can be expected from digital and environmental provisions whose impact may be related to a smaller subset of goods. Regarding environmental provisions, one might expect that products considered as environmentally relevant are the ones which are more significantly impacted by these provisions. The identification of this subset of products is based on Zugravu-Soilita (2018). More specifically, this product list combines different proposals put forward by several WTO members and international agencies[9] for the classification of environmental goods based on Harmonised System (HS) six-digit codes.

[9] Environmentally Preferable Products, Clean Technologies, Cleaner Technologies and Products, End-of-pipe products, and other EGs.

TABLE 6.3 *Heterogeneity by income levels of partners (beginning and end of period).*

	Non-HIC in 2000		HIC in 2000		Non-HIC in 2020		HIC in 2020	
	Imports	Exports	Imports	Exports	Imports	Exports	Imports	Exports
PTA dummy	0.0213	0.236**	-0.139	0.184	0.288***	0.160	−0.475***	0.265**
	(0.118)	(0.111)	(0.135)	(0.177)	(0.0919)	(0.132)	(0.167)	(0.132)
No. of digital provisions	−0.00420	0.0105**	0.00275	0.00539	−0.00110	0.0101*	−0.0135	0.00127
	(0.00797)	(0.00486)	(0.00668)	(0.00921)	(0.00394)	(0.00597)	(0.0149)	(0.00572)
No. of environ. provisions	−0.000278	−0.00680**	0.000335	−0.00554	−0.00493**	−0.00431	0.0105	−0.00459
	(0.00455)	(0.00267)	(0.00330)	(0.00457)	(0.00240)	(0.00345)	(0.00764)	(0.00316)
Country-Year FE	Yes	Yes	Yes	Yes	Yes	Yes	Yes	Yes
Partner-Year FE	Yes	Yes	Yes	Yes	Yes	Yes	Yes	Yes
Country-Partner FE	Yes	Yes	Yes	Yes	Yes	Yes	Yes	Yes
Error-clust. ctry-part.	Yes	Yes	Yes	Yes	Yes	Yes	Yes	Yes
Observations	22,068	21,748	11,626	10,297	16,929	17,483	16,765	14,562
R-squared	0.931	0.920	0.952	0.932	0.941	0.920	0.937	0.929

Robust standard errors in parentheses. *** $p < 0.01$, ** $p < 0.05$, * $p < 0.1$.

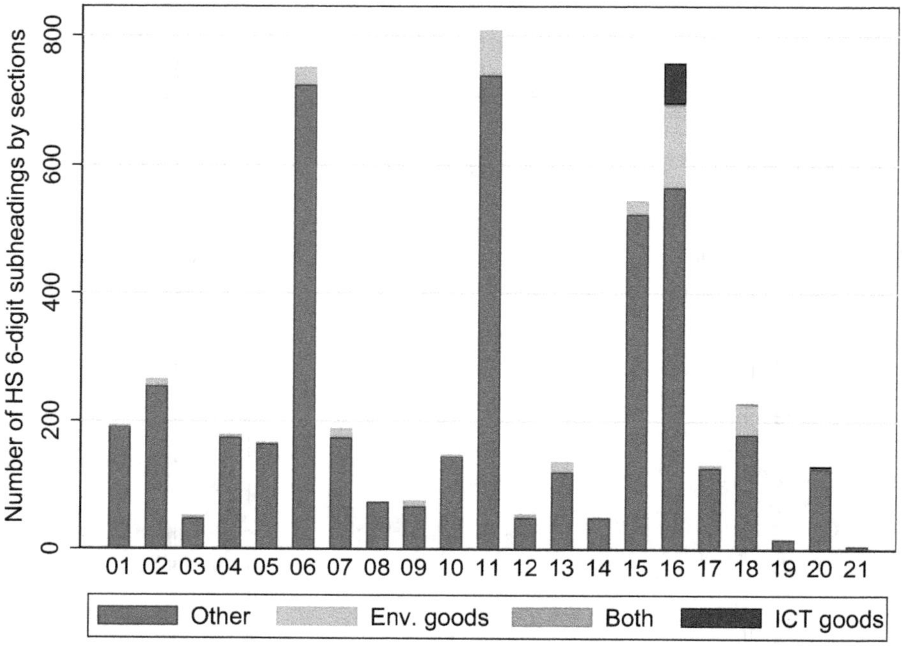

FIGURE 6.9 Environmental and ICT product categories across HS sections.
Source: Authors' illustration based on OECD (2019).

The conversion of this list to the 1997 HS nomenclature yields 364 environmental HS six-digit product categories. Regarding digital provisions, the list of ICT goods in the OECD Handbook for Measuring Digital Trade (2019) is used. After conversion, this results in sixty-four 'digital' or rather ICT products. It is true that these products are not the only ones to be affected by digital provisions, and they may not even be targeted directly by these provisions. However, the analysis presented here follows the current 'standard' in the literature. There is a minor overlap of products between the two lists, which includes office machines (HS 847290), photosensitive semiconductor devices (HS 854140), electrical machines and apparatus (HS 854380), and lasers other than laser diodes (HS 901320).

Figure 6.9 indicates that although environmental goods are present in most of HS sections, they account for more than 5 per cent of HS product categories in sections XI (Chemicals and Allied Industries), IX (Wood and Wood Products), XI (Textiles), XIII (Footwear), XV (Metals), XVI (Machinery and Electrical), and XVIII (Precision Instruments). These are the same HS sections concerned with the presence of ICT goods. The assumption here is that the impact of digital and environmental provisions should be more sizeable for these HS sections. The remaining analysis is limited to these HS sections, further restricting the sample.

Table 6.4 combines specifications run for aggregate values in Tables 6.1 and 6.2. The impact of PTAs and provisions on imports remains not statistically significant.

TABLE 6.4 *Impact of selected HS sections.*

	Selected sample		Regionally		Extra-regionally	
	Imports	Exports	Imports	Exports	Imports	Exports
PTA dummy	0.108	0.464***	−0.0320	0.496**	0.434**	0.253*
	(0.112)	(0.121)	(0.105)	(0.231)	(0.181)	(0.140)
No. of digital provisions	0.00124	0.0114**	−0.00104	0.0190	0.0105	0.0164***
	(0.00502)	(0.00555)	(0.00396)	(0.0122)	(0.00846)	(0.00620)
No. of environ. Provisions	−0.00273	−0.0124***	0.000435	−0.0163***	−0.0132***	−0.0126***
	(0.00287)	(0.00344)	(0.00244)	(0.00626)	(0.00498)	(0.00435)
Country-Year FE	Yes	Yes	Yes	Yes	Yes	Yes
Partner-Year FE	Yes	Yes	Yes	Yes	Yes	Yes
Country-Partner FE	Yes	Yes	Yes	Yes	Yes	Yes
Error-clust. ctry-part.	Yes	Yes	Yes	Yes	Yes	Yes
Observations	28,714	20,796	21,915	14,624	6,799	6,160
R-squared	0.951	0.931	0.953	0.919	0.948	0.964

Robust standard errors in parentheses. *** $p < 0.01$, ** $p < 0.05$, * $p < 0.1$.

However, the results for exports are confirmed qualitatively and estimates are larger, confirming a protectionist behaviour for environmental provisions.

While considering regional and extra-regional differences, imports from regional partners are the only configuration not to achieve any statistical significance. The structure of results is almost identical for the different types of trade flows, although digital provisions only play a significant role for exports out of the region. PTAs have a positive impact on the different trade flows, and environmental provisions show a negative impact.

Table 6.5 considers the impact of partners with high-income status at the beginning and at the end of the period, as previously illustrated in Table 6.3. The economic development of partners is key to achieving a positive impact of PTAs on exports while imports do not depict a clear pattern. The positive impact of digital provisions is limited to developed countries, while the negative impact of environmental provisions is reflected in almost all trade flows.

As another attempt to understand the impact of these provisions on the composition of trade flows, the share of the aggregated export or import flows for the selected HS sections that is related to environmental and ICT goods is calculated. The dependent variable in this case is bounded between 0 and 100, following closely the approach proposed by Brandi et al. (2020).

The results in Table 6.6 do not indicate any 'greening' of these trade flows, neither a 'digitalising' of them. The most consistent effect to be identified is the negative impact of PTAs, on average, on the 'greening/digitalising' of imported values.

6.7 CONCLUSION

This chapter takes a close look at the design and the effects of digital and environmental provisions in Latin American PTAs. To give some context, a brief discussion on the, rather heterogeneous, domestic landscape of digital and environmental policies in Latin America is provided. This heterogeneity is also found in the design of digital and environmental provisions in Latin American PTAs. Overall, however, a positive link can be observed: countries with more ambitious digital policies also tend to be more ambitious in their environmental policies, and *vice versa*, both at the domestic and international trade policy levels. An empirical investigation into the effects of PTA design differences on the volume and composition of trade flows yields a number of interesting insights. Digital provisions in Latin American PTAs are found to increase exports, while environmental provisions are associated with a decline in such trade flows. For imports, no such results of statistical significance can be detected. Neither does the analysis provide statistically significant evidence for a 'greening' or 'digitalising' of trade flows – that is, on the composition of international trade.

TABLE 6.5 *Heterogeneity by income levels of partners (beginning and end of period) on selected HS sectors.*

	Non-HIC in 2000		HIC in 2000		Non-HIC in 2020		HIC in 2020	
	Imports	Exports	Imports	Exports	Imports	Exports	Imports	Exports
PTA dummy	0.217	0.447***	−0.230*	0.334	0.336***	0.445***	−0.345*	0.395**
	(0.150)	(0.143)	(0.120)	(0.264)	(0.130)	(0.172)	(0.192)	(0.197)
No. of digital provisions	0.00317	0.00839	−0.000487	0.0461***	0.00859*	0.00964	−0.0101	0.0213*
	(0.00651)	(0.00584)	(0.00587)	(0.0120)	(0.00444)	(0.00711)	(0.00952)	(0.0113)
No. of environ. provisions	−0.00679*	−0.00975**	0.00283	−0.0270***	−0.0111***	−0.00971**	0.00812**	−0.0165***
	(0.00398)	(0.00402)	(0.00315)	(0.00602)	(0.00381)	(0.00477)	(0.00410)	(0.00600)
Country-Year FE	Yes	Yes	Yes	Yes	Yes	Yes	Yes	Yes
Partner-Year FE	Yes	Yes	Yes	Yes	Yes	Yes	Yes	Yes
Country-Partner FE	Yes	Yes	Yes	Yes	Yes	Yes	Yes	Yes
Error-clust. ctry-part.	Yes	Yes	Yes	Yes	Yes	Yes	Yes	Yes
Observations	18,168	13,862	10,546	6,920	13,650	11,125	15,064	9,661
R-squared	0.941	0.934	0.966	0.932	0.952	0.934	0.951	0.933

Robust standard errors in parentheses. *** $p < 0.01$, ** $p < 0.05$, * $p < 0.1$.

TABLE 6.6 *PTAs and greening/digitalising trade.*

	Selected sample		Regionally		Extra-regionally	
	Imports *share*	Exports *share*	Imports *share*	Exports *share*	Imports *share*	Exports *share*
PTA dummy	−4.867***	−2.708	−5.019**	0.287	−5.999**	0.0537
	(1.775)	(2.162)	(2.307)	(4.342)	(2.592)	(1.811)
No. of digital provisions	0.121*	−0.0944	−0.0182	0.0404	0.186*	−0.129
	(0.0660)	(0.0812)	(0.0911)	(0.136)	(0.0996)	(0.0798)
No. of environ. provisions	−0.00216	0.0695	0.0676	−0.0425	−0.0252	0.0416
	(0.0401)	(0.0447)	(0.0536)	(0.0767)	(0.0612)	(0.0474)
Country-Year FE	Yes	Yes	Yes	Yes	Yes	Yes
Partner-Year FE	Yes	Yes	Yes	Yes	Yes	Yes
Country-Partner FE	Yes	Yes	Yes	Yes	Yes	Yes
Error-clust. ctry-part.	Yes	Yes	Yes	Yes	Yes	Yes
Observations	26,909	18,282	20,361	12,373	6,548	5,887
R-squared	0.671	0.706	0.656	0.729	0.705	0.671

Robust standard errors in parentheses. *** $p < 0.01$, ** $p < 0.05$, * $p < 0.1$.

There are a number of avenues for future research on this topic. One limitation that future research may address is related to the nature of digital and environmental provisions in PTAs. The analyses outlined in this chapter focus primarily on the scope, or the number, of such provisions included in PTAs. A more fine-grained classification of provisions according to their purpose and/or legal enforceability would surely add considerable value to the debate. This may also contribute to a deeper understanding of the identified effects of PTA design on exports and imports. Notwithstanding these limitations, it is hoped that this chapter contributes to an increasingly active debate on the link between digitalisation and environmental sustainability, and the economic impacts associated with it.

REFERENCES

Aaronson, S. A. and P. Leblond 2018. "Another Digital Divide: The Rise of Data Realms and its Implications for the WTO," *Journal of International Economic Law* 21(2): 245–272.

Azmeh, S., C. Foster and J. Echavarri 2020. "The International Trade Regime and the Quest for Free Digital Trade," *International Studies Review* 22(3): 671–692.

Berger, A C. Brandi, C., J.-F. Morin and J. Schwab 2020. "The Trade Effects of Environmental Provisions in Preferential Trade Agreements." In: C. Beverelli, J. Kurtz and D. Raess (Eds.), *International Trade, Investment, and the Sustainable Development Goals*. Cambridge: Cambridge University Press, pp. 111–139.

Blümer, D., J.-F. Morin, , C. Brandi and A. Berger 2020. "Environmental Provisions in Trade Agreements: Defending Regulatory Space or Pursuing Offensive Interests?" *Environmental Politics* 29(5): 866–889.

Brandi, C., J.-F. Morin and F. Stender 2022. "Do Greener Trade Agreements Call for Side-Payments?" *The Journal of Environment & Development* 31(2):111–138.

Brandi, C., J. Schwab, A. Berger and J.-F. Morin, J.-F. 2020. "Do Environmental Provisions in Trade Agreements Make Exports from Developing Countries Greener?" *World Development* 129: 104899

Burri, M. and R. Polanco 2020. "Digital Trade Provisions in Preferential Trade Agreements: Introducing a New Dataset," *Journal of International Economic Law* 23(1): 187–220.

Climate Policy Database 2023. *Climate Policy Database*. Cologne and Berlin: New Climate Institute. Available at: https://climatepolicydatabase.org/.

Digital Trade Integration Database 2022. *Digital Trade Integration Database*. Florence: European University Institute. Available at: https://dti.eui.eu/.

DürA., L. Baccini and M. Elsig 2014. "The Design of International Trade Agreements: Introducing a New Dataset," *The Review of International Organizations* 9(3): 353–375.

Elsig, M. and S. Klotz 2021. "Digital Trade Rules in Preferential Trade Agreements: Is There a WTO Impact?" *Global Policy* 12(S4): 25–36.

2022. "Initiator Conditions and the Diffusion of Digital Trade-Related Provisions in PTAs," *International Interactions* 48(2): 292–308.

Gao, H. 2018. "Digital or Trade? The Contrasting Approaches of China and US to Digital Trade," *Journal of International Economic Law* 21(2): 297–321.

Hollway, J., J.-F. Morin and J. Pauwelyn 2020. "Structural Conditions for Novelty: The Introduction of New Environmental Clauses to the Trade Regime Complex," *International Environmental Agreements: Politics, Law and Economics* 20(1): 61–83.

Jinnah, S. and J.-F. Morin 2020. *Greening Through Trade: How American Trade Policy Is Linked to Environmental Protection Abroad*. Cambridge, MA: MIT Press.

López, D., B. Condon and F. Muñoz 2020. "The New Rules on Digital Trade in Latin America: Regional Trade Agreements." In WTO (Eds.), *Adapting to the Digital Trade Era: Challenges and Opportunities*. Geneva: World Trade Organisation, pp. 214–231.

Morin, J.-F., C. Blümer, C. Brandi and A. Berger 2019. "Kick-Starting Diffusion: Explaining the Varying Frequency of PTAs' Environmental Clauses by Their Initial Conditions," *World Economy* 42(9): 2602–2628.

Morin, J.-F., A. Dür and L. Lechner 2018. "Mapping the Trade and Environment Nexus: Insights from a New Dataset," *Global Environmental Politics* 18(1):122–139.

OECD 2019. *Handbook on Measuring Digital Trade*. Paris: Organisation for Economic Co-operation and Development.

Polanco, R. 2021. "Regulatory Convergence of Data Rules in Latin America." In M. Burri (Ed.), *Big Data and Global Trade Law*. Cambridge: Cambridge University Press, pp. 268–300.

Thorstensen, V. and V. Delich 2020. "Convergence on E-commerce: The Case of Argentina, Brazil and MERCOSUR." In WTO (Eds.), *Adapting to the Digital Trade Era: Challenges and Opportunities*. Geneva: World Trade Organisation, pp. 232–253.

UN 2016. *Framework Agreement on Facilitation of Cross-Border Paperless Trade in Asia and the Pacific. Resolution/Adopted by the Economic and Social Commission for Asia and the Pacific*. Bangkok: United Nations Economic and Social Commission for Asia and the Pacific. Available at: https://digitallibrary.un.org/record/3882345?ln = en.

UN 2021. "Quantifying the Environmental Benefits from Paperless Trade Facilitation," *UNCTAD Transport and Trade Facilitation Newsletter* No. 92. Geneva: United Nations

Conference on Trade and Development. Available at: https://unctad.org/news/quantifying-environmental-benefits-paperless-trade-facilitation.

UN 2022. *Digital and Sustainable Trade Facilitation: Global Report 2021*. Bangkok: United Nations Economic and Social Commission for Asia and the Pacific. Available at: www.unescap.org/kp/2022/untf-survey-2021-global.

WCO 2021. *How Digital Tools Can Improve Compliance with SPS Measures*. Brussels: World Customs Organisation. Available at: https://mag.wcoomd.org/magazine/wco-news-94/digital-tools-compliance-sps-measures/.

WEF 2022. *Digitalization is the Key that Can Unlock Net-Zero for Industry*.Geneva: World Economic Forum. Available at: www.weforum.org/agenda/2022/05/digitalization-key-net-zero-schneiderelectric/.

WTO 2021. *Digital Technologies and Trade*.Geneva: World Trade Organisation. Available at: www.wto.org/english/tratop_e/dtt_e/dtt-environment_e.htm.

Zugravu-Soilita, N. 2018. "The Impact of Trade in Environmental Goods on Pollution: What Are We Learning from the Transition Economies' Experience?" *Environmental Economics and Policy Studies* 20(4): 785–827.

7

Trade Law Impact on Food Security in Latin America

Colombia's 2016 Peace Agreement Case

José Manuel Álvarez Zárate, María Camila Camargo Moncayo, Sofía Urrea Zuluaga and Diana Maria Beltrán Vargas

7.1 INTRODUCTION

The Colombian Government signed a Peace Agreement with the Fuerzas Armadas Revolucionarias de Colombia (FARC)[1] guerrilla group on 26 November 2016 to end a civil war after more than fifty years of internal conflict. The Peace Agreement contains six chapters intended to create the necessary transformations to find a stable and lasting peace with the FARC. These chapters include obligations that the state agreed on with the rebels, some of which require enacting new general and specific agricultural policies that demand profound reforms of the existing domestic policies. The first chapter of the Peace Agreement contains a *Comprehensive Rural Reform* (CRR), which is expected '[to] contribute to the structural transformation of the rural areas, closing the gaps between the countryside and the city and creating conditions of well-being and good living for the rural population' (Colombian Government FARC-EP 2016, p. 7). It also includes 'the obligation to progressively realise the human right to healthy, nutritional and culturally appropriate food' or in other words, the progressive realisation of the 'right to food' (ibid., p. 32). Thus, the Peace Agreement adopted a specific principled approach regarding the development of the rural economy, emphasising the importance of reciprocity, cooperation, and solidarity in the resulting trade relationships (Ministerio de Agricultura y Desarrollo Rural 2022, p. 16) and providing obligations that aim to ensure food security (Colombian Government FARC-EP 2016).[2] Such an approach potentially stands in contrast to a long-standing economic rationale underlying the creation of

[1] Fuerzas Armadas Revolucionarias de Colombia ('Revolutionary Armed Forces of Colombia').

[2] See Peace Agreement paragraph 4.1.3.6 regarding the programmes for substitution of illicit narcotic crops. These comprehensive development plans for crop substitution and environmental regeneration require the participation of communities – men and women – in the planning, implementation, and evaluation.

the World Trade Organization (WTO) and preferential trade agreements (PTAs) that are based on principles such as progressive trade liberalisation (Baggaley 1998).[3]

International trade rules have generally imposed obligations on states related to agricultural policies. As a result, 'policy space' to regulate domestic food production to adopt social policies has some restrictions. In ongoing discussions on how trade is a means to guarantee food security worldwide,[4] the UN Special Rapporteur on the Right to Food has pointed out that the WTO's Agreement on Agriculture (AoA) (WTO 1995a) created more obstacles to trade by allowing a concentration on certain firms and preventing farmers from participating fairly and effectively with their goods (Fakhri 2020, par. 27–31). For instance, specific instruments such as market access concessions (AoA, Art. 4) and safety and quality regulations can be used for protectionist purposes, creating barriers for member states to fulfil their right to food (Hawkes and Plahe 2013). In other words, trade regulations such as Article 4.2 potentially limit states' policy space to revert tariff reductions that affect the food market to guarantee the right to food. Also, measures such as the European Green Deal create new barriers to some agricultural exports from the Global South.[5] Thus, as we will explain, trade agreements are compatible with the rural reform established with the FARC in the Peace Agreement.

One of the main aims of the CRR is to identify different alternatives to international trade at local, regional, and national levels, based on the concept of rural territory as a socio-historical context in which the communities play a leading role in the definition of the development and improvement of their living conditions (Colombian Government FARC-EP 2016). The CRR's main aim is to guarantee the right to food for local communities through the development of a rural economy (market) according to the particular needs of the population that inhabit such communities. Under the definition of *Rurality* it is implied that it is only possible to guarantee the right to food with 'rural development' (CISAN 2022, p. 28) which focuses on production and supply within regions creating a high enough food self-

[3] See WTO Preamble, par. 5: 'Determined to preserve the basic principles and to further the objectives underlying this multilateral trading system'. Baggaley (1998) puts it as follows: 'Multilateral free trade has taken on increasing global importance with the passage of such agreements as the NAFTA, the EU, the GATT, and the recent transformation of the latter into the WTO. The underlying principle of each is progressive trade liberalization in all fields of economic activity, including those which are more prone to protectionist forces such as agriculture'.

[4] See Preamble, par. 6. Agreement on Agriculture, which recognises the need to take account of food security in ongoing negotiations. For example, in the 27–28 March 2023 meeting of the Agriculture Committee, WTO Members said that they were maintaining a focus on food security (to intensify their efforts to address the severe food security crisis, which is especially challenging for least developed countries (LDCs) and net food-importing developing countries (NFIDCs).) www.wto.org/english/news_e/news23_e/agri_28mar23_e.htm

[5] See https://commission.europa.eu/strategy-and-policy/priorities-2019-2024/european-green-deal/sustainable-use-key-natural-resources_es.

sufficiency. This might go beyond *food security* understanding used for trade purposes in the AoA, as will be explained below.

This chapter examines the limits that international trade law – in particular, the WTO legal framework and PTAs – could create to uphold the right to food in the process of implementation of the Peace Agreement. It also addresses the degree to which Colombia can use its 'policy space' in light of its international commitments to achieve/strengthen the right to food of its people. In the end, we conclude that the rural reform plan included in the Peace Agreement is compatible with international trade agreements and such treaties do not hinder that plan.

The first section focuses on how international trade law policies are linked with food security and tend to collide with the right to food. Second, we describe the Peace Agreement structure and explain the scope for guaranteeing food security and food sovereignty. The third section specifies how the Peace Agreement enshrines the right to food as an objective. The following section reviews the obligations established in the WTO Agreement on Agriculture and in PTAs in the context of the Colombian post-conflict. Finally, we conclude that implementing the Peace Agreement Policies regarding the right to food falls under Colombia's policy space as provided by international trade agreements.

7.2 THE RIGHT TO FOOD AND TRADE LAW POLICIES

The right to food is recognised as 'the fundamental right of everyone to be free from hunger'[6] under Article 11 of the *International Covenant on Economic, Social, and Cultural Rights*. Other human rights treaties have adopted this concept also,[7] which the jurisprudence[8] and doctrine have developed. The Special Rapporteur on the right to food has defined the right to food following a more sociological perspective inherent to our life in society:

> It is the right for everyone to celebrate life through their meals with each other in communion. One of the most important ways that a community defines

[6] International Covenant on Economic, Social and Cultural Rights, Art. 11.2. United Nations (1966).

[7] Other examples include Convention on the Elimination of All Forms of Discrimination against Women New York, 18 December 1979, Preamble; Convention on the Rights of the Child, Art. 24; Convention on the Rights of Persons with Disabilities, Arts. 25, 28; Additional Protocol to the American Convention on Human Rights in the Area of Economic, Social and Cultural Rights Arts. 12 and 17.

[8] Initially, the right to food was recognised and developed by national courts. For instance, the Colombian Constitutional Court has analysed the scope of the right to food and food security in decisions such as C-028/2018, C-644/2012, C-209/2016, and C-077/2017, among others; regarding international courts, recently the Inter-American Court of Human Rights has analysed the right to adequate food in the decision *Case of the Indigenous Communities of the Lhaka Honhat (Our Land) Association v. Argentina (Merits, reparations and costs) February 6, 2020, par.* 210–221.

> itself is through what, how, when and with whom they eat. Communities are made through shared holidays, memories, recipes, palates and manners of eating. Through these food practices, people create their social and political institutions. (Fakhri 2020, par. 9)

The right to food is relevant to our societies, yet it might be negatively impacted by trade regulations at the international and domestic levels. At the same time, trade regulations also help to satisfy all kinds of human needs, including those concerning food supply. For instance, trade might help uphold the right to food in countries with limited domestic agriculture production where food supply relies mostly on imports. In other cases, trade may affect the right to food when domestic food prices increasingly depend on the global food market, which in turn negatively affects the local production of food (FAO 2010, p. 22).

It is important to note that the Agreement on Agriculture does not refer to the right to food but to *food security* (AoA, Preamble and Art. 20). The WTO Committee on Agriculture has defined it[9] following the 1996 Rome Declaration on World Food Security as: '… when all people, at all times, have physical and economic access to sufficient, safe and nutritious food to meet their dietary needs and food preferences for an active and healthy life' (FAO 1996). In this way, trade is considered a fundamental tool for achieving food security (Ibid.)[10] because the trading system allows for the 'policy space' to establish food policies as part of the right to development.[11] In that sense, even though international trade rules (within the scope of the WTO and PTAs) are not focused on enhancing the right to food but on *food security*, pursuing the right to food through local policies is not forbidden as long as these comply with the trade disciplines and commitments provided in the agreements.

The concept of *food security* is embodied in the AoA. Even though it is only mentioned in the preamble of the referred Agreement,[12] it is a pillar of the obligation to continue negotiations, as provided in Article 20. c (non-trade concerns).[13]

9 Such definition can be found on the WTO webpage in the section related to Food Security. See www.wto.org/english/tratop_e/agric_e/food_security_e.htm

10 See FAO (1996, par. 13): '… reaffirm that a peaceful, stable and enabling political, social and economic environment is the essential foundation which will enable States to give adequate priority to food security and poverty eradication'.

11 On the right to development, see Álvarez (2015).

12 AoA, Preamble 'Noting that commitments under the reform programme should be made in an equitable way among all Members, having regard to non-trade concerns, including food security and the need to protect the environment …'

13 AoA, Article 20. 'Recognizing that the long-term objective of substantial progressive reductions in support and protection resulting in fundamental reform is an ongoing process, Members agree that negotiations for continuing the process will be initiated one year before the end of the implementation period, taking into account:

…

(c)non-trade concerns, special and differential treatment to developing country Members, and the objective to establish a fair and market-oriented agricultural trading

Colombian PTAs do not mention food security or the right to food. However, PTAs generally preserve the Parties' ability to safeguard public welfare, and they were built 'on their respective rights and obligations under the Marrakesh Agreement Establishing the World Trade Organization and agreements to which they are both parties'.[14]

Recently, there has been a growing interest on the part of the WTO regarding the food security of its members. Indeed, for the organisation, it is fundamental to address how international trade could help to solve problems of scarcity and distribution, especially when the world is going through a food crisis worsened by the Covid-19 pandemic and current international conflicts.[15] Nevertheless, according to the Special Rapporteur on the right to food, the WTO system puts several limitations on fulfilling this right.[16] A fundamental limitation is that the AoA aims to enhance trade among its members rather than addressing their particular food needs (Yigzaw 2015, p. 175–176; Fakhri 2020, par. 23). In the existing international trade legal framework (WTO and PTAs), the rights of companies and traders are privileged over the rights of consumers and small-scale farmers. It enhances privileged firms by keeping and safeguarding the interests of those who have the power within the food production chain (Fakhri 2020, par. 27–28) instead of people's needs.

The international discussion about this potential collision of rights also needs to consider access and input legitimacy issues, and that all voices are heard. For example, during the Conference of the Parties (COP) 26 in Glasgow, the Director General of the WTO, Ngozi Okonjo-Iweala, highlighted the importance of trade in addressing issues such as climate change and the food crisis (WTO 2021d). However, during the same meeting, only big corporations were invited to participate (Barret 2021; James et al. 2021), without any consideration of how these firms can influence the public policies adopted by the states on how to address the food crisis or climate change (even though the Conference of the Parties (COP) was fundamentally about the latter). Other international organisations may play a role in this debate. Margulis has recently documented that interventions by four different UN organisations – the Food and Agriculture Organization (FAO), the World Food Programme (WFP), the Office of the High Commissioner for Human Rights (OHCHR), and the Special Rapporteur on the Right to Food (SRRTF) – had an important role in agricultural trade liberalisation (Margulis 2023).

system, and the other objectives and concerns mentioned in the preamble to this Agreement' (underlined out of text).

14 See Colombia – United States Trade Promotion Agreement Preamble.

15 The amount of news related to agriculture and food security has increased since 2020, explained also by the Covid-19 pandemic as well as the food crisis derived from the Russian Invasion of Ukraine: www.wto.org/english/news_e/archive_e/fsec_arc_e.htm

16 United Nations Special Rapporteur on the Right to Food, in its 2020 Report called 'The Right to Food in the Context of International Trade Law and Policy'. The same potentially applies in the context of PTAs.

Regardless of the criticism, states are legally obliged to consider the AoA, other WTO Agreements, and PTAs when adopting suitable trade regulations that fulfil their food needs and must identify the policy space within these rules. According to FAO, although states count on policy space to guarantee food security, they need to use it more effectively (Matthews 2015). In that sense, FAO has affirmed that: 'WTO rules are not intended to restrict the policy objectives of its members with respect to food and agriculture, but rather to discipline the use of policy measures which have adverse spillover effects on other countries. It is often possible to pursue policy objectives with instruments which are not restricted under WTO disciplines (Matthews 2015, p. 5)'.

Even though the right to food is not explicitly set in WTO rules and PTAs, the call for *food security* is provided, for example, in the preamble of these agreements, which with the evolution of the concept should reflect the understanding of this right as a whole. The definition of *food security* has been enriched since the 1970s (FAO 2002); it used to be limited to guaranteeing food access to a particular population. Nowadays, it also requires *availability* and is linked to concepts such as *food sovereignty*, *food democracy*, and, indeed, the right to food. The evolution of the idea of food security has opened the door to include all these elements in trade policies when necessary.

Under those considerations, national policies that aim for food security must guarantee the right to food and comply with the WTO legal framework (particularly the AoA), which aims to avoid market and trade distortions. There must be a proper balance to achieve both goals. With this purpose in mind, recently, the WTO adopted the *Ministerial Declaration on the Emergency Response to Food Insecurity*, which recognises the right of member states to adopt measures to increase *food security* considering their impact on the whole market and under the Organization's legal framework (WTO 2022).[17]

7.3 THE PEACE AGREEMENT SCOPE

The main problems for the rural population in Colombia recognised in the Peace Agreement are, among others, the extreme land concentration, which emphasises the inequality in access to property rights that causes polarised social structures (Guereña 2016, p.10), food insecurity, deep gender inequality, and several marketing barriers that affect the commercialisation of their products (CISAN 2022, p. 12), which have to be solved to achieve a lasting peace. Because of the conflict, the

[17] WTO 2022: '5. We resolve to ensure that any emergency measures introduced to address food security concerns *shall minimize trade distortions as far as possible*; be temporary, targeted, and transparent; and be notified and *implemented in accordance with WTO rules*. Members imposing such measures *should take into account their possible impact on other Members*, including developing countries, and particularly least-developed and net food-importing developing countries' (text italicized by authors).

economic development of several countryside zones has stagnated for a long time. Therefore, the Colombian state needs to change the economic conditions of people living in depressed rural areas and must implement strong policy measures to solve the food insecurity and marketing barriers that agricultural production faces, such as transportation and logistics problems arising from years of abandonment of disputed territories that have hindered production and marketing of agricultural products within Colombia and their exports.

There is a correlation between states' exposure to internal conflicts and the deterioration of their food security due to direct war effects, such as violence, insecurity, and displacement (Abebe 2021), as the Special Rapporteur on the right to food concluded in his report on 'Conflict and the right to food'. The report gave 'an account of how different forms of violence in food systems harm people and generate the conditions that lead to human rights violations' (Fakhri 2022) and how violence makes more people poor, vulnerable, and marginalised (Ibid., par 3).

The armed confrontation in Colombia has been a conflict over land (Reyes 2016) in rural areas. According to the Unified Registry of Victims ('Registro Único de Víctimas' – RUV), there are approximately 8,219,403 victims of forced displacement due to events that occurred from 1985 to 31 December 2021 (Unidad para las Víctimas 2022). Peasants and farmers left rural areas in significant numbers, worsening economic production in such zones. Therefore, reforming rural areas is a crucial aspect of the Peace Agreement in Colombia. By granting access and usage rights to land, along with providing the necessary resources to cultivate it effectively, it is possible to address the root causes of the conflict in Colombia and pave the way for its resolution. The CRR is expected to contribute to the rural areas' structural transformation, 'closing the gaps between the countryside and the city and creating conditions of well-being and good living for the rural population' (Colombian Government FARC-EP 2016, p. 7). The CRR has four pillars (Colombian Government FARC-EP 2016):

- Pillar 1: A quantitative and qualitative land use and access increase.
- Pillar 2: Establishing special development programmes with a regional perspective.
- Pillar 3: The development of national plans to reduce poverty and extreme poverty in the countryside, centred on increasing productivity and consolidating the transition from an informal to a formal rural labour market (Ministerio de Agricultura y Desarrollo Rural 2019). This pillar recognises the fundamental economic role of the peasant, the family, and the community in rural development.
- Pillar 4: Food and nutritional security are at the centre of the entire effort to transform the countryside. This pillar acknowledges the significance of recognising the advantages of improved nutrition in rural areas, where agricultural production has increased.

Hence, this reform is crucial for the transition to peace, as 'recovery from conflict and its effects is not only about raising agricultural production and productivity – availability of food – but also about increased access to food' (Flores 2004, p. 16). In that regard, the Peace Agreement has provided a cross-cutting adoption of the food policy objectives through a system for the progressive realisation of the right to food conceived by the Agreement, specifically, the National Plans described above. It means that all the measures under the Peace Agreement related to the right to food must follow these policies. It is stated: 'It is necessary to ensure that all national plans comply in a cross-cutting manner with the objectives of the proposed food and nutrition policy, through a system that articulates them in the territories' (Colombian Government FARC-EP 2016, Point 1.3.4).

The following presents an analysis of one of the plans developed from pillar 3 of the Agreement. We aim to explore one of the most significant measures related to the right to food, which has been implemented thus far within the framework of the Peace Agreement.

7.4 RIGHT TO FOOD MEASURES UNDER THE PEACE AGREEMENT THAT MAY BE RELATED TO TRADE

7.4.1 *The National Rural Plan of the System for the Progressive Guarantee of the Right to Food (SGPDA)*

The social and economic situation of the rural population in Colombia is worrying. Besides the abovementioned high concentration of land ownership, other main problems are the low labour remuneration and the difficulties in income generation. In addition, the lack of adequate infrastructure, poor agricultural modernisation (lack of modern farm techniques), insufficient access to credit, barriers to commercialisation, limited development of science and technology, and the consequences of the armed conflict have generated a substantial gap in this segment of the population (CISAN 2022).

As mentioned, the Peace Agreement's third pillar called for developing national plans to reduce poverty in the countryside. That led to the formation of the *National Rural Plan of the System for the Progressive Guarantee of the Right to Food* (SGPDA)[18] as a fundamental tool for transforming the territories. Its principal aim is to promote the well-being of the population living in the country's rural and dispersed areas (CISAN 2022; Ministerio de Agricultura y Desarrollo Rural, Ministerio de Comercio, Industria y Turismo, Ministerio de Salud y Protección

[18] The SGPDA is an inter-sectoral policy instrument that promotes, facilitates, and manages the coordination and articulated action between the sectors and social actors. It allows for the different spheres and territorial levels to have responsibilities and competencies in the formulation, implementation, monitoring, evaluation, and control of public policies related to the dimensions of the human Right to Food.

Social 2022). The Intersectoral Commission on Food and Nutritional Security heads the implementation and monitoring of the SGPDA. This is the highest governing authority for food and nutritional security in Colombia.

The Commission is composed of the Minister of Agriculture, the Minister of Health, the Minister of Commerce, the Minister of Education, the Minister of Environment, the Minister of Housing, the Minister of Equality and Equity, the Director of the National Planning Department, the Director of the Administrative Department for Social Prosperity, the Director of the Colombian Institute of Family Welfare (or their delegates), the Director of the Administrative Department of the Presidency of the Republic, and a member of the Colombian Association of Nutrition Faculties (Decree Law 264 of 2023, Ministry of Agriculture and Rural Development).

The SGPDA is in line with *the Mission for the Transformation of the Colombian Countryside*,[19] whose findings identified the main obstacles to the commercialisation processes of agricultural products as: 'the lack of appropriate institutions, the lack of infrastructure, the lack of standards and adoption of good practices, the abuse of dominant positions in certain parts of the supply chains, and the lack of information' (DNP 2016). This Mission is an initiative of the National Government created in 2015, intending to formulate concrete public policies for the Colombian countryside over the next twenty years (MTC 2015). Like the Peace Agreement, this initiative embraces a comprehensive and multisectoral approach to rural development, extending beyond agriculture and livestock.

The SGPDA recognises food security as a fundamental human right, and it is considered the focal point of the entire effort to transform the Colombian countryside by strengthening local and regional markets and creating strategies against hunger. The SGPDA has three main objectives (Ministerio de Agricultura y Desarrollo Rural 2022):

1. To create a system that allows the implementation of the human right to food in rural areas by strengthening the coordination between government entities and citizens.
2. To ensure families' and communities' adequate food availability and accessibility.
3. To improve production and commercialisation conditions by promoting and consolidating local and regional markets and supporting agroecological practices.

This plan is effective until 2031 and aims to achieve its goals by implementing actions that consider both territorial and individual approaches. These actions are

[19] A national project led by the Planning National Department (DNP in Spanish) to determine the public policy guidelines about rural development.

designed to reduce poverty, enhance community participation, and foster coordinated efforts across various territorial areas to support sustainable social development.

1. Territorial approach: The formulation and implementation of this plan have prioritised territories profoundly affected by the internal Colombian conflict; 170 municipalities, grouped into sixteen sub-regions, were prioritised (Colombian Government FARC-EP 2016).
2. Individual approach: The formulation and implementation of this plan prioritise peasant and rural communities with a gender and ethnic approach (CISAN 2022).

Furthermore, community-based participation is a constitutive and cross-cutting element in the right-based approach (CISAN 2022). Thus, a bottom-up participatory planning process must be applied for its formulation and implementation. This means that its performance must incorporate the food systems and methods traditionally developed by rural communities.

7.4.2 *Implemented Measures within the SGPDA*

Within the SGPDA, nine national plans[20] were established to ensure the three components of the right to food that have been developed from international instruments[21]:

i. Availability: The possibility for individuals to feed themselves, either directly by exploiting the productive land or other natural sources of food or through well-functioning distribution, processing, and marketing systems that can move food from the place of production to where it is needed, according to demand (United Nations Committee on Economic, Social and Cultural Rights 1999).
ii. Access: Ensure physical and economic access to food. The first implies that food should be accessible to everyone by removing geographical and infrastructural barriers, particularly those affecting vulnerable groups (CISAN 2022). The second means that the food costs to maintain an adequate diet should not be so excessive that it may compromise the ability to fulfil other essential personal or family needs (United Nations Committee on Economic, Social and Cultural Rights 1999).
iii. Adequacy: It means that food should meet each person's dietary needs, considering their age, living conditions, health, ethnic differences, occupation, gender, and socio-cultural context (Office of the United Nations High Commissioner for Human Rights 2010).

[20] The plans have a national scope but will be implemented with a preference for the prioritised territories (those where the internal conflict mostly took part).

[21] E/C.12/1999/5: General Comment No. 12 on the right to adequate food. Committee on Economic, Social and Cultural Rights.

TABLE 7.1 *National plans related to the food policies provided in the Peace Agreement*

Right to food component	Related national plan
Availability	National Irrigation and Drainage Plan for the Peasant, Family and Community Economy National Plan for Technical and Technological Integral Assistance and the Promotion of Research National Roads Plan for Regional Integration National Plan for the Promotion of the Commercialisation of the Production of the Peasant, Family and Community Economy under the Responsibility of the Ministry of Agriculture National Plan for Rural Electrification National Plan for the Promotion of Solidarity Economy and Rural Cooperatives Environmental Zoning Plan
Access	Plan to Support and Consolidate Income Generation from the Peasant, Family and Community Economy.

Source: Translated by the authors. Information from CISAN (2022).

These national plans are directly connected with the Peace Agreement's CRR. According to the latter, food policy in rural areas is based on creating welfare conditions through implementing national plans for comprehensive reform to overcome poverty and close rural-urban gaps (Table 7.1) (Colombian Government CSIVI 2017, p. 30).

The Colombian Government started implementing these national plans between 2020 and 2021 through resolutions (norms/standards issued by government institutions), establishing specific measures to be adopted at the national and regional levels. They are financed mainly with resources from the Colombian state's general budget.

These plans aim to transform the agricultural economy at its core, requiring local communities to define and shape the process. According to the Colombian Ministry of Agriculture, excessive intermediation in the agricultural chain has impacted the marketing conditions of peasant, family, and community economies, coupled with small traders' low associative capacity and vertical integration. In Colombia, peasant, family, and community products have low insertion levels in local, regional, and national value chains (Ministerio de Agricultura y Desarrollo Rural 2019). Therefore, these policies acknowledge the need to build supportive intermediary channels that strengthen short marketing channels (farmers' markets) as an option to reduce excessive intermediation. Through these plans, the Peace Agreement looks for the recognition and inclusion of a traditional peasant economy at local, regional, and national levels. Hence, these plans look to strengthen institutional initiatives for production chains and 'short marketing circuits'.

Short marketing circuits represent a trade model focused on the direct sale of products, minimising intermediation. The end consumer acts as the buyer, acquiring locally produced goods. Concurrently, production chains seek to establish connections between local businesses and agro-industrial companies to supply raw materials (Ministerio de Agricultura y Desarrollo Rural 2019). They are centred around selling fresh or seasonal products such as fruits and vegetables. There is little or no intermediation between producers and consumers because they are generally close, so the sale price is lower (FAO et al. 2018).

In addition, such models provide for the co-financing of projects through productive alliances and commercial infrastructures such as marketplaces, create public–private partnerships, promote those products through a national brand, and provide technical assistance. These plans grant a central role to the participation of rural families and communities, encouraging the development and strengthening of new public policy management modalities grounded in acknowledging diverse population groups, safeguarding national production, and coordinating various economic and social sectors.

The following sections will explore if these national plans and the Peace Agreement's CRR are compatible with Colombian international trade obligations, in particular under the WTO Agreement on Agriculture. We will also identify whether they provide enough policy space to implement the peace agreement measures related to the right to food.

7.5 WTO – AGREEMENT ON AGRICULTURE

7.5.1 *Obligation to Notify Domestic Support Measures under the Peace Agreement*

The AoA does not prohibit domestic support of agriculture but regulates these measures to establish a fair and market-oriented agricultural trading system. Information sharing between trading partners is expected to play an essential role in levelling the playing field and supporting inclusive trade (WTO 2018). Regarding domestic agricultural support measures, WTO members have agreed to reduce the level of support (van den Bossche and Zdouc 2022, p. 956). For that purpose, they must notify domestic support measures and new or modified exempt measures (G/AG/2 and G/AG/2/Add.1), including their total Aggregate Measurement of Support (AMS).[22] A member shall be considered to comply with its domestic support

[22] 'The 'Aggregate Measurement of Support' means the annual level of support, expressed in monetary terms, provided for an agricultural product in favour of the producers of the basic agricultural product or non-products specific support provided in favour of agricultural producers in general, other than support provided under programmes that qualify as exempt from reduction under Annex 2 to the AoA (WTO ANALYTICAL INDEX, Agreement on Agriculture – Article 1)'.

reduction commitments in any year in which its domestic support in favour of agricultural producers expressed in terms of current total AMS does not exceed the corresponding annual or final bound commitment level specified in the member's schedule (AoA, Art. 6.3).

All national support measures favouring agricultural producers must be notified and are subject to the WTO rules and those of the AoA. Under the general multilateral legal framework of the WTO, there is a process of examination of the extent to which the country must notify trade measures and if they are compatible with the treaty obligations or whether exception regimes are applicable. This is part of the transparency principle enshrined in the WTO as an integral aspect of the system. According to the WTO, 'agricultural trade had been a major element in global development, and multilateralism and [the] WTO had been playing an important role in ensuring the transparency and predictability of the system' (WTO 2018, p. 5).

Notifications must follow the specific commitments in each member's schedule (WTO 1995b, 1995c, 1996). Domestic support commitments must be notified annually (AoA, Art. 18.2). However, for new or modified domestic measures, notification requirements are ad hoc, meaning they are due only when a specific measure is introduced or about to be introduced (AoA, Art. 18.3).

The tendency of non-submission of notifications or the long delays in the submission by developing countries indicates the technical difficulties in compiling their notification (Konandreas and Mermigkas 2014). It is also a reflection of a policy choice related to ambiguities in the interpretation and meaning of the elements of the domestic support obligations, especially that of the calculation of the AMS. Regarding measures Colombia has been taking and will need to take under the Peace Agreement, not all measures are needed to be notified; thus, it must be determined which measures Colombia should notify the WTO about.

On 1 June 2021, Colombia notified the WTO of all the domestic support measures implemented under the Peace Agreement, even those that do not have a trade impact or are based on non-trade objectives. It also notified the WTO of the total AMSs and the measures exempt from the reduction commitment under Articles 18.2 and 18.3 of the AoA. Among the measures exempted from the reduction commitment, Colombia included those related to the Special and Differential Treatment and Development Programs (AoA, Art. 15). In this regard, the Colombian Government issued a general note establishing: 'Following the signing on 24 November 2016 of the Peace Agreement with the FARC, Colombia increased budgets to implement programs for the substitution of illicit crops' (G/AG/N/COL/73). Colombia reiterated the same note for 2018, 2019, and 2020 (G/AG/N/COL/74, G/AG/N/COL/75, G/AG/N/COL/76).

Even if the notification obligation under WTO Agreements is not applicable, Colombia stated that it might be necessary to notify some measures implementing the Peace Agreement. Even though that agreement does not provide for export- or import-directed measures, the SGPDA sets guidelines to adopt measures for protecting and encouraging national production through internal support measures with a territorial and personal approach. This is an explicit domestic support measure that might be notified. Under the considerations mentioned, the following section will examine whether the measures implemented under the SGPDA are framed under the category exceptions that Colombia should notify, or if there are other applicable exemptions under the AoA. The parameters that Colombia should comply with when implementing future measures related to the SGPDA will also be considered.

7.5.2 *Exemption from the Reduction Commitments*

Figure 7.1 illustrates the rules outlined in the WTO Agreement on Agriculture by which states may identify in which cases domestic support measures in favour of agricultural producers are or are not subject to reduction commitments.

Domestic support measures in agriculture are defined by the WTO Glossary Term, as 'any domestic subsidy or other measure which acts to maintain producer prices at levels above those prevailing in international trade; direct payments to producers, including deficiency payments, and input and marketing cost reduction measures available only for agricultural production'. They are commonly classified as non-tariff measures, defined as 'all policy interventions other than tariffs that can potentially affect the quantities and the prices of internationally traded goods' (UNCTAD 2010). Despite the absence of trade objectives, international trade can be influenced by non-tariff measures from domestic regulations that address market failures, such as information asymmetries or negative externalities (UNCTAD 2019).

These measures may have no or minimal distortive effect on trade or have trade-distorting effects. Therefore, some domestic support-exempted categories exist in the so-called 'blue box' and 'green box' measures. The 'blue box' measures are direct

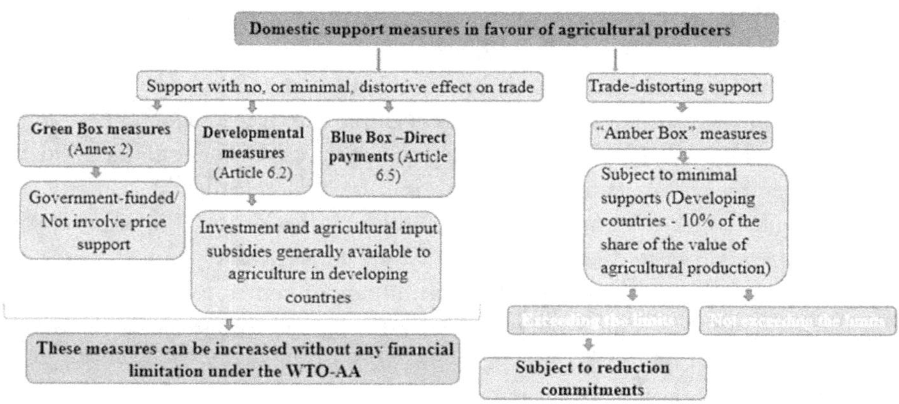

FIGURE 7.1 Domestic support measures of the AoA.
Source: created by the authors based on the AoA and Annex 2.

payments under production-limiting programmes not subject to the commitment to reduce domestic support as long as they comply with the requirements enshrined in Paragraph 5 of Article 6 of the Agriculture Agreement.[23] The measures that do not distort trade or, at most, cause minimal distortion, qualify as 'green box' measures. They can be increased without any financial limitation as long as they comply with the below-mentioned requirements. All green box measures for which exemption is claimed must comply with two general criteria: (i) government-funded (not by charging consumers higher prices); (ii) not including price support to producers or transfers from consumers; and (iii) comply with policy-specific criteria depending on the type of measure[24] (AoA Annex 2).

The programmes tend to be not targeted at particular products and include direct income supports for farmers unrelated to current production levels or prices. They could also be environmental protection and regional development programmes (WTO n.d.2). Developing countries have additional special treatment related to governmental stockholding programmes for food security and subsidised food prices for poor urban and rural populations. This exemption covers programmes not targeted at products and includes direct income support for farmers decoupled from current production levels or prices (AoA, Annex 2 Nos. 3–4.).

If the domestic support measures do not fit into any AoA-exempted categories, they must comply with the *minimis* percentage to be exempted from the reduction commitments agreed upon by the WTO members. Following the AoA rules, minimal domestic support by any state members is allowed for product-specific or non-product-specific. This threshold for developing members is 10 per cent of the total value of production of a basic agricultural product during the relevant year for product-specific, and 10 per cent of the value of that member's total agricultural output for non-product specific for developing countries (AoA, Art. 6, para. 4).

All domestic support measures favouring agricultural producers that do not fit into the exempt categories nor comply with the minimum support level, fall into the so-called 'amber box'[25] and are subject to the total AMS reduction commitments.

23 These payments shall not be subject to the commitment to reduce domestic support if: '(i) such payments are based on fixed area and yields; or (ii) such payments are made on 85 per cent or less of the base level of production; or (iii) livestock payments are made on a fixed number of head'.

24 These types include general services, public stockholding for food security purposes, domestic food aid, direct payments to producers, decoupled income support, government financial participation in income insurance and income safety-net programmes, payments (made either directly or by way of government financial participation in crop insurance schemes) for relief from natural disasters, structural adjustment assistance provided through producer retirement programmes, structural adjustment assistance provided through resource retirement programmes, structural adjustment assistance provided through investment aids, payments under environmental programmes, and payments under regional assistance programmes.

25 'Amber box' measures are all domestic supports except those in the blue and green boxes. These include measures to support prices, or subsidies directly related to production quantities (WTO n.d.1.).

The above AoA rules provide the legal framework to develop and implement the right to food through the domestic support measures provided in the Colombian Peace Agreement. Even though that agreement and its programmes on food security and the right to food fall under the 'non-trade' concern measures concept, the issued regulation for implementing the Peace Agreement (the SGPDA) might raise questions on its potential trade impacts.

Colombian Peace Agreement's measures satisfy the requirements to qualify as 'green box' measures.

First, the SGPDA complies with the general requirement of being government-funded. Colombia's General Budget is the primary source of the SGPDA, complemented by the territorial sources. The funding and participation for the implementation of the Peace Agreement are divided into (1) the General Budget of the Nation 36 per cent; (2) the General System of Participation[26] 29.2 per cent; (3) the General System of Royalties[27] 15.2 per cent; (4) own resources of the territorial entities 4.3 per cent; (5) non-repayable international cooperation funds[28] 8.9 per cent; and (6) resources from the private sector 6.4 per cent (Colombian Government CSIVI 2017, p. 217). None are directed at a single region, product, or peasant community. CRR will receive most of the funding of this investment with an 85.4 per cent share of the total Peace Agreement investment (Colombian Government CSIVI 2017, p. 213). In implementing the Peace Agreement, the National General Budget has targeted different kinds of investments in the agricultural sector and rural development (Colombian Government CSIVI 2017). For example, the General System of Participation has financed access to safe drinking water and basic sanitation, and the General System of Royalties is a supplementary source of the territorial entities (Colombian Government CSIVI 2017, p. 221).

Second, the SGPDA and associated national plans also comply with the requirement not to provide direct price support for products. These are non-trade measures as they pursue social and development objectives and do not provide for export- or import-directed measures. Instead, they focus on protecting and encouraging national production through internal support measures guided by the territorial and personal approach. The income and technical support for farmers, the preferential treatment to women and ethnic communities, and the fair-trade standards

[26] These are the resources that the nation transfers to territorial entities, as mandated by the constitution, with the purpose of satisfying basic needs in education, health, potable water, and basic sanitation, primarily (Minvivienda).

[27] These are the resources from the exploitation of non-renewable natural resources allocated to territorial entities by the nation.

[28] The national government, by means of Decree Law 691 of 2017, established the Colombia in Peace Fund. This fund aims to facilitate the effective management of resources allocated to post-conflict efforts, sourced from diverse national and international channels. These include contributions from the United Nations System Fund, the European Union Post-Conflict Fund, as well as other non-governmental entities, international agencies, and donations from other states.

TABLE 7.2 *Policy-specific criteria applicable to the national plans of the SGPDA.*

National rural plan of the system for the progressive guarantee of the right to food		
Right to food component	**Related national plan**	**Category of measure exempted from the AoA**
Availability	National Irrigation and Drainage Plan for the Peasant, Family and Community Economy	Green Box: General services – Infrastructure services, including water supply facilities (para. 2, subparagraph g, Annex 2)
	National Plan for Technical and Technological Integral Assistance and the Promotion of Research	Green Box: General services – Research and training services (par. 2, subparagraph c, Annex 2)
	National Roads Plan for Regional Integration	Green Box: General services – Infrastructure services, including roads and other means of transport (par. 2, subparagraph g, Annex 2)
	National Plan for the Promotion of the Commercialisation of the Production of the Peasant, Family and Community Economy under the Responsibility of the Ministry of Agriculture	Green Box: General services – marketing and promotion services (par. 2, subparagraph f, Annex 2)
	National Plan for Rural Electrification	Green Box: General services – Infrastructural services, including electricity (par. 2, subparagraph g, Annex 2)
	National Plan for the Promotion of Solidarity Economy and Rural Cooperatives	Green Box: Payments under regional assistance programmes (par. 13, Annex 2)
	Environmental Zoning Plan	Green Box: Payments under environmental programmes (par. 12, Annex 2)

Source: AoA, created by the authors.

included in the plans are not related to current production levels or prices of the products either.

Third, regarding the policy-specific criteria, we identified the type of measure exempted under Annex 2 of the AoA that applies to each of the national plans related to the food policies provided in the Peace Agreement:

As indicated in Table 7.2, the aforementioned national plans are within the scope of paragraphs 2, 12, and 13 of Annex 2 of AoA, establishing the basis for exemption from the reduction commitments. Policies in the general service category involve support in relation to programmes which provide services or benefits to the rural community; the plans placed in this category were designed to grant general benefits for peasants in rural communities related to infrastructure, training, and access to basic services. Particularly, the National Plan for the Promotion of a Solidarity Economy[29] has supported public policies to ensure the bargaining power of the peasants, such as the creation of programmes with technical assistance to support the creation of organisations (Ministerio del Trabajo 2020a), which provides preferential treatment to women and indigenous communities but is not directed at the prices of products.

The National Plan for the Promotion of Commercialization[30] also strengthens institutional initiatives for short marketing circuits, creating public–private partnerships, and promoting products through a national trademark. Technical assistance and the articulation of family farms with agro-industrial companies (private or public) to provide raw materials are also included (Ministerio de Agricultura y Desarrollo Rural 2019). Its main objective is to promote the integration of the Peasant, Family, and Community Economy (ECFC) in local, regional, and national value chains through alternative marketing schemes and eliminating information asymmetries. The National Plan complements this with technical and technological integral assistance and the promotion of research for agricultural production.

Additionally, the National Plan for the Promotion of Solidarity Economy and Rural Cooperative is exempted by the 'Payments under regional assistance programs' category, following AoA Annex 2 (13), because (i) it is limited to producers in disadvantaged regions, clearly identifiable by the territorial approach of the Peace Agreement; (ii) its support does not condition the type or volume of production, on the contrary, it is based on ensuring the bargaining power of the peasants through organisations to become part of the production chain and; (iii) the measures are available to all the producers but grant some specific support to women and ethnic communities.

Finally, the Environmental Zoning Plan is also exempted by the 'Payments under environmental programs' following AoA Annex 2 (12) because it is an environmental management instrument for territorial planning and administration. It is a guideline for decisions made by local and regional authorities (Ministerio de Ambiente y Desarrollo Sostenible 2021), and it is subject to the government's environmental programmes.

In sum, following the policy-specific criteria and conditions set out in Annex 2 of the AoA, these plans fully comply with WTO rules; thus, they are within Colombia's policy space to regulate.

[29] Public policy that establishes the guidelines for promoting an economy based on solidarity, cooperation, and association as instruments for the integration and socio-economic revitalisation of territories. It aims to enhance the living conditions of rural communities within the framework of the Peace Agreement (Ministerio del Trabajo 2020b).

[30] Public policy that seeks to promote the integration of Peasant, Family, and Community Economy into local, regional, and national value chains through the improved use of alternative marketing schemes addressing information asymmetries (Ministerio de Agricultura y Desarrollo Rural 2019).

In addition to measures covered by the Green Box, two other categories of domestic support measures derived from the Peace Agreement are exempt from reduction commitments under the AoA: specific development measures in developing countries and certain direct payments under production-limiting programmes (Art. 6.2 and 6.5 of the AoA). The notification made by Colombia to the WTO Committee on Agriculture for the period 2017 to 2020 (WTO 2021a, 2021b, 2021c, 2023), after the Peace Agreement was signed, follows Article 6.2 of the AoA, which allows measures taken by developing country members to encourage diversification from growing illicit narcotic crops since Colombia created budgets to implement programmes for the substitution of illicit crops. The aforementioned national plans represent the public policies that the Colombian state aims to implement to ensure the right to food within the framework of the Peace Agreement. Generally, the measures included in those plans are not direct subsidies to export but development policies to alleviate poverty in rural areas.

Due to the mandatory bottom-up participatory planning process under the SGPDA, Colombia should incorporate an appropriate institutional mechanism that integrates all decisions to be taken within the framework of these national plans to identify future measures that must be notified to the WTO Committee on Agriculture and must comply with the reduction commitments.

There should be no significant challenges to implementing the SGPDA under the scope of Annex 2 of the AoA, as long as it does not involve product-specific support. If Colombia, as a WTO developing country member, wants to introduce a product-specific policy within the implementation of the Peace Agreement, one path to being exempted from the reduction commitments would be using the *de minimis* criteria provided in the AoA. But in some cases, the *de minimis* criteria may not be adequate for pursuing specific food policy objectives. In the Bali Ministerial Conference, the G33 claimed that 'agriculture in developing countries is not a commercial operation but is carried out mainly by small-scale and resource-poor farmers with no other source of livelihood' (Konandreas and Mermigkas 2014).

7.6 CONCLUSIONS

At first glance, the international trading system does not seem to restrict agricultural policies designed to enhance social and economic livelihood of marginalised communities. However, should those policies be directed to export goods, legal limitations could potentially arise. Thus, programmes to implement the Colombian Peace Agreement related to the right to food, particularly those that aim to guarantee food security of peasants, count with a broad policy space under international trade law. In particular, the AoA does not constitute an obstacle to a farming and food policy in the process of implementing the commitments under the Peace Agreement.

Thus, it is crucial to closely monitor the alignment of regulatory measures in the upcoming years with the framework granted by the AoA. The right to food-related measures under the Peace Agreement will be in force until 2031 and might gain a certain complexity in time as they aim to strengthen the rural economy. Therefore, there is a possibility that implementing the Peace Agreement in the future will require measures that are not under the scope of the AoA, resulting in measures that may conflict with this agreement, other rules in WTO law, or similar ones included in PTAs. Protective measures, such as increasing tariffs, import limitations, and or restrictions on some products, for instance, could be implemented to aid emerging domestic industries competing with bound importers.

In this respect, government officials need to be careful when issuing any regulation related to the right to food under the Peace Agreement and the trade law policies to avoid the breach of either substantive obligations, such as discrimination, or procedural obligations, such as failing to notify a measure. By adhering to these responsibilities, officials can prevent potential trade disputes.

The Peace Agreement is a chance for Colombian society to build a more equalitarian society, enhancing affected communities and allowing them to benefit from the whole economic system. But the spectre of the international trading system (WTO Agreements and PTAs) should not be overlooked in implementing this particular aspect of the Peace Agreement.

The Peace Agreement has imposed on the Colombian Government the task of enacting policies which pose changes in the national economic system as it is obliged to include rural communities in the whole agricultural production chain. It is to be seen if giving land, empowering farmers to produce, transform their products, and add value beyond production for their success will allow them in the future to export to foreign markets.

REFERENCES

Abebe, W. 2021. Food Insecurity in the Horn of Africa and Its Impact on Peace in the Region, Institute for Peace and Security Studies (IPSS) Policy Brief, vol. 15-02, https://ipss-addis.org/wp-content/uploads/2021/03/Policy-Brief-Food-Insecurity-in-the-Horn.pdf, March 2021.

Álvarez, J. M. 2015. "The In Dubio Pro Development Principle: A Right to Development in Trade and Investment Regimes," *Denver Journal of International Law & Policy* 43(4): 333–356.

Baggaley, N. 1998. "Trade Liberalization Under GATT, the NAFTA and the EU. Selected Topics," *Journal of Comparative International Management* 1(1):3–22.

Barret, G. 2021. "COP26: Indigenous Peoples, Protests, and a Call to End the War on Nature," UN News, https://news.un.org/en/story/2021/11/1105102, 6 November.

CISAN (Comisión Intersectorial de Seguridad Alimentaria y Nutricional) 2022. *Plan Nacional Rural del Sistema para la Garantía Progresiva del Derecho a la Alimentación. Comisión Intersectorial de Seguridad Alimentaria y Nutricional.*www.icbf.gov.co/system/files/v2.plan_nacional_rural_del_sgpdha_conanexo.pdf.

Colombian Government CSIVI 2017. *Plan marco de implementación del Acuerdo Final. Comisión de Seguimiento, Impulso y Verificación del Acuerdo Final.*

Colombian Government FARC-EP 2016. *Acuerdo Final para la Terminación del Conflicto y la Construcción de una Paz Estable y Duradera*. Translation available at www.peaceagreements.org/wview/1845/Final%20Agreement%20to%20End%20the%20Armed%20Conflict%20and%20Build%20a%20Stable%20and%20Lasting%20Peace.

DNP (Departamento Nacional de Planeación) 2016. *El Campo Colombiano: Un Camino Hacia el Bienestar y la Paz. Informe Detallado de la Misión Para la Transformación del Campo Colombiano*. Bogotá: Departamento Nacional de Planeación; Nuevas Ediciones S.A.

Fakhri, M. 2020. The Right to Food in the Context of International Trade Law and Policy. United Nations Special Rapporteur on the Right to Food, A/75/219, 22 July 2020.

Fakhri, M. 2022. *Conflict and the Right to Food. United Nations Special Rapporteur on the Right to Food*, A/HRC/52/4029, 29 December 2022.

FAO 1996. Rome Declaration on World Food Security and World Food Summit Plan of Action: World Food Summit, FAO (063)/F688 www.fao.org/3/w3613e/w3613e00.htm.

2002. "Trade Reforms and Food Security: Conceptualising the Linkages." www.fao.org/3/y4671e/y4671e06.htm#bm06.

2010. "Fact Sheet N°34 The Right to Adequate Food." www.ohchr.org/sites/default/files/Documents/Publications/FactSheet34en.pdf.

FAO, OPS, WFP, UNICEF 2018. "Panorama de la seguridad alimentaria y nutricional en América Latina y el Caribe 2018," http://iris.paho.org/xmlui/handle/123456789/49616.

Flores, M. 2004. "Conflicts, Rural Development and Food," ESA Working Paper No. 04-02.

Guereña, A 2016. "Unearthed: Land, Power and Inequality in Latin America," Oxfam International, November 2016.

Hawkes, S. and J.K.Plahe 2013. "Worlds Apart: The WTO's Agreement on Agriculture and the Right to Food in Developing Countries," *International Political Science Review / Revue internationale de science politique* 34(1): 21–38.

James, W. et al. 2021. "Big Crowds Rally in Rainy Glasgow for COP26 Climate Action," Reuters. www.reuters.com/business/cop/thousands-rally-rainy-glasgow-cop26-climate-action-2021-11-06/, 6 November 2021.

Konandreas, P. and G.Mermigkas 2014. *WTO Domestic Support Disciplines: Options for Alleviating Constraints to Stockholding in Developing Countries in the Follow-up to Bali*.www.fao.org/3/i3819e/i3819e.pdf.

Margulis, M. E. 2023. *Shadow Negotiators: How UN Organizations Shape the Rules of World Trade for Food Security*. Stanford: Stanford University Press.

Matthews, A. 2015. "The State of Agricultural Commodity Markets 2015–2016," FAO 2015 I5224E/1/12.15. www.fao.org/3/i5224e/i5224e.pdf.

Ministerio de Agricultura y Desarrollo Rural 2019. *Plan Nacional para la Promoción de la Comercialización de la Producción de la Economía Campesina, Familiar y Comunitaria*, Bogotá. www.minagricultura.gov.co/Normatividad/Resoluciones/RESOLUCI%C3%93N%20NO.%20000006%20DE%202020.pdf.

2022. *Plan Nacional de Asistencia Integral Técnica, Tecnológica y de Impulso a la Investigación*, Bogotá, 2 May 2022.

Ministerio de Agricultura y Desarrollo Rural, Ministerio de Comercio, Industria y Turismo, Ministerio de Salud y Protección Social 2022. *Resolución Conjunta 213 de 2022 Por la Cual Se Adopta el Plan Nacional Rural del Sistema para la Garantía Progresiva del Derecho a la Alimentación*, Bogotá, 13 July 2022.

Ministerio de Ambiente y Desarrollo Sostenible 2021. *Resolución 1608 de 2021 por el cual se adopta el Plan de Zonificación Ambiental Derivado del Acuerdo Final de Paz*, Bogotá.

Ministerio del Trabajo 2020a. Plan Nacional de Fomento a la Economía Solidaria y Cooperativa Rural. Bogotà. https://portalparalapaz.gov.co/wp-content/uploads/2022/07/Archivo-Digital-07-Plan-Nacional-de-Fomento.pdf.

2020b. *Resolución 2950 de 2020 Por el cual se adopta el Plan Nacional de Fomento a la Economía Solidaria y Cooperativa Rural y Se Dictan Disposiciones para su Implementación*, Bogotá.

MTC (Misión para la Transformación del Campo). 2015. Informe. Bogotá D.C., septiembre de 2015, https://colaboracion.dnp.gov.co/CDT/Agriculturapecuarioforestal%20y%20pesca/Estrategia%20de%20Competitividad%20para%20el%20Sector%20Agropecuario%20V2015-10-23.pdf

Office of the United Nations High Commissioner for Human Rights 2010. *The Right to Adequate Food*. www.ohchr.org/sites/default/files/Documents/Publications/FactSheet34en.pdf.

Reyes, A. 2016. *La reforma rural para la paz*. Penguin Random House.

Unidad para las Víctimas 2022. *Las xifras que presenta el Informe Global sobre Desplazamiento 2022, 19 May 2022*. www.unidadvictimas.gov.co/es/registro-y-gestion-de-informacion/las-cifras-que-presenta-el-informe-global-sobre-desplazamiento#:~:text=La%20cifra%20reportada%20por%20el,31%20de%20diciembre%20de%202021.

United Nations 1966. *International Covenant on Economic, Social, and Cultural Rights, General Assembly Resolution 2200A (XXI)*.www.ohchr.org/en/instruments-mechanisms/instruments/international-covenant-economic-social-and-cultural-rights.

United Nations Committee on Economic, Social and Cultural Rights 1999. *General Comment N°12: The Right to Adequate Food (Art. 11 of the Covenant)*.www.refworld.org/docid/4538838c11.html.

UNCTAD. 2010. *Non-tariff Measures: Evidence from Selected Developing Countries and Future Research Agenda. United Nations publication, New York and Geneva*. https://unctad.org/system/files/official-document/ditctab20093_en.pdf

UNCTAD. 2019. *International Classification of Non-Tariff Measures, United Nations publication, New York and Geneva*. https://unctad.org/system/files/official-document/ditctab2019d5_en.pdf.

Van den Bossche, P. and W.Zdouc 2022. *The Law and Policy of the World Trade Organization. Text, Cases, and Materials*. Cambridge: Cambridge University Press.

WTO (n.d.1).*Notifications Portal. Open Trade Data*. Accessed Member Profile: Colombia. https://notifications.wto.org/es/status-by-member/colombia.

1995a. Agreement on Agriculture. Geneva: WTO, 1 January 1995.

1995b. “Committee on Agriculture – Notification Requirements and Formats,” G/AG/2, 30 June 1995.

1995c “Committee on Agriculture – List of ‘Significant Exporters’ for the Purposes of the Notification Requirements in respect of Export Subsidy Commitments,” G/AG/2/Add.1, 16 October 1995.

1996. “Obligaciones de Notificación: Agricultura,” G/AG/W/24, 18 April 1996.

2018. Agriculture Policy Landscape Symposium, Summary Report, 13–14 June 2018. www.wto.org/english/tratop_e/agric_e/sumreport_agww18_e.pdf.

2021a. “Committee on Agriculture – Notification – Colombia – Domestic Support – Table DS:1 – Calendar Year 2017,” G/AG/N/COL/73, 02 June 2021.

2021b. “Committee on Agriculture – Notification – Colombia – Domestic Support – Table DS:1 – Calendar Year 2018,” G/AG/N/COL/74, 2 June 2021.

2021c. "Committee on Agriculture – Notification – Colombia – Domestic Support – Table DS:1 – Calendar Year 2019," G/AG/N/COL/75, 2 June 2021.
2021d. "DG Okonjo-Iweala Highlights Trade's Role in Ambitious and Just Climate Action at COP26", 2 November 2021. www.wto.org/english/news_e/news21_e/clim_02nov21_e.htm.
2022. "Ministerial Declaration on the Emergency Response to Food Insecurity" WT/MIN (22)/28; WT/L/1139, 22 June 2022.
2023. "Committee on Agriculture – Notification – Colombia – Domestic Support – Table DS:1 – Calendar Year 2019," G/AG/N/COL/76, 30 March 2023.
Yigzaw, D. 2015. "WTO Agricultural Trade and the Unfulfilled Promise of Development," *South Carolina Journal of International Law and Business* 11(2): 163–225.

8

How Preferential Trade Agreements Are Perceived in Chile: From Love to Hate in a Single Step?

Dorotea López and Andrés Bórquez[1]

8.1 INTRODUCTION

Chile is recognized worldwide for its broad and extensive network of preferential trade agreements (PTAs). According to data from Chile's Undersecretary of International Economic Relations (2022), 95 percent of exports go to markets that have signed PTAs with Chile, and these exports are responsible for more than 17 percent of new jobs. This strategy of actively negotiating market access through PTAs is a key pillar of Chile's foreign economic policy and is central to the implementation of its development model, particularly after the return to democracy in 1990. The negotiation of PTAs has enabled Chile to engage with international markets, leading to further trade liberalization. Since the 1990s, the strategy has enjoyed a high degree of national consensus and very low degree of politicization. In recent years, however, questions have arisen, particularly after the protests of October 2019 and the subsequent process of constitutional rewriting. For example, the social outburst and disagreement with the current economic model and its distributive effects led to a high debate on the Comprehensive and Progressive Agreement for Trans-Pacific Partnership/Trans-Pacific Partnership (CPTPP/TPP), which was finally approved in parliament in 2023. From 2018 to 2023, expressions of civil disorder have been multiplied in the media and social networks. Questions have arisen regarding the continuation of signing PTAs.[2] The objections mainly come from concerns regarding the unequal distribution of benefits from trade openness and demands to implement a more active development policy. This opposition to trade policy as usual, primarily from public and civil society organizations, played an important role in the 2021 general elections when voters rejected the traditional parties and ultimately elected the youngest president in

[1] This work was funded by ANID Millennium Science Initiative Program NCS2022_053 Millennium Nucleus on the Impacts of China in LAC (ICLAC).

[2] The terms "preferential trade agreements" and "free trade agreements" are used interchangeably throughout this chapter.

Chilean history. During his campaign and first year in government, he raised the need to rethink trade policy, and in particular his apprehensions about some provisions in agreements such as the TPP and about the treaty modernization project with the European Union (EU).

However, this study finds that a positive perception of PTAs still seems to be dominant in many segments of the private sector and in key government authorities. The political-economy literature has studied the features that shape public and elite perceptions toward free trade, focusing on various economic and sociotropic factors, and mainly for the cases where the EU and the United States were involved. Chile is a particularly interesting case to study, as free trade has long been seen as an important and successful element of its export-led growth economic model, and it has enjoyed significant public support. Yet, after the October 2019 demonstrations there has been a significant shift in public debate over the role of free trade in Chile, with significant concerns about its distributional and social effects becoming key topics. Much of these concerns catalyzed opposition to the CPTPP.

To determine to what degree perceptions toward PTAs have in fact changed, this chapter develops a mixed methodology based on stakeholder's surveys, expert interviews, and media analyses. First, a stakeholder survey was conducted. Second, a content analysis of the two main Chilean newspapers was carried out covering the past five years to identify changes in media coverage over time. Finally, the results were contrasted with interviews with key stakeholders, such as former trade diplomats – Chilean Ambassadors to the World Trade Organization (WTO), Undersecretary of International Economic Relations Directors, and government officials – academics, and scholars at higher education institutions.

This chapter finds skepticism increasing, but at a low rate, among large segments of Chilean societies. Civil society laments negative distributional effects and costs on society and demands more access and inclusion to trade policy formulation and implementation. Also visible are continued fears that increasing market integration could lead to important structural changes in the future.

This disquiet has been more evident recently than at other times in its history, possibly because of the social and productive results of the Chilean model and the high expectations that trade policy would lead to structural economic changes. During the social unrest of October 2019, the number of TPP opponents and of anti-TPP slogans seen on banners or written on the walls of streets was striking. The debate regarding ratification and implementation of this agreement featured more prominently in the media than had any of the previously signed agreements. However, this does not seem to be evidence of a radical change in the perception of the country's trade policy.

The chapter is divided into four sections. The first reviews the literature on perceptions regarding trade agreements. In the second section, the trajectory of Chile's trade policy is described to provide understanding of key moments in time where turning points in general perceptions have occurred. In the third, the results of the surveys, the media analysis, and the interviews are presented and discussed. Finally, some conclusions are presented.

8.2 LITERATURE ON PERCEPTIONS OF PTAS

Past literature has examined the factors shaping people's attitudes toward free trade for at least two decades. These explanations range from classical economic models of factors of production to nationalism, fear of foreign cultures, and gender differences, amongst others (Kuznetsov 2015). One area in which new studies have emerged is analyzing how PTAs shape attitudes toward trade liberalization. Initially, attention has been paid to identifying what makes some people support trade liberalization and others oppose it, and to characterizing the mechanisms behind this formation of preferences. There are different approaches ranging from direct economic self-interest to those that stress sociotropic concerns, as well as noneconomic concerns, which include cultural or social factors that shape attitudes.

The economic approach to people's perceptions of trade liberalization predicts that individuals act and behave based on their income, which is related to factors of production or factor endowments possessed (Rogowski 1989; Irwin 1995; Hiscox 2001; O'Rourke and Sinnott 2001; Scheve and Slaughter 2001; Margalit 2012). Yet, in recent years, this conventional wisdom has been challenged by a variety of studies showing that noneconomic factors matter as well. This work suggests that there are many other factors, not directly related to economic aspects, that may explain the observed variation in public opinion about free trade, including education, culture, gender, and nationalism (Mansfield et al. 2002; Walter 2021).

Regarding noneconomic factors, education has received ample attention that effects attitudes toward trade. Hainmueller and Hiscox (2006) argue for example that education increases knowledge about the general benefits of trade to the economy, boosting support for trade liberalization among the more educated. Another differentiating factor is people's age and their aversion to what is new.

Gender has been singled out as well as an important factor because women are systematically less inclined than men to favor trade liberalization (O'Rourke and Sinnott 2001; Scheve and Slaughter 2001; Drope and Chowdhury 2014). In addition, Drope and Chowdhury (2014) find that it is not women, per se, who favor protectionism, but, more precisely, economically vulnerable women because, as the factor endowment approach suggests, women are more sensitive than men to issues of economic security. More recent work demonstrates that women remain systematically less likely to favor trade because they are affected indirectly. Mansfield et al. (2015) argue that "this gender difference is rooted in attitudes toward competition, relocation, and involvement in world affairs."

Moreover, several authors highlight social and cultural consequences. Individuals who are concerned with these social-cultural effects are more disposed to view economic integration as harmful (Wehner 2007; Margalit 2012; Baccini 2019).

Other studies find that respondents' positive perception (or support) for trade liberalization is found to have a strong negative correlation with patriotic, nationalist, and chauvinistic views (O'Rourke and Sinnott 2001; Mayda and Rodrik 2005; Mayda et al. 2007). Similarly, Mansfield and Mutz (2009) found that the impact of nationalism on trade preferences must be considered, given the tendency for some individuals and cultures to be ethnocentric and isolationist.

The literature regarding the role of interest groups that support or oppose trade has been well developed in the case of the European Union and the United States (Grossman and Helpman 2002; Dür and Mateo 2014; Gheyle and De Ville 2019; De Bièvre and Poletti 2020; De Bièvre et al. 2020). These contributions increase our understanding of the interaction among lobbying groups, public opinion, and the increasing legitimizing pressure of trade agreements.

Some studies demonstrate that country characteristics seem to matter in the public's eyes. Dür and Huber (Chapter 3) find that political ideology, and to a lesser extent, geopolitical concern, seem to play a role in determining which individuals are viewed as favorable PTA partners. Citizens in developing countries prefer countries that are culturally similar, democratic, and consider security issues and high environmental and labor standards (Spilker et al. 2016; Cherry 2018; DiGiuseppe and Kleinberg 2019; Bush and Prather 2020). For example, Minard and Landriault (2015) find that the public is unwilling to support treaties with China due to the characteristics of the regime's political system.

In short, the perception of trade policy, of which PTAs are an integral part, will depend, then, on several factors including levels of education, culture, exposure, and economics. Individuals' views about the effect of liberalization are driven by sociotropic concerns, rather than a direct assessment of the effect of trade liberalization in purely economic terms (Kuznetsov 2015).

In this context, the world has seen a rising backlash against globalization. Recent research shows, that contrary to a popular narrative, the backlash is not associated with a large swing in public opinion against globalization but is rather a result of its politicization (Walter 2021). Both material and nonmaterial causes drive the globalization backlash, and these causes interact and mediate each other. The consequences are shaped by the responses of societal actors, national governments, and international policymakers. These results are more complex if we distinguish between the perceptions of elites and citizens. A recent study, published by Dellmuth et al. (2022), mapped legitimacy beliefs toward six key international organizations, among them the UN, drawing on elite and citizen survey data from Brazil, Germany, the Philippines, Russia, and the United States. They found a notable elite–citizen gap for all six organizations studied in four of the five countries. This gap between what contemporary elites and citizens think about globalization might bode ill for the future of global institutions and trade agreements.

This section has limited itself to reviewing some of the findings in the literature that studies the perception vis-à-vis free trade, focusing on PTAs. As seen, there is limited literature for Latin America. In the following sections we will assess to what degree a change in attitudes in Chile can be explained by existing arguments, or whether additional country- or context-specific factors need to be brought in.

8.3 CHILEAN TRADE POLICY

Trade policy in Chile is an essential part of its foreign and economic policies. Even more so, it is considered a key element of the development strategy since integration into the world economy has been seen as a growth engine. Thus, various contributions to trade policy have reflected the growing importance in the framework of Chilean foreign policy (Frohmann 1991; Agosin 1993; Hachette 1993; Velasco and Tokman 1993; Sáez and Valdés 1999; Lopez et al. 2022).

During Pinochet's regime, under the paradigm of liberalism, an aggressive trade opening plan was implemented. Given the country's partial international isolation, the government followed both a path of unilateral reduction of tariff and nontariff barriers on the one hand (Hachette 2000; Ffrench-Davis 2003) and of multilateral negotiations within the framework of the General Agreement on Tariffs and Trade (GATT) on the other (Jara 2005; López and Muñoz 2018).

With the return of democracy in 1990, the foreign affairs priorities of Chile were an expression of a political discussion that placed emphasis on finding a consensus on a development model and increasing trade relations with countries. This reasoning was initially marked by the narrative of "international reinsertion" (Tomassini 1990; Heine 1991). Along with the decision to maintain and deepen the neoliberal model, a strong push led to the negotiation of PTAs as well as the strengthening of the idea of joining subregional integration schemes such as Mercosur or the Andean Pact (DIRECON 2009). The main objective was to speed up the integration of Chile into the world economy after years of international isolation during the dictatorship period. In fact, since the third United Nations Conference on Trade and Development which took place in Santiago in 1972, Chile has enjoyed a society-wide consensus on the importance of integration in the world and cooperating closely with other trading partners (UNCTAD 1973).

In 1990, with the beginning of the democratic period, the country started a process of bilateral negotiations (Economic Complementarity Agreements (ECAs)), focused mainly on goods, within the framework of the Latin American Integration Association (LAIA).[3] This process became known as "open regionalism" (Rojas and Solis 1993; Van Klaveren 1994) and guided Chile's economic integration model when Chile was a young democracy seeking PTAs with the major markets in the world. These

[3] Examples: Argentina (ECA 16) and Mexico (ECA 17) in 1991, with Colombia (ECA 24 – 1993), Venezuela (ECA 23 – 1993), Bolivia (ECA 22 – 1993), Ecuador (ECA 32 – 1994), Peru (ECA 38 – 1998), Cuba (ECA 42 – 2008), and the Free Trade Agreement with Central America (PTA) (ratified between 2002 and 2012).

agreements rested on a discourse focused on Latin American integration. This has been defined in the trade policy of Chile as a different strategy to accelerate the economic integration process (Wilhelmy and Durán 2003).

For several years there was wide consensus over the virtues of an open integration strategy. However, a few critical voices were raised during the negotiations with Mercosur between 1994 and 1996. Few sectors that still maintained protection (e.g., in agriculture) were in direct competition with imports from the South American bloc. To address internal pressures from the import-competing sectors and unions, the government compensated groups that claimed to be damaged through increased competition (Porras 2003). This was done to appease opposition while the decision was taken to submit the signed agreement to Congress for ratification, even though this was not needed within the framework of the LAIA (Porras 2003). The opposition consisted mainly of the National Agricultural Society (SNA) and of interest groups that did not want the country to be subject to a common tariff regime and instead favored another type of "insertion" model.

After Mercosur, the trade debate centered around a potential membership of Chile in the North American Free Trade Agreement (NAFTA) (López and Muñoz 2018; Lagos 2001; Porras 2003; DIRECON 2009). In this case, the government saw NAFTA as a more attractive agreement to join than Mercosur. However, the internal resistance of unions in the United States, together with the fact that President Clinton failed to obtain the necessary fast-track authority from the US Congress, complicated Chile's inclusion in this treaty. As a result, the Chilean government began separate negotiations with Mexico and Canada. Thus, Chile signed a PTA with Canada in 1997. This agreement proved to be very important since it provided a seal of approval signaling that Chile was continuing its strategy of active economic integration. It also kept open the possibility of joining NAFTA at a later stage. In 1998, it broadened its economic complementation agreement[4] (ACE) with Mexico, bringing it even closer to a trade agreement model more applied by Northern countries. The last NAFTA country with which Chile signed a PTA was the United States in 2003. It was wide-ranging and one of the most progressive trade treaties at the time, because it was one of the first to include provisions on labor and environment.

After these initial successes, momentum to negotiate PTAs continued. Civil society and the business community appeared to support the idea that this was the path to growth and development. Thus, in 2003, the Economic Partnership Agreement with the European Union was signed, which expanded the classical trade treaty structure by incorporating political, economic, and cooperation aspects.[5]

4 This is a term used by Latin American countries in the bilateral agreements they enter into with each other to reciprocally open their goods markets, which fall within the legal framework of the Latin American Integration Association (ALADI). They aim at a greater opening of markets than the Partial Scope Agreements, but less than the Free Trade Agreements.

5 The modernization of this agreement started in 2021 and finalized in 2023.

The decade of the 2000s was characterized by the increasing emergence and role of Asian economies on the international stage, what the Economic Commission for Latin America and the Caribbean (ECLAC) would later refer to as the "Asian factory" phenomenon. In addition, China entered the scene with its accession to the WTO in 2001, eventually becoming the largest economic actor in world trade. In 2004, Chile hosted the sixteenth (XVI) annual meeting of the Forum for Asia-Pacific Economic Cooperation (APEC) in Santiago, with the motto of *One Community, Our Future*. This was of great symbolic importance, as it was the first time that an Andean country held the presidency of the organization.

Chile has continued to focus extensively on the Asia-Pacific region. In April 2004, a PTA between Chile and South Korea was concluded. Shortly after, in 2006, an agreement with the People's Republic of China was finalized.[6] During that same year, negotiations of the Strategic Economic Partnership Agreement with Brunei Darussalam, New Zealand, and Singapore, known as P4 (the predecessor of the TPP-11 initiative), were concluded.

These were years of intense activity for trade policy. In 2007, a partial scope economic agreement with India and an Economic Association Agreement with Japan entered into force. The partial agreement with India includes trade disciplines in limited areas of market access, rules of origin, customs procedures, safeguards, and dispute settlement while in contrast, the PTA with Japan has had a broader scope, including disciplines on services, intellectual property, and investment among others. In 2008, a PTA with Panama was signed, while in 2009, PTAs with Peru and Colombia came into force, through a process of expansion of the ECAs. These agreements include most of the disciplines that each country commits to in their PTAs with the United States and go beyond goods and services. Similar agreements were later finalized with Australia (2009), Malaysia (2012), Hong Kong, Vietnam (2014), and Thailand (2015).

In 2009, based on the P4, the United States pushed to shape a regional agreement that would have broad membership and high standards (Gallegos Zúñiga and Polanco 2013). Australia, Canada, Japan, Malaysia, Peru, and Vietnam joined this project. It was an ambitious agreement and one that included a large number of issues that have caused internal debates, such as the strengthening of intellectual property rights, a new deal for state-owned enterprises, which is based on the principle of competitive neutrality and seeks to harmonize the internal policies of each Member State in this matter. Likewise, a chapter on small- and medium-sized companies is included, which is novel since it is the first time that there are provisions on this topic, and its content is informative although it does not fall under the dispute resolution chapter of the agreement.

6 This agreement has been under continuous negotiations since then. In 2010, a Supplementary Agreement on Trade in Services entered into force. A Supplementary Agreement on Investment is in force since 2017. A Modernization Protocol entered into force in 2019.

Today, Chile has a network of thirty-three trade agreements of different depths and scopes. More recently, it has embarked on modernizing some of these and has explored the inclusion of new topics such as gender and the digital economy, among others. Within the context of modernizing the agreement with Canada, important progress was made by including a chapter on gender and trade, which was signed in 2016. This chapter was included for the first time in any world agreement in the PTA with Uruguay. The attention to gender is closely linked to the leadership of President Michelle Bachelet, who served as president from 2014 to 2018 (López and Muñoz 2021). As a result, Chile has been an active participant in the creation of a technical group on gender and trade in the Pacific Alliance and in the APEC Forum. More precisely, in the APEC's Roadmap on Women and Inclusive Growth, Canada, Chile, and New Zealand established the Inclusive Trade Action Group (ITAG) on the sidelines of the 2018 APEC leaders' summit. Chile has also been engaged actively in another new issue area: the digital economy. In 2020, Chile was the first country to sign the Digital Economy Partnership Agreement (DEPA), an agreement on the digital economy that the Chilean Undersecretariat for International Economic Relations (SUBREI) has highlighted as innovative in its structure and negotiation.[7]

Chile has continued its policy of entering into trade agreements, in 2022, the PTAs with Brazil and Ecuador, countries which usually are reluctant to engage in any trade negotiations, came into force. It is also working on the modernization of its agreements, such as with Mexico; finalized the agreement with Paraguay in 2024; and is in negotiations with India, among others.

However, not all trade projects have been free of criticism. When Chile began to study the "modernization" of the Agreement with the European Union, as well as during the TPP negotiations, some controversial issues emerged – concerned with topics such as natural resources and investor-state dispute settlement (ISDS).

On natural resources, the EU proposed an article on export prices, which would have prevented Chile from offering preferential prices for lithium and other raw materials to companies offering "value added." Regarding the resolution of investment disputes, the government considered signing "side letters" to exclude recourse to ISDS, following New Zealand's practice. However, this strategy yielded few results. Chile reached such an agreement just with New Zealand on February 17, 2023, and, apparently, similar side letters with Mexico and Malaysia, although they are not publicly available.

Whereas politicization has increased over the years, overall support for trade has not in any significant way decreased but rather increased, as various surveys have documented. The Public Studies Center (CEP) has developed and conducted a national public opinion survey about attitudes and perceptions of the population since 1987.[8] Some questions in the survey focus specifically on free trade. The data in 2023 has

7 Subsecretaría de Relaciones Económicas Internacionales (SUBREI). www.subrei.gob.cl/home.

8 For further information, www.cepchile.cl/opinion-publica/encuesta-cep/sobre-encuesta-cep/que-es-la-encuesta-cep/.

shown that 72 percent of the respondents considered that Chile can have access to better products, thanks to international trade;[9] 81 percent agree that Chile should continue to expand trade with other countries; and 68 percent consider that foreign investment should be encouraged.

When questions relate to imports more specifically, the CEP surveys actually show that compared to twenty years ago, more people see imports in a positive way. When the statement was formulated as follows: "Chile should limit the import of foreign products to protect its national economy," 58 percent of respondents answered that they strongly agreed with the statement. By 2022, the level of agreement with the statement fell from 58 percent to 43 percent. The size of the group that neither agrees nor disagrees increases slightly from 14 percent to 18 percent, and the percentage that strongly disagrees with the statement increases from 22 percent to 36 percent.

Similarly, the surveys conducted by the Inter-American Development Bank (IDB), through the Latinobarómetro cross-regional survey, reveal that popular support for international trade remains strong, with 73 percent of citizens in 2018 in favor of increasing trade. However, surveys also show that if politicians warn of job losses due to lower trade barriers, and if the media and social media promote such arguments, support for trade may wane through such framing effects. This also means that the stability of preferences might be somewhat volatile, and it makes a difference how, and by whom the arguments for and against free trade, are presented.

In summary, since the implementation of what has been defined as the neoliberal model during the 1970s, trade liberalization and international insertion have benefited from a broad consensus. With respect to PTAs, some disagreement became visible as witnessed in the talks with Mercosur on agricultural liberalization, with New Zealand on dairy products, as well as with the United States on investment protection. But in general, the opposition was largely limited to affected sectors. These concerns were addressed by the government and therefore did not spill over to significant public discussions. This changed with the debates about TPP, where the involvement of Chilean society was evidently greater, also driven by a notable increase in news coverage. This led to greater politicization and a questioning of the dominant "neoliberal model."

8.4 PERCEPTION OF PTAS: INSIGHTS FROM A STAKEHOLDER SURVEY, MEDIA ANALYSIS, AND INTERVIEWS

The recent emergence of increased politicization of trade agreements in Chile can be observed in both discussions and debates in the traditional media and on social media. Trade policy is today a more salient issue among different stakeholders than

9 This high support is only slightly lower than in 2003 where 78 percent of the respondents agreed with this statement. Similarly, respondents who disagreed with the statement, "Thanks to free trade, Chile can have access to better products" increased from 5 percent to 13 percent.

it was prior to the TPP. To identify the perception of trade and PTAs and potential shifts, this study uses insights from three complementary sources.

First, data from an elite stakeholder' survey provides valuable insights on elite perceptions. The sample consists of fifty-one respondents ranging from trade diplomats, academics, and private sector representatives. Second, the chapter carries out a media content analysis to capture the PTAs' politicization over time. Third, information from twenty-one in-depth interviews with experts on Chile's trade policy is used to complement the analysis. The interview partners are drawn from a mix of former trade diplomats (Chilean ambassadors to the WTO, SUBREI Directors, and government officials), academics, and scholars at higher education institutions. Due to confidentiality reasons, the interviews have been anonymized.

Regarding the elite survey, the response rate has been 17 percent, totaling fifty-one overall, and are valid responses to the questionnaires sent to experts. The sample consists of 74 percent men and 24 percent women. The questionnaire was sent by email with a purposive sampling. Moreover, 52 percent of the sample live in the Metropolitan Region, 46 percent in other regions, and only 2 percent outside Chile. Regarding the educational level, 16 percent hold a doctoral degree, 46 percent a master's degree, 62 percent a bachelor's degree, and one had only finished high school education. The data was collected between March and August 2022.

The print media review was conducted through a content analysis including the two newspapers with the largest readership in Chile: *La Tercera* and *El Mercurio*, from January 1, 2017, to August 8, 2022. After subscribing to the journals to access the historical files, a total of forty-six relevant news items were identified through the search functions for subscribers of each journal. Subsequently, a sentiment analysis was carried out following Bardin (2002) to identify positive and negative news. In addition, concepts and their frequency were mapped out. As for the general procedure of sentiment analysis, the news was manually separated into positive and negative in relation to how much they promoted or opposed trade agreements. Figure 8.1 provides an overview of thirty-one news with positive sentiments and fifteen with negative sentiments. As the frequency analysis shows, we divided different concepts falling in the positive and negative categories, respectively, and counted the number of times they were mentioned (frequency) (see Figure 8.2).

The purpose of the twenty-one interviews with specialists in Chilean trade policy experts was to deepen our understanding regarding the identified issues in the survey and the media review. These interviews also made it possible to contrast the critical views of PTAs found in public discourse with those of the experts. The interviews were conducted in person as well as remotely. The questionnaire was semi-structured with an emphasis on exploratory questions. The authors are cognizant that for former officials, their support in favor of liberalization and a policy of openness may be conditioned by their experiences occurring during the military regime where the country was closed to international trade.

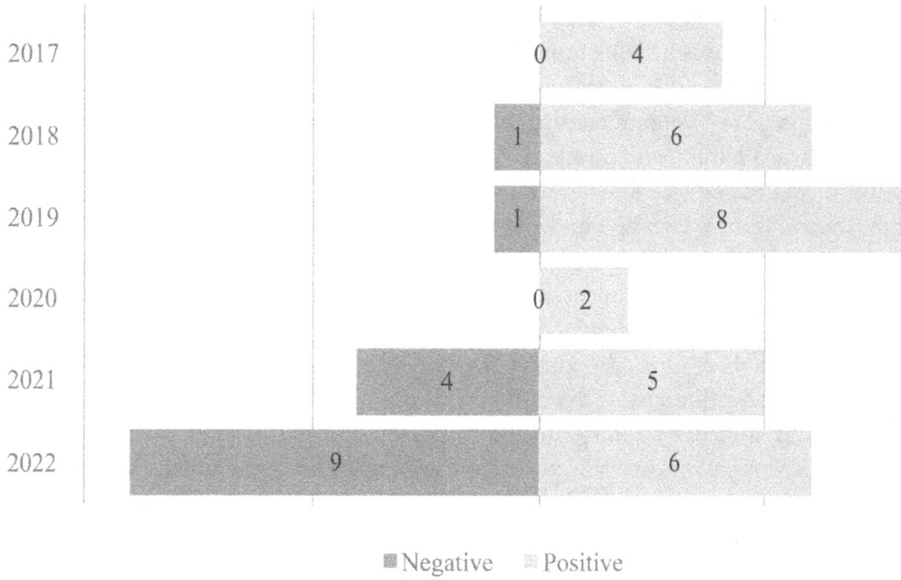

FIGURE 8.1 Content analysis of print media.
Source: Created by the authors based on the survey results.

8.4.1 *General Perception Regarding Trade and PTAs*

We proceed by first conducting a comparative analysis with the data collected from the three different methods to identify the importance attributed to international trade. The survey data shows that respondents overwhelmingly see trade as "very important" (96 percent), and only one respondent considers it to be "fairly important" and one respondent "indifferent." This confirms that integration into international markets is still perceived to be a very positive strategy by trade experts. Approval drops a bit when the question focuses on PTAs specifically, with 84 percent of respondents indicating that they are "very important" and only one respondent that they are "fairly important." One possibility is that this reflects growing negative sentiments toward the TPP/CPTPP after 2019 or a minority view of a fairly limited impact on society.

Using the data retrieved from the two main newspapers, we observe that since 2017 the number of news items addressing PTAs in general has increased consistently, indicating that the issue has potentially become more salient. We observe a drop in attention for 2020, when the COVID pandemic likely took center stage and PTA negotiations were also stalled. Also, 65 percent of the news items could be classified as positive in their description of trade agreements.

Between 2017 and 2020, news items with a positive message outnumbered negative ones, even during the period of social unrest in 2019, when opposition to the

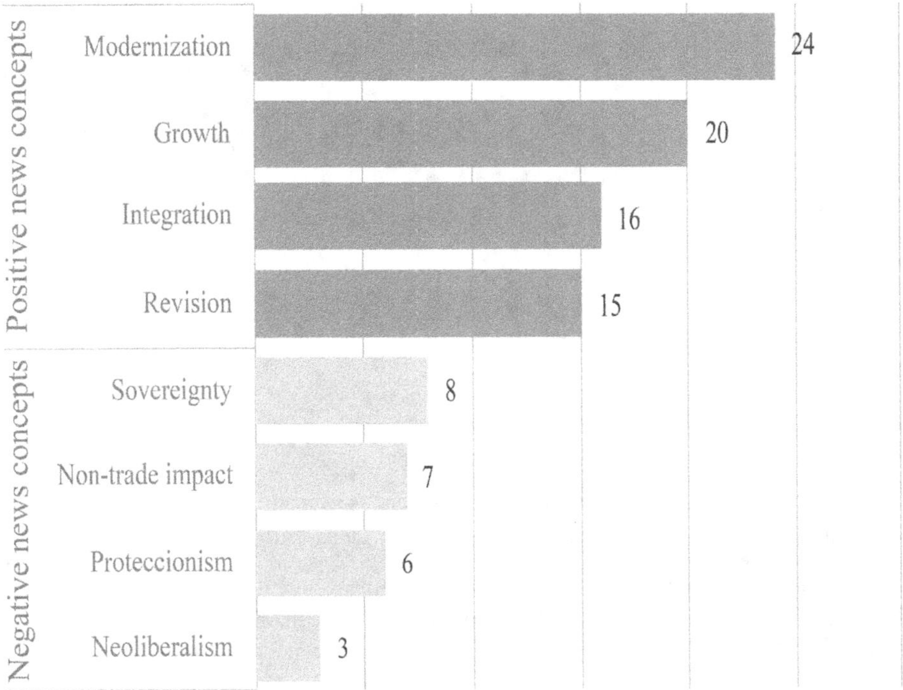

FIGURE 8.2 Positive and negative news concepts.
Source: Created by the authors based on the survey results.

TPP was observed (Figure 8.3). The trend started to shift in 2021 and in 2022 we see a steep rise in negative news. It is important to consider that both newspapers are privately owned and are considered to editorially reflect conservative and right-leaning positions. Therefore, the negative news trends could also be explained by opposition to President Boric's type of trade policies, something these newspapers have questioned since the presidential campaign.[10]

As Figure 8.3 shows, after 2020 the negative news increased in frequency. This could be related to the 2019 social movements directly questioning the neoliberal economic model and, as a representation of this, the network of PTAs. During the political campaign and the first year of President Boric's administration, there was a lot of criticism of the so-called free trade policy of former governments. What was also questioned was the dependence and reliance on exporting natural resources, in particular copper.

Turning to interviews, in general, trade experts hold the view that PTAs have benefited the country because they have improved market access, led to growth due

[10] For more information: Público.es "La derecha mediática chilena contra la constitución": . www.publico.es/politica/derecha-mediatica-chilena-constitucion.html

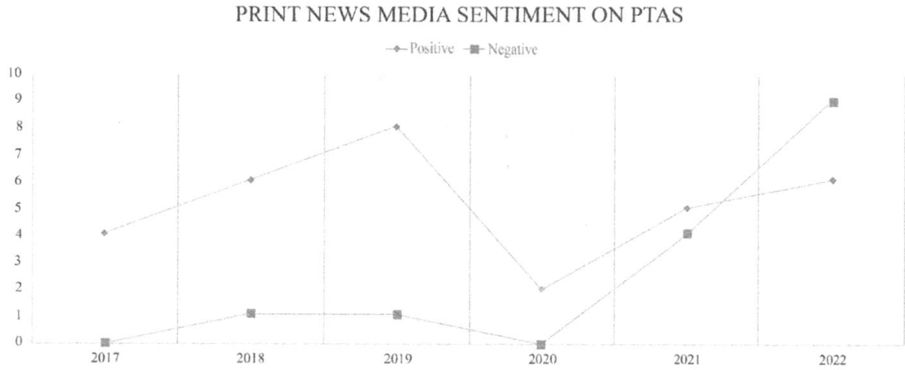

FIGURE 8.3 Print news media sentiment on PTAs.
Source: Created by the authors based on the survey results.

to the reduction of tariffs and trade barriers, lowered consumer prices, and strengthened Chile's position abroad. One respondent illustrates this sentiment

> well: In general, Chile's trade policy – what it was, and what has been Chile's integration strategy in commercial economic matters during the last three decades – has been fundamental for the country's growth. It has been a pillar from the point of view of its contribution in terms of expanding markets. . . . In addition, it seems to me that it has given the country a brand. (Interviewee No. 5)

Most interviewees, when asked to share their view on PTAs, held that they were a tool to boost exports and imports of the country for two main reasons: (i) because of tariff reductions and the elimination of trade barriers and (ii) by allowing the exchange of goods and services in profitable conditions and without discrimination. Overall, there is a strong perception that PTAs have positive effects for both producers and consumers as they provide better development opportunities for the country because the economy becomes more competitive. The rest of the respondents, close to 40 percent, answered that PTAs were just agreements between two countries, but they did not elaborate more on their effects.

Below, we show the results of a "word cloud" that summarizes the most used words when respondents were asked about the meaning of a PTA for them. We can see that answers are oriented around economic and trade concepts. And the answers tend to describe PTAs economic objectives.

We contrast above word cloud (Figure 8.4) with a second one (Figure 8.5) drawing from the media analysis. We can see that for this data, the most common words are not necessarily related to classic economic concepts except for the term "growth." Also, trade-related and non-trade issues tend to appear most frequently. The results show that the "survey respondents" are focusing on economic matters, whereas the right-leaning media is covering many noneconomic objectives, such as sovereignty, democracy, and potentially the costs as evidenced by the word "consequence."

FIGURE 8.4 Word cloud 1 – Concepts related to PTA.
Source: Created by the authors based on the survey results.

FIGURE 8.5 Word cloud 2 – Concepts in the news regarding PTA.
Source: Created by the authors based on the survey results.

In the survey, the respondents were also asked explicitly what positive attributes they give to the agreements, providing a set of multiple-choice answers. Table 8.1 shows the responses according to frequency. The most critical aspects are closely related to the fact that they are associated with facilitating investments, trade in goods and services, and supporting diversification in export baskets.

TABLE 8.1 *The contribution of PTAs.*

Free Trade Agreements contribute to	Frequency
Facilitating foreign investment	38
Strengthening export of services	38
Diversifying exports of products	32
Promoting the participation of regions in the foreign market	29
Receiving transfer of technology	28
Stimulating national innovation	25
Improving national industry	25
Enhancing the quality of employment	22
Reducing social inequality	15
Consolidating female labor insertion	14
Improving environmental protection	10

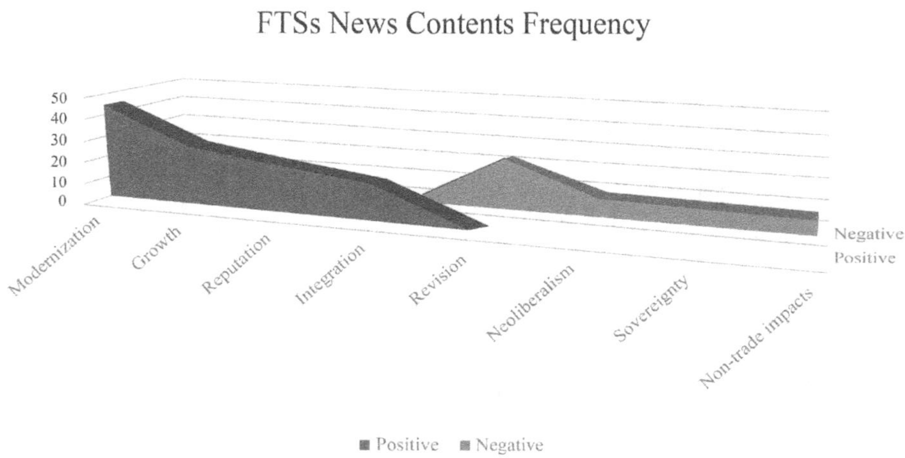

FIGURE 8.6 Media analysis.
Source: Created by the authors based on the survey results.

If we focus on the data from the content analysis of the media, the most frequently used words related to PTA effects were country-reputation, sovereignty, neoliberalism, revise, trust, democracy, growth, protectionism, incorporation of new topics, integration, negative consequences of updated PTAs, negative impacts of PTA. These are broader than the expressions found in the responses to our questionnaire, where the topics were primarily commercial in nature.

Taking a closer look at the media content analysis, we see the different categories also in Figure 8.6 and how they are associated with positive and negative attributes of the agreements.

In the following, we look in more detail at some of the categories.

8.4.1.1 Modernization

In the first category, modernization,[11] most of the news items reviewed suggested that Chile continues on the path of deepening and expanding the network of agreements. In particular, it must strengthen its bilateral ties and not abandon its path toward lifting barriers in order to increase trade. The government should continue improving the existing agreements, exploring new topics (e.g., gender), and strengthening economic relationships.

8.4.1.2 Growth

On growth, the second-most mentioned category, the role of PTAs was underscored as a fundamental element in the country's growth and development, terms that were used synonymously in most cases. Export-led growth is also pictured as a stimulus to employment and innovation, as well as higher wages. PTAs were also described as instruments that make the economy more dynamic, as they help increase the availability of products for consumers, lead to lower prices, and improve access to technologies.

8.4.1.3 Integration

Interesting to note is the perception that PTAs are an obstacle to integration within Latin America, particularly with Mercosur. This perception may be shaped by the Chilean government's argument that Chile could not join Mercosur as a full member because of the common tariff imposed. However, Chile wanted to join NAFTA, and increase relations with more open economies and developed countries.

8.4.1.4 Revision

Since 2019, the idea of opting for unilateral revisions of PTAs and the possibility of derogation of existing commitments received increased attention in the public debate. This then resulted in a counter-campaign by different sectors, arguing that such a move would damage the country's image or reputation. Furthermore, during the period in 2021 in which the work of the Constitutional Convention took place, the discussion of considering to go through the PTAs was present in the media analysis.

[11] The difference between modernization and revision is that modernization is when both parties decide to improve the treaty, that is, update or renegotiate some issues. Conversely, revision is unilateral, meaning that one of the parties requests a review from the other party – a country requires the other country to make changes.

8.4.1.5 Sovereignty

The most critical view can be observed in relation to the sovereignty category. Many news items pointed out that the agreements impose conditions that limit the countries' freedom of action. These comments are related to criticism leveled against the TPP, such as the lack of civil society participation in the negotiations, an argument expressed for the first time in any PTA negotiation process.

The fact that Congress can only authorize trade talks and reject outcomes of the negotiations without being involved in the process of negotiations began to be questioned. Some of the criticism regarding the lack of the parliament's involvement went hand in hand with negative views on job protection, concerns about the lack of inclusiveness, and unbalanced distributive impacts.

Contrasting these media views with information from the elite interviews, we observe that the latter shows more pragmatism when it comes to sovereignty. Interviewees pointed out, for instance, that any treaty or agreement naturally implies ceding some degree of sovereignty. Yet, none of the treaties that Chile has signed restricted its core ability to act or its sovereignty. Indeed, specific clauses in the treaties provide protection in this respect. One interviewee stated the following: *The WTO in general and all the bilateral treaties that Chile has signed explicitly state that the regulatory capacity of the State remains intact, that is, there is no limitation of sovereignty* (Interviewee 4).

Equally, all the interviewees pointed out that the most negative perceptions of the plurilateral treaties were due more to the political situation after 2019, the constitutional discussion, and the approval of the TPP, than being a concrete criticism of specific PTAs. The following three responses by interviewees illustrate this stance:

> *That break is determined by the TPP, not by the type of agreement. There is not a criticism against multilateralism per se, but it is a criticism against the TPP.* (Interviewee 1)

> *This is because the discussion focused on the TPP, but I don't see why public opinion can understand the difference between a bilateral or plurilateral agreement.* (Interviewee 2)

> *In particular, with the TPP there has been an ideologically-centered criticism with no real foundation and that is related to the investor-state situation, but it is something ideological.* (Interviewee 14)

8.4.2 *Specific Perceptions regarding PTA Provisions*

Dür et al. (2023) argue that interest groups' positions toward trade agreements depend on the specific design features of trade agreements. Depending on which issues are covered in a trade agreement, a group may be supportive of that agreement. In the survey we asked the participants to indicate how important an

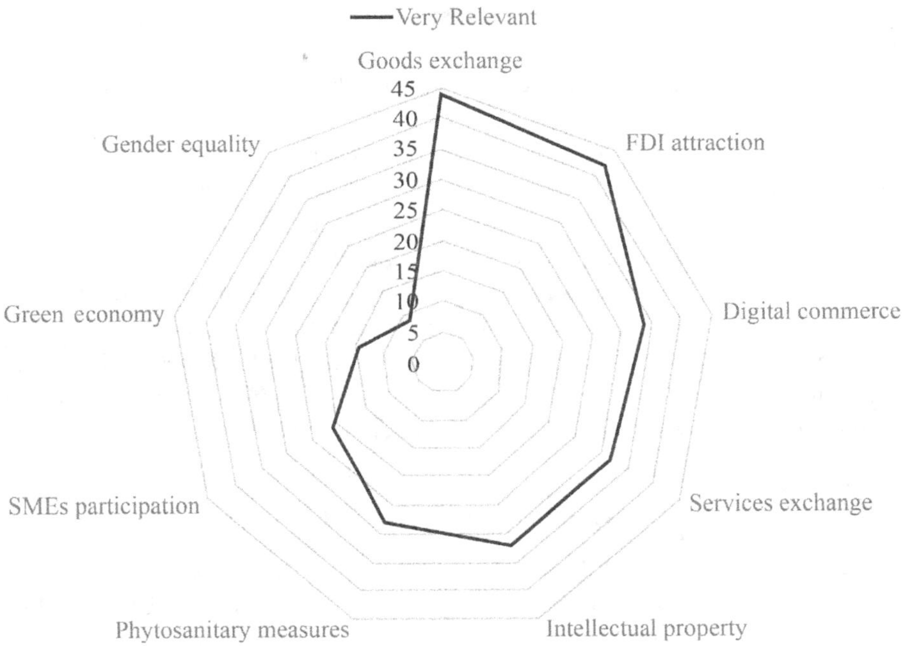

FIGURE 8.7 How important is a PTA for the following reasons.
Source: Created by the authors based on the survey results.

agreement is in relation to different objectives. A list was provided, and they were asked to rate them according to their relevance (see table in the Appendix). This allowed us to make a comparison and to rank their importance. In Figure 8.7, the results are shown according to the order of importance from the highest to the lowest.

8.4.2.1 Intellectual Property, FDI Promotion, and Digital trade

The most supported categories are Foreign Direct Investment (FDI) promotion, digital commerce, intellectual property, phytosanitary measures, and services trade. The category "Small and Medium enterprises" received support but to a lesser degree. This finding is consistent with one of the criticisms against PTAs that they have not been a substantial instrument to strengthen the role of Small and Medium Enterprises (SMEs). The increasing inclusion of SMEs and trade in services, however, could be explained by the willingness of recent governments to improve opportunities for service providers, increase export diversification, and reflect the important role of agriculture, and smaller-scale farmers, in the Chilean economy.

The importance given to FDI promotion could be both positive and negative. On the one hand, concerns about the slowing of investment (as also present in media reports) would suggest more importance to FDI concerns. On the other hand, the salience of FDI is also related to increasing concerns about private investors suing the Chilean state and therefore needing clear rights and obligations in the PTAs.

When it comes to the increasing importance of digital trade that entered the political debate in Chile, this is often related to the role of media platforms, the taxing of international streaming services, such as Netflix, but also more generally important to digitalization as an effect of the pandemic.

Finally, the moderate attention to "intellectual property" could be a result of the debates during the TPP negotiations. In one interview, it was argued that Chile lost out in terms of intellectual property in the PTA with the United States. In this sense, it was mentioned that the PTAs can have a chilling effect on public policies in the country, especially those related to the promotion of industrial policies.

8.4.2.2 Gender and Green Economy

From the survey, we observe that gender and green economy topics appear to be less relevant. By contrast, these topics are frequently covered in the media. From the interviews, we can gather some more nuanced perspectives on their growing importance. Some suggest that Chile should aspire to similar levels of ambition as witnessed in most developed countries.

One interviewee put it as follows: *It is important and necessary that these issues [gender] are included in the agreements. Above all for a small or at the most a middle-sized country like ours [Chile]* (11).

However, although interviewees differed on the effectiveness of integrating these nontraditional issues into PTAs, they shared the view that these topics needed more attention.

Gender: In recent years gender policies have become a more important topic in Chile. This is in line with the contribution by Bahri (Chapter 4), who shows that several countries, including Chile, have been at the forefront of incorporating gender provisions in PTAs. Similarly, the chapter by Caceres and Munoz (Chapter 9) demonstrates that trade agreements enhance women's service sector employment, which can have positive effects, potentially, for the goal of gender equality. Figure 8.8 plots perception of survey respondents about the PTA relevance for gender equality according to their place of residence (urban vs. rural).[12] The data shows that survey respondents who reside in rural areas are slightly more in agreement that PTAs are relevant for gender equality.

The generational rift is less evident in perceptions of the gender perspective. However, there is a tendency for younger generations such as millennials

[12] Chile is divided into sixteen regions; Santiago is in the Metropolitan Region, where 43 percent of the urban population lives.

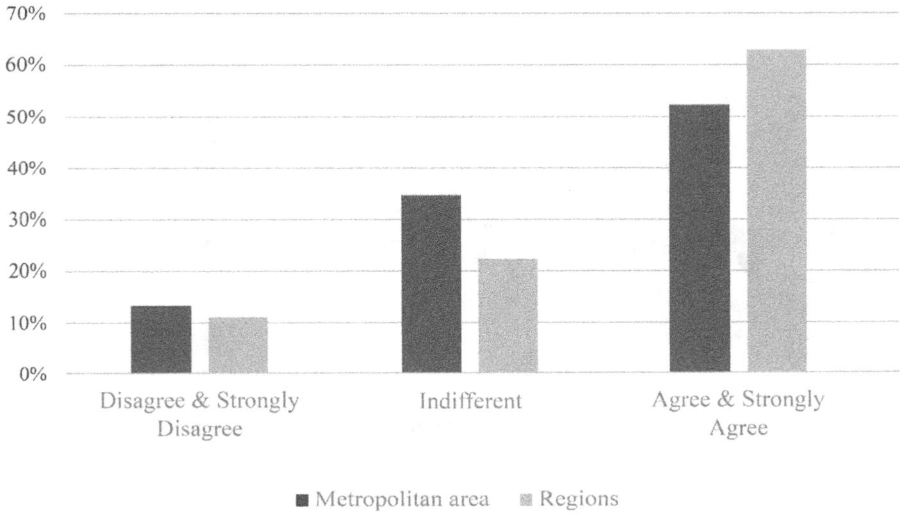

FIGURE 8.8 Importance of PTAs on gender equality.
Source: created by the authors based on the survey results.

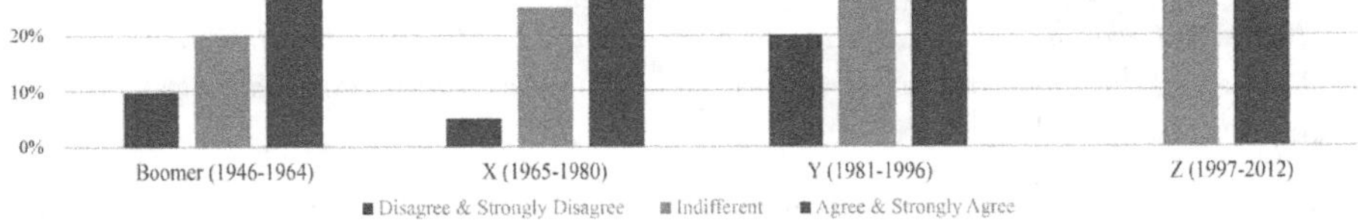

FIGURE 8.9 Perceptions on gender equality.
Source: Created by the authors based on the survey results and age range categories of Pew Research Center. Millennials 1981–1996, Z Generation 1997–2012, X Generation 1965–1980, Baby Boomers 1946–1964.[13]

(category Y) to agree less that PTAs have a positive impact on reducing gender gaps (Figure 8.9).

The interviewees mentioned that these differences in perception observed between generations are mainly due to specific life experiences. One interviewee shared the following explanation:

> *This is partly because the list of concerns is different for an older generation than it is for a younger generation. For example, the challenges related to the environment and climate change were not so dramatic a few years ago.* (Interviewee 2)

[13] For purposes of interpretation, we are cautious as the size of the samples is small.

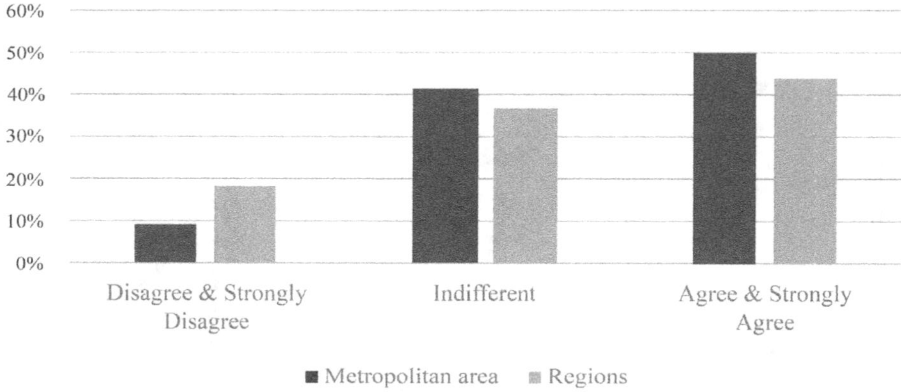

FIGURE 8.10 Importance of PTAs for the green economy by respondents' location.
Source: Created by the authors based on the survey results.

Moreover, some interviewees added that, although the millennial generation is, in comparison to other age groups, more critical in its views of free trade and international treaties, this does not mean that they want more protectionist measures to be applied. On the contrary, this is a generation that enjoys freedom of choice. It could be argued then that millennials' critiques are directed more at the standards used in international trade on issues such as the environment, gender, or labor rights than at trade itself. One interviewee stated the following:

> *Millennials are a generation that operates in a tremendously open and connected world. They are a very libertarian generation, with a position towards life in which they want freedom of expression and thought and are free to consume what they want. And even if they have critical views, that does not translate into formulas that amount to protectionism.* (Interviewee 3)

Green economy: The survey also focused on the relevance of the topic of green economy to be included in PTAs. Similar to gender provisions, more and more PTAs in Latin America include environmental provisions as documented in the chapter by Klotz and Ugarte (Chapter 6). Results of the survey show that most respondents considered this topic important (57 percent). When focusing on survey respondents' place of residence, we observe that outside the Metropolitan Region[14], the support for the statement that PTAs are significant for the green economy received less support. Also, 19 percent of people living outside the Metropolitan Region found no relevance in relation to the green economy (see Figure 8.10).

Looking more closely at the survey data on whether any generational difference exists in perceptions of the role of PTAs in matters related to the green economy, the results are mixed. As far as perception of the green economy is concerned, younger

[14] More than 40 percent of the population is concentrated in the Metropolitan Region.

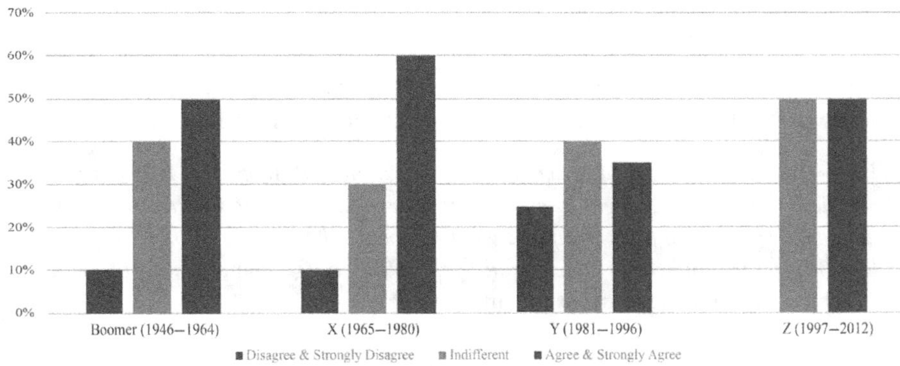

FIGURE 8.11 Perceptions on the green economy.
Source: Created by the authors based on the survey results and age range categories of Pew Research Center.

generations are more skeptical regarding the role that this type of agreement can play on this issue. As shown in Figure 8.11, a smaller percentage of both millennials (Generation Y) and Generation Z respondents agree that PTAs support the green economy. Older generations such as baby boomers and Generation X, meanwhile, tend to be more in agreement that PTAs have a positive relationship with the green economy.[15] This may be a result of the priority given to environmental issues, which have become an increasingly important part of people's lives over time.

8.4.2.3 Other Relevant Regional Results

The survey found a difference in perception between people from Chile's more urban regions and the Metropolitan Region. The experts pointed out that the difference may be due to the different role played by the regions compared to the Metropolitan Region in the production of the different goods that Chile exports. It is important to recall that the mining sector is highly concentrated in the north of the country, being close to 60 percent of the country's exports. And the south center regions are the main agricultural exporters, representing the second-most important commercial sector for Chile. One interviewee stated the following:

> *People from the Regions, not from Santiago or Metropolitan Region,*[16] *are much closer to their personal experience with export results. Because 80% of the goods that Chile exports come from the regions.* (Interviewee 1)

[15] According to Beresford Research, generations are groups of people born within the same fifteen- to twenty-year span. These are divided into four categories: Generation X is anyone born from 1965 to 1980. Baby boomers are anyone born from 1946 to 1964. Millennials are anyone born from 1981 to 1996. Generation Z is anyone born from 1997 to 2012. *Source*: www.beresfordresearch.com/age-range-by-generation/.

[16] Chile is divided into sixteen regions; the Metropolitan one concentrates 43 percent of the urban population.

People are more likely to benefit from exports, for example in terms of employment.

On the scope that PTAs should cover, opinions differed as well amongst interview partners. Some voices were particularly skeptical about issues beyond the core objective of trade liberalization as captured in the following statement:

> *PTAs are not an instrument of economic policy to solve all problems. ... I am a bit skeptical that PTAs can help to correct gender issues. The same applied to climate change. I would be in favor of alternative instruments; the fact is that those issues are lost among the hundreds of articles and chapters that a PTA contains ..., It is better to explore more ad hoc instruments.* (Interviewee 2)

8.4.2.4 Additional Insights from Interviews

In this final section, we briefly discuss additional views shared by interviewees that might deserve further exploration. First, regarding the increasing politicization of Chile's trade policy and the negotiation of PTAs, the interviewees did not consider this development negatively. There was no opposition to citizens and civil society showing more interest in trade policy as illustrated by the following statement:

> *Ideologization is not bad in itself, in the sense that it does not seem bad to me that an agreement becomes politicized when it is discussed. I understand that this gives it more content. ... We have even gained something from all that happened with the TPP—we have made people talk about issues that they had never talked about ... that is a positive side-effect."* (Interviewee 11)

Second, it was also stressed that information needs to be fact-driven and should lead to better knowledge. This aspect was also prominent in the media coverage, in which it was pointed out that the issues, being rather technical, were more difficult for the general population to understand, making it more likely that misinterpretations would occur, or fake news would spread. This was captured by the following statement:

> *There is a lot of ignorance about the content of the treaties, caricatures have been made about them that do not help the discussion much.* (Interviewee)

Third, while the TPP led to increased politicization, the content of TPP was not that novel as stated by one interview partner:

> *While the TPP is a complicated agreement with many technical chapters hard to understand for the public, the TPP in reality has the same content as found in many of the treaties that have been previously signed.* (Interviewee 3)

8.5 CONCLUSIONS

This chapter has shown that the past consensus view related to Chilean trade policy has undergone a change. However, contrary to our expectations, the views regarding

PTAs are not as negative as expected due to the social outbreak/unrest in 2019 and the politicization over TPP. It seems that many of the issues raised by the protesters were not necessarily related to the PTAs itself.

Our results from different data sources suggest that Chileans' elites and media seem to have reached a consensus that PTAs are necessary for economic growth. The perceptions of PTAs are still dominantly positive, whereas the media coverage has tended to become more negative. The chapter finds that not even the most critical voices related to PTAs seek to return to protectionist policies; rather they demand that PTAs become more inclusive and focused on achieving development objectives. Specifically, they show strong preferences for sovereignty, democracy, gender, and the environment. Clearly, further research is needed to better capture the degree of individuals' knowledge and understanding of PTA effects.

The results further suggest that the population from Chile's regions and older generations have a more positive perception of PTAs, mainly due to the importance of the exporting sector in rural areas. The results also show the older the individuals the more positive their assessment. This may be explained by their exposure to successful trade liberalization after the military regime. The criticism of younger generations needs to be interpreted as nuanced, as they don't oppose trade per se, but wish to see more attention paid to the environment, gender, or community rights, and the impact of trade on development. It also suggests, related to the trade policy literature, that older generations' attitudes reflect more egocentric and economic preferences, while younger generations are increasingly driven by sociotropic preferences.

Finally, this chapter calls for more research into public opinion and how it will affect the conduct of trade policy in Chile in the future. Will a more informed and engaged public demand changes for the future content of PTAs and treaty partners? How will policymakers engage with a more politicized trade policy environment? And finally, will PTAs remain a dominant instrument of shaping trade cooperation, or will new instruments arise?

REFERENCES

Agosin, M. 1993. "Beneficios y costos potenciales para Chile de los acuerdos de libre comercio," *Revista Estudios Públicos* 52: 101–126.

Baccini, L. 2019. "The Economics and Politics of Preferential Trade Agreements," *Annual Review of Political Science* 22: 75–92.

Bardin, L. 2002. *Análisis de contenido*. Madrid: Akal.

Bush, S. and L. Prather 2020. "Foreign Meddling and Mass Attitudes toward International Economic Engagement," *International Organization* 74(3): 584–609.

Cherry, J. 2018. "The Hydra Revisited: Expectations and Perceptions of the Impact of the EU-Korea Free Trade Agreement," *Asia Europe Journal* 16(1): 19–35.

De Bièvre, D. and A. Poletti 2020. "Towards Explaining Varying Degrees of Politicization of EU Trade Agreement Negotiations," *Politics and Governance* 8(1): 243–253.

De Bièvre, D., P. Garcia-Duran, L. J. Eliasson and O. Costa O. 2020. "Politicization of EU Trade Policy across Time and Space," *Politics and Governance* 8(1): 239–242.

Dellmuth, L. and J. Tallberg 2021. "Elite Communication and the Popular Legitimacy of International Organizations," *British Journal of Political Science* 51(3): 1292–1313.

Dellmuth, L., J. A. Scholte, J. Tallberg and S. Verhaegen 2022. "The Elite–Citizen Gap in International Organization Legitimacy," *American Political Science Review* 116(1): 283–300.

DiGiuseppe, M. and K.B. Kleinberg 2019. "Economics, Security, and Individual-Level Preferences for Trade Agreements," *International Interactions* 45(2): 289–315.

Dirección General de Relaciones Económicas Internacionales (DIRECON) 2009. *Chile 20 Años de Negociaciones Comerciales*. Santiago: Direcon.

Drope, J. and A. Chowdhury 2014. "Economic (In)Security and Gender Differences in Trade Policy Attitudes," William Davidson Institute Working Papers Series. https://ideas.repec.org/p/wdi/papers/2014-1067.html

Dür, A. and G. Mateo 2014. "Public Opinion and Interest Group Influence: How Citizen Groups Derailed the Anti-Counterfeiting Trade Agreement," *Journal of European Public Policy* 21(8): 1199–1217.

Dür, A., R. Huber, G. Mateo and G. Spilker 2023. "Interest Group Preferences towards Trade Agreements: Institutional Design Matters," *Interest Groups & Advocacy* 12(1): 48–72.

Ffrench-Davis, R. 2003. *Entre el neoliberalismo y el crecimiento con equidad. Tres décadas de políticas económicas en Chile*, 3ª edición. Santiago: JC Sáez Editor.

Frohmann, A. 1991. "Nuevas formas de concertación regional no institucionalizadas: Contadora y el Grupo de los Ocho," *Revista Mexicana de Política Exterior* 31: 22–38.

Gallegos Zúñiga, J. and R. Polanco Lazo 2013. "Evolución jurídica de la política comercial de Chile", *Revista de Derecho Universidad Finis Terrae* 1(2): 52–53.

Gheyle, N. and F. De Ville 2019. "Outside Lobbying and the Politicization of the Transatlantic Trade and Investment Partnership." In D. Dialer and M. Richter (Eds.), *Lobbying in the European Union: Strategies, Dynamics and Trends*. Berlin: Springer, pp. 339–354.

Grossman, G. M. and E. Helpman 2002. *Interest Groups and Trade Policy*. Princeton: Princeton University Press.

Hachette, D. 1993. "Estrategias de globalización del comercio," *Estudios Públicos* 51: 45–85.

2000 "La reforma comercial". In F. Larraín and R. Vergara (Eds.), *La transformación económica de Chile*. Santiago: Centro de Estudios Públicos, pp. 295–338.

Hainmueller, J. and M. J. Hiscox 2006. "Learning to Love Globalization: Education and Individual Attitudes toward International Trade," *International Organization* 60(2): 469–498.

Heine, J. 1991. *La reforma del Estado latinoamericano en los ochenta: Algunas reflexiones y proposiciones metodológicas*. CEPAL. https://hdl.handle.net/11362/33734.

Hiscox, M. J. 2001. "Through a Glass and Darkly: Attitudes toward International Trade and the Curious Effects of Issue Framing," *International Organization* 60(3): 755–780.

Irwin, D. 1995. "Industry or Class Cleavages over Trade Policy? Evidence from the British General Election of 1923," National Bureau of Economic Research. NBER Working Paper.

Jara, A. 2005. "Las virtudes de la promiscuidad: La apertura comercial de Chile." In A. Estevadeordal and T. Macau (Eds.), *Regionalismo global: Los dilemas para América Latina*. Barcelona: Fundació CIDOB, pp. 89–122.

Kuznetsov, I. 2015. *People's Perception of Free Trade and Economic Sophistication*. Louisiana State University (LSU) and Agricultural and Mechanical College. LSU Master's Theses 2574, https://repository.lsu.edu/gradschool_theses/2574.

Lagos, R. 2001. "Chile en un mundo en cambio," *Foreign Affairs en español* 1(1): 67–81.

López, D. and F. Muñoz 2018. "La inserción Económica Internacional de Chile y sus Desafíos. In: Chile mirando hacia su futuro. Cambios futuros por venir. *Revista de la Sociedad Suiza de Americanistas No 77 (2016–2017)*. https://www.sag-ssa.ch/bssa/pdf/LARevista_2016-2017_No77.pdf

2021. "Trade Finance Constraints as a Barrier for Chilean Services Internationalization," *Tec Empresarial* 15(1): 2–19.

Lopez, D. et al. 2022. *China's Trade Policy in Latin America: Puzzles, Transformations and Impacts*. Cham: Springer

Mansfield, E. and D. Mutz 2009. "Support for Free Trade: Self-Interest, Sociotropic Politics, and Out-Group Anxiety," *International Organization* 63(3): 425–457.

Mansfield, E., H. Milner and P. Rosendorff 2002. "Why Democracies Cooperate More: Electoral Control and International Trade Agreements," *International Organization* 56(3): 477–513.

Mansfield, E., D. Mutz and L. Silver 2015. "Men, Women, Trade, and Free Markets," *International Studies Quarterly* 59(2): 303–315.

Margalit, Y. 2012. "Lost in Globalization: International Economic Integration and the Sources of Popular Discontent," *International Studies Quarterly* 56(3): 484–500.

Mayda, A. and D. Rodrik 2005. "Why Are Some People (and Countries) More Protectionist than Others?," *European Economic Review* 49(6): 1393–1430.

Mayda, A. M., K. H. O'Rourke and S. Sinnott 2007. "Risk, Government, and Globalization: International Survey Evidence," NBER, Working Paper.

Minard, P. and M. Landriault 2015. "Internet Use, Voter Turnout, and Party Preference across Four Regime Types in East Asia," *Taiwan Journal of Democracy* 11(2): 75–108.

O'Rourke, K. H. and R. Sinnott 2001. "The Determinants of Individual Trade Policy Preferences: International Survey Evidence [with comments and discussion]", Brookings Trade Forum 2001, Brookings Institution Press. www.jstor.org/stable/25063160.

Porras, J. I. 2003. *La estrategia chilena de acuerdos comerciales: Un análisis político*. Serie Comercio Internacional 36, Comisión Económica para América Latina y el Caribe (CEPAL). https://hdl.handle.net/11362/4376.

Rogowski, R. 1989. *Commerce and Coalitions: How Trade Affects Domestic Political Alignments*. Princeton: Princeton University Press.

Rojas, F. and L.G. Solís 1993. "Entre la intervención y el olvido: Las relaciones entre Centroamérica y Estados Unidos," *Anuario de Estudios Centroamericanos* 19(1): 5–22.

Sáez, S. and J. G. Valdés 1999. "Chile y su política comercial 'lateral'," *Revista de la CEPAL* 67: 81–94. https://hdl.handle.net/11362/12169.

Scheve, K. and M. Slaughter 2001. "What Determines Individual Trade-Policy Preferences?" *Journal of International Economics* 54(2): 267–292.

Spilker, G., T. Bernauer and V. Umaña 2016. "Selecting Partner Countries for Preferential Trade Agreements: Experimental Evidence from Costa Rica, Nicaragua, and Vietnam, *International Studies Quarterly* 60(4): 706–718.

Tomassini, L. 1990. "La política internacional después del Muro," *Estudios Internacionales* 23(91): 281–338.

UNCTAD III 1973. Actas de la conferencia de las naciones unidas sobre comercio y desarrollo tercer período de sesiones Santiago de Chile, 13 de abril–21 de mayo de 1972 volumen I informe y anexos.

Van Klaveren, A. 1994. "Chile: La política exterior de la transición," *América Latina Internacional* 1(2): 47–64.

Velasco, A. and M. Tokman 1993. "Opciones para la política comercial chilena en los'90," *Estudios Públicos* 52: 53–99.

Walter, S. 2021. "The Backlash against Globalization," *Annual Review of Political Science* 24: 421–442.

Wehner, L. 2007. "Los TLC de Chile. Estrategias y tácticas de negociación," *Iberoamericana* (2001-) 7(28): 153–157.

Wilhelmy, M. and R. Durán 2003. "Los principales rasgos de la política exterior chilena entre 1973 y el 2000," *Revista de ciencia política* (Santiago) 23(2): 273–286.

Appendix

Questionnaire

What does a PTA mean?
What do you think are the reasons why the government decides to sign a PTA?
Do you believe that PTAs are important for the development of the country?
How important do you think trade with other countries is for Chile's development?
PTAs contribute to:

Reduce social inequalities
Improve environmental protection
Improve domestic industry
Improve the quality of domestic employment
Strengthen female labor participation
Encourage local innovation
Promote the participation of the regions in foreign trade
Facilitate foreign investment
Technology transfer
Diversify the export of products
Strengthen the export of services

How important is a PTA for the following reasons?

Goods trade
Services trade
Phytosanitary measures
Gender equality
SMEs participation
FDI promotion
Green economy
Digital commerce
Intellectual property

9

Chile's PTA Services Impact Assessment Looking beyond Trade Flows

Women's Employment Participation

Felipe Muñoz and Javiera Cáceres

9.1 INTRODUCTION

Preferential trade agreements (PTAs) are usually viewed as policy devices that can help increase trade flows between countries and promote economic growth and development. In recent decades, however, a progressive expansion of PTAs has been witnessed, both in the number of economies that participate, and in the topics they address and the depth of obligations that are agreed upon (Mansfield and Pevehouse 2013; Chacha and Nussipov 2022). From originally mostly trade-only treaties, PTAs have become complex instruments that address aspects of trade liberalization and a variety of non-trade issues, many of which can impact domestic regulations (Limão 2007; Lechner 2016; Milewicz et al. 2018; Lake and Krishna 2019).

Including provisions related to trade in services is a good reflection of these agreements' evolution (Marchetti and Roy 2008; Roy 2014). Due to their characteristics and modes of international trade supply, service agreements contain provisions that consolidate market access and nondiscriminatory regulations concerning foreign competitors and domestic suppliers (Francois and Hoekman 2010; López and Muñoz 2016). Service provisions are different from those for trade in goods in that they typically affect regulations of a domestic nature that act as a barrier to trade. To date, the nature and drafting of these provisions and the lack of disaggregated trade data have made it difficult to assess their impact (Francois and Hoekman, 2010). Moreover, it has been recognized that reforms driven by PTAs may go beyond those governing international trade flows, for which impact assessments should not be limited to bilateral exchanges of goods.

At the same time, there is an increasing awareness of the differentiated impact of trade policy and PTAs on men and women (Brussevich 2018; World Bank and WTO 2020; Cáceres et al. 2021). Economies have an inherently "gendered structure," making it important to assess economic policies' impact on gender inequality (Ridgeway and Correll 2004; Ridgeway 2011; Rai 2018; Momsen 2019). Specifically, while some economic policies may contribute to reducing gender disparities and enhancing women's economic autonomy, others may have a negative impact, increasing the gaps between different population groups, such as men and women (Cáceres and Muñoz 2023a).

This chapter looks at the case of Chile to analyze the impact of the inclusion of service provisions in PTAs on the gendered structure of the economy. Chile is characterized by both an open economy based on a dense PTA network and deep gender inequalities. Chile has further been recognized as a small open economy whose economic development strategy was based on the integration of international trade, with an active policy toward the use of PTAs, including service provisions (López and Muñoz 2015, 2020; López et al. 2020). Over the years, Chile has built one of the largest PTA networks worldwide, which in 2022 reached thirty-three agreements with sixty-five economies, covering developed and developing economies in the Americas, Europe, Asia, and Oceania, which represented 67 percent of the world population and 88 percent of the global gross domestic product (GDP) (SUBREI 2022). At the same time, the country faces substantial disparities between men and women, with inequalities that range from unequal participation in labor markets and wages earned from these activities to the uneven allocation of housework and gender differences in time use (De Paula 2018; Fuentes and Vergara 2018).

The chapter's objective is to assess the impact of the inclusion of trade in service provisions on the participation of women in the labor force, particularly within the services sector. In the case of Chile, women tend to have more robust involvement in tertiary activities (services) rather than primary (mining, forestry, aquaculture) or secondary (mainly mining processed goods). Following previous studies that have linked trade in services and gender (Sauvé 2020; Johannesson and Nordås 2021), this chapter works with the hypothesis that the inclusion of solid service provisions within PTA may enhance the development of this sector and should, in turn, have a positive impact for women's employment. For this reason, a more substantial effect of PTA on women's employment rather than men's should be observed, which should help reduce the gender gaps in this sector.

To address these conjectures, the chapter builds on two streams of literature. On the one hand, it engages with scholarship that focuses on the drafting and inclusion of service provisions in trade agreements. On the other hand, it speaks to research on the gendered impact of trade agreements, particularly in women's employment. The chapter is structured as follows. The first section reviews the literature regarding the economy as a gendered structure, its implication for trade policy, particularly for trade in services, and how Chile has included this topic in its PTAs. The second section presents some stylized facts on the evolution of women's participation in the Chilean economy. In the third section, the methodological framework of analysis is discussed. The fourth section presents and discusses the chapter's key results, which is that the inclusion of solid service provisions in PTAs could enhance the development of this sector and positively impact women's employment. The results from the estimations suggest that the inclusion of deep service provisions in Chilean PTAs positively impacted women's employment, particularly in the services sector. For men, the results showed a negative or nonsignificant effect. Finally, when analyzing the impact of these provisions on gender gaps, it shows that these agreements have contributed to reducing gender gaps in the workforce.

9.2 GENDERED IMPACT OF TRADE POLICY

9.2.1 *Gender and Trade*

While traditional theories of international and development economics do not directly address the existence of a gender-differentiated impact of economic and trade policies, it has become increasingly relevant to assess how these policies affect men and women differently. The "gender neutral" approach toward economics has been increasingly challenged (Elson 1993; Benería 1995). New theoretical and policy works highlight that human interactions are embedded in social contexts, dominated by norms and preconceptions leading to gender-based regimes. In this sense, there are social constructs related to gender, which foster segregation of jobs, division of labor, and differences in social positions in authority, among others (Ridgeway and Correll 2004).

The first challenges to traditional economic theories came from liberal feminist approaches toward international development, in which authors' stated that the marginalized position of women in the economy could be explained due to their lower pay compared to men (Boserup 1970). Along these lines, they argued that including gender equality would reinforce the development processes, empowering the different stakeholders in the economy (Buvinic 1976; Tinker and Bramsen 1976; Rogers 2005). As a gendered structure in the economy is recognized, heterodox approaches, such as basic needs theory, human capability theory, and ecofeminism theory, have also incorporated gender differences as a critical element in understanding socio-economic relationships. These theories have generated increased attention to the power relations within households and how this can affect labor issues, including women's decision to participate in the workforce as well as the nature of that participation (Calasanti and Bailey 1991; Davies and Carrier 1999; Rai 2018).

For example, analyzing labor issues regarding the basic needs[1] approach often overlooks family power relations. However, human capability theory offers a comprehensive approach that includes legal, political, and human rights (Nussbaum

[1] The basic need approach to development was framed in the 1970s and 1980s, aiming to prioritize fulfilling the basic needs of all the people within development policies and international cooperation actions (Hoadley 1981; Stewart 1985; Streeten 1979).

and Sen 1993; Sen 2001). The latter approach challenges the traditional view of the family, in which there is a common understanding and even distribution of tasks and activities. It highlights the impact of gender relations on women's participation in the workforce. Ecofeminist theory takes this a step further in the context of sustainable development and advocates for an interdependent, anti-patriarchal model (Dreze and Sen 1990; Lahar 1991; Arriagada 2002; Elias and Roberts 2018; Rai 2018). Theories on women and gender in development increasingly influence current economic perspectives. Gender equality is now a central topic, with an increasing focus on gender mainstreaming as the strategy to achieve it (Cáceres and Muñoz 2023b).

The underlying idea of gender approaches is that the economy functions as a "gendered structure" where both market and non-market activities impact its development (Ridgeway and Correll 2004; Ridgeway 2011; Rai 2018; Momsen 2019). Der Boghossian (2019) emphasizes that women experience unequal pay, underrepresentation, and barriers such as limited access to formal loans. The normative construction and division of responsibilities between men and women result in a division of paid and unpaid tasks that give way to an unequal distribution of resources and rewards in the economy. The context in which social relations are inscribed forms gender relations, conditioning the division of labor, differences within economic activities, and social authority, among others (Ridgeway and Correll 2004).

Likewise, it is essential to recognize that the differences in women's access to resources – productive, financial, technology, and information – limits their ability to take advantage of gains from international trade and the possibility of expanding participation in domestic and international markets. In this way, understanding how social context affects gender relations permits the establishment of frameworks to empower women to benefit from the changes caused by international trade. This understanding will enable the formulation of public policies that promote the positive effects of international trade, strengthen women's economic autonomy, and reduce existing gender inequalities (Bezanson and Luxton 2006; Rai and Waylen 2014). Therefore, promoting gender equality by increasing women's participation in the economy is a common theme and strategy discussed by world leaders and development agencies.

International trade affects women and men differently depending on their economic positions as workers, traders, producers, consumers, etc. The roles assigned to women and men impact their economic autonomy, empowerment, and well-being. At the same time, various studies show that gender inequality affects the performance and competitiveness of economies (Juhn et al. 2014; Audi and Ali 2017; UNCTAD 2017; Bøler et al. 2018; Kis-Katos et al. 2018; Nasser de Carvalho 2020; Sauvé 2020). In this context, international trade has proven instrumental in promoting faster, sustainable economic development, as long as policymakers acknowledge the complex relationship between trade and gender and incorporate the necessary policies to guarantee even participation and distributional benefits. Gender-responsive trade policies can ultimately open new opportunities for women as employees and entrepreneurs (UNCTAD 2020).

In recent years, there has been increased attention to the gendered impact of trade policies (Keating 2004; Gibb 2008; Frohmann 2017), as well as increased interest in the inclusion of gender-sensitive provisions within trade agreements (Zarrill 2017; Bahri 2019, 2020; Cáceres et al. 2021; Laperle-Forget 2022). Although the literature on the links between gender inequalities and trade is not conclusive, it has been determined that increasing the participation of women in economic activities can help reduce poverty and increase their income levels. This is because women's participation leads to higher levels of economic activity and economic autonomy (Novta and Wong 2017; WTO 2017b; CEPAL 2021). The literature has begun to analyze the impacts of trade policies on gender gaps, paying particular attention to their impact on poverty, wage differences, and feminized economic sectors (Çagatay 2001; Fontana 2009). In particular, it is recognized that high levels of gender inequality are associated with countries with less commercial intensity and diversification (Kazandjian et al. 2019). Using data on employment and wages, various authors have studied how trade liberalization can reduce the gap in employment participation, or wages, between men and women by strengthening sectors that are intensive in female labor or by expanding demand for work in the economy (Berik et al. 2004; Arndt et al. 2006; Villalobos and Grossman 2008; Menon and Van der Meulen Rodgers 2009).

In the 1990s, PTAs began progressively incorporating gender-related provisions through general provisions, specific chapters, and gender mainstreaming. The first references to the relationship between gender and trade in PTAs can be found in the instruments linked to labor issues and eliminating discrimination between men and women in workplaces and equal pay (Monteiro 2018). The first chapter on trade and gender contained in a PTA – worldwide – was included in the Free Trade Agreement (FTA) between Chile and Uruguay in 2017. From here, the literature has focused on the analysis of the incorporation of gender in other preferential agreements and regional integration processes (López and Muñoz 2018; López et al. 2019; Cáceres et al. 2021).[2]

The year 2017 also marked a turning point in incorporating gender issues in the World Trade Organization (WTO). In December, at the 11th WTO Ministerial Conference held in Buenos Aires, Argentina, 118 members and observers supported the Buenos Aires Declaration on women and trade to eliminate obstacles to women's economic empowerment (WTO 2017a). The declaration is based on the

[2] For a further discussion on South America's approach toward the inclusion of gender provisions within preferential trade agreements, see the chapter by Amrita Bahri, "Making Trade Agreements Work for Women: What's Behind the South American Approach?" (Bahri, Chapter 4). This chapter reviews which other regions include gender-related commitments in their trade agreements, and how South America has emerged as a frontrunner in drafting trade agreements with various kinds of gender commitments.

gender and trade chapters contained in Chile's agreements with Uruguay and Canada. It follows what is expressed in goal 5 of the Sustainable Development Goals (SDGs) and the United Nations Convention on the Elimination of All Forms of Discrimination Against Women. Although the incorporation of the gender perspective has been slow at the multilateral level, mainly due to the complexity of reaching consensus, notable advances have been seen at a preferential level in the past decade.

9.2.2 *Gender and Trade in Services*

There is consensus that services have contributed to economic development as inputs to other productive activities and end-user consumption (Cali et al. 2008; Francois and Hoekman 2010; UNCTAD 2010). Therefore, they have become integral to trade policymaking, particularly negotiating PTAs. Trade in services faces barriers that differ from trade in goods (Borchert et al. 2013; Benz and Jaax 2022). Specifically, because services are intangible, they do not need to cross borders physically, nor are they observable before purchase or physically storable, and their production and consumption typically occur in the same location. Thus, barriers to trade in services differ from those to goods, as they are not typically imposed on the border but rather at the domestic level. For this reason, services-related provisions do not have the same structure or impact as provisions for goods (Hoekman 2006; Francois and Hoekman 2010). Because of this, service commitments in international agreements do not involve tariff reductions but aim to consolidate countries' policies and regulations vis-à-vis services.

Nevertheless, these agreements anchor openness and provide clear frameworks for developing the services sector for the benefit of domestic and foreign providers of services. In recent years, following the increasing mainstreaming of a gender perspective within trade policy, the literature has analyzed how trade in services impacts men and women differentially. Sauvé (2020) points out that services could become a source of inclusive growth, particularly when looking into the skills and job positions that women may hold. A robust services sector could enhance women's participation in the workforce. Using data from India, Johannesson and Nordås (2021) found that services sectors had lower wage gaps than those related to manufacturing. Furthermore, expanding services trade reduces wage gaps, contributing to more inclusive economic growth and development.

In the past decades, Chile has built an extensive network of PTAs to guarantee market access for its main export products and expand and diversify its export basket (López and Muñoz 2015; Albertoni et al. 2022). Within this strategy, services have been identified as a sector where the country could specialize, moving away from primary commodities linked to mineral extraction and agriculture. For this purpose, Chile has included services as a pillar of its trade negotiation mandates. While some commitments were made during the Uruguay Round in the context of the General

Agreement on Trade in Services (GATS), Chile was not an active participant in multilateral service negotiations. Instead, the inclusion of services as an important issue within the negotiation mandates of Chilean trade agreements began in the mid-1990s when the country was pursuing its failed incorporation into the North American Free Trade Association (NAFTA). This process led to the first negotiations for a comprehensive FTA with Canada and Mexico, including topics beyond market access for goods, such as services, intellectual property, and investment (Muñozet al. 2021). By December 2022, out of thirty-three agreements signed by Chile, twenty-three include service provisions (SUBREI 2022).

Some common characteristics can be described when looking into the services-related content of Chilean PTAs. First, Chile has included these provisions in dedicated chapters on cross-border services. They have been complemented by specific chapters for sectors and topics such as telecommunications, financial services, transport services, movement of natural persons, and e-commerce. Mode 3 (commercial presence) is covered by chapters dedicated to investment.[3] While all chapters follow the same structure and include standard provisions and definitions, the main difference is using positive or negative list approaches (Muñoz et al. 2021). When comparing Chilean agreements to others using data from the design of trade agreements (DESTA) project (Dür et al. 2014), Chilean PTAs stand out regarding their degree of commitment and levels of liberalization. The country's PTAs contain the main elements that characterize deep services integration, including references to GATS, national treatment and most favored nation provisions, sectorial provisions, and a relatively low number of excluded sectors.

It is recognized that an important element regarding service provisions in trade agreements is that beyond the additional liberalization achieved through these instruments, they bound economies' existing policies (Findlay et al. 2005; Hoekman and Mattoo 2013), which signal economies trajectories and reinforce reforms that may have been adopted unilaterally. Moreover, the agreements following negative list approaches tend to liberalize all service trade except sensitive areas, including specific sectors or modes of provisions (especially Mode 4).[4] Chile made significant efforts to liberalize its services sector starting in the early 2000s. The openness of Chile's services sector was mainly bound in the first agreements signed during the early 2000s, particularly in the FTA with the United States. Since the subscription of this agreement in 2003, Chile has used it as a template for upcoming negotiations, following its structure and trade liberalization commitments, being

[3] During the Uruguay Round, to establish a classification of services, the document W120 was produced, which recognized four modes of services: Mode 1: cross-border provision, Mode 2: consumption abroad, Mode 3: commercial presence, and Mode 4: presence of natural persons. Mode 3 corresponds to providing a service through commercial presence in the territory of any other country.

[4] Mode 4: The presence of natural persons corresponds to the provision of a service through the presence of natural persons in the territory of any other country.

recognized as a landmark concerning services liberalization. While some liberalization has been achieved in the latter agreements, we should not expect a huge effect at the margin with each additional PTA. However, the net effect of all these PTAs is potentially quite profound. Finally, while the objective to diversify the Chilean export basket has not achieved the expected results (López et al. 2020; López and Muñoz 2020; Prieto et al. 2011), it is believed that the inclusion of service provisions within trade agreements may have helped to foster the participation of women in the economy, as men could have moved toward other economic activities and the expansion of domestic services.

9.3 FEMALE LABOR PARTICIPATION IN CHILE: STYLIZED FACTS

While the previous section reviewed the incorporation of service provisions within Chilean PTAs, this section presents some stylized facts regarding the participation of women in the Chilean workforce. This section mainly investigates the involvement of women in the services sector and the evolution of the participation gender gaps in the country. Data from other Latin American countries are included as a comparative basis of analysis. The studied period comprises thirty-two years, from 1990 until 2021, covering all democratic governments following the military dictatorship in Chile and the period in which most preferential trade liberalization took place (López and Muñoz 2015).

Despite decades of sustained economic growth and poverty reduction, Chile has been described as an unequal country in terms of income and wealth (Contreras 2003; Contreras and Ffrench-Davis 2012; Mieres Brevis 2020). The roots of inequality in the country may be explained by factors such as income disparities, uneven capital accumulation, educational gaps, social networks, and access to social services and infrastructure, amongst others (Núñez and Tartakowsky 2011; Contreras et al. 2019; Flores et al. 2020; Gutiérrez and Muñoz 2022). Furthermore, this inequality affects indigenous populations and women most, particularly when reviewing income disparities (Agostini et al. 2010; Gammage et al. 2014; Rodríguez 2017). One cause of this difference may be explained by the uneven participation of women in the formal workforce (Undurraga 2011; Ipsen 2022).

As shown in Figure 9.1, Chile's female workforce participation is one of the lowest in the world (Contreras and Plaza 2007; Rau 2010). Since 1990, men's participation in the labor force has stayed at over 70 percent, except during the COVID-19 crisis, which dropped to 65 percent in 2021. On the contrary, women's participation has never surpassed the 50 percent threshold. In the early 1990s, women's participation in the labor force was only 31 percent, slowly increasing to 37 percent by the end of that decade. The commodity boom of the 2000s created rapid growth in the women's labor force (Ocampo 2008), which grew over 10 percent in a decade, reaching maximum participation of 49.5 percent in 2019, just before the COVID-19 pandemic. As social and economic activity

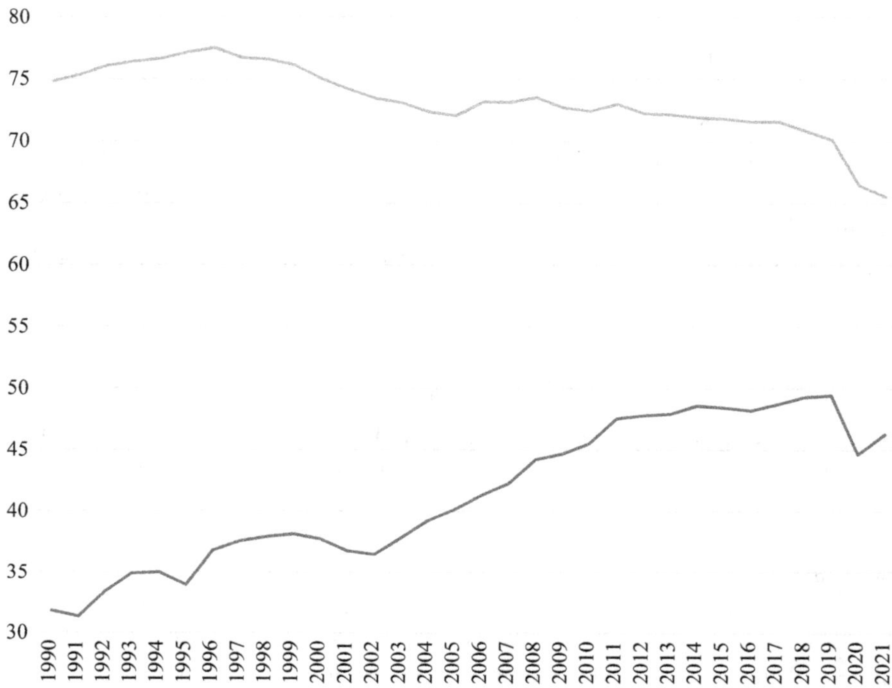

FIGURE 9.1 Women's and men's participation in the Chilean labor force (ILO estimates). 1990–2021.
Source: Authors' elaboration based on World Bank (2022).

restrictions were enacted to control the COVID-19 pandemic, these policies profoundly impacted labor participation.

This impact was uneven between genders (Arteaga-Aguirre et al. 2021; Velasco 2021). While men's participation in the labor force dropped by four percentage points, representing a 5.7 percent reduction, for women participation decreased by five percentage points, representing a 10 percent overall reduction. Hence, both the absolute and relative impact of the COVID-19 pandemic on men's and women's work participation was stronger for women than men, increasing the gaps between both groups.

Participation of women in the workforce in Chile is among the lowest in Latin America. As shown in Figure 9.2, in 1990, Chilean women's participation in the workforce was the second lowest (31.2 percent), only topped by Ecuador (28,1 percent), but a total fifteen percentage points lower than El Salvador, which had the highest participation rate (49.6 percent). In thirty-two years, between 1990 and 2021, women's participation grew in all Latin American economies. In the case of Chile, women's participation rate rose to 46.7 percent but still ranks among the lowest in the region. For example, Brazil's rose from 44 percent to 64.7 percent,

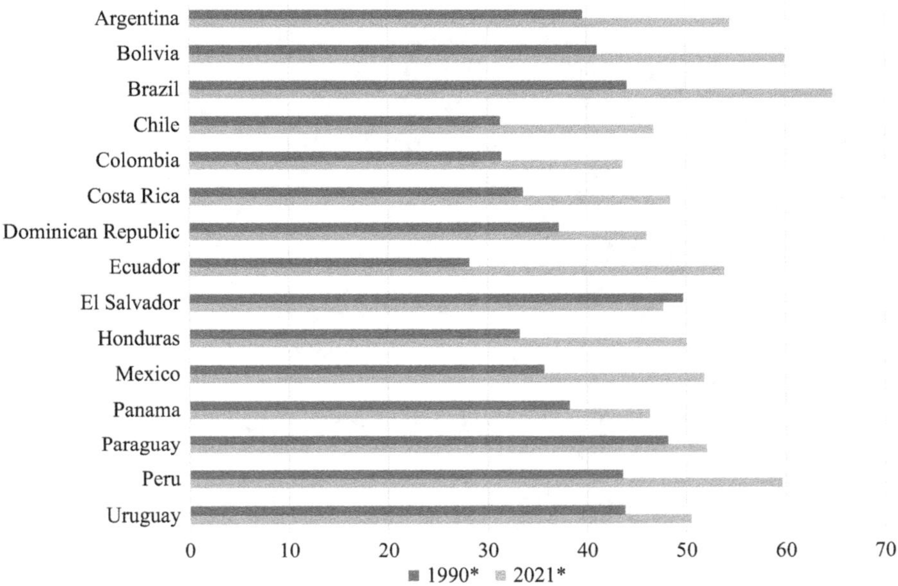

FIGURE 9.2 Women's participation in the workforce. Selected Latin American economies (ILO estimates). 1990/2021*
Source: Authors' elaboration based on World Bank (2022).
Note: *Data for Bolivia, Dominic Republic, El Salvador, Honduras, and Uruguay correspond to 2020.

currently making it the region's highest. During this period many countries – including Brazil, Bolivia, Peru, Argentina, Ecuador, Paraguay, Mexico, Uruguay, and Honduras – passed the 50 percent threshold. Chile and countries such as Colombia, Panama, and the Dominican Republic still have participation rates of less than 50 percent. Nevertheless, it must be stated that the figures reflect the impact of the COVID-19 crisis, which reduced women's participation in the workforce throughout the region. However, this does not change that Chile still has a gap in women's participation vis-à-vis other Latin American economies.

Concerning the participation of women in the services sector, Figure 9.3 shows that most women in the workforce in Chile, approximately 85.1 percent in 2019, are employed in the services sector. This information reflects the gendered structure of the overall economy, as most women are expected to engage in domestic and care activities and, therefore, do not participate prominently in industrial activities. Their participation in agricultural activities is mainly linked with subsistence and familiar agriculture or informal activities such as harvesting during spring and summer.

Although the increased participation of women in the Chilean workforce has reduced the gender gap in the labor force in the Chilean labor market, the gap continues to be among the highest in the Latin American region. As shown in Figure 9.4, the total workforce gender gap (the rate of men participating in the labor

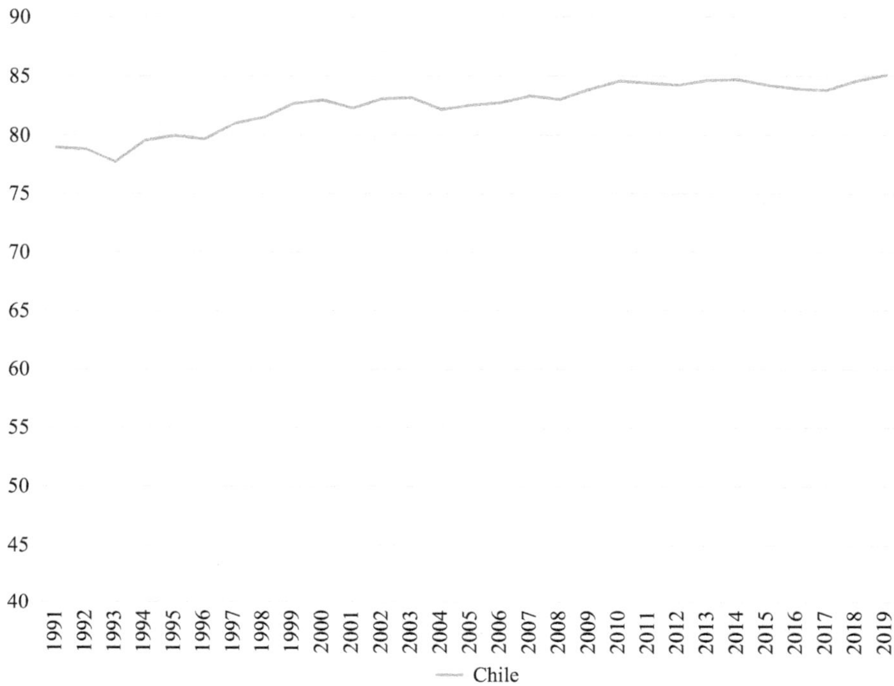

FIGURE 9.3 Women's participation in the services sector, as a share of total women's employment. Chile. 1991–2019.
Source: Authors' elaboration based on World Bank (2022).

market compared to women) has decreased from over 40 percent in the first years of the 1990s to almost 20 percent by the end of 2021. Within the services sector, there was a ten-point gender gap at the beginning of the 1990s, but parity was achieved in the early 2010s. Since then, the gap has fluctuated within two points for men and women, which reflects normal year-to-year variations.

9.4 THEORETICAL ASSUMPTIONS AND HYPOTHESIS

The theoretical assumption that expanded trade in services may increase women's labor participation is grounded in the understanding of the unique characteristics of the service sector and its alignment with the existing skill sets and employment preferences of women. Traditionally, the service industry has been considered more inclusive and flexible, often offering part-time, remote, or flexible working arrangements that appeal to women who may juggle work with family responsibilities (Steiger and Wardell 1995; Leschke 2015; Stichter 2016). As global trade in services grows, driven by technological advancements and the increasing digitization of many service roles, new opportunities arise for women to engage in the workforce

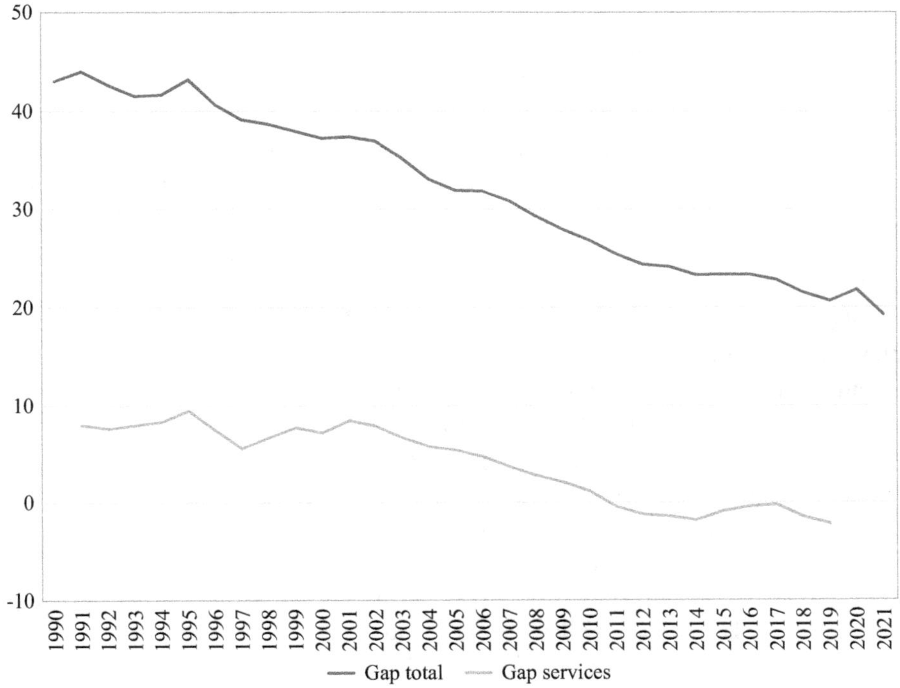

FIGURE 9.4 Gaps in women's and men's labor participation (total and services). 1990–2021.
Source: Authors' elaboration based on World Bank (2022).

(Krieger-Boden and Sorgner 2018; Larsson and Viitaoja 2019; Charles et al. 2022). One of the main characteristics of services and digital trade is that this expansion may not be limited by geographical boundaries (as it happens for goods), allowing women to participate in the global economy from their local environments. The growth in service trade could potentially lead to a higher demand for new skills, resulting in increased employment opportunities for women. This alternative, in turn, can contribute to greater economic independence and empowerment for women, further promoting gender equality in the workforce (Foley and Cooper 2021; Parmer 2021). However, it is important to note that this positive outcome is contingent on supportive policies and frameworks that ensure fair employment practices and address any gender biases in the workplace.

Moreover, trade agreements that specifically encompass services can significantly influence the job market by creating new opportunities and setting the standards for labor practices. Including services-related provisions within these agreements may lead to a surge in demand for service-oriented jobs, many of which align closely with the sectors where women traditionally have a stronger presence or competitive advantage. For instance, women have historically played a dominant role in sectors like healthcare and education. The liberalization of these services through trade agreements can lead to a proliferation of jobs in these sectors, potentially increasing employment opportunities for women.

PTAs can also include provisions directly addressing gender-related issues (Bahri 2019; López et al. 2019; Cáceres and Muñoz 2023b). These might involve encouraging gender equality in the workplace, promoting women's entrepreneurship, and ensuring equitable treatment in employment. This approach can create an enabling environment that increases women's participation in the labor force and enhances their status within it. However, it is crucial to recognize that the positive impacts of trade agreements on women's labor participation are not automatic. They depend significantly on how these agreements are structured and implemented. A conscious effort must be made to ensure these agreements are inclusive and consider the unique challenges and barriers women face in the workforce. This effort includes addressing wage gaps, supporting skill development, and ensuring access to necessary resources and technology. With thoughtful implementation, trade agreements that include services have the potential to be a powerful tool in promoting gender equality and empowering women economically.

From here, this chapter aims to understand the impact of PTAs on women's labor participation, particularly those with service provisions. Using Chile as a case study, due to its long-lasting trade policy openness and relatively low female participation in the workforce, the following working hypotheses are stated:

H1: The subscription of PTAs with deep service commitments might increase women's labor force participation in Chile.

H2: The subscription of PTAs with deep service commitments might reduce the gender gap in labor force participation in Chile.

9.5 METHODOLOGICAL APPROACH AND DATASET

Having outlined the theoretical basis of our research and reviewed the main trends of women's participation in Chile's labor market, this section briefly presents our methodological approach. Following the literature (Sauré and Zoabi 2014; Gaddis and Pieters 2017; Rocha and Winkler, 2019), the chapter proposes the following model specification to capture the impact of including deep services commitments in Chilean PTAs on female labor participation and workforce gender gaps:

$$y_{k,t} = \delta_k + \alpha t + \beta T_{k,t} + X'_{kt}\gamma + u_{k,t} \qquad (9.1)$$

where k indicates country and t periods (years). The dependent variable $y_{k,t}$ is set to describe female labor participation or gender gaps in the workforce. The model specification presented in equation (9.1) proposes both trade ($\beta T_{k,t}$) and country-specific x ($X'_{kt}\gamma$) control variables. Two parameters of interest are included as explanatory variables: a dummy variable to capture the existence of a PTA covering deep service provisions (D_ser), taking value 1 for those countries having PTA with deep service provisions in force in year *t*, and an interaction variable identifying those provisions for the case of Chile (I_ser_cl), so to have a differentiated effect for this country. These variables are constructed from revising PTAs using existing coding datasets and the authors' analysis and classification of commitments (Dür et al. 2014; Muñoz et al. 2021). Hence, it is said that a PTA includes deep services provisions if the commitments covered by the agreement include references to GATS, national treatment and most favored nation provisions, sectorial provisions, and a relatively low number of excluded sectors. The latter variable intends to capture the impact of these provisions on Chilean labor force participation to correctly assess the effect on women's involvement in the country.

Therefore, equation (1) can be restated as follows:

$$y_{k,t} = \alpha_t + \beta LnGDP_{k,t} + \beta ser_{va_{k,t}} + \beta ser_{exp_{k,t}} + \beta D_{ser_{k,t}} + \beta I_{ser}cl_{k,t} + u_{k,t} \qquad (9.2)$$

where $y_{k,t}$ represents the dependent variable, for which six specifications have been selected and constructed using information from the World Bank and the International Labor Organization statistical datasets. First, the ratio of women's labor participation (wom_par) and participation in the services sector (wom_par_s) are included. Both indicators were chosen due to gendered structures; women tend to participate more actively in the services sector. Second, to test whether there are differentiated impacts between men and women, the same indicators for men are included (men_par and men_par_s, respectively). Finally, differential participation indicators are included to observe gaps between men and women in the workforce and the services sector (gap and gap_ser, respectively). In addition to the chapter's parameters of interest, as control variables, equation (9.2) includes the natural logarithm of the country's k GDP in year t ($LnGDP_{k,t}$), the share of services in their gross domestic value added ($ser_{va_{k,t}}$), and the value of export services ($ser_{exp_{k,t}}$) extracted from the World Bank's World Development Indicators dataset.

Having set the model to be estimated, to test the chapter's hypotheses, a panel dataset comprising seventeen countries in Latin America was built for the period 1990 to 2021. The sample selection was based on an ad hoc selection of control countries that matched with observable and unobservable similarities to the country under study, Chile. Economic and export structures, economic cycles, and women's participation in economic activity were the most important factors. From here, it is shown that Latin American economies have faced similar economic development processes (Hofman 2000; Bértola and Ocampo 2012), and particularly those in South America have similar trade patterns, with a high dependency on the export of natural resources, including mineral and agriculturally based commodities (Cypher 2010; Svampa 2013; Giraudo 2020). Following the crisis in the decade of 1980s, various countries in the region have followed an active integration process, including the signing of PTAs with regional and overseas partners (Agosin and

Ffrench-Davis 1993; Choksi et al. 2019; Cornick et al. 2020). Finally, while Chile has a lower share of female participation in the region's labor force, Latin America's countries share substantial gender inequalities, including access to the formal labor market (Costa et al. 2009; Alonso 2020).

9.6 RESULTS AND DISCUSSIONS

A generalized least square regression was used to estimate the value of the coefficients associated with the control parameters, considering the nature of the data. Table 9.1 shows the results for the six specifications of the dependent variable. The first model uses women's participation in the workforce as a dependent variable, aiming to understand how services PTAs may impact the participation of women in the various economic activities of the countries. First, we may point out that, while positive as expected, coefficients associated with GDP and services exports are not statistically significant. This result presents some challenges in its interpretation, as it would be expected that a higher economic activity could be linked to an increased participation of women in the workforce. A possible explanation for this may be the

TABLE 9.1 *Results Generalized Least Squares (GLS) regression.*

Dep. var.	Women part.	Women part. in services	Men part.	Men part. in services	Gap labor part.	Gap services part.
Natural logarithm GDP	1.13 (0.23)	0.98 (0.160)	0.759 (0.142)	3.179*** (0.000)	−1.33 (0.182)	1.313** (0.040)
Service value added	−0.18*** (0.004)	−0.25 (0.60)	−0.17*** (0.000)	0.07** (0.021)	0.004 (0.935)	0.113** (0.012)
Services exports	0.90 (0.228)	1.28** (0.02)	0.524 (-0.069)	0.278 (0.471)	−0.619 (0.376)	−0.751 (0.145)
Dummy services	−0.36 (0.649)	−0.98* (0.09)	0.037 (0.905)	−0.225 (0.568)	0.483 (0.508)	0.673 (0.221)
Interaction dummy services Chile	0.10** (0.041)	0.07** (0.047)	−0.034* (0.078)	-0.020 (0.421)	−0.142*** (0.002)	−0.94*** (0.007)
Trend	0.29*** (0.000)	0.31*** (0.000)	−0.197*** (0.000)	0.052* (0.068)	−0.438*** (0.000)	−0.251*** (0.000)
R^2	0.1264	0.3570	0.029	0.3716	0.2893	0.2163
Obs.	537	537	537	537	537	537
Groups	17	17	17	17	17	17

Note: Standard deviation in parenthesis. * 10 percent significance; ** 5 percent significance; *** 1 percent significance.

selected pool of countries (i.e., Latin American economies), in which for relatively smaller economies, women tend to have higher participation in employment due to being the sole contributor to their households, and many times in informal activities which are not well registered.

On the other hand, the coefficient associated with the share of services in the economy's value added is negative and statistically significant. This result may be counterintuitive, as a higher share of services in the economy would imply a higher use of labor, and normally the service economy is a sector in which women have relatively higher participation. When one looks into the parameters of interest, it is noted that the dummy variable associated with agreements with strong service provisions is negative and non-statistically significant. This parameter would imply that lower participation of women in the workforce would be expected for those economies subscribing to a PTA with service provisions. Nevertheless, as shown, the hypothesis that the parameter's value is zero cannot be rejected. Moreover, when looking specifically into the case of Chile, the main case study of this chapter, the value of the parameter associated with the country's interaction term with services PTA shows a positive and statistically significant relationship. Hence, the data suggest that the subscription of PTAs with strong service provisions for Chile has positively impacted women's participation in the workforce. This result reinforces the chapter's first working hypothesis, as the inclusion of service provisions in PTA would increase the participation of women in the workforce, as shown for Chile. This could be explained by the expansion of tradable sectors' activity and the overall economic growth associated with these agreements, which have implicated an increase in the demand for productive factors, including labor.

The second model specification uses the participation of women in the services sector as a dependent variable, as the inclusion of deep service provisions in PTA should positively impact the development of this sector in signatory countries and, therefore, expand the participation of women in this market. The estimation shows that GDP (positive coefficient) and the share of services in the economy (negative coefficient) are not statistically significant. Nevertheless, the export of services is positive and statistically significant, with an associated coefficient of 1.28, meaning that an increase in 1 percent of services exports would be associated with a 1.28-point increase in women's participation in the services sector. This result is interesting, as it may show a link between the development of a more robust export services sector and the increased participation of women in this sector's workforce. The interpretation of the coefficients associated with the variables of interest shows that, while the inclusion of service provisions would be linked with lower participation of women in the services sector for other countries, this would be the opposite for Chile. The service dummy's result suggested that including deep service provisions in PTA would reinforce this sector and, therefore, increase demand for productive factors, including women's labor. This alternative is suggested for Chile's case. On the one hand, these results can be explained by the fact that the sample may present in terms of economic output and the subscription of PTAs, as the smaller economies in the sample have subscribed to PTAs. In contrast, countries such as Argentina or Brazil – the biggest economies in the sample – have not engaged in these agreements. Besides, the econometric specification could be over-representing lagged results. An AR(1) model is estimated below to overcome the second hypothesis.

The third and fourth models replicate the previous analysis, using men's participation in the labor market and the services sector, respectively. For the participation of men in the labor market, results are equivalent to those for women, except for the interaction term for Chilean PTAs, which is negative and statistically significant. This result, while counterintuitive, can be explained due to the high participation rate of men in the economy before signing these agreements. In the 1990s, Chile's economy grew by double digits, expanding the demand for various productive factors, including labor. In the decade of the 2000s, while the expansion of GDP continued, it was also accompanied by an increase in tertiary education enrollment and women's participation. These factors may explain a relative drop in men from the workforce.

Nevertheless, it must be stated that the share of men participating in the workforce continues to be higher than that of women, for which this decrease associated with the subscription of PTA may not be interpreted as an overall decrease in work participation but a relatively smaller increase for women. Finally, the fifth and sixth models are particularly interesting, as they reflect the changes in gender gaps in labor market participation. For both models, the coefficient associated with Chile's subscription of PTAs with deep service provisions (Interaction dummy services Chile) shows a negative and significant value. These values, representing a reduction in the gap between men and women, reaffirm the hypothesis that these agreements have been functional in reducing gender disparities as they expand women's participation in the workforce, both in general and in the services sector.

The presence of an autoregressive model can be one of the main problems with econometric estimations based on panel data. This may be the case when the model's past values predict future values, which can be stated for various economic variables – particularly those related to labor markets – as there are a series of determinants that do not allow for a quick change or that have little or no variation in their values (including the existence of contracts and inertia). As seen in Table 9.1, the Trend parameter is statistically significant for all specifications, suggesting an autoregressive model is present. For this reason, the equation (9.2) is rerun using a GLS with an autoregressive process, AR(1), in which the value of the actual observation is based on the immediate past one. Results of this second estimate are presented in Table 9.2 for the six specifications of the dependent variable. Overall, it can be stated that no significant changes are observed between both specifications, as most coefficients have values and statistical significance similar to the previous equations. The main difference in women's participation in

TABLE 9.2 *Results GLS regression with AR(1) disturbances.*

Dep. var.	Women part.	Women part. in services	Men part.	Men part. in services	Gap labor part.	Gap services part.
Natural logarithm GDP	0.617 (0.564)	0.630 (0.454)	−2.758*** (0.000)	3.733*** (0.000)	−1.919 (0.092)*	1.412** (0.045)
Service value added	−0.149* (0.077)	0.025 (0.699)	−0.139*** (0.000)	0.176*** (0.003)	−0.036 (0.651)	0.052 (0.390)
Services exports	3.528*** (0.000)	3.950*** (0.000)	2.151*** (0.000)	1.537*** (0.006)	−4.193*** (0.000)	−2.446*** (0.000)
Dummy services	0.807 (0.403)	0.521 (0.490)	−0.593 (0.103)	0.387 (0.553)	−1.378 (0.128)	−0.742 (0.292)
Interaction dummy services Chile	0.126* (0.067)	0.117** (0.031)	−0.067* (0.079)	0.042 (0.422)	−0.196*** (0.002)	−0.126** (0.014)
R^2	0.3153	0.3153	0.0137	0.4929	0.4808	0.2387
Obs.	537	537	537	537	537	537
Groups	17	17	17	17	17	17

Note: St. dev. in parenthesis. * 10 percent significance; ** 5 percent significance; *** 1 percent significance.

the labor force is that the coefficient associated with services exports is positive and highly significant under the new specification. The coefficient of interest, Interaction dummy services Chile, continues to be positive and statistically significant, reinforcing the hypothesis that these agreements promote women's participation in the Chilean labor market. Similar conclusions can be drawn regarding women's participation in the services sector, with the positive and high significance of the parameters associated with services exports and Chilean PTAs.

When one looks into men's participation, the main conclusion is that service exports positively impact men's participation, and the inclusion of deep service provisions in trade agreements has a negative effect on men's workforce participation and is nonsignificant for the services sector. More notable results are found when analyzing gender gaps in labor participation. On the one hand, services exports have a largely negative and significant coefficient for the total labor and services sector. This result would reinforce the idea that the higher the export of services, the lower the gender gaps in the labor market would be observed, as higher demand for productive resources would lead to a more egalitarian participation of men and women in the economy. The same conclusion can be drawn for a parameter associated with Chilean PTAs with deep service provisions, as both specifications show a negative and statistically significant coefficient. Overall, the results support the chapter's hypotheses, as the coefficients associated with Chilean PTAs positively impact women's participation and negatively impact gender gaps. Therefore, it could be concluded that these agreements foster the development of the services sector, enhance the participation of women, and help reduce gender disparities.

9.6.1 *Robustness Checks*

Two alternative methodologies are presented below to check the robustness of the previously shown results. First, to eliminate possible unobservable country-fixed effects that may impact the estimations, the first differences of the variables were taken, such that the model presented in equation (9.2) can be rewritten as:

$$\Delta y_{k,t} = \alpha_t + \beta \Delta LnGDP_{k,s} + \beta \Delta ser_{va_{k,s}} + \beta \Delta ser_{exp_{k,s}} + \beta D_{ser_{k,t}} + \beta I_{ser} cl_{k,t} \qquad (9.3)$$

where the subscript s denotes the change within periods $t - t - 1$; results for this alternative specification are shown in Table 9.3 for the variable of interest (Interaction dummy services Chile). While not all parameters are reported, it can be stated that, except for the coefficient associated with participation in the services sector gap, all results are statistically significant. When looking at women's participation in the workforce and the services sector, the existence of PTAs with deep service provisions is associated with a substantial increase in women's labor participation in Chile. While this is not looking directly into economic growth, these findings may support the hypothesis that these agreements foster economic development, as they show that they may increase women's participation in the workforce. Particularly in a country such as Chile, where men's participation in the workforce was already high before the signing of these agreements, the potential to grow in the services economy is mainly related to creating opportunities for women to occupy jobs in the services sector.

In contrast, the results given in Table 9.3 show that the existence of PTAs with deep service sector provisions is associated with a reduction in men's labor force.

TABLE 9.3 *Results difference-in-differences regression.*

	Women part.	Women part. in services	Men part.	Men part. in services	Gap labor part.	Gap services part.
Interaction dummy services Chile (1 vs 0)	3.534*** (0.950)	2.706** (0.997)	−0.922* (0.510)	−1.972** (0.790)	−1.189** (0.503)	−0.455 (0.285)

Note: St. dev. in parenthesis. * 10 percent significance; ** 5 percent significance; *** 1 percent significance; ATET estimate adjusted for covariates, panel effects, and time effects.

This result may be counterintuitive, as agreements should increase labor participation. To account for this phenomenon, two explanations are presented. First, during the 1990s, the Chilean economy was overheating, for which the labor market in the 2000s was adjusting, increasing the share of the population acceding to formal tertiary education instead of joining the workforce after high school. Second, the increasing participation of women in the economy, particularly in the services sectors, has begun to level the field. While there is still a profound participation gap in the overall workforce, this has been reduced in the services sector. These explanations are consistent with the results of the final two specifications, in which signing PTAs with deep service provisions reduces the overall gap in labor markets. In contrast, this effect is statistically nonsignificant for the services sector, as the gap between men and women is lower in this sector. Nevertheless, the services sector comprises various activities, and it may be pointed out that women are still mainly employed in domestic, reproductive, and care jobs. For this, a detailed analysis of the subsectors in which men and women are employed within the services sectors could bring additional light to reducing gender gaps in the economy.

A second method used as a robustness check for this chapter is a synthetic control method (SCM). The SCM is proposed as an alternative method to estimate the impact of the independent variable on the dependent variable. This method relies on constructing a synthetic control of the outcome variable to compare pretreatment and aftertreatment results (Abadie et al. 2010; Billmeier and Nannicini 2013; López et al. 2022). Based on the database built for the estimations, a synthetic Chile was constructed from countries that have not signed PTAs with strong service provisions. As for determining the treatment year, the Chile–United States agreement has been identified as a milestone for its structure, extent, and policy implications. Therefore, the year 2003 is used as a threshold. Figure 9.5 presents the results for the SCM for the six specifications of the dependent variable. The first two graphs (Figures 9.5a and 9.5b) show the results for women's participation in the workforce and women's participation in the workforce of the services sector. The SCM is inconclusive regarding the difference between the treated and non-treated units in these two scenarios. In both cases, a positive trend can be observed throughout the studied period, including the decrease caused by the COVID-19 pandemic at the end of the series. While this result does not suggest a significant impact of PTAs, it is still positive and does not rule out previous conclusions.

Moreover, from an examination of the following graphs (Figures 9.5c and 9.5d), it can be stated that for men's participation, there is indeed a negative impact on their labor participation, as suggested by previous methods. The values in the *y*-axis are scaled for each graph, for which the reduction of men's participation oscillates between 65 percent and 80 percent, while for women, it was between 30 percent and 50 percent. This result is relevant because, for men, it can be stated that full occupation has been achieved. Not all men over fifteen years old are expected to be actively part of the workforce, as some may still be studying, retired, or taking care of

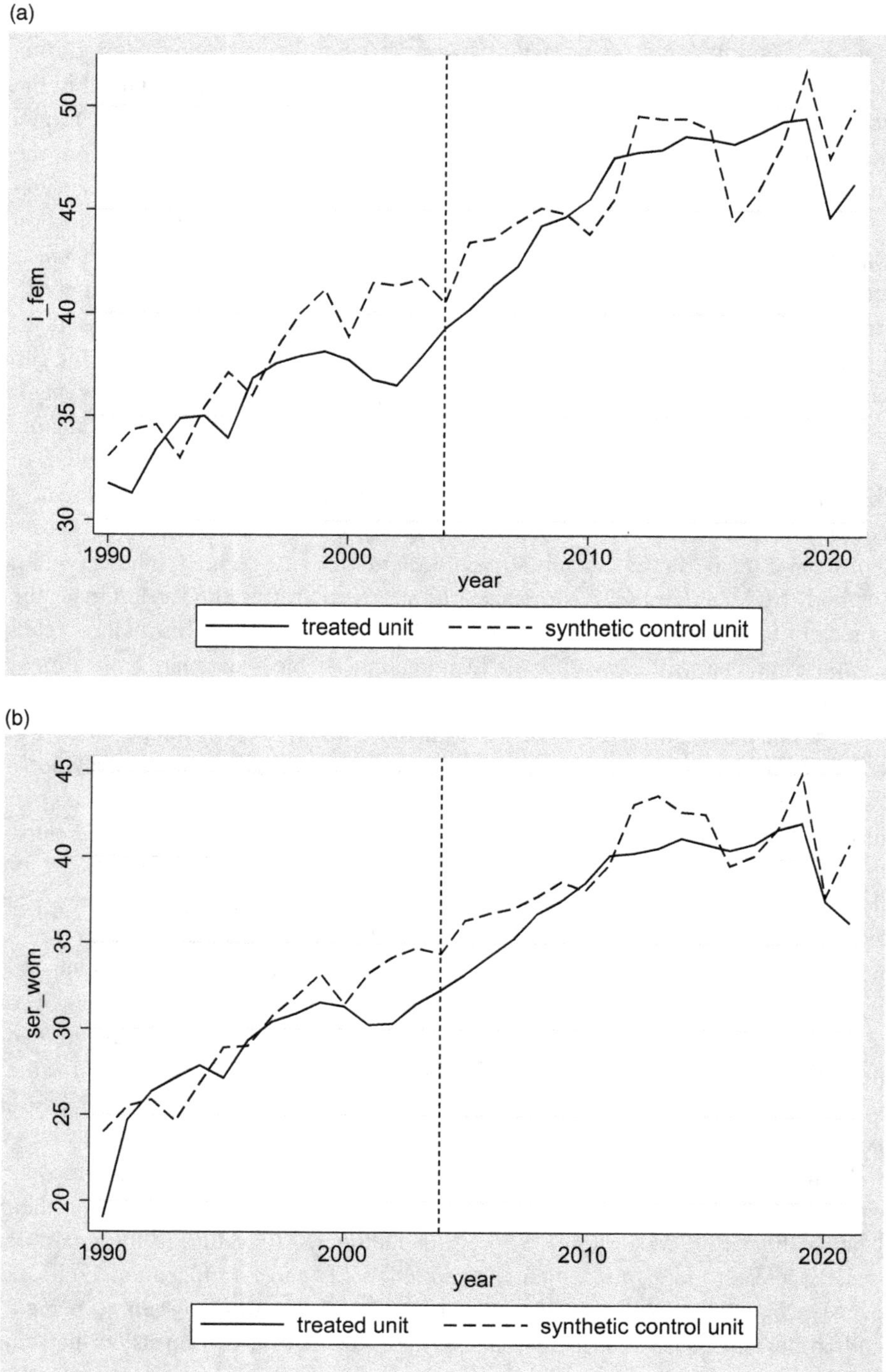

FIGURE 9.5 Synthetic control method results. (a) Women's labor participation, (b) women services' sector participation. (c) men's labor participation, (d) men services'

(c)

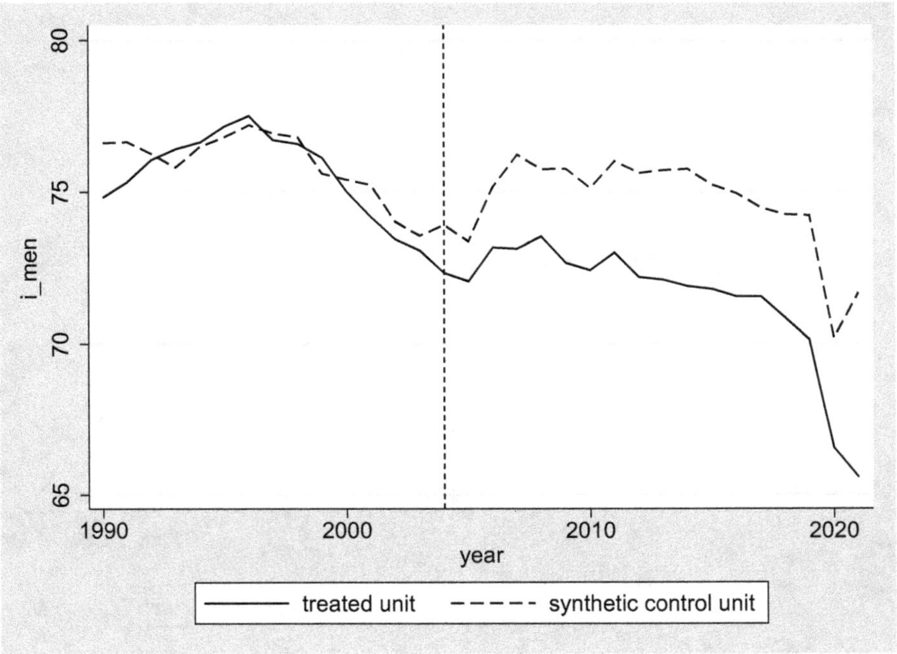

(d)

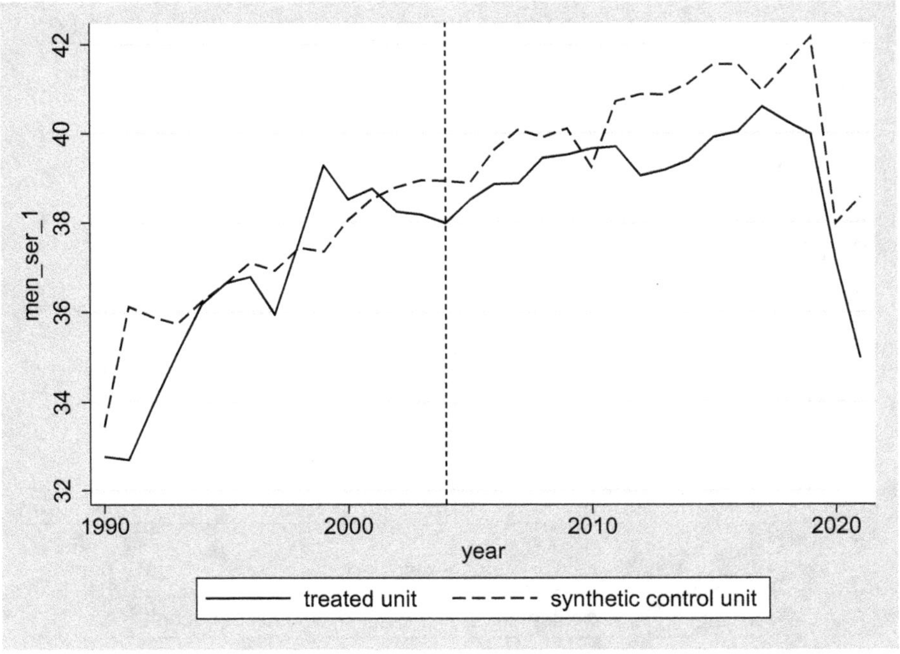

FIGURE 9.5 (*cont.*) sector participation, (e) gender gap in labor participation and (f) gender gap services' sector participation.
Source: Authors' estimations.

(e)

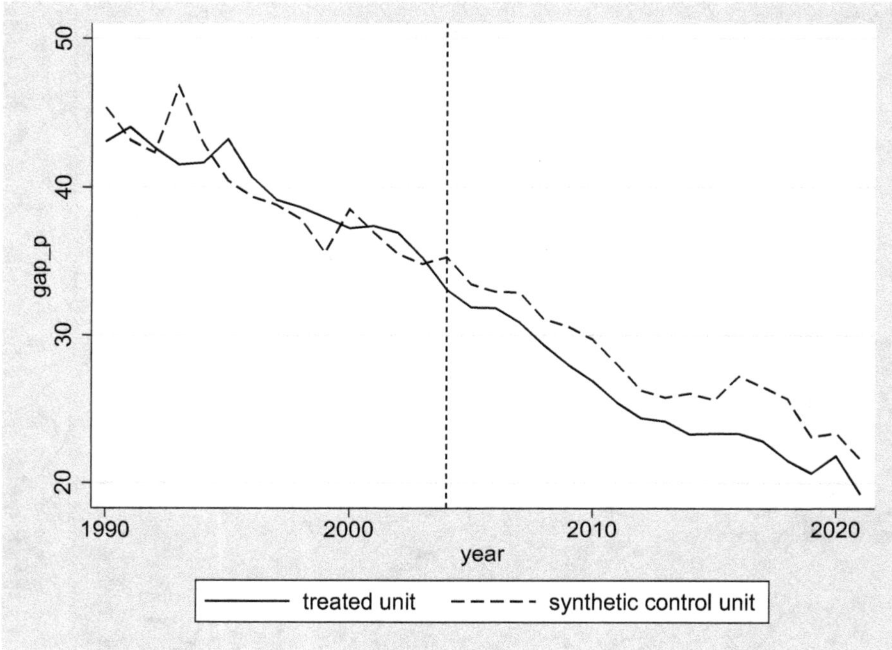

(f)

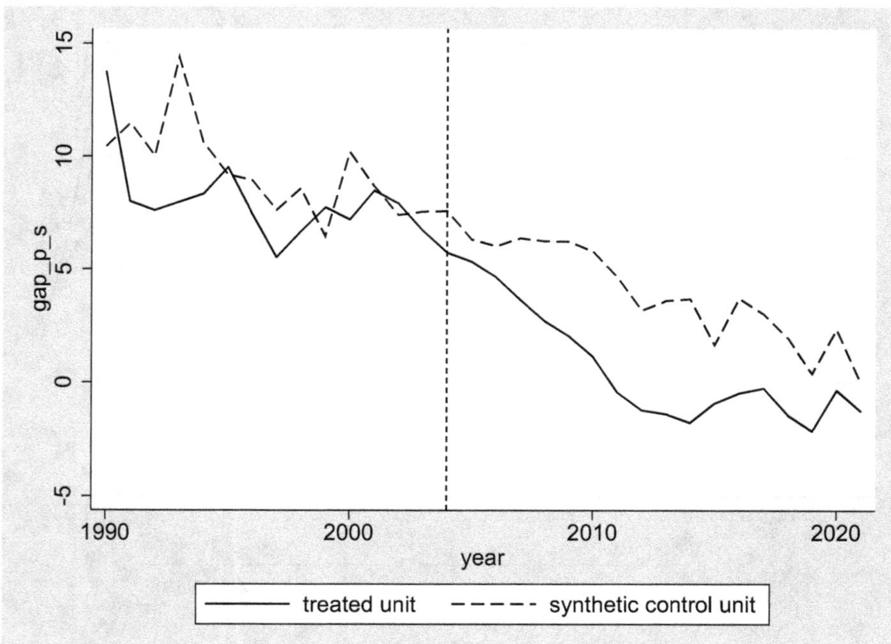

FIGURE 9.5 *(cont.)*

domestic activities. The most interesting results are found in the specifications looking into gaps in the workforce.

Figures 9.5e and 9.5f show that the treated unit values are lower for overall labor and services sector participation. These values reinforce the hypothesis that PTAs with strong service provisions have positively impacted the reduction of gender gaps by fostering this sector and, through it, the participation of women in the economy. Furthermore, this effect can be understood as both the growth of women's participation and the relative reduction of men's participation. Both effects imply a decrease in the gender gap in Chilean labor markets.

9.7 FINAL REMARKS

The uneven distribution of wealth and income between men and women is one of the main challenges of current economic policymaking. This is a long-lasting problem developed and developing economies pursuing sustainable development objectives face. To overcome this situation, understanding the economy as a gendered structure becomes a valuable tool to study the causes of inequalities and how different policies, amongst them trade policies, impact gender disparities.

The purpose of this chapter was to analyze how the inclusion of service provisions in PTAs affects the gendered structure of the economy in Chile. The working hypotheses that guided the research were that the inclusion of solid service provisions in PTAs might enhance the development of this sector and positively impact women's employment. Hence, a more substantial impact of PTAs on women's employment than on men's should be encountered, which should help reduce the gender gaps in this sector. The estimations' results suggest that including deep service provisions in Chilean PTAs positively impacted women's employment, particularly in the services sector. For men, the results showed a negative or nonsignificant effect. Finally, when analyzing the impact of these provisions on gender gaps, it shows that these agreements have contributed to reducing gender gaps in the workforce.

These results reinforce the idea that strengthening the services sector allows for a relatively higher expansion of women's employment compared to men, reducing gender gaps. Before signing the agreements, men in Chile already showed high labor participation, so there was less potential or scope for an increase in occupation. Therefore, women can benefit the most from the economic expansion resulting from trade agreements. This increased participation is the first step toward a more gender-balanced economy. It shows that trade policy can become instrumental in reducing gender gaps.

In a broader sense, the results reinforce the thesis that their impact beyond trade flows should be considered when analyzing PTAs. Following Dür et al. (2014), the design of these agreements extends into matters beyond trade, including the institutional organization of the economy in areas such as labor, environment, and competition policy. Therefore, a careful examination of their results in those issues should be considered, especially when governments' objectives go far beyond the expansion of trade flows, and in which these flows are an instrument for promoting inclusive and sustainable development.

Nevertheless, it must be stated that the results of this chapter looked at aggregate data, for which new avenues of research need to be explored. First, even though female labor force participation increased in Chile, this does not mean that the gendered structure of economic activity has been completely dismantled. While women's participation in the workforce increased, this participation is primarily within the services sector. We do not know if these jobs are concentrated around jobs linked to reproductive and care activities, which might reinforce traditional gender norms. Moreover, the services sector comprises high-value-added activities requiring specialized jobs and low-value-added activities in which employment is focused on low-skill positions. Therefore, increased participation in the services sector, per se, does not necessarily imply a better economic position. Second, the results only reflect workforce participation but not the remuneration of this participation.

Gender gaps are not reduced to participation but also wages and working conditions. Even though a more significant number of women participate in formal jobs, this does not necessarily imply that the salaries are similar, for which huge gaps could still be observed. Third, other related issues, such as domestic and unpaid work, are not considered within current statistics. Evidence suggests that women sacrifice their time in the workforce, as they still take care of most domestic and unpaid household activities. This situation leads to an uneven distribution of unpaid tasks and the prevalence of gender differences in time spent in remunerated and unpaid activities. So, while this chapter provides insights into the effects of trade agreements and service provisions on women's labor participation, much more research is needed to understand the causes and consequences of gender disparities.

The chapter also opens new avenues for future research on how trade agreement design and implementation may become instrumental in achieving gender equity objectives. First, while the chapter looked into agreements with service provisions, it was stated that new PTAs are increasingly including gender-related provisions, either in general terms, as part of existing chapters, or even as new chapters in the agreements.[5] Hence, it may be necessary to understand if service chapters and service-related provisions may also benefit from a gender perspective and, if so, how existing commitments should be modified to meet gender equity objectives. Second, the chapter benefits from the case of Chile, which may be considered an outlier in terms of its trade policy. Therefore, new analysis covering other economies facing different challenges concerning their trade policies and gender structures may contribute to a better understanding of the relationship between trade policy,

[5] For a further discussion, see Bahri (Chapter 4).

services, and gender equity. Third, in times of economic and political turmoil, getting to know the impacts of trade agreements beyond trade flows may allow us to extend the discussion on these international instruments. Moreover, it is likely that if PTAs are linked with the consecution of other objectives such as sustainability, environment protection, or gender equity, the general population may positively perceive them.

REFERENCES

Abadie, A., A. Diamond and J. Hainmueller 2010. "Synthetic Control Methods for Comparative Case Studies: Estimating the Effect of California's Tobacco Control Program," *Journal of the American Statistical Association* 105(490): 493–505.

Agosin, M. and R. Ffrench-Davis 1993. "La liberalización comercial en América Latina," *Revista de la CEPAL* 50: 41–62.

Agostini, C., P. Brown and A. Roman 2010. "Poverty and Inequality among Ethnic Groups in Chile," *World Development* 38(7): 1036–1046.

Albertoni, N., D. López, M. Montt, F. Muñoz and A. Rebolledo 2022. "The Not-So-Boring Political Economy of Trade Policy in Chile." In J. Cornick, J. Frieden, M. Mesquitao and E. Stein (Eds.), *Political Economy of Trade Policy in Latin America*. Washington: IADB, pp. 107–138.

Alonso, R. C. 2020. "Las desigualdades de género en el centro de la solución a la pandemia de la COVID-19 y sus crisis en América Latina y el Caribe," *Análisis Carolina* 2020(20): 1–14.

Arndt, C., S. Robinson and F. Tarp 2006. "Trade Reform and Gender in Mozambique," *Nordic Journal of Political Economy* 32: 73–89.

Arriagada, I. 2002. "Cambios y desigualdad en las familias latinoamericanas," *ECLAC Review* 77: 143–161.

Arteaga-Aguirre, C., V. Cabezas-Cartagena and F. Ramírez-Cid 2021. "Mujeres, teletrabajo y estrategias de cuidados en el contexto de pandemia en Chile," *Revista* CS(35): 11–39.

Audi, M. and A. Ali 2017. "Gender Gap and Trade Liberalization: An Analysis of Some Selected SAARC Countries," MPRA Paper 83485.

Bahri, A. 2019. "Measuring the Gender-Responsiveness of Free Trade Agreements: Using a Self-Evaluation Maturity Framework," *Global Trade Customs Journal* 14(11/12): 517–527.

Bahri, A. 2020. "Women at the Frontline of COVID-19: Can Gender Mainstreaming in Free Trade Agreements Help?" *Journal of International Economic Law* 23(3): 563–582.

Benería, L. 1995. "Toward a Greater Integration of Gender in Economics," *World Development* 23(11): 1839–1850.

Benz, S. and A. Jaax 2022. "The Costs of Regulatory Barriers to Trade in Services: New Estimates of Ad Valorem Tariff Equivalents," *Economics Letters* 212: 1–3.

Berik, G., Y. van der Meulen and J. Zveglich 2004. "International Trade and Gender Wage Discrimination: Evidence from East Asia," *Review of Development Economics* 8(2): 237–254.

Bértola, L. and J. A. Ocampo 2012. *The Economic Development of Latin America since Independence*. Oxford: Oxford University Press.

Bezanson, K. and M. Luxton 2006. *Social Reproduction: Feminist Political Economy Challenges Neo-liberalism*: Montreal: McGill-Queen's Press-MQUP.

Billmeier, A. and T. Nannicini 2013. "Assessing Economic Liberalization Episodes: A Synthetic Control Approach," *Review of Economics Statistics* 95(3): 983–1001.

Bøler, E. A., B. Javorcik and K. H. Ulltveit-Moe 2018. "Working across Time Zones: Exporters and the Gender Wage Gap," *Journal of International Economics* 111: 122–133.

Borchert, I., B. Gootiiz and A. Mattoo 2013. "Policy Barriers to International Trade in Services: Evidence from a New Database," *The World Bank Economic Review* 28(1): 162–188.

Boserup, E. 1970. *Women's Role in Economic Development*. New York: St. Martin's Press.

Brussevich, M. 2018. "Does Trade Liberalization Narrow the Gender Wage Gap? The Role of Sectoral Mobility," *European Economic Review* 109: 305–333.

Buvinic, M. 1976. *Women and World Development: An Annotated Bibliography*. London: Overseas Development Council.

Cáceres, J. and F. Muñoz 2023a. "The Gendered Impact of COVID-19 Crisis in Latin America." In P. Baisotti and P. Moscuzza (Eds.), *Reframing Globalization After COVID-19. Pandemic Diplomacy amid the Failure of Multilateral Cooperation*. Sussex: Sussex Academic Press, pp. 66–96.

Cáceres, J. and F. Muñoz 2023b. "South America's Leadership in Gender Mainstreaming in Trade Agreements." In A. Bahri, J.-Y. Remy and D. López (Eds.), *Trade Policy and Gender Equality*. Cambridge: Cambridge University Press, pp. 267–291.

Cáceres, J., F. Muñoz, B. Alarcón, L. Chávez, M. Fierro, L. Guzmán, … T. Rogaler 2021. "Propuestas para la incorproación de disposiciones de género en el Protocólo adicional de la Alianza del Pacífico," *Integración y Comercio* 25: 47–75.

Çagatay, N. 2001. *Trade, Gender and Poverty*: New York: UNDP.

Calasanti, T. M. and C. A. Bailey 1991. "Gender Inequality and the Division of Household Labor in the United States and Sweden: A Socialist-Feminist Approach," *Social Problems* 38(1): 34–53.

Cali, M., K. Elis and D. Willem 2008. "The Contribution of Services to Development and the Role of Trade Liberalisation and Regulation," Overseas Development Institute Working Paper 298.

CEPAL 2021. *Perspectivas del comercio internacional de América Latina y el Caribe. La integración regional es clave para la recuperación tras la crisis*. Santiago: CEPAL.

Chacha, M. and A. Nussipov 2022. "The Breadth–Depth Trade-Off and Varieties of Preferential Trade Agreements," *Journal of Common Market Studies* 60(3): 821–844.

Charles, L., S. Xia and A. P. Coutts 2022. "Digitalization and Employment," *International Labour Organization Review* 1–53.

Choksi, A. M., M. Michaely and D. Papageorgiou 2019. "The Design of Successful Trade Liberalization Policies." In A. Köves and P. Marer (Eds.), *Foreign Economic Liberalization. Transformations In Socialist And Market Economies*. London: Routledge, pp. 37–56.

Contreras, D. 2003. "Poverty and Inequality in a Rapid Growth Economy: Chile 1990–1996," *Journal of Development Studies* 39(3): 181–200.

Contreras, D. and R. Ffrench-Davis 2012. "Policy Regimes, Inequality, Poverty and Growth: The Chilean Experience, 1973–2010," WIDER Working Paper.

Contreras, D. and G. Plaza 2007. *Participación laboral femenina en Chile. ¿Cuánto importan los factores culturales?*. Series Documentos de Trabajo, No. 235 Universidad de Chile.

Contreras, D., G. Otero, J. Díaz and N. Suárez 2019. "Inequality in Social Capital in Chile: Assessing the Importance of Network Size and Contacts' Occupational Prestige on Status Attainment," *Social Networks* 58: 59–77.

Cornick, J., J. Frieden, M. Mesquita Moreira and E. H. Stein 2020. *Political Economy of Trade Policy in Latin America*. Washington: IADB.

Costa, J., E. Silva and F. Vaz 2009. "The Role of Gender Inequalities in Explaining Income Growth, Poverty and Inequality: Evidence from Latin American Countries," Working Paper 52, International Policy Centre for Inclusive Growth.

Cypher, J. M. 2010. "South America's Commodities Boom: Developmental Opportunity or Path Dependent Reversion?" *Canadian Journal of Development Studies/Revue canadienne d'études du développement* 30(3–4): 635–662.

Davies, L. and P. J. Carrier 1999. "The Importance of Power Relations for the Division of Household Labour," *Canadian Journal of Sociology/Cahiers canadiens de sociologie* 24(1): 35–51.

De Paula, C. 2018. *Gender Gaps in Chile: An Overview*. Washington: The World Bank.

Der Boghossian, A. 2019. "Trade Policies Supporting Women's Economic Empowerment: Trends in WTO Members," WTO Staff Working Paper ERSD-2019-07.

Dreze, J. and A. Sen 1990. *Hunger and Public Action*. New York: Clarendon Press.

Dür, A., L. Baccini and M. Elsig 2014. "The Design of International Trade Agreements: Introducing a New Dataset," *The Review of International Organizations* 9(3): 353–375.

Elias, J. and A. Roberts 2018. *Handbook on the International Political Economy of Gender*. Cheltenham: Edward Elgar Publishing.

Elson, D. 1993. "Gender-aware Analysis and Development Economics," *Journal of International Development* 5(2): 237–247.

Findlay, C., S. Stephenson and F. J. Prieto 2005. "Services in Regional Trading Arrangements." In P. Macrory, A. Appleton and M. Plummer (Eds.), *The World Trade Organization: Legal, Economic and Political Analysis*. New York: Springer, pp. 1888–1907.

Flores, I., C. Sanhueza, J. Atria and R. Mayer 2020. "Top Incomes in Chile: A Historical Perspective on Income Inequality, 1964–2017," *Review of Income and Wealth* 66(4): 850–874.

Foley, M. and R. Cooper 2021. "Workplace Gender Equality in the Post-Pandemic Era: Where to Next?" *Journal of Industrial Relations* 63(4): 463–476.

Fontana, M. 2009. "The Gender Effects of Trade Liberalization in Developing Countries: A Review of the Literature." In M. Bussolo and R. D. Hoyos (Eds.), *Gender Aspects of the Trade Poverty Nexus. A Macro-Micro Approach*. Washington: The World Bank, pp. 25–50.

Francois, J. and B. Hoekman 2010. "Services Trade and Policy," *Journal of Economic Literature* 48(3): 642–692.

Frohmann, A. 2017. "Gender Equality and Trade Policy," SECO Working Paper 24/2017.

Fuentes, A. and R. Vergara 2018. "Brecha salarial de género: Evolución en el período 1990–2017," *Puntos de Referencia* 490: 1–8.

Gaddis, I. and J. Pieters 2017. "The Gendered Labor Market Impacts of Trade Liberalization Evidence from Brazil," *Journal of Human Resources* 52(2): 457–490.

Gammage, S., T. Alburquerque and G. Durán 2014. *Poverty, Inequality and Employment in Chile*. Geneva: ILO.

Gibb, H. 2008. *Mainstreaming Gender in Trade Policy*. Paper produced for the 13th Meeting of the APEC Women Leaders Network May 12–14, 2008 Arequipa, Peru.

Giraudo, M. E. 2020. "Dependent Development in South America: China and the Soybean Nexus," *Journal of Agrarian Change* 20(1): 60–78.

Gutiérrez, V. and F. Muñoz 2022. "Desigualdad económica en Chile en el contexto de la Agenda 2030: Análisis de las acciones públicas," *Estudios internacionales (Santiago)*, 54(203): 87–127.

Hoadley, J. S. 1981. "The Rise and Fall of the Basic Needs Approach," *Cooperation and Conflict* 16(3): 149–164.

Hoekman, B. 2006. "Liberalizing Trade in Services: A Survey," World Bank Policy Research Working Paper 4030.

Hoekman, B. and A. Mattoo 2013. "Liberalizing Trade in Services: Lessons from Regional and WTO Negotiations," *International Negotiation* 18(1): 131–151.

Hofman, A. A. 2000. "*The Economic Development of Latin America in the Twentieth Century*. Santiago: ECLAC.

Ipsen, A. 2022. "Gendered Labor Legacies of Authoritarian Neoliberalism: Chile's Double Crisis," *Gender, Work & Organization* 31(4): 1–20.

Johannesson, L. and H. K. Nordås 2021. "Services Trade: The Great Gender Equaliser?" *Foreign Trade Review* 56(3): 341–363.

Juhn, C., G. Ujhelyi and C. Villegas-Sanchez 2014. "Men, Women, and Machines: How Trade Impacts Gender Inequality," *Journal of Development Economics* 106: 179–193.

Kazandjian, R., Kolovich, L., Kochhar, K. and M. Newiak 2019. "Gender Equality and Economic Diversification," *Social Sciences* 8(4): 1–24.

Keating, M. 2004. *Gender, Development, and Trade*. Oxford: Oxfam.

Kis-Katos, K., J. Pieters and R. Sparrow 2018. Globalization and Social Change: Gender-Specific Effects of Trade Liberalization in Indonesia," *IMF Economic Review* 66(4): 763–793.

Krieger-Boden, C. and A. Sorgner 2018. "Labor Market Opportunities for Women in the Digital Age," *Economics* 12(1): 1–8.

Lahar, S. 1991. "Ecofeminist Theory and Grassroots Politics," *Hypatia* 6(1): 28–45.

Lake, J. and P. Krishna 2019. "Preferential Trade Agreements: Recent Theoretical and Empirical Developments." In A. Banerjee (Ed.), *Oxford Research Encyclopedia of Economics and Finance*, pp. 1–31. Retrieved from https://oxfordre.com/economics/view/10.1093/acrefore/9780190625979.001.0001/acrefore-9780190625979-e-323.

Laperle-Forget, L. 2022. *WTO Database on Gender Provisions in Regional Trade Agreements*. Geneva: WTO.

Larsson, A. and Y. Viitaoja 2019. "Identifying the Digital Gender Divide: How Digitalization May Affect the Future Working Conditions for Women:" In A. Larsson and R. Teigland (Eds.), *The Digital Transformation of Labor*. London: Routledge, pp. 235–253.

Lechner, L. 2016. "The Domestic Battle over the Design of Non-Trade Issues in Preferential Trade Agreements," *Review of International Political Economy* 23(5): 840–871.

Leschke, J. 2015. "Non-standard Employment of Women in Service Sector Occupations: A Comparison of European Countries." In W. Eichhorst and P. Marx (Eds.), *Non-standard Employment in Post-industrial Labour Markets: An Occupational Perspective*. Cheltenham: Edward Elgar, pp. 324–352.

Limão, N. 2007. "Are Preferential Trade Agreements with Non-trade Objectives a Stumbling Block for Multilateral Liberalization?" *The Review of Economic Studies* 74(3): 821–855.

López, D. and F. Muñoz 2015. "Cuarenta años de apertura comercial chilena," *Cuadernos americanos: Nueva epoca* 4(154): 125–151.

López, D. and F. Muñoz 2016. "El comercio de servicios y el desarrollo: Una discusión en curso," *Sociedad y economía* 30: 255–280.

López, D. and F. Muñoz 2018. "Trade Policy and Women in the Pacific Alliance," *Agenda Internacional* 25(6): 133–150.

López, D. and F. Muñoz 2020. "Chile: Tensión entre políticas sectoriales y horizontales." In N. Mulder, K. Fernández-Stark and M. Álvarez (Eds.), *Gobernanza y desempeño exportador de los servicios modernos en América Latina y la India*. Santiago: CEPAL, pp. 93–118.

López, D., J. M. Ahumada and F. Muñoz 2020. "State Neutrality, Business Elite and the Lack of Export Services Development in Chile: An Exploratory Qualitative Analysis," *Organizations and Markets in Emerging Economies* 11(21): 152–172.

López, D., F. Muñoz and J. Cáceres 2019. *Gender Inclusion in Chilean Free Trade Agreements*. Santiago: Institute of International Studies, University of Chile.

López, D., F. Muñoz and J. Cáceres 2022. "Chile-Korea Free Trade Agreement: A Synthetic Control Assessment," *CEPAL Review* 138: 131–150.

Mansfield, E. and J. Pevehouse 2013. "The Expansion of Preferential Trading Arrangements," *International Studies Quarterly* 57(3): 592–604.

Marchetti, J. and M. Roy 2008. "Services Liberalization in the WTO and in PTAs." In J. Marchetti and M. Roy (Eds.), *Opening Markets for Trade in Services: Countries and Sectors in Bilateral and WTO Negotiations*. Cambridge: Cambridge University Press, pp. 61–112.

Menon, N. and Y. Van der Meulen Rodgers 2009. "International Trade and the Gender Wage Gap: New Evidence from India's Manufacturing Sector," *World Development* 37(5): 965–981.

Mieres Brevis, M. 2020. "La dinámica de la desigualdad en Chile: Una mirada regional," *Revista de análisis económico* 35(2): 91–133.

Milewicz, K., J. Hollway, C. Peacock and D. Snidal 2018. "Beyond Trade: The Expanding Scope of the Non-Trade Agenda in Trade Agreements," *Journal of Conflict Resolution* 62(4): 743–773.

Momsen, J. 2019. *Gender and Development*. London: Routledge.

Monteiro, J.-A. 2018. Gender-related Provisions in Regional Trade Agreements. Retrieved from Geneva: www.econstor.eu/bitstream/10419/191640/1/1047566001.pdf.

Muñoz, F., J. Cáceres and S. Rojas 2021. *Manual de exportación de servicios y aprovechamiento de tratados de libre comercio*. Santiago: SUBREI.

Nasser de Carvalho, P. 2020. "Critical Analyses of International Trade Liberalization and Links between International Trade and Gender," *Mural Internacional* 11(1–13): e53034.

Novta, N. and J. Wong 2017. *Women at Work in Latin America and the Caribbean*: Washington DC: International Monetary Fund.

Núñez, J. and A. Tartakowsky 2011. "The Relationship between Income Inequality and Inequality of Opportunities in a High-inequality Country: The Case of Chile," *Applied Economics Letters* 18(4): 359–369.

Nussbaum, M. and A. Sen 1993. *The Quality of Life*. New York: Clarendon Press.

Ocampo, J. A. 2008. "El auge económico latinoamericano." *Revista de ciencia política (Santiago)* 28(1): 7–33.

Parmer, L. L. 2021. "The Road to Gender Equality: Persisting Obstacles for American Women in the Workforce," *The Psychologist-Manager Journal* 24(2): 85–96.

Prieto, F. J., S. Sáez and A. Goswami 2011. "The Elusive Road to Service Export Diversification: The Case of Chile." In S. Sáez (Ed.), *Exporting Services: A Developing Countries Perspective*. Washington: World Bank, pp. 309–360.

Rai, S. 2018. "Gender and Development." In J. Elias and A. Roberts (Eds.), *Handbook on the International Political Economy of Gender*. London: Edward Elgar Publishing, pp. 142–158.

Rai, S. and G. Waylen 2014. *New Frontiers in Feminist Political Economy*. London: Routledge.

Rau, T. 2010. "El trabajo a tiempo parcial en Chile," *Economía chilena* 13(1): 39–59.

Ridgeway, C. 2011. *Framed by Gender: How Gender Inequality Persists in the Modern World*. Oxford: Oxford University Press.

Ridgeway, C. and S. Correll 2004. "Unpacking the Gender System: A Theoretical Perspective on Gender Beliefs and Social Relations," *Gender Society* 18(4): 510–531.

Rocha, N. and D. E. Winkler 2019. "Trade and Female Labor Participation: Stylized Facts Using a Global Dataset," World Bank Policy Research Working Paper 9098.

Rodríguez, J. 2017. "The Political Economy of Income Inequality in Chile since 1850." In L. Bértola and J. Williamson (Eds.), *Has Latin American Inequality Changed Direction? Looking over the Long Run*. Cham: Springer, pp. 43–64.

Rogers, B. 2005. *The Domestication of Women: Discrimination in Developing Societies*. London: Routledge.

Roy, M. 2014. "Services Commitments in Preferential Trade Agreements: Surveying the Empirical Landscape." In P. Sauvé and A. Shingal (Eds.), *The Preferential Liberalization of Trade in Services*. London: Edward Elgar, pp. 15–36.

Sauré, P. and H. Zoabi 2014. "International Trade, the Gender Wage Gap and Female Labor Force Participation," *Journal of Development Economics* 111: 17–33.

Sauvé, P. 2020. "Gendered Perspectives on Services Trade and Investment," *Journal of World Trade* 54(4): 481–502.

Sen, A. 2001. *Development as Freedom*: Oxford: Oxford Paperbacks.

Steiger, T. L. and M. Wardell 1995. "Gender and Employment in the Service Sector," *Social Problems* 42(1): 91–123.

Stewart, F. 1985. "A Basic Needs Approach to Development." In F. Stewart (Ed.), *Planning to Meet Basic Needs*. London: Springer, pp.1–13.

Stichter, S. 2016. "Women, Employment and the Family." In L. McDowell and J. Sharp (Eds.), *Space, Gender, Knowledge: Feminist Readings*. London: Routledge, pp. 327–342.

Streeten, P. P. 1979. *Basic Needs: Premises and Promises*. Washington: World Bank.

SUBREI 2022. *Acuerdos comerciales*. Retrieved from www.subrei.gob.cl/acuerdos-comerciales/acuerdos-comerciales-vigentes.

Svampa, M. 2013. "Consenso de los commodities y lenguajes de Valoración en América Latina," *Nueva Sociedad* (244): 30–46.

Tinker, I. and M. B. Bramsen 1976. *Women and World Development*. Washington: Overseas Development Council.

UNCTAD 2010. *Services, Trade and Development*. Geneva: UNCTAD.

2017. "The New Way of Addressing Gender Inequality Issues in Trade Agreements: Is It a True Revolution?" Retrieved from Geneva: https://unctad.org/system/files/official-document/presspb2017d2_en.pdf.

2020. "COVID-19 Requires Gender-equal Responses to Save Economies," Retrieved from https://unctad.org/en/pages/newsdetails.aspx?OriginalVersionID=2319.

Undurraga, R. 2011. Between Family and Work: Women's Participation in the Labour Market in Chile, PhD thesis. Coventry: University of Warwick

Velasco, J. 2021. "Los impactos de la pandemia de la Covid-19 en los mercados laborales de América Latina," *Compendium: Cuadernos de economía yadministración* 8(2): 99–120.

Villalobos, L. D. and F. B. Grossman 2008. "Did the Trade Reform Bring about Gender Wage Equality in Mexican Industry?" Paper presented in the VI Globelics Conference at Mexico City, September 22–24 2008.

World Bank 2022. *World Development Indicators*.

World Bank and WTO 2020. *Women and Trade: The Role of Trade in Promoting Gender Equality*. Washington: The World Bank.

WTO 2017a. "Buenos Aires Declaration on Women and Trade Outlines Actions to Empower Women." Retrieved from www.wto.org/english/news_e/news17_e/mc11_12dec17_e.htm.

2017b. *Gender Aware Trade Policy*. Retrieved from www.wto.org/english/news_e/news17_e/dgra_21jun17_e.pdf.

Zarrilli, S. 2017. "The New Way of Addressing Gender Equality Issues in Trade Agreements: Is It a True Revolution?" UNCTAD. Retrieved from ICTSD's Network of Experts. https://unctad.org/system/files/official-document/presspb2017d2_en.pdf?utm_source=chatgpt.com.

10

Food Labelling Regulation of the Pacific Alliance Members

Víctor Saco

10.1 INTRODUCTION

Over the past decade, several Latin American countries have increasingly turned to mandatory labelling of processed foods. This has been in response to public health concerns about rising levels of obesity in the population, particularly among children. The main aim of these regulations is to provide consumers with appropriate information about foods that are high in sugar, salt or fat. To this end, all of Pacific Alliance members – Chile, Colombia, Mexico and Peru – have adopted specific labelling as a public health approach. The approach taken in these countries has been to use labels that are similar to the 'STOP' transit symbol but in black. This type of legislation first appeared in Chile and was later adopted by Peru, Mexico and Colombia, as well as by other Latin American countries such as Uruguay and Argentina, and its use is currently being discussed in Costa Rica.

The purpose of this chapter is twofold: first, to explore patterns in the legislative trends observed in selected Pacific Alliance countries regarding the labelling of foods containing certain ingredients related to non-communicable diseases and, second, to examine whether this new stop sign approach can evolve into a new legal standard that other countries in the region are likely to follow. This chapter builds on previous work that conducted a comparative case study of Peru and Chile (Boza et al. 2020). The main intention is also to focus on Mexican and Colombian legislation, because current developments in Colombia suggest a strong diffusion effect and a quasi-emergence of a Latin American standard for this type of food labelling.

This chapter has two parts: first, I present the legislation enacted in four Pacific Alliance countries; second, I discuss how a common standard on the specifics of food labelling has emerged in Pacific Alliance member states, suggesting important diffusion effects. Focusing on diffusion, I find that the degree and speed of adoption

I would like to thank Rodrigo Polanco and Manfred Elsig for their guidance and inputs. I also want to thank Sofia Boza for spearheading this project with me some years ago.

is strongly influenced by three main factors: the authority of the World Trade Organization (WTO) Agreement on Technical Barriers to Trade (TBT) as enforced in discussions in the TBT Committee, the work of health-related organizations, and previous foreign domestic legislation. The fact that the Latin American countries applying this standard are members of the Pacific Alliance is also an indicator that this forum has facilitated diffusion through diplomatic and technical exchanges.

10.2 REGULATIONS IN CHILE, PERU AND MEXICO

The regulation of front-of-package labelling (FOPL) for nutrition, which I examine in this chapter, is characterized by the use of a specific form of the transit sign 'STOP'. This sign was first introduced in Chile. This was followed by Peru, Mexico and Colombia, in chronological order. The regulations adopted in the first three countries are described below, leaving the case of Colombia for a new section.

10.2.1 *The Case of Chile*

Chile was the first country of the Pacific Alliance members to implement the STOP sign on FOPL. The pertinent Chilean law was approved in 2012 and came into effect in 2016.[1] Figure 10.1 provides an illustration of its design.

The law and its implementing decree (Decree 13) define that these warnings must be present on all food products sold on the Chilean market, whether local or imported, if the product contains an excess of 'critical nutrients' for sodium, sugar, saturated fat and calories. However, some foods are exempt from labelling, such as foods sold in bulk, fractionated or prepared at the point of sale. Table 10.1 provides an overview of the thresholds and the timeframe for implementation as set out in the regulation.

Table 10.1 shows the two categories regulated by Decree No. 13: solids and liquids. The thresholds for critical nutrients are set in portions of 100 grams for solids and in portions of 100 millilitres for liquids. The decree provides for a transition period to gradually reduce the amount of critical nutrients until 2019.

Nutrition labelling was only one of the three pillars of Law 20606. The other two were (ii) a ban on advertising to protect children and (iii) a programme to promote and educate about healthy lifestyles. By way of example, the law prohibits any advertising aimed at children under the age of 14, when the food is subject to mandatory labelling (the octagonal symbol). This also means that companies will not be allowed to offer free toys or other similar promotional strategies related to the products. In addition, labelled products may not be sold or distributed in schools.

[1] Ley 20606, sobre composición nutricional de los alimentos y su publicidad. www.bcn.cl/leychile/navegar?idNorma = 1041570. This law was implemented through Decree 13 of 2015; see Decreto 13, Modifica Decreto Supremo N° 977, de 1996, Reglamento Sanitario de los Alimentos. www.bcn.cl/leychile/navegar?idNorma = 1078836&idVersion = 2022-07-14&idParte = .

FIGURE 10.1 Warning labelling – Chile.
Note: Top right: 'High in Sugar'; top left: 'High in Saturated Fats'; bottom left: 'High in Salt'; and bottom right 'High in Calories', all in an octagonal label with a black background and white border that also contains the words 'Ministry of Health' for each nutrient in excess.
Source: Decreto 13 of 2015 (n 2).

10.2.2 *The Case of Peru*

Peru was the second Pacific Alliance country to introduce the octagonal 'STOP' signs. The law was passed in May 2013,[2] one year after Chilean law (2012). However, it was not until 2019 that the implementing regulation was issued and therefore the law really came into force.[3]

2 Law 30021, "Law for the Promotion of Healthy Nutrition for Children and Teenagers applies to processed food and non-alcohol beverages", enacted May 17, 2013. www.gob.pe/institucion/congreso-de-la-republica/normas-legales/118470-30021.

3 Supreme Decree No. 017-2017-SA, which establishes the technical specifications for consigning advertising warnings on processed foods that exceed the established technical parameters

TABLE 10.1 *Thresholds of 'critical nutrients'*

Nutrient11	Classification	From the date of implementation (26 June 2016)	24 months after implementation (26 June 2018)	36 months after implementation (26 June 2019)
Calories	Solid (kcal/100 g)	350	300	275
	Liquid (kcal/100 ml)	100	80	70
Sodium	Solid (mg/100 g)	800	500	400
	Liquid (mg/100 ml)	100	100	100
Sugar	Solid (g/100 g)	22.5	15	10
	Liquid (g/100 ml)	6	5	5
Saturated fats	Solid (g/100 g)	6	5	4
	Liquid (g/100 ml)	3	3	3

Regarding signs, Peruvian law has some similarities with Chilean law. The signs consist of an octagonal shape with a black background and a white border. The difference is that the Peruvian signs add an additional box below the 'STOP' sign that reads: 'Avoid its excessive consumption' or 'Avoid its consumption', depending on the case (Figure 10.2).

The Peruvian law targets four types of critical nutrients – sugar, sodium/salt, saturated fat and trans-fat – in foods and soft drinks. On this point, the Peruvian labelling differs from the Chilean one; the Chilean 'High in Calories' has been replaced by the Peruvian 'High in Trans-Fat'. Saturated fats, sugar and salt are common to both laws.

Also, the Peruvian law differs from the Chilean one, since in the case of saturated fats, sugar, the octagonal signs are accompanied by a box that reads 'excessive consumption of the product should be avoided'. If the product contains trans-fats, the text in the box is: 'Avoid its consumption'. According to Peruvian law, this is the way to provide consumers with 'clear, legible, conspicuous and understandable' information.

As in the case of Chile, the Peruvian regulation works with limits and thresholds that are quasi-identical. The thresholds will also decrease over time, after a thirty-nine-month period. As in the case of Chile, the regulations apply differently to solid and liquid products. Table 10.2 provides an overview:

As in the case of Chile, some foods are exempted. The Peruvian law does not apply to unprocessed foods, which are described in the law as products in a 'natural state'. Other similarities include the promotion of nutrition education and sports in

and in the media according to the Regulation of the Law on the Promotion of Healthy Eating for Children and Adolescents. https://busquedas.elperuano.pe/dispositivo/NL/2191835-1.

FIGURE 10.2 Warning labelling – Peru.
Note: First line from left to right: 'High in Saturated Fats'; 'High in Sugar'; 'High in Salt' and in the box 'Avoid Its Excessive Consumption'. In the second line: 'High in Trans-Fats' and 'Avoid Its Excessive Consumption'.
Source: Supreme Decree No. 017-2017-SA (n 4).

schools. And in the case of marketing to children under the age of sixteen, the law prohibits promotional activities such as the use of toys, gifts or prizes to encourage consumption, or the use of characters admired by children. In Peru, only 'healthy foods' can be sold in schools. In summary, a comparison of the Chilean and Peruvian regimes reveals a high degree of similarity with only minor differences.

10.2.3 *The Case of Mexico*

The Mexican law was passed in March 2020, partially enacted in October 2020 and fully enacted in April 2021.[4] Similar to Chile and Peru, it includes octagonal signs to warn customers of adverse health effects. However, the law will be under continuous evaluation until 2025 and may be adjusted during that time.

4 NOM-051-SCFI/SSA1–2010. www.dof.gob.mx/normasOficiales/4010/seeco11_C/seeco11_C.htm

TABLE 10.2 *Thresholds of 'critical nutrients'*

Nutrient	Classification	6 months after the approval of the Manual of Advertising Warnings[5] (18 December 2018)	39 months after the approval of the Manual of Advertising Warnings (18 December 2021)
Sodium	Solid (mg/100 g)	800	400
	Liquid (mg/100 ml)	100	100
Sugar	Solid (g/100 g)	22.5	10
	Liquid (g/100 ml)	6	5
Saturated fats	Solid (g/100 g)	6	4
	Liquid (g/100 ml)	3	3
Trans-fats		According to the actual regulation[6]	According to the actual regulation

Note: The technical parameters applicable after thirty-nine months can be updated according to new information based on scientific evidence.

The law provides for three phases of implementation: the first phase was from October 2021 to September 2023, the second phase is defined from October 2023 to September 2025, and the third and final phase begins in October 2025. The aim of the phases is to implement the regulation gradually and to evaluate its impact on an ongoing basis. The difference between the phases lies in the evaluations that are made to the products, depending on the critical nutrients that are included. In the first phase, all products with sugars, fats and sodium are evaluated. In the second phase, only sugars and fats are evaluated. Finally, in the third phase, all critical nutrients are evaluated.

Regarding the signs, the first difference with the Peruvian and Chilean regulations is that the Mexican law has five octagonal signs. Sugar, salt/sodium and saturated fat are common in Chile, Peru and Mexico. The other two signs are for calories and trans-fats. Mexican legislation uses the four signs from Chile and adds the trans-fat octagon from the Peruvian regulation. (Peruvian law warns of the 'content' of trans-fats, while Mexican law of the 'excess' of them.) There is an interesting adaptation that can be observed here, as the Mexican regulation draws clearly from the two previous regulations.

5 Supreme Decree N° 012-2018-SA, published on 16 June 2018, approved the "*Manual de Advertencias Publicitarias en el marco de lo establecido en la Ley N° 30021, Ley de promoción de la alimentación saludable para niños, niñas y adolescentes, y su Reglamento aprobado por Decreto Supremo N° 017-2017-SA.*" The Decree entered into force the day after its publication.

6 Peru enacted in 2016 (July 27) a norm to gradually reduce to eliminate the use of trans-fats in processed foods (Supreme Decree N° 033-2016-SA).

TABLE 10.3 *Thresholds of 'critical nutrients' in Mexico*

	Calories	Sugars	Saturated fats	Trans-Fats	Salt
Solid products, by 100 g of product Liquid products, by 100 ml of product	≥275 kcal in total ≥70 kcal in total or ≥ 8 kcal of free sugars	≥10% of the total energy originating from free sugars	≥10% of the total energy originating from saturated fats	≥1% of the total energy originating from trans-fats	≥ 1 mg of sodium per kcal or ≥ 300 mg Drinks without calories ≥ 45 mg of sodium
The product should use	**EXCESS IN CALORIES**	**EXCESS IN SUGAR**	**EXCESS IN SATURATED FATS**	**EXCESS IN TRANS-FATS**	**EXCESS IN SALT**

FIGURE 10.3 Warning labelling – Mexico[7].
Note: From top left to bottom right: 'Excess in Calories', 'Excess in Salt', 'Excess in Trans-Fats', 'Excess in Sugar' and 'Excess in Saturated Fats'.

In Mexico, octagonal labels also have a black background and require a text box to include the name of the Ministry of Health using a polygonal border, as shown in Figure 10.3.

As in the case of Chile and Peru, Mexico also sets thresholds for critical nutrients. If a product, liquid or solid, exceeds the thresholds, the product should carry one or more octagonal symbols. The Mexican thresholds are listed in Table 10.3.

Despite important similarities, the Mexican regulation also contains minor differences compared to the Peruvian and Chilean legislation. The Mexican regulation introduces an additional scheme based on the size of the package. While Figure 10.3 shows the warning labels that are mandatory for packages larger than 40 cm^2, another warning label applies to smaller packages[8], as shown in Figure 10.4.

The special labelling for smaller packages or 'mini-signs' is an innovation of the Mexican legislation in relation to the previous two countries, Chile and Peru. This

[7] Numeral 4.5.3.4 de la MODIFICACIÓN a la Norma Oficial Mexicana NOM-051-SCFI/SSA1–2010. In "Manual de la MODIFICACIÓN a la Norma Oficial Mexicana" NOM-051-SCFI/SSA1–2010.

[8] Article 4.5.3.4.1 Norma Oficial Mexicana NOM-051-SCFI/SSA1–2010.

FIGURE 10.4 Warning labelling in smaller packages[9]
Note: From left to right, 1, 2, 3, 4 and 5, the word 'signs'.

CONTIENE EDULCORANTES, NO RECOMENDABLE EN NIÑOS

FIGURE 10.5 Additional warning labelling – sweeteners.[10]
Note: left side: 'contains sweeteners, not recommended for children'.

CONTIENE CAFEÍNA - EVITAR EN NIÑOS

FIGURE 10.6 Additional warning labelling – caffeine.[11]
Note: 'contains caffeine, avoid in children'.

"Este producto no contiene sellos ni leyendas".

FIGURE 10.7 Positive labelling.[12]
Note: 'This product contains no signs or legends'.

innovation can address the criticism of some companies that are against using labels on small packages because they may affect the space they had for their brands and commercial images. At the same time, it allows people to still have information about the critical ingredients present in the products.

Smaller signs could have a greater impact in the case of Peru, for example. In Peru, because its regulation is based on the weight of the products and not on the size, small presentations of the products are not required to carry the octagonal

[9] Numeral 4.5.4.2 de la MODIFICACIÓN a la Norma Oficial Mexicana NOM-051-SCFI/SSA1–2010. In "Manual de la MODIFICACIÓN a la Norma Oficial Mexicana" NOM-051-SCFI/SSA1–2010. www.gob.mx/cms/uploads/attachment/file/654130/MANUAL_DE_LA_MODIFICACION_NOM-051_.pdf

[10] Numeral 4.5.3.4 de la MODIFICACIÓN a la Norma Oficial Mexicana NOM-051-SCFI/SSA1–2010. In "Manual de la MODIFICACIÓN a la Norma Oficial Mexicana" NOM-051-SCFI/SSA1–2010.

[11] Ibid.

[12] Numeral 4.1.4. Bis de la MODIFICACIÓN a la Norma Oficial Mexicana NOM-051-SCFI/SSA1–2010, Especificaciones generales de etiquetado para alimentos y bebidas no alcohólicas preenvasados, información comercial y sanitaria, publicada el 5 de abril de 2010. www.dof.gob.mx/normasOficiales/8150/seeco11_C/seeco11_C.html

signs; a box containing ten chocolates must carry the octagonal signs, but none of the ten packages of the chocolate bars must bear signs.

Another innovation in the Mexican regulation is that Mexico has gone beyond the octagonal signs and introduced new signs: a sign for caffeine, another for sweeteners, and the so-called positive signs. This can be seen in Figures 10.5, 10.6 and 10.7. These signs do not exist in Chilean or Peruvian regulations.

In the case of Figures 10.5 and 10.6, these labels are additional to the respective octagon. If a product contains trans-fats and uses sweeteners, the product packaging should bear the octagonal trans-fat symbol and below it the Figure 10.5 symbol. The labels in Figures 10.5 and 10.6 are intended to prevent children from consuming these products, which is the reason for the warning 'not recommended for children' (Figure 10.5) or 'avoid in children' (Figure 10.6).

In this sense, the most relevant difference in the Mexican law is the introduction of 'positive' labelling for products that do not have STOP signs or caffeine or sweeteners; these signs were introduced in the first amendment to the Mexican law in 2021.[13] In this case, 'positive' does not mean beneficial to health but wants to publicize that a product has no signs.

The above discussion shows that both Peru and Mexico have closely followed and adapted their labelling schemes to their predecessor(s). From the first mover (Chile), labelling has begun to diffuse, and nine years after the Pan American Health Organization (PAHO) said that 'the new Mexican labelling as the best model currently available'.[14] In the next section, we focus on the most recent law adopted among the Pacific Alliance members to see if a tipping point has been reached, while this new standard has the potential to spread quickly to other jurisdictions. The case of Colombia will help prove this.

10.3 COLOMBIAN REGULATIONS: THE CONSOLIDATION OF THE OCTAGONAL WARNING SIGNS

In this section, we turn to another and final Pacific Alliance member that has recently begun to regulate critical nutrient excesses. It is interesting to observe that the regulation has clearly been shaped and influenced by previous regulation in Pacific Alliance countries. We see a diffusion of regulatory practice. Of particular note is the recognition of the mandatory nature of the practice, specifically the use of octagonal warning labels. This is reflected in the case of Colombia, where even minor attempts to deviate from previous practice have been challenged in the domestic courts, resulting eventually in a mandatory labelling system that is virtually

[13] Numeral 4.1.4. Bis de la MODIFICACIÓN a la Norma Oficial Mexicana NOM-051-SCFI/SSA1–2010, Especificaciones generales de etiquetado para alimentos y bebidas no alcohólicas preenvasados, información comercial y sanitaria, publicada el 5 de abril de 2010. www.dof.gob.mx/normasOficiales/8150/seeco11_C/seeco11_C.html.

[14] BBC. "*Etiquetado de alimentos: qué cambia con la nueva normativa de México inspirada en Chile (y qué resultados dio en el país sudamericano)*". 1 Oct 2020.

TABLE 10.4 *Thresholds of 'critical nutrients' in Colombian regulation*[15]

Nutrient	Solids (100 g)	Liquids (100 ml)
Sodium (mg)	≥ = 400	≥ = 150
Added sugars (g)	≥ = 10	≥ = 5.0
Saturated fats (g)	≥ = 4.0	≥ = 3.5

FIGURE 10.8 Warning labelling in Colombian law under Decree 810.
Note: From left to right: 'High in Added Sugars', 'High in Salt/Sodium' and 'High in Saturated Fats'. Inside the white background reads 'Minsalud', which is the short form for 'Ministry of Health'.

identical to that of other Pacific Alliance members. In the following lines, I will examine the different stages of the regulations, the changes due to judicial involvement, and finally some observations on what mix of factors explains this almost completely copy-paste health regulation.

Colombia has the most recent regulations on warning labels of the Pacific Alliance member countries. In June 2021, the Ministry of Health issued Resolution 810, which regulates the labelling of products. Resolution 810 introduced a new standard for the FOPL for 'critical nutrients', and similar to the regulations in Chile, Peru and Mexico, the warning labels must be used when the product, whether liquid or solid, exceeds certain thresholds. In the case of Colombia, these thresholds are shown in Table 10.4.

If a product is to be sold in the Colombian market and exceeds the above table limits, it should bear a sign that at the time of Resolution 810 looks like in Figure 10.8.

Another sign included in the Colombian Resolution 810 is a positive labelling option for products produced according to best nutritional practices. The Mexican regulation also included a 'positive' sign, but in that case the sign indicated the absence of an octagonal warning sign, in the case of Colombia the 'positive' sign is only given if the product has a lower content of sodium, sugar or saturated fat. The Colombian 'positive' label is shown in Figure 10.9.

[15] Ministerio de Salud y Protección Social. Resolución 0000810 de 2021 (16 JUN 2021). Table 17, pages 42–43.

FIGURE 10.9 Positive labelling in Colombian law.[16]

Just one month after the Ministry of Health issued Resolution 810, in July 2021, the Colombian Congress passed Law 2120. This law instructed the Colombian government to regulate in detail, among other things, the labelling of processed foods that exceed healthy levels of critical nutrients. Politically, this meant a confrontation between the executive and legislative branches.

Following the publication of Law 2120, a group of NGOs requested a judicial process (*Acción de cumplimiento*) against Resolution 810. Among the challenged provisions of the Resolution was the warning label (round shapes), as shown in Figure 10.7. Regarding the warning signs, the plaintiffs argue that the octagonal shape of the warning signs should be followed in Colombia, and not the round signs.[17]

The plaintiffs' main argument was that the signs of Resolution 810 did not comply with the requirements of Article 5 of the new law, since the Resolution had a lower hierarchy than the law. Specifically, and with respect to warning signs, that the round signs and the way they were designed in Resolution 810 were not as 'clear, visible, legible, easily identified and understood by consumers' as the octagonal sign and did not meet the requirements of the new law.

On 27 October 2022, the Colombian Council of State, the highest court in administrative matters, issued its ruling on the *Accion de cumplimiento*.[18] Although the Court did not indicate which is the best type of symbol for labelling, it ordered the Ministry of Health to issue a new regulation in accordance with Law 2021, since Resolution 810 cannot regulate Law 2021, as it precedes the former. On 13

[16] Ministerio de Salud y Protección Social. Resolución 0000810 de 2021 (16 JUN 2021). "Figura 7. Forma del sello positivo". Pages 47–48.

[17] Previous to the *Acción de Cumplimiento*, another judicial procedure was started a *Proceso de Nulidad* where the plaintiffs indicated, referring to the PAHO that the "the most effective model is octagonal labeling." Consejo de Estado. Sala de lo Contencioso Administrativo. Centro de Estudios de Derecho, Justicia y Sociedad (Dejusticia) vs Ministerio de Salud y Protección Social. (Demanda) 17 Nov 2021, at 11, fn 5.

[18] Consejo de Estado. Sala de lo Contencioso Administrativo. Sección Quinta. Radicación n.° 25000-23-41-000-2022-00942-01. Bogotá D.C., veintisiete (27) de octubre de dos mil veintidós (2022). During the pleadings, the Colombian Executive accepted that it had already planned to change the warning labels for the octagonal-shaped symbols and adopt the Pan American Health Organization (PAHO) profile model (at 8).

TABLE 10.5 *Updated thresholds in Colombian regulation*[19]

Nutrient	Solid (100 g) – semisolids	Liquids (100 ml)
Sodium	≥ = 1 mg and/or ≥ = 300 mg/100 g 300 mg/100 g for packaged raw meat with added salt/sodium	≥ = 1 mg/Kcal Or ≥40 mg of sodium per each 100 ml – beverages without alcohol and no energy supply
Sugars	≥ = 10% of the total energy coming from free sugars	≥ = 10% of the total energy coming from free sugars
Saturated fats	≥ = 10% of the total energy coming from saturated fats	≥ = 10% of the total energy coming from saturated fats
Trans-fats	≥ = 1% of the total energy coming from trans-fats	≥ = 1% of the total energy coming from trans-fats
Sweeteners	Any quantity of sweeteners	Any quantity of sweeteners

FIGURE 10.10 Warning labelling in Colombian law under Decree 2492.
Notes: From left to right: 'High in Salt/Sodium', 'High in Sugars', 'High in Saturated Fats', 'Excess in Trans-Fat' and 'Contains Sweeteners'. All are accompanied by the legend 'Minsalud', which is the short form for 'Ministry of Health'.

December 2022, The Ministry of Health issued Resolution 2492 to comply with the ruling.[20] Resolution 2492 modified some articles of Resolution 810, including those regulating warning signs, and adopted the octagonal shape (Figure 10.10).

Along with the change in symbols, the thresholds for a product to carry one of these symbols were also changed. These updated thresholds emulate the limits

[19] Ministerio de Salud y Protección Social. Resolución Número 2492 de 2022 (13 DIC. 2022).
[20] Ministerio de Salud y Protección Social. Resolución Número 2492 de 2022 (13 DIC. 2022).

TABLE 10.6 *Comparison between limits in critical nutrients in the four Pacific Alliance members – solid products of 100 g*

	Chile	Peru (2021)	Mexico	Colombia
Sodium	800 mg/100 g	400 mg in 100 g	≥1 mg of sodium per kcal or ≥300 mg in 100 g	≥ = 1 mg and/or ≥ = 300 mg/100 g
Sugars	22.5 g/100 g	10 g in 100 g	≥10% of the total energy originating from free sugars	≥ = 10% of the total energy coming from free sugars
Saturated fats	6 g/100 g)	4 g in 100 g	≥10% of the total energy originating from saturated fats	≥ = 10% of the total energy coming from saturated fats
Trans-fats	No octagonal sign	Another law	≥1% of the total energy originating from trans-fats	≥ = 1% of the total energy coming from trans-fats
Calories	350 kcal/100 g	No octagonal sign	≥275 kcal in total	No octagonal sign
Sweeteners	No octagonal sign	No octagonal sign	No octagonal sign	Any quantity of sweeteners

* Elaborated by the author.

already established in the cases of Chile, Peru and Mexico. Table 10.5 shows the new thresholds according to Article 5 of Resolution 2492 of 2022.

In the previous paragraphs, I have documented the advertising warning regulations in the Pacific Alliance countries. I chose the Pacific Alliance as an example because all of its members currently have the same octagonal warning system without having coordinated it at the Pacific Alliance level. (It is possible that there will be coordination in the future for a regulation on this matter.) The octagonal warning signs are the first common regulation; a second issue common to these four countries is the thresholds that apply when the octagonal signs are exceeded. Among the four countries, the limits are not only similar, but they show an evolution: the most recent regulation is stricter than the previous ones; for example, in the case of sodium/salt the limit has passed from 800 mg to 300 mg in ten years (Chile 2012 to Colombia 2022), as seen in Table 10.6.

10.4 THE LATIN AMERICAN STANDARD FOR LABELLING PROCESSED FOODS: OCTAGONAL WARNING LABELS

The octagonal warning signs can be seen as a contribution to the front packaging regulation in international trade law, from Latin American countries. The thesis I propose, based on the information presented previously, is that diffusion happened among the four countries. My starting point is Gilardi's definition of diffusion as 'the interdependent process that is conducive to the spread of policies' (Gilardi 2012). Diffusion of international policy refers to a situation 'when government policy decisions in a given country are systematically conditioned by prior policy choices made in other countries' (Simmons et al. 2006, quoted by Gilardi 2012).

I consider that diffusion, in this case study, has three stages: a first stage that I call 'creation', starting in 2012 by Chile; a second stage, 'consolidation', having as examples, in an early stage, Peru and ending in the case of Mexico; and a final stage, 'enforcement', where the case of Colombia is very relevant. The stages are a manifestation of two types of arguments supporting the choice of octagonal warning signs. The first argument is the scientific basis to support the use of the signs, the second is the coercive nature or legal force of the signs. Both arguments have been developed and refined over more than ten years.

10.4.1 *Diffusion of the Octagonal Warning Signs in Latin America*

According to Gilardi, this can occur via diffusion mechanisms that can be grouped into four categories: coercion, competition, learning and emulation. Of these, I consider the most appropriate for the octagonal label warning signs to be learning and emulation mechanisms. The **learning** mechanism

> emphasizes the process whereby policy makers use the experience of other countries to estimate the likely consequences of policy change. Before a policy is introduced, its consequences are by definition uncertain. [For] Policy makers . . . other countries can also be a useful source of information. Looking at outcomes in countries that have already introduced the policy, and maybe comparing them with those of countries that have not adopted it, can be a way for policy makers to evaluate what will likely happen if they choose to pursue the new policy. (Gilardi 2012)

The **emulation** mechanism requires that political actors shift from the 'logic of consequences' to the 'logic of appropriateness'. According to the former, 'actors choose among alternatives by evaluating their likely consequences' (March and Olsen 1998; Checkel 2005, both works quoted by Gilardi 2012).

The learning mechanism is more explicit in what I call the 'consolidation phase' of the octagonal signs that Peru and Mexico learnt from the Chilean experience. For example, Peru, as a WTO member, knew that the Chilean Law was questioned by more than ten WTO members (including the United States and the European Union (EU)) in different TBT Committee meetings between 2013 and 2016 (Thow 2017, 565; Boza et al. 2020). Similarly, Mexico knew that the Peruvian law raised 'specific trade concerns' fourteen times between 2013 and 2017, expressed by ten members within the same committee (Argentina, Brazil, Canada, Colombia, Costa Rica, EU, Guatemala, Mexico, Switzerland and the United States). Prior to adopting its own legislation in 2018, Mexico criticized Peru's octagonal warning signs stating at the time 'that this "stop sign" could cause confusion among consumers because: (a) the purpose of the nutrient information was to provide consumers with data on the nutrients contained in the food in order to make informed decisions when purchasing food' (WTO 2018; Boza et al. 2020).

Peru learnt from the concerns expressed by other countries about the Chilean legislation, as well as from internal criticism. Peru established a period of five years between the general disposition of the law and the finalization of the specific rules in the implementation of the regulation, giving stakeholders the opportunity to provide input and to adapt to the law.

Another example of the diffusion learning mechanism is related to the criticism in the WTO TBT Committee regarding the transparency and costs of the measure. For example, the EU argued at the TBT Committee in 2013 that 'adapting to the new labelling requirements would require significant investments for manufacturers and a redesign of packaging for some product categories that have not yet been defined' (WTO 2014) (Boza et al. 2020). To address the lack of transparency in the measures, Peru allowed de facto five years of adjustment because the regulation that complemented it was five years late, but the regulation allowed another three years of adjustment. Mexico and Colombia also have adjustment periods (see above for the three phases in the case of Mexico). Also, in order to avoid criticism of transparency, a significant number of non-governmental organizations, associations, chambers of commerce and companies participate in the consultation process. In the case of Mexico, for example, a list of participants can be found in the text of the law.[21]

Apart from the diffusion learning mechanism, there are also examples of the emulation mechanism of diffusion. The Colombian case is the most evident example of this. In the emulation mechanism, diffusion occurs because countries evaluate the consequences of their policies or laws. The Colombian case shows how diffusion mechanisms operate: these health protection measures travel from one Pacific Alliance country to the other. But Colombian law also illustrates that domestic interest groups might use judicial means to prevent governments from straying from established models. In the case of Colombia, the shift from using round to octagonal warning signs clearly demonstrates the evaluation of consequences, including legal implications that will be discussed later in this chapter.

10.4.2 *Scientific and International Legal Grounds Supporting Octagonal Warning Signs in Latin America*

Diffusion theory can help explain the reasoning behind political decisions. However, it is important for politicians, congressmen and decision-makers to support their arguments with scientific evidence. In addition, for states with international commitments, decisions must also be supported by international law. For example, when it comes to labelling requirements for product packaging, the commitments

[21] NOM-051-SCFI/SSA1–2010.

made under the TBT Agreement of the WTO are relevant. Furthermore, the TBT Agreement requires that any measures affecting product labelling be supported by technical and scientific evidence.

10.4.2.1 The WTO TBT Agreement

All members of the Pacific Alliance are also members of the WTO and are therefore bound by the TBT Agreement.[22] Article 2.2 of the TBT Agreement requires parties to ensure that their labelling regulations, which constitute technical regulations, do not create unnecessary obstacles to international trade. Parties also have an obligation to notify the WTO about technical regulations that may affect trade relations. Importantly, regulations that might raise concerns about WTO members are labelled Specific Trade Concerns and are regularly discussed in the TBT Committee.

According to Article 2.2 of the TBT Agreement, technical regulations should not create technical barriers and should not be more trade-restrictive than necessary to achieve a legitimate objective, all the while taking into account the risks that non-fulfilment would create. The four Pacific Alliance members have different reasons for implementing mandatory food labelling, but all are pursuing legitimate goals. The last statement is not contrary to the TBT Agreement, as this treaty does not provide an exhaustive list of public policy objectives that states can protect. Therefore, it is not limited to protecting only health.

In Chile, the objective stipulated by law for using octagonal signs is to inform the population about the nutritional composition of foods that contain excessive amounts of nutrients linked to the development of obesity and other non-communicable diseases. Another goal is to regulate food advertising, particularly targeting children under 14. For the Peruvian law, the objective is to promote and protect public health. In the case of Mexico, the regulation has two objectives for the use of octagonal signs: information and consumer protection. The law seeks to 'establish commercial and health information that should be clear and truthful' (Article 1). The Mexican law does not mention health objectives. Finally, the objective of the Colombian law is to promote health and a healthy food environment, as well as the prevention of non-communicable diseases and the promotion of healthy eating habits. In this case, and contrary to what happens in Mexico, 'accurate information' is not the objective of the regulation.

The regulations of all four Pacific Alliance member states align with the goals of the TBT Agreement, satisfying the first part of TBT article 2.2. However, demonstrating that the octagonal signs are a 'no less trade restrictive measure', as per the second part of Article 2.2, is a complex and contested task (Kapterian 2010). It is not sufficient, as in the case of Peruvian law, to refer to the WTO TBT Agreement and

[22] The TBT Agreement is also integrated completely into chapter 6 of the Pacific Alliance Additional Protocol re-enforcing the importance of TBT commitments.

Decision 562 of the Andean Community,[23] which confirms the agreement of the law and the decree with these international treaties.

To prove that the octagonal warning signs are not too trade-restrictive, it is important to prove that the measure is proportionate. In response to concerns raised at the TBT Committee, Chile and Peru demonstrated that although there were trade effects, they were not disproportionate. First, because during the initial years of implementing this measure in the Andean countries, the consumption of products with the seals did not decrease dramatically. Some producers utilized this opportunity to modify their product mix, resulting in a shift in consumption from processed products to healthier options without seals (*sin sellos*).

In Peru, prior to the COVID-19 pandemic, a study conducted in July 2019 found that 67 per cent of Peruvians reduced or replaced their consumption of products with the octagonal warning. A study by Kantar, which concluded in September 2019, showed that consumers chose to buy fewer food products with warnings of saturated fats and sugar (Luna 2019; Boza et al. 2020). Despite the reduction in consumption, these products continue to be sold. In Mexico, a comparable outcome occurred in 2021, with 72 per cent of consumers finding the octagonal symbols helpful and comprehensible. Additionally, sales of cereals not classified as products with octagonal signs increased from 5.9 per cent to 11 per cent as producers modified their production methods and reduced the use of critical nutrients (El Poder del Consumidor 2021).

There are additional arguments regarding the proportionality of the measure that extend beyond its less-restrictive nature. For example, during a TBT meeting, the US representative to the WTO expressed disappointment that Peru had chosen a labelling approach that failed to educate consumers about the role of different nutrients in a healthy and balanced diet (WTO 2018; Boza et al. 2020). Transparency is one such argument. While other criticisms have been raised, there is currently no contentious case before the WTO. However, several authors have presented arguments related to the proportionality of octagonal warning signs that could be used in such cases. It is important to note that these arguments are purely academic at this time[24].

Proportionality is related to the scientific arguments of the states. The next section pays particular attention to the role of and interaction in global and regional health and trade institutions. These organizations have played an important transmission role as experts regularly interacted and learnt from experiences in other countries with similar health-related concerns. For instance, Article 5 of the Colombian reformulated law 2120 states that the front label should include a warning label 'which should have a high preventive effect, be clear, visible, legible, easily identified and understood by

[23] Decision 562 of the Commission of the Andean Community. "Guidelines for the preparation, adoption and application of technical regulations in the member countries of the Andean Community and at the community level" of 25 of June 2003.

[24] For Mexico (Bahri and Charvel 2021), Chile (Araya et al. 2019) and Colombia (Villa García and Quiroz 2023).

consumers, and contain clear messages warning the consumer of excessive levels of critical nutrients'. Article 5 continues stating that the 'Ministry of Health and Social Protection, will regulate the technical parameters of this libelling, … based on the best scientific evidence available. … For this purpose, it may take into account the scientific evidence provided by the World Health Organization (WHO)'.

10.4.2.2 Health Standards: WHO and PAHO

The World Health Organization (WHO) and the PAHO are responsible for addressing health issues and developing standards. In 2016, PAHO introduced a nutrient profiling model that identifies processed and ultra-processed products as those with excessive amounts of sodium, free sugars, sweeteners, total fat, saturated fats or trans-fats (PAHO 2016). The PAHO considers that the best option to transmit information to the consumers is in the way the octagonal signs do, because the signs are clear, direct and simple. Also, the PAHO highlighted the benefits of the octagonal system over other warning systems:

> No evidence is provided to support the argument that the traffic light system offers consumers more choice or that it makes it easier to read and understand the nutritional components of products compared to other systems. In fact, some independent scientific data have shown the opposite: the use of the traffic light system has proved less effective in informing consumers when products contain excessive amounts of sugars, fats or sodium, compared to the nutrition warning system (28, 52, 54) adopted in Chile, Mexico, Peru and Uruguay, and proposed for use in Brazil, Canada and other countries. (PAHO 2020, at 17)

It is a sign of diffusion that PAHO has advocated for the use of octagonal signs, following the example of Peru and Chile, which have already implemented similar laws. This is a common occurrence as diffusion is not limited to states: 'In political diffusion, all kinds of actors from professionals to politicians, journalists and pundits seek to influence both the spin of policy evaluations and the issue-definition with reports, lobbying, interventions in the political debates, campaigning and so on. The whole process is less structured and more complex because it involves many actors and it spans the whole policy cycle' (Gilardi and Wasserfallen 2019).

However, it is important to note that PAHO recommendations are not mandatory, and even the WHO does not have a mandatory FOPL system. In contrast, octagonal signs are not forbidden. Nevertheless, the WHO does provide guidelines for warning labelling of food products. According to WHO, 'Guiding principles and framework manual for front-of-pack labelling for promoting healthy diets':

> Principle 7: The FOPL system should be interpretive, based on symbols, colours, words or quantifiable elements.
>
> Principle 8: The design of FOPL systems should be understandable to all population subgroups, and should be based on the outcome of consumer testing, evidence of system performance and stakeholder engagement (WHO 2019, 18)

If a government plans to develop a new FOPL system, the WHO proposes a checklist to guide implementation. The guidelines explicitly refer to the Chilean approach in the first part and state:

> Review the elements of existing systems that are considered to be more effective or less effective in supporting consumers to make informed food purchases and healthier eating choices (using published evidence or primary consumer studies of the usefulness of FOPL system elements, including format such as design and content). The three main categories of systems that can be compared are:
> - interpretive systems such as the multiple traffic light labelling system (United Kingdom), Nutri-Score system (France) and warning system (Chile); [underlined by author]
> - non-interpretive systems such as percentage reference intakes (European Union); and
> - hybrid systems such as the Health Star Rating (Australia and New Zealand). (WHO 2019, 19)

The WHO acknowledges the Chilean model as one that can be followed by other states in the world. The WHO endorsement might have supported the regional diffusion in Latin America.

> The report further states: Much of the available evidence on the performance of FOPL in guiding consumers to identify healthier food products comes from developed countries and has tended to focus on the comparison of interpretive (particularly multiple traffic light labels) and non-interpretive nutrient-based systems. Furthermore, evidence suggests that system performance may be moderated by its familiarity in the marketplace, such that increased familiarity with a system improves its understanding. However, emerging findings of primary research studies, in particular from Latin American countries, provide new evidence on the potential effectiveness of other types of systems, including other interpretive nutrient-based systems, summary indicator systems and hybrid systems. Hence, the generalizability of research findings on a FOPL system's performance across countries may be variable, given differences in prior exposures. It is prudent for countries to undertake consumer testing of proposed FOPL systems to ensure their suitability for the target market [underline not in the original]. (WHO 2019, 17)

This statement is in line with the recommendations outlined in the WHO document 'Implementing nutrition labelling policies of WHO', which emphasizes the importance of respecting publicity, transparency and stakeholder relations when implementing an FOPL (WHO 2021). The octagonal system also adheres to the Codex Alimentarius Regulations, which prohibit the provision of false, misleading, or deceptive information that may create an erroneous impression of its character (Codex Alimentarius, Principle 1, CXS-1-1-1985).

It is evident from the dates of the WHO and PAHO documents that the octagonal warning labels used by the Pacific Alliance countries have had an impact and are now considered a model to emulate. These warnings do not contradict the guidelines of these international organizations. Although PAHO and WHO standards are not mandatory, it is reasonable to assume that the standardization work of multilateral and regional intergovernmental health organizations supports the direction of the mandatory labelling system. Additionally, discussions in the WTO have helped to address concerns early on and may have led to policies that are certainly less trade-restrictive.

When comparing the legislative projects of Pacific Alliance member states, it is important to note that none of them directly mention the countries that inspired their labelling policies. However, the existence of boilerplating or close alignment across the cases provides indirect evidence of diffusion mechanisms at play. Regarding specific diffusion mechanisms, one popular mechanism discussed in political science literature is 'learning' (Gilardi and Wasserfallen 2019). Countries observe the development and implementation of policies in other countries and learn from the consequences of those policies. If the outcomes are positive, such as a high degree of policy acceptance and little opposition, they update their beliefs and are likely to pursue similar strategies to achieve their public policy objectives. It seems likely that the significant time gap between the acceptance of the law and the implementation regulations was intentional. This gap allows for extensive participation and consultation by interested parties in the final design of the measures. It also provides an opportunity to learn from debates in other countries and within international organizations.

To enhance the diffusion across countries, it would be beneficial to discuss the common regulation of FOPL in the Technical Barriers to Trade Committee of The Pacific Alliance. This committee coordinates positions on TBT matters among its members in the WTO and shares regulatory experiences in informal settings. The feasibility of a common regulation on octagonal warning can be inferred from the precedent set by Decision 9 of 2020[25].

Decision No. 9 of the Pacific Alliance TBT Committee adds to the Additional Protocol to the Pacific Alliance Framework Agreement an Annex on the Elimination of Technical Barriers to Trade in Food Supplements. The Decision provides guidance on regulating the labelling of food supplements. However, it does not provide in-depth information on octagonal signs. It proposes common criteria for the information that should be shared, such as the measure of 100 grams to oblige the sharing of information on critical nutrients and the mention of the five types of critical elements seen in the Colombian case. Point 13 regulates what refers to 'positive' mentions or statements. These decisions and statements will help to protect the health measures from criticism and promote the use of labelling models in the region.

10.5 CONCLUSIONS

By 2023, it is clear that octagonal nutrition warning FOPL has become a standard in most Latin American countries. Although this chapter only presents Pacific Alliance

[25] Decisión N°9 de la Comisión de Libre Comercio del Protocolo Adicional al Acuerdo Marco de la Alianza del Pacífico. https://alianzapacifico.net/download/decision-no-9-anexo-suplementos-alimenticios-eliminacion-de-obstaculos-tecnicos/.

member countries, it is worth noting that Argentina and Uruguay also use octagonal labelling. Additionally, Panama, Brazil, Jamaica and Canada are currently discussing its use (Sanchez et al. 2018).

Latin America has been contributing to international trade law with the use of octagonal warning signs for the past ten years. This regulation was first introduced in Chile in 2013 and was initially criticized before the TBT Committee. The octagonal standard is now widely accepted, but it was not always the case during its consolidation period. At first, Chile and Peru relied on cross-fertilization to advance their legislation due to the lack of clear recommendations beyond those expressed by PAHO in 2016 and 2020. Later on, the Mexican and Colombian processes were aided by the work of these international organizations. These last two processes were not easy. The Mexican food industry criticized the project and was later accused of paying for biased studies.[26] In the Colombian case, private parties initiated a lawsuit that set an important precedent for achieving the labelling change, thanks to PAHO.

The diffusion of laws among Pacific Alliance members did not result in copy-pasting. Instead, there is evidence of evolution and improvement in the regulations. The Mexican regulation followed the criteria of Chile and Peru by setting thresholds and using octagonal signs but also introduced 'positive signs' for products without critical nutrients. Similarly, the Colombian regulation used positive signs and included additional warnings. Colombia broke from the previous standards of Chile, Mexico and Peru and tried to adopt a new approach but lately changed and followed the octagonal signs and positive signs.

Additionally, it is important not to overlook the role of the WTO and the initial criticisms of Chile and Peru, including Mexico, which later adopted the system it had criticized years earlier. The member states of the Pacific Alliance undoubtedly used the criteria of the TBT Agreement to prevent criticism of their legislation. They did this by consulting with the private and public sectors, discussing at length at the legislative level, referencing international standards, and allowing for judicial or administrative review of the process. For example, in Colombia, there is judicial review, while in Peru, administrative review is available.

In conclusion, this chapter discusses the development of a new labelling system led by Chile and adopted by several Latin American countries. The system has become a standard and could serve as a model for countries both within and outside the region. It has been tested in the WTO and is consistent with international health standards. Ultimately, this could be taken as a successful example of balancing trade and health concerns.

[26] Alianza por la salud alimentaria. Corporaciones de alimentos y bebidas traen "ciencia chatarra" a México para negar daños a salud y combatir el impuesto (2015). https://alianzasalud.org.mx/2015/09/corporaciones-de-alimentos-y-bebidas-traen-ciencia-chatarra-a-mexico-para-negar-danos-a-salud-y-combatir-el-impuesto/.

REFERENCES

Araya, S., A.Elberg, C.Noton and D.Schwartz. 2019. "Identifying Food Labeling Effects on Consumer." https://ssrn.com/abstract=3195500, accessed on 10 November 2023.

Bahri, A. and S.Charvel 2021. "The Mexican Front-of-Pack Labeling Reform: Is it Compatible with International Trade Law?." *Journal of World Investment & Trade*22(2): 223–248.

Boza, S., R.Polanco and V.Saco. 2020. "Front-of-package Nutrition Labelling. In Latin America: Review of the Cases of Chile and Peru." *Boletim do Instituto de Saúde* (BIS) 21(1): 141–150.

Checkel, J. 2005. "International Institutions and Socialization in Europe: Introduction and Framework." *International Organization*59(4): 801–826.

Codex Alimentarius. 1985. CODEX STAN 1-1985. General Standard for the Labelling of Prepackaged Foods.

El Poder del Consumidor. 2021. "A un año de su implementación, el etiquetado frontal de advertencia ha traído cambios positivos indiscutibles en México." https://elpoderdelconsumidor.org/2021/09/a-un-ano-de-su-implementacion-el-etiquetado-frontal-de-advertencia-ha-traido-cambios-positivos-indiscutibles-en-mexico/, accessed on 10 November 2023.

Gilardi, F. 2012. "Transnational Diffusion: Norms, Ideas, and Policies." In: W.Carlsnaes, T. Risse and B. Simmons (Eds.), *Handbook of International Relations*. Thousand Oaks: SAGE Publications.

Gilardi, F. and F.Wasserfallen 2019. "The Politics of Policy Diffusion." *European Journal of Political Research* 58(4): 1245–1256

Kapterian, G. 2010. "A Critique of the WTO Jurisprudence on 'Necessity." *ICLQ* 59: 89–127.

Luna, F. 2019. "Etiquetado: Primeros resultados en autoservicios". Kantar Noticias 12/09/2019. https://www.kantarworldpanel.com/pe/Noticias/Etiquetado-Primeros-resultados-en-autoservicios, accessed on 10 November 2023.

March, J. G. and J. P.Olsen 1998. "The Institutional Dynamics of International Political Orders." *International Organization* 52(4): 943–969.

PAHO (Pan American Health Organization). 2016. "Nutrient Profile Model". Washington, DC, 2016, https://iris.paho.org/handle/10665.2/18621

PAHO. 2020. "Front-of-Package Labeling as a Policy Tool for the Prevention of Noncommunicable Diseases in the Americas. Washington, DC, 2020, https://iris.paho.org/handle/10665.2/52740

Sánchez, K., N.Balderas, A.Munguia and S.Barquera 2018. *El etiquetado de alimentos y bebidas: La experiencia en Mexico*. Instituto Nacional de Salud Pública.

Simmons, B., F. Dobbin and G. Garrett 2006. "Introduction: The International Diffusion of Liberalism." *International Organization* 60(4): 781–810.

Thow, A-M, A. Jones, C. Hawkes, I. Ali and R. Labonté 2017. "Nutrition Labelling Is a Trade Policy Issue: Lessons from an Analysis of Specific Trade Concerns at the World Trade Organization." *Health Promotion International* 33: 561–571.

Villa, I. and A.Quiroz 2023. *Etiquetado frontal de advertencia en Colombia y México: Un estudio a la luz del derecho comparado*. Monografía para optar por el título de abogadas de la Universidad EAFIT.

WHO 2019. "Guiding Principles and Framework Manual for Front-of-Pack Labelling for Promoting Healthy Diets." www.who.int/publications/m/item/guidingprinciples-labelling-promoting-healthydiet, accessed on 10 November 2023.

2021. "Implementing Nutrition Labelling Policies: A Review of Contextual Factors." www.who.int/publications/i/item/9789240035089, accessed on 10 November 2023.

2018. "Minutes of the meeting of 8–9 November 2017." https://alianzasalud.org.mx/wp-content/uploads/2018/05/omc-bloqueo-mx-vs-etiquetado-peru-30-04-18.pdf, accessed on 20 February 2020.

11

The Political Economy of Investment Protection Reform in South American PTAs

Julia Calvert

11.1 INTRODUCTION

In 2012, the United Nations Conference for Trade and Development (UNCTAD) proclaimed that a new generation of investment policy was emerging, one in which governments recognised the need to harness foreign investment in ways that better promoted sustainable and inclusive development. A key challenge for governments, they observed, was the need to bring international investment agreements (IIAs) into line with these objectives. As it stood, IIAs were 'focused almost exclusively on protecting investors and [did] not do enough to promote investment for development' (UNCTAD 2012, 7). Efforts to reform investment protection standards have grown rapidly in national and multilateral institutions since the report. These reforms range from incremental modifications to the wording and scope of key provisions to paradigm-shifting changes that aim to transform the way foreign investment is governed.[1] Investment chapters in preferential trade agreements (PTAs) have come to the forefront of reform efforts amid the declining popularity of bilateral investment treaties (BITs). What do they represent to the future of investment protection?

This chapter examines trends in the formulation of PTA investment chapters in South America, where governments were some of the first to experience the costs of BITs. Until recently, South America was the most litigated region by foreign investors under BITs, having since fallen behind Europe. As the number of BIT claims brought against South American governments grew, so too did public pressure for reform. Governments responded to these pressures differently. Ecuador, Bolivia and Venezuela took the unprecedented move of terminating BITs and/or withdrawing from enforcement mechanisms like the International Centre for the Settlement of Investment Dispute (ICSID) Convention (although

[1] On reform typologies, see Roberts (2018).

Ecuador since rejoined). Colombia, Chile and Peru stayed the course and expanded their investment protection commitments. Examining the political economy of international investment law reform through the formulation of South American PTAs can help us understand the role and capacity of capital-importing countries in reshaping investment protection standards in the new reform era.

This chapter makes two primary arguments. One is that domestic factors matter in shaping the articulation of investment protection commitments, even in countries that have traditionally been seen as rule-takers in trade and investment negotiations. Arguably, the legitimacy crisis now confronting international investment law has created more political space for domestic actors and institutions to shape investment lawmaking, which has contributed to experimentation with new reforms. However, the epistemic and political influence of extra-regional trade partners continues to weigh heavily on treaty-making programmes in all but Brazil, where officials are seeking to change foreign investment governance. The second argument this chapter makes is that increased variation in PTA contents may exacerbate the challenges governments face in promoting sustainable and inclusive development. On one hand, incremental reforms incorporated into investment chapters may help governments preserve greater policy space. On the other hand, increased diversity in the IIA universe can reduce the clarity of governments' investment protection commitments and increase compliance problems. This lack of clarity may pose significant risks, especially for Peru, Chile and Colombia, which have expanded investor access to investor–state dispute settlement (ISDS).

The next part of this chapter provides contextual background by discussing the rise of PTA investment chapters amid the declining popularity of BITs. Section 11.2 focuses on the post-2012 'reform era' and details the kinds of reforms reflected in South America's PTA investment chapters. Section 11.3 discusses the drivers of these reforms, focusing on the formation of countries' reform preferences and the role of domestic norms and actors. The final section concludes.

11.2 THE RISE OF INVESTMENT CHAPTERS

In the post-war era, most South American countries fiercely opposed the standards of investment protection then championed by the United States (US) and Europe. Suspicion of foreign investors and the predominance of state-led development models favoured more protectionist management of domestic investment markets. The tide began to turn by the 1980s. Much of South America warmed to the idea that foreign investment could bring economic growth. As a result, governments looked for quick and efficient means of attracting it. Signing IIAs became the method of choice, due in part to their endorsement by influential capital-exporting countries and international organisations (Poulsen 2015; Usynin and Gáspár-Szilágyi 2018; Berge and St. John 2021). Almost 300 IIAs were concluded by South American governments in the 1990s, a leap from the handful of agreements

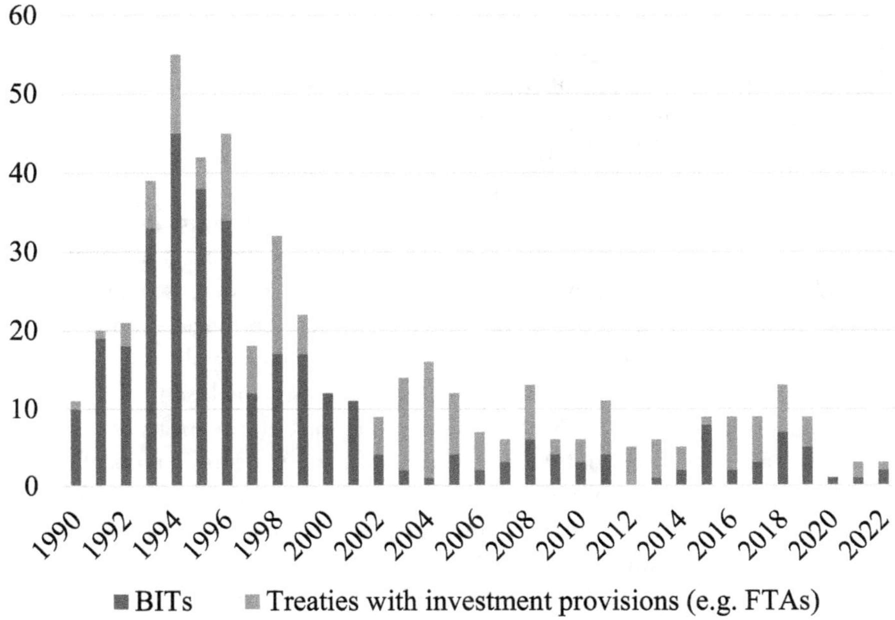

FIGURE 11.1 IIAs signed by South American countries 1990–2022.
Source: Author created using data from UNCTAD (2022a).

that existed in the previous decade (UNCTAD 2005, 15). Most of these agreements took the form of BITs that were similar in nature and scope. They were short in text with broad definitions (e.g. of investors and investment) and vaguely worded standards of treatment that included most-favoured nation, national treatment, fair and equitable treatment, full protection and security. They also included compensation requirements for expropriation, all of which were backed by ISDS (Polanco Lazo 2016, 82).[2] Under ISDS, governments agreed to arbitrate investment disputes through third-party institutions, enabling investors to bring legal claims against them directly.

Yet, the wave of treaty signings was short-lived. Fewer than ten BITs were concluded annually after 2001, a sharp drop from the mid-1990s when forty-five agreements were signed in one year alone (see Figure 11.1). A common explanation for the declining popularity of the BIT pertains to the rise in ISDS cases. Most South American governments had experienced at least one investor claim by the early 2000s, just as treaty formulation began to slow. Scholars argue that investor claims delivered clearer and more salient information about the potential costs of BITs, leading governments to be more cautious in their treaty-making programmes

[2] On the global drivers of treaty formulation in this period, see Elkins et al. 2006; Allee and Peinhardt 2014; Simmons 2014.

(Poulsen 2015), and generating demands for reform (Haftel and Thompson 2018).[3] The decline in BIT signings, therefore, reflected a process of political learning whereby governments and civil society groups became more aware of the major design flaws in BITs and the potential costs they might impose.

Indeed, criticism of BITs and the ISDS system by civil society groups, academics and practitioners grew quickly in the early 2000s, leading some to proclaim a legitimacy crisis in international investment law (cf Franck 2005; Penhardt and Wellhausen 2016; Landford and Fauchauld 2018). Critics expressed concern over the ambiguity and breadth with which investment rules were written, which allowed, they argued, foreign investors to challenge a wide range of government measures as a violation of their treaty rights. This ambiguity also bestowed on international arbitrators considerable interpretative power, which some feared they would use to the benefit of investor claimants (Franck 2005; Spears 2010, 1040; Schill 2017, 653). That most international arbitrators are trained in commercial law and come from a handful of prestigious (Western) institutions generated the risk that arbitrators would favour commercial interpretations of investment rules without assigning adequate significance to public interests (like human rights) and the unique challenges faced by low- and middle-income countries when interpreting the facts of a dispute (Franck 2007; Sornarajah 2008; Waincymer 2009; Nunnenkamp 2017). The practice of double hatting – when one person serves as an arbitrator in one case and corporate counsel in another – established direct incentives for international arbitrators to favour investors in their judgements (Kapeliuk 2012, 274; Puig and Shaffer 2018, 366).

Other concerns pertained to the single-liability principle and forum-shopping. The single-liability principle refers to the fact that under BITs, states assume all the obligations with very narrow grounds upon which they could hold investors liable for their own wrongdoing (Yazbek 2010, 104–105; Alschner 2018, 240). Forum-shopping, the practice of locating operations in a country with a wide array of, or more stringent, BITs, meant that investors could exploit the patchwork of BITs to enhance their power over host-governments. Critics cautioned that these factors, combined with the exorbitant costs of ISDS proceedings would contribute to regulatory chill whereby governments fail to introduce or amend policies for fear of a costly and protracted legal battle (Spears 2010; Tienhaara 2018; Thakur 2021).

Ecuador, Bolivia and Venezuela famously reacted to these concerns by terminating BITs and/or withdrawing from the ICSID Convention. Other governments continued to deepen their commitments to investment protections, albeit in a different form. Indeed, bucking the decline in BIT signings was a rise in the number of investment chapters concluded as part of broader PTAs. Between 2001 and 2011,

3 Studies find that governments were largely unaware of the potential costs of BITs when they signed onto them and current governments had little knowledge of the investment protection commitments made by their predecessors (cf. Poulsen 2015; Sattorova 2018; Calvert 2022).

TABLE 11.1 *PTAs signed by South American countries 2001–2011*

- 2010 Bolivia-Mexico
- 2002 Chile-EU
- *(1997 BIT w Austria; 1992 Belgium-Luxembourg Economic Union; 1994 Croatia; 1995 Czech Republic; 1993 Denmark; 1993 Finland; 1992 France; 1991 Germany; 1996 Greece; 1997 Hungary; 1993 Italy; 1998 Netherlands; 1995 Poland; 1995 Portugal; 1995 Romania; 1991 Spain; 1993 Sweden; 1996 United Kingdom)*
- 2003 Chile-European Free Trade Association
- *(2003 Chile-Iceland BIT; 1993 Chile-Norway BIT; 1999 Chile-Switzerland BIT, all (i))*
- 2003 Chile-Korea*(i)
- 2003 Chile-US*(i)
- 2005 Chile-China (followed by 2008 supplementary agreement on investment)*(i)
- 2005 Chile-New Zealand, Singapore and Brunei Darussalam
- *(1999 New Zealand BIT)*
- 2006 Chile-Colombia*(i)
- 2006 Chile-Panama
- *(1996 Chile-Panama BIT)*
- 2006 Chile-Peru*(i)
- 2007 Chile-Japan*(i)
- 2008 Chile-Australia*(i)
- *(1992 Chile-Malaysia BIT)*
- 2009 Chile-Turkey
- *(1998 BIT signed but not in force)*
- 2010 Chile-Malaysia
- 2011 Chile-Vietnam
- *(1999 BIT signed but not in force)*
- 2006 Colombia-US*(i)
- 2007 Colombia-Northern Triangle*(i)
- 2008 Colombia-EFTA*
- 2008 Colombia-Canada*(i)
- 2005 Mercosur-Peru
- 2007 Mercosur-Israel
- 2010 Mercosur-Egypt
- 2003 Peru-Thailand
- *(1991 Peru-Thailand BIT) (i)*
- 2006 Peru-US*(i)
- 2008 Peru-Canada*(i)
- 2008 Peru-Singapore*(i)
- 2009 Peru-China*(i)
- 2010 Peru-EFTA*
- 2010 Peru-Korea*(i)
- 2011 Peru-Costa Rica*(i)
- 2011 Peru-Japan
- *(co-exists w 2008 Peru-Japan BIT) (i)*
- 2011 Peru-Mexico*(i)
- 2011 Peru-Panama*(i)
- 2003 Uruguay-Mexico*(i)

Source: Author created using data from UNCTAD 2022.
Note: *contains investment chapter; (i) provides for ISDS.

South American governments signed thirty-four PTAs with reciprocal commitments, more than 60 per cent of which contained an investment chapter. And all but two of these chapters contained ISDS provisions. It seems somewhat contradictory that PTA investment chapters grew while BITs declined. Yet, as illustrated in Table 11.1, only a minority of countries – namely Chile, Colombia and Peru – were responsible for the growth.[4] Bolivia and Mercosur member countries continued to exclude them from their PTAs, while Ecuador and Venezuela abstained from trade agreements entirely.

[4] Chile, Peru and Colombia also signed BITs after 2001, sometimes for the purpose of treaty updating. Peru signed five BITs, its most recent being that with Japan in 2008. Chile has signed four more BITs, most recently with Hong Kong in 2015. Colombia being a relative late-comer to investment treaty-making, concluded 15 BITs after 2005, the most recent of which was with Spain in 2021. Therefore, while PTA investment chapters had become increasingly popular, they did not displace BITs entirely.

In some ways, PTA investment chapters signed in this period represented an early phase in the reform of international investment law. For the most part, they were written with greater detail and clarity than first-generation BITs and incorporated a limited recognition of social objectives. In some instances, investment chapters replaced BITs that were increasingly seen as outdated. Chile replaced its 1997 BIT with Korea with the 2003 Chile-Korea PTA investment chapter, which contains more precise definitions of key terms and standards. For instance, it stipulates investment characteristics and narrows the treaty's scope and coverage.[5] The treaty also recognises environmental concerns. Article 10.18 on Environmental Measures stipulates that:

> 1. Nothing in this Chapter shall be construed to prevent a Party from adopting, maintaining or enforcing any measure otherwise consistent with this Chapter that it considered appropriate to ensure that an investment activity is undertaken in a manner sensitive to environmental concerns.
> 2. The Parties recognise that it is inappropriate to encourage investment by relaxing domestic health, safety or environmental measures.

The 1997 Chile-Korea BIT made no reference to the environment or related concerns in its vaguely worded nine-page text.

Yet, most PTA investment chapters also deepened government commitments to investment liberalisation. Investment chapters provide pre- and post-establishment rights to national treatment and most-favoured nation status, while BITs typically provide only post-establishment rights. Pre-establishment rights increase the onus placed on governments for investment liberalisation. For instance, pre-establishment rights to national treatment require that governments provide foreign investors equal access to the domestic market even before an investment is made, which affects foreign investment admissions and vetting processes. This prevents governments from imposing approval requirements or sectoral caps on the quantity of incoming foreign direct investment (FDI). Investment chapters also more often prohibit the use of performance requirements, such as those related to export volumes and technology transfer, tools that advanced economies used to promote development in the past (Chang 2004). Therefore, while PTA investment chapters afforded governments more precision in their investment protection commitments, they also demanded greater liberalisation of domestic investment markets.

Extra-regional partners, particularly in North America, had a large impact on the contents of these chapters. For instance, the 2003 Chile-Korea PTA mentioned

[5] For instance, Article 10.2.4 of the Chile-Korea PTA stipulates that:

> Nothing in this Chapter shall be construed to prevent a Party from providing a service or preforming a function such as law enforcement, correctional services, income security or insurance, social security or insurance, social welfare, public education, public training, health and childcare.

above shares 80 per cent of its text with an earlier PTA signed between Chile and Mexico (1998) and 75 per cent of its text with the 1996 Chile-Canada PTA. Both of these investment chapters were modelled after the 1992 North American Free Trade Agreement (NAFTA), which itself heavily reflected US preferences.[6] NAFTA's chapter 11 on investment set a new precedence in its scope and coverage, particularly in relation to investment liberalisation. It was also written with greater detail and clarity than most BITs at the time. The Chile-Korea PTA article on environmental measures is virtually identical to that of NAFTA's chapter 11, which the US pushed for as a means to ensure that Mexico did not lower environmental standards to attract FDI. Canada, Mexico and the US used their bargaining power to push chapter 11 standards southwards through the negotiation of PTAs with South American partners. Yet, South American treaty signers were not unwilling adherents. Chile embraced the NAFTA gold-standard model, integrating into its own treaty-making programme.

The US also diffused some of the incremental reforms it adopted to its own model BIT post-NAFTA. The 2006 Peru-US PTA and the 2003 Chile-US PTA share 92 per cent of their text and carried forward NAFTA's gold-standard, but with key changes that later appeared in the 2004 US model BIT. For instance, a key innovation of the 2004 US BIT model was the incorporation of a qualified fair and equitable treatment standard (see Schwebel 2011).

In some countries, the decline of the BIT was met with the rise of the PTA investment chapter. The question is: why were government officials in Chile, Colombia and Peru less responsive to the emerging legitimacy crisis in international investment law than their counterparts elsewhere? And, to what extent has their stance on PTA investment chapters changed in the new reform era?

11.3 PTA INVESTMENT CHAPTERS IN THE REFORM ERA

Since 2012, South American governments have signed twenty-one PTAs, including bilateral and mega-regional agreements. Chile and Colombia continued to lead PTA signings, followed by Peru. Mercosur countries and Ecuador signed fewer agreements while Bolivia and Venezuela abstained completely. As Table 11.2 illustrates, slightly over half (11) of the agreements contain investment chapters, down from 60 per cent in the previous decade. Of the eleven PTAs with an investment chapter, ten contain ISDS provisions. Therefore, among those countries that continue to include investment chapters in their PTAs – namely, Chile, Peru and Colombia – there continues to be a loose consensus on the merits of retaining the ISDS system. However, it should be noted that twenty-four per cent of the PTAs concluded in this period do not contain an investment chapter nor co-exist with a

[6] Based on data provided by the Electronic Database on Investment Treaties. See Alschner et al. (2021).

TABLE 11.2 *PTAs signed by South American countries 2012–2023*

2018 Brazil-Chile*
2012 Chile-Hong Kong
(*2016 Chile-Hong Kong BIT*)
2013 Chile-Thailand
2016 Chile-Uruguay
(*2010 Chile-Uruguay BIT*)
2017 Chile-Argentina*(i)
2017 Chile-Indonesia
2020 Chile-Ecuador
2021 Chile-Paraguay
(*1995 Chile-Paraguay BIT*)
2012 Colombia-Peru-Ecuador-EU**
(*2009 Colombia-Belgium-Luxembourg BIT; 2014 Colombia-France BIT; 2007 Colombia-Peru BIT; 2021 Colombia-Spain BIT; 2014 Pacific Alliance Protocol; 2005 Peru-Belgium-Luxembourg BIT; 1995 Peru-Germany BIT; 1995 Peru-Finland BIT; 1994 Peru-Denmark BIT; 1994 Peru-Netherlands BIT; 1994 Peru-Spain BIT; 1994 Peru-Portugal BIT; 1994 Peru-Italy BIT; 1994 Peru-Czechia BIT; 1993 Peru-France BIT*)
2013 Colombia-Costa Rica*(i)
2013 Colombia-Israel*(i)
2013 Colombia-Korea*(i)
2013 Colombia-Panama* (i)
2017 Colombia-Mercosur
2019 Colombia-Ecuador-Peru-UK
(*2010 Colombia-UK BIT; 1993 Peru-UK BIT*)
2018 Comprehensive and Progressive Transpacific Partnership*(i)
2018 Ecuador-European Free Trade Association
2014 Pacific Alliance*(i)
2022 Pacific Alliance-Singapore*(i)
2015 Peru-Honduras*(i)
2018 Peru-Australia*(i)

Source: author created using data from UNCTAD (2022a)
Note: *contains an investment chapter; ** Ecuador joined in 2017; (i) provides for ISDS

BIT. This is an uptick from the 15 per cent of PTAs without investment protections between treaty partners signed in the previous decade, suggesting that trade liberalisation may be becoming disentangled from the issue of investment protection.

The year 2012 did not mark a historic juncture in international investment law amongst treaty signers. Most treaty drafters did not depart in substantial ways from traditional investment protection standards. Rather, most PTA investment chapters continued the trend towards incremental reform. Like pre-2012 PTAs, they encompass more precise definitions of key terms than first-generation BITs, such as investment and investor, and clarify substantive protections, including those related to fair and equitable treatment and indirect expropriation. It is noteworthy however that there are strong similarities between some agreements concluded after 2012 and those concluded before it. For instance, the 2013 Colombia-Korea PTA shares 76 per cent of its content with the 2003 Chile-US PTA (Alschner et al. 2021).

More generally, though, the degree of similarity across PTA investment chapters has declined slightly over time. No PTA signed after 2012 shares more than 76 per cent of its content with another agreement, and the vast majority of agreements are closer in content to other PTAs signed after 2012. This is likely because the kinds of incremental reforms that governments are experimenting with have grown, and their usage and wording vary across agreements. For instance, Colombia's recent PTA investment chapters with Costa Rica and Korea use an asset-based definition of investment, while the Colombia-Panama PTA investment chapter adopts a slightly more restrictive enterprise-based definition. The Colombia-Costa Rica PTA and the Colombia-Panama PTA exclude matters of taxation from the substantive scope of the treaty, but the Colombia-Korea PTA does not (although it does exclude subsidies, grants and government procurement).

It is now common for investment chapters to include procedural amendments that reduce coverage over sensitive policy areas or economic sectors and increase the transparency of arbitral proceedings. Yet, procedural reforms also vary. The Colombia-Korea PTA establishes an alternative dispute resolution mechanism alongside ISDS and disallows the submission of arbitral claims concerning disputes of a certain nature, for instance, involving measures 'appropriate to ensure that investment activity … is undertaken in a manner sensitive to environmental concerns' (Article 8.11). The Colombia-Costa Rica PTA does neither of these things, but it does contain stronger transparency requirements, including the public release of arbitral documents.

Another key change pertains to the incorporation of language concerning corporate social responsibility (CSR) and social objectives. Arguably, this is also where we see the greatest variation across investment chapters. The first South American PTAs to include explicit articles on CSR were the Colombia-Canada PTA and the Peru-Canada PTA, both signed in 2008. Eight of the eleven investment chapters concluded post-2012 contain such articles, suggesting South American governments have adopted them as commonplace.[7] It should also be noted, however, that CSR standards continue to depend on voluntary compliance by investors. As such, recent investment chapters do not necessarily revise the single-party liability principle. Whether they expand the grounds upon which host-states can bring successful counterclaims has yet to be seen. New provisions related to the right to regulate, environmental protection and sustainable development feature widely in post-2012 investment chapters. These provisions are meant to empower arbitral tribunals to decide case details in light of their impact on public interest matters in the hopes that governments will preserve more policy space. Yet, there is strong variation in the use of these provisions. For instance, the Colombia-Costa Rica PTA references labour standards and CSR but does not reference governments' right to regulate beyond the treaty preamble. The Colombia-Korea PTA does not reference labour standards nor CSR but explicitly recognises the right to regulate outside of the treaty preamble.

One of the most notable changes in the post-2012 reform era is the conclusion of mega-regional PTAs with investment chapters. Investment chapters of both the Comprehensive and Progressive Agreement for Trans-Pacific Partnership (CPTPP)

[7] The only PTA investment chapters not to include CSR are the 2013 Colombia-Israel PTA, the 2013 Colombia-Korea PTA and the 2015 Peru-Honduras PTA.

and the Pacific Alliance Additional Protocol share important similarities, which is perhaps unsurprising, given that the founding countries of the Pacific Alliance include two CPTPP members. They carry forward the trend towards incremental reform, but there are also some notable differences between them. For instance, the agreements differ in the restrictions placed on the use of performance requirements,[8] in their articles on expropriation,[9] and in provisions on CSR.[10] Unlike the Pacific Alliance protocol, the CPTPP investment chapter also includes an article on subrogation (Article 9.13) and explicitly provides for counterclaims in ISDS proceedings (Article 9.19.2). In broad strokes, these agreements represent the consolidation of existing investment protection standards, given they largely preserve existing norms.

Variation in the wording and scope of incremental reforms suggests that international investment law has entered a phase of experimentation as governments seek to strike the right balance between investment protection and promoting sustainable development. However, this variation may reduce the overall clarity of governments' investment protection commitments and create new compliance problems (and greater costs). Slight changes in the wording of investment rules can generate different arbitral outcomes. For instance, Ecuador lost a US$ 75 million ISDS case to US-based Occidental after changes it made to the system of tax credits given to oil companies. It won a favourable judgement in an almost identical ISDS case brought by Canada-based EnCana. The different outcomes were due to the fact that Article XII(I) of the Canada-Ecuador BIT had more explicit language exempting matters of taxation from treaty coverage than the US-Ecuador BIT, under which Occidental brought its claim. The impact of these variations on arbitral outcomes means that governments have slightly different obligations to investors according to the IIA under which a claim is brought. In the context of limited resources, governments may struggle to monitor and enforce their compliance with their different commitments at the national level.

A second notable departure from pre-2012 trends are IIAs signed by Brazil, as in the 2017 Intra-Mercosur Investment Facilitation and Cooperation Protocol (herein referred to as 'the Mercosur Investment Protocol') and the 2018 Chile-Brazil PTA investment chapter. These agreements closely follow the Cooperation and Facilitation Investment Agreement (CFIA) model released by Brazil as the cornerstone of its treaty-making programme in 2015. Brazil's CFIAs are explicitly focused

8 Technology purchase requirements are included in the kinds of performance requirements prohibited in the CPTPP investment chapter and are not addressed in the Pacific Alliance protocol.

9 Article 9.8.6 on Compensation and Expropriation in the CPTPP Investment Chapter explicitly addresses the matter of issuing, renewing or maintaining a subsidy or grant. No similar article appears in the Pacific Alliance protocol.

10 The agreements contain similarly worded articles on 'Corporate Social Responsibility and 'Investment and Environmental, Health and other Regulatory Objectives'; however, unlike the CPTPP, the Pacific Alliance protocol includes them in a separate section C and explicitly excludes them from dispute resolution mechanisms.

on investment facilitation as opposed to investment protection and liberalisation. They exclude standard investment protections, including the highly controversial 'fair and equitable treatment' and 'full protection and security' standards, in favour of provisions aimed at encouraging cooperation between contracting parties on investment-related matters, the establishment of institutions that enhance communication between investors and host-governments (i.e. national focal points or Ombudspersons), and the implementation of dispute prevention mechanisms. CFIAs also reference CSR and forgo ISDS, providing for state-to-state dispute settlement instead.

The Mercosur Investment Protocol and the Brazil-Chile PTA investment chapter possess many of these characteristics. Article 4 of the Mercosur Investment Protocol explicitly excludes the standards of fair and equitable treatment, full protection and security and the pre-establishment phase from the agreement. The same standards are absent from the Brazil-Chile PTA. Against the rising number of PTA investment chapters with incremental reforms are, therefore, a select number of IIAs that incorporate paradigmatic change. Roberts (2018) defines paradigmatic reforms as those which establish a new framework for resolving foreign investment disputes as an alternative to the ISDS system. Both treaties meet this criterion in excluding ISDS provisions, but they also surpass it in shifting the policy debate over foreign investment governance from one of investment protection to one of creating a conducive business environment through enhanced transparency and cooperation. The latter approach arguably preserves greater policy space for governments to use domestic mechanisms that aim to attract and govern foreign investment in ways that promote sustainable and inclusive development.

That Chile agreed to Brazil's preferred investment rules as the basis for the 2018 PTA investment chapter bodes well for Brazil's ability to scale up its CFIA model. However, Chile has pursued international rules on investment facilitation alongside its focus on investment protection and tends not to see them as competing. The Chilean government has been a keen advocate of a Multilateral Agreement on Investment Facilitation for Development inside the World Trade Organisation. Chile has also been particularly flexible towards the preferences of its treaty partners, having recently agreed with Canada to ISDS in the context of the CPTPP while also accepting the EU's proposed multilateral investment court in the context of the EU-Chile Advanced Framework Agreement. While most of Colombia and Peru's PTAs include investment chapters (67 per cent and 71 per cent of PTAs, respectively), 55 per cent of Chile's PTAs do not and instead restrict investment rules to matters of trade in services and government procurement.[11] The exclusion of investment

[11] This trend is a continuation from the decade prior. Only 7 of the 14 PTAs Chile signed between 2001 and 2011 contained investment chapters, but all agreements without an investment chapter co-exist with a BIT. In the case of the Chile-Vietnam PTA and the Chile-Turkey PTA, the BITs are not in force.

chapters in Chilean PTAs reflects the fact that investment flows between Chile and many of its post-2012 partners are covered by a co-existing BIT, some of which were concluded in the run-up to the PTA negotiations.[12] However, Chile also signed three of the five PTAs that did not include an investment chapter nor co-exist with a BIT. The only Colombian and Peruvian PTAs to exclude investment chapters are those concluded with Ecuador and Europe (i.e. the Peru-Ecuador-Colombia-EU PTA and the closely associated Peru-Ecuador-Colombia-UK PTA),[13] but Colombia and Peru already have BITs in force with the UK and major capital-exporting EU member countries.

It should be noted that South American governments also pursued systemic reforms that aimed to further institutionalise the ISDS system. South American governments announced their intention to construct an alternative ISDS system under the banner of the Union of South American Nations (UNASUR) in 2010 that would rival ICSID. Their proposal included a new centre for investor–state arbitration, a code of conduct for arbitrators and mediators and a counselling centre for investment disputes. The arbitration centre was to include an appellate tribunal through which member states could submit arbitral judgements to review in the hopes that it would add greater consistency and predictability to the application of investment rules (Fiezzoni 2011). UNASUR representatives met to finalise the agreements in January 2016; however, momentum behind the initiative faded as political support for UNASUR waned amongst key member states. The initiative has since been shelved entirely, suggesting that governments have moved away from the idea of finding a regional answer to the reform question.

Post-2012, the IIA network in Latin America, looks increasingly diverse. First-generation BITs have been layered and sometimes replaced with second- and third-generation PTA investment chapters that encompass a wide range of reforms. Most IIAs now reflect a dominant preference for incremental reform, but paradigmatic reforms are appearing at the margins. Reforms of any degree may help governments better preserve public interests with promising results for sustainable and inclusive development given the significant limitations of first-generation BITs. However, they also threaten to further fragment an already complex area of international law. The danger then is that reform efforts are exacerbating – not alleviating – the very challenges that may hamper governments' abilities to meet development goals. What is driving these trends is the subject of the next section.

12 Chile's PTA with Uruguay and Hong Kong for instance built on pre-existing BITs signed in 2010 (when it was updated) and 2016, respectively. The Chile-Brazil PTA built on an investment facilitation agreement signed in 2015 and Chile and Paraguay had a BIT dating back to 1995.

13 The exclusion of an investment chapter from the 2012 Colombia-Peru-Ecuador-EU PTA, the derivative 2019 Colombia-Peru-Ecuador-UK PTA, and the 2017 Colombia-Mercosur PTA reflected opposition to incremental reforms in Ecuador and Brazil and questions around EU competence in negotiating investment chapters in EU PTAs (cf Usynin and Gáspár-Szilágyi 2018, 8–10).

11.4 THE DRIVERS OF REFORM

In accounting for PTA trends, we can differentiate between what governments want (their preferences) and what they agree to (treaty outcomes). Trade preferences are the set of rules that governments believe will generate the greatest economic and political benefits. They are informed by interest groups, political leadership (e.g. ideology and societal linkages), and beliefs about trade and investment liberalisation. Treaty outcomes are often an amalgam of country trade preferences, inter-state power politics and efficiency-seeking behaviour. All governments tend to sacrifice some of what they want to secure higher-order preferences. How much a government sacrifices is the result of uneven bargaining power (Putnam 1988). At the same time, the complexity of trade and investment rules and scarce government resources creates incentives for governments to rely on 'boilerplate' provisions found in their own IIAs or in those of treaty partners (Peacock et al. 2019).

The similarities across many post-2012 PTA investment chapters suggest that governments continue to rely on standardised language in their treaty drafting, even as these standards slightly change. Peacock et al. (2019) argue that this kind of behaviour stems from efficiency-seeking behaviour as governments seek to lower negotiating and drafting costs, and incorporate accumulated knowledge into an increasingly complex and nuanced set of agreements. Bargaining power dynamics also continued to shape the content of most South American PTAs, with the exception of those signed by Brazil. Post-2012 saw several instances in which these governments negotiated PTA investment chapters in a position of weaker bargaining power. In the TPP negotiations, Chile and Peru were disadvantaged relative to wealthier trade partners like the US, Australia, Canada, Japan and New Zealand.[14] The US, in particular, had a strong influence over that agreement, having used its bargaining power to shape the investment chapter after its own model BIT.[15] After the US withdrew in 2017, the CPTPP investment chapter went relatively unchanged. Exceptions include slight modifications to the definition of covered investment and a narrower scope to ISDS coverage.[16] Colombia was also arguably at a disadvantage when it signed agreements with Israel and Korea in 2013, which favoured incremental reform and preserved ISDS.

Yet, Chile, Colombia and Peru were not pulled towards more stringent investment protection standards that they otherwise did not support. That Chile, Peru and Colombia themselves supported these standards (albeit in a modified form) is evidenced by South-South PTAs and BITs signed in this period. Stark differences

[14] Negotiations towards the CPTPP were launched in 2008 under the banner of the Transpacific Partnership, but the final agreement was not signed until 2016.

[15] A text analysis by Alschner and Skougarevskiy (2015, 3) found that the TPP investment chapter shared 82 per cent of its text with the 2006 US-Colombia FTA, its closest relative.

[16] Side letters exempting New Zealand from ISDS coverage with its primary investment partners were also signed.

TABLE 11.3 *ISDS cases involving South American countries as respondents under IIAs*

Country*	Cases as respondent	Cases as home-state	Year of first claim against (outcome)	Wins	Losses	Settled or discontinued	Pending
Argentina	62	5	1997 (investor win)	6**	19	28	9
Bolivia	17	1	2002 (settled)	0	3	10	4
Chile	7	9	1998 (investor win)	3	2	0	2
Colombia	20	4	2016 (investor win)	5	1	1	13
Ecuador	24	0	2002 (settled)	6	8	4	7
Paraguay	3	0	1998 (State win)	1	1	1	0
Peru	31	3	1998 (settled)	6	2	4	19
Uruguay	5	1	1998 (State win)	4	0	0	1
Venezuela	53	1	1996 (investor win)	12	17	10	14

Source: Author created using data from UNCTAD (2022b).

in development status and market size did not characterise other PTA negotiations where incremental reforms were included. They were also included in investment chapters where South American governments arguably had the advantage, as in the case of the Peru-Honduras PTA and the Colombia-Costa Rica PTA. Chile may have had an advantage in PTA negotiations with Uruguay and Paraguay, but the parties addressed investment protection in stand-alone BITs with incremental reforms. That all three countries negotiated a stringent investment chapter with incremental reforms as the basis of the Pacific Alliance agreement further illustrates this point. Bargaining power and efficiency seeking therefore helped shape the content of many South American PTAs in the reform period, but they do not explain why governments were willing to negotiate these agreements in the first place nor their continued support for standard investment protections. Here, it is necessary to consider other factors.

Another explanation for incremental reform preferences in these countries pertains to their experience in ISDS. As illustrated in Table 11.3, the countries vary in the timing and frequency of investor claims. Peru faced its first ISDS case in 1998, and it has been sued relatively frequently. As of January 2023, at least thirty-one ISDS cases have been brought against the country under IIAs. Chile faced its first claim in 1998, but it has faced fewer total claims overall (seven). Colombia experienced its first ISDS case in 2016, but claims against the country grew quickly, reaching twenty ISDS cases by 2023. All three governments have won more cases than they lost, and the awards rendered against them have been relatively small.[17] Peru has won six cases (with costs) and lost two, settling or having discontinued four additional cases. Chile lost its first case, but the US$ 10 million paled in comparison to the US$ 515 million sought by the investor in that dispute. In total, Chile has won three cases and lost two, with two more cases pending. Colombia has won five of the cases, lost one and the others are pending.

The incremental reforms adopted by governments suggest a degree of policy learning about the dangers of overly broad and ambiguous treaty provisions (Haftel and Thompson 2018). According to Rivas (2013, 195), who headed Colombia's treaty model drafting and Free Trade Agreement (FTA) negotiations in the Ministry of Trade, updates to Colombia's 2017 model BIT were in part a result of the wave of treaty claims brought against it. A positive track record in ISDS proceedings may confirm for officials the overall benefits of their investment protection commitments and the impartiality of ISDS, in turn generating preferences for incremental reforms that retain the perceived benefits of the existing system. Countries that have terminated BITs (as in Ecuador) or withdrawn from ICSID have poor track records in ISDS proceedings.

Yet, investor claims do not alone explain the extent or timing of government reform preferences. It does not explain why Colombia updated its BIT model in 2006, 2008 and 2011, well before its first ISDS case. Outside of Peru, Chile and Colombia, governments that have not lost an ISDS case prefer systemic or paradigmatic reform. For instance, Indonesia refused to renew BITs with a host of partners despite having never lost an ISDS case.[18] Australia announced a ban on ISDS provisions under its Labour government in 2015, having only faced one claim, which it won (Calvert and Tienhaara 2022). Other governments like Argentina, which lost several costly ISDS cases, did not pursue paradigmatic reforms. Reform preferences, therefore, do not map neatly onto countries' arbitral records.

Another explanation for reform preferences pertains to countries' domestic landscapes and pressures. That government officials in Peru, Colombia and Chile held similar reform preferences after investor claims suggests that they may have been responding to similar domestic factors. One of these factors pertains to the normative beliefs held by the policymakers themselves.

Normative ideas – for instance, about the merits of economic liberalism and the appropriateness of IIAs in attracting FDI – serve as the filter through which individuals determine what they want to see in the information that confronts them. As such, they are key drivers of confirmation bias. In theories of bounded rationality, the habit of individuals to assign greater significance to information they 'want' to

[17] Awards have not yet surpassed US$ 20 million, a relatively small sum in comparison to the billion-dollar awards rendered against other governments.

[18] Indonesia has been sued seven times, winning 3, settling or discontinuing 3. In Al Warraq v Indonesia, the Indonesian government was found liable but no damages were awarded.

believe is referred to as confirmation bias or motivated reasoning (Poulsen 2015, 26). The key here is that different normative priors can orient confirmation bias in different ways, leading to competing interpretations of the same information (Calvert 2022). This is why two countries that win in ISDS proceedings may view their investment protection commitments in a different light. That Chile, Colombia and Peru continued to expand their investment treaty commitments while other countries with positive track records in ISDS proceedings did not reflects the potential influence of different normative belief systems.

That government officials across all three countries shared a normative commitment to investment protections, and international arbitration, is evident in the statements made by officials in relation to ISDS cases. Here, state discourse across the countries bears striking similarities. Namely, state officials tended to affirm the state's commitment to extant international legal obligations and praised the authority of arbitral tribunals while highlighting the countries' positive track records in ISDS proceedings. For example, in response to Colombia's loss in an ISDS case brought by mining giant Glencore, officials from the National Agency for the State's Legal Defense, which manages the state's response to investor claims, stated that the Agency 'respects and recognises the powers of international institutions and is convinced of the use of [these] dispute resolution mechanisms that resolve cases more promptly' (El Tiempo 2020). The statement was made even while the Agency sought annulment of the award.

When Chile was presented with a new ISDS claim in 2021, government officials emphasised Chile's 'undisputed track record as a country that offers its investors a treatment consistent with its international obligations', a claim that was 'supported by the fact that [Chile] has faced a very low number of investment arbitrations as defendants and has been victorious in all but one of the cases' (Peña 2021). In response to Peru's loss in an ISDS case brought by Canadian mining company Bear Creek, former Minister of Economy and Finance Alonso Segura dismissed criticism of the award, arguing that: 'In reality, [the losses] are healthy because it is part of the rules of the game of being a country with strong investment. These cases in which we have effectively lost were those where there were arguments to lose, but we won the majority. That's the way it works' (Lozano 2019).

These statements can be interpreted as an effort by government officials to reduce the reputational fallout resulting from ISDS cases. However, the fact that officials felt beholden to these pressures suggests they continued to see value in foreign investment attraction and believed that the current system of investment protection was the most appropriate means of attracting it. While they are sensitive to criticism of IIAs and the ISDS system, their belief overall in the merits of investment protections as enshrined in international law means that they are more likely to view the problem as a need to 'fine-tune' the existing system. In other countries, like Ecuador, government officials emphasised the sovereignty costs associated with IIA commitments in their calls for systemic and paradigmatic reforms (cf Calvert 2022).

This is not to say that normative beliefs are a causal driver of treaty outcomes, rather that they play a role in determining policymakers' first-order preferences and, in doing so, make them more or less susceptible to supporting incremental reforms in the context of PTA investment chapters. However, for particular beliefs to acquire significance in policymaking processes, they require favourable actors and institutions (Béland 2009). The political economy of trade and investment policy in Peru, Colombia and Chile differs in important ways, but each country provides (at least until recently) a conducive environment for the dominance of pro-market belief systems.

In Chile, there has historically been a broadly held consensus between mainstream political parties on the merits of IIAs and the ISDS system. This consensus formed in the 1990s in the wake of the dictatorial and right-wing government of Augusto Pinochet. Pinochet initiated a process of rapid economic liberalisation, restructuring economic sectors and state institutions to facilitate market-led development. Following Pinochet's defeat in a 1988 plebiscite, left- and right-leaning political parties converged on a set of norms that would guide democratic renewal. The 'Chilean consensus' was formed around a belief in the sanctity of the rule of (international) law and the idea that electoral democracy was best complemented by free-market economics (Fermandois 2011, 37). Pose (2019) attributes the consensus to the initial success of structural adjustment under Pinochet and to pro-market technocrats, who helped embed support for free-market economics in key bureaucratic institutions. Business associations were initially lukewarm towards government plans to negotiate PTAs, but over time those who won out from trade liberalisation became fervent supporters of the integrationist agenda, leaving the consensus unchallenged.

Support for trade and investment liberalisation remained strong within the political class over time. Two decades of centre-left leadership under the Concertación failed to generate substantive departures in foreign economic policy despite its strong ties to labour and other left-leaning groups who were critical of PTAs. Heading into the reform period, Chile was led by the centre-right coalition of Sebastián Piñera (2010–2014, 2018–2022), a keen advocate of economic liberalisation. Piñera was replaced by the centre-left government of Michelle Bachelet (2006–2010, 2014–2018), which continued the pro-trade agenda even while moderating neoliberal measures in areas of social policy.

Recently, it appeared that Chile would fail to ratify the CPTPP agreement and complete negotiations with the EU on a modernised trade agreement due to opposition from civil society and smaller left-leaning political parties who opposed ISDS. Critics feared the agreements would empower multinational corporations while disadvantaging indigenous groups and workers. Gabriel Boric, who firmly opposed the CPTPP as a member of the Chamber of Deputies, promised to veto the agreement if elected president. Once Boric came to power in 2022, he retracted his promise out of respect for the democratic process, which saw the CPTPP agreement pass through two legislative bodies.[19] Boric's decision to ratify the agreement confirms the normative link between electoral democracy and free-market economics that has been embedded in Chilean political institutions. As first observed by Polanco Lazo (2016, 133), the Chilean legislature has continued to ratify all PTAs with support across mainstream political parties.

In Peru, economic elites and technocrats have a stronger hold over the reform debate than elected politicians. Politicians in Peru tend to be more inexperienced than their counterparts in Chile and Colombia and they often lack the backing of an institutionalised political party. The dominance of foreign economic policy by technocrats and economic elites in Peru reflects the historic influence of the Fujimori model of market-led development. In the 1990s, the semi-autocratic government of Albert Fujimori adopted a sweeping and rapid programme of economic reform in what became known as the 'Fujishock'. Fujimori reformed state institutions to ease his agenda, appointing outward-looking elites trained in prominent Western institutions and previously employed in international financial institutions to key bureaucratic and political posts. Technocratic elites and economic advisors defended the model over changes in government while entrenching economic integration as a cornerstone of Peruvian foreign policy. Technocrats had strong ties to Peru's business community, in particular the domestic representatives of foreign-owned companies, who influenced trade and investment policy through corporatist and personalist linkages.

As a result, Peru's support for traditional investment protection standards remained stable despite the election of political leaders who were themselves critical of trade and investment liberalisation. Ollanta Humala (2011–2016), a left-leaning candidate of indigenous descent, denounced the TPP negotiations in his presidential campaign. Over time, the Humala government embraced the TPP negotiations and signed onto the Pacific Alliance agreement. Centre-right presidents deeply committed to trade and investment liberalisation were also elected, rotating power with left-leaning figures. Notable was Alan García (2006–2011), who was backed by the American Popular Revolution Party (APRA), Peru's oldest and most institutionalised political party. The point, however, is that Peru demonstrated remarkable consistency in its reform preferences across changes in the executive branch due largely to the influence of bureaucratic and economic elites and weakness in the political party system, which meant opposition parties did not form an effective veto point in legislative debates on investment policy (see Calvert 2022).

A slightly different constellation of actors and institutions dominates reform debates in Colombia. Colombia too embarked on a period of economic and

[19] The CPTPP passed through congress with a narrow vote of approval, namely by members of centrist parties on the left and right (seventy-seven in favour and sixty-eight against). The senate also voted in favour of the agreement but with a stronger majority (twenty-seven in favour, ten against, one abstention).

bureaucratic reform, which escalated in the 1990s according to neoliberal dictates. As in Peru and Chile, bureaucratic modernisation empowered pro-market technocrats in foreign economic policy circles who promoted economic integration (Villaveces-Niño and Caballero-Argáez 2020). For the most part, technocrats saw willing proponents of trade and investment liberalisation in the executive branch. Post-2000, Colombian elections saw to power right-leaning governments whose foreign policy was closely aligned with that of the US (although to varying degrees).[20] That government officials took inspiration from US trade agreements in their redesign of Colombia's model IIA reflects a broader and more historic deference to US foreign policy. Rivas (2013, 195) notes that trade negotiators learnt the importance of more detailed provisions during the Colombia-US FTA negotiations, which inspired changes in Colombia's 2006 model BIT. However, Colombian officials did not blindly follow the US. The impetus for BIT model updating also came from a bureaucratic impulse to keep up with international trends in PTA investment chapters. Model drafters also reviewed ICSID awards and decisions and consulted closely with UNCTAD officials concerning the incremental reforms made by other governments. More recently, the Constitutional Court has also weighed into the reform debate in demanding the issuance of interpretative statements to enhance the compatibility of certain substantive investment protections with the Colombian constitution (see Suárez Ricuarte 2019).

Interest groups have influenced the country's trade agenda and its IIA programme, but they have sometimes served as roadblocks. For instance, opposition from influential interest groups to a proposed PTA with China in 2012 led to the demise of that agreement. As a substitute, the executive branch focused its efforts on pushing forward the ratification of the Colombia-China BIT, which had been left outstanding since 2008 (Long et al. 2019). Generally, investment liberalisation is less contested by interest groups, which may have reinforced support for BITs. The executive branch is, therefore, not isolated from interest group pressure, but political leaders exert more independent influence over the reform debate than in Peru insofar as it is their preferences that matter. This was most recently illustrated by changes to Colombia's IIA programme after the 2022 election of Gustavo Petro. Petro, a left-leaning economist and former guerrilla fighter, has called for the renegotiation of Colombia's PTAs with a focus on rewriting investment protection clauses that threaten the environment.

In 2023, the Petro government signed a BIT with Venezuela despite international condemnation of the Maduro regime. It is likely that that agreement was the result of political strategising by Petro, given the need for Venezuelan cooperation in Colombia's ongoing peace talks with the Ejército de Liberación Nacional (ELN, National Liberation Army). Most importantly, the BIT provides for ISDS despite the

20 This alignment reflected the US governments' historic footprint in the country, and contemporary security arrangements aimed at combatting narco-trafficking.

previous rejection of that system by the Maduro government. However, the treaty substantially modifies key protections by emphasising the limits of those protections and the parties' regulatory powers. It also excludes several traditional substantive protections, that critics identify as the most problematic, such as fair and equitable treatment, full protection and security and most-favoured nation treatment. Who dominates reform processes therefore varies in important ways across Peru, Colombia and Chile. However, the common factor is that all of these actors had subscribed, until recently, to the merits of strong investment protections.

The impact of domestic beliefs on IIA reform is also evidenced by the case of Brazil. Brazil is one of the few countries that has never ratified a traditional IIA. Although it signed a swath of BITs in the 1990s, legislators voted against the agreements for fear that they would constrain national policy space and favour foreign investors over their domestic counterparts. Concern for the equal treatment of national and foreign investors is an enduring legacy of the Calvo Doctrine, a nineteenth-century doctrine which held that foreign nationals should not be given privileged access to supra-national institutions through which to resolve legal disputes with their hosts since domestic investors had been given no such privilege. Brazilian officials have long rejected ISDS on this basis. The national treatment norm largely persisted in the political class. One explanation for its endurance pertains to FDI attraction. FDI inflows to Brazil accelerated over time despite the country's failure to ratify BITs. According to Vidigal and Stevens (2018, 486–487), success in attracting FDI likely confirmed for political elites the BITs were not necessary to secure an economic advantage.

Brazil launched a new treaty-making programme in 2015 under the leadership of Dilma Rousseff (2011–2016) based around the CFIA. The launch of Brazil's CFIA model appears to have been driven by interest group pressure and a growing preference for regional and global integration. Brazil's business community expanded rapidly over the past two decades, particularly in the areas of agriculture and natural resources. As a result, Brazil became a significant exporter of FDI, particularly to other global South economies. By the 2010s, Brazilian investors had begun pushing the government for rules that would ease their outward investment. Domestic norms continued to have a strong impact. Namely, the CFIA model avoids infringing on the national treatment norm by focusing squarely on the issue of investment facilitation and forgoing investment protection and ISDS entirely. According to Moraes and Cavalcante (2021), much of the business community accepted the principle of equal treatment and did not press for BIT-like investment protections. They instead sought frameworks that would encourage governments to strengthen their business environment for investment and reduce the transaction costs associated with navigating bureaucracies and opaque regulation.

Arguably, the legitimacy crisis in international investment law has created more space for policy experimentation in South America as governments face less pressure to adhere to a one-size-fits-all set of investment protections. The bargaining power of extra-regional players and their epistemic influence in leading incremental reform continues to weigh heavily in treaty-signing countries. However, the domestic politics of investment policy continues to change, and it will have important ramifications for the future of international investment law.

11.5 CONCLUSION

Momentum towards the reform of international investment law has grown since 2012. Governments are seeking ways to better protect their policy space and prevent frivolous investor claims. Yet there appears to be little consensus on the extent of reforms required. In Colombia, Peru and Chile, governments tend to view IIAs as consistent with their development goals, at least until recently. As such, they have favoured incremental reforms and advanced them in a new generation of PTAs. But they have also been responsive to the demands and institutional realities of regional and extra-regional partners. As a result, PTA investment chapters vary in their contents (although, in most instances, to slight but significant degrees), and a growing number of PTAs exclude them entirely. Outside of these countries, reform preferences range from systemic to paradigmatic. Brazil's CFIA model poses the most successful example of paradigmatic reform in the region. To date, it is the only alternative IIA model to inform a PTA investment chapter, but it appears to be overlapping with – not displacing – traditional investment protection standards.

The spaghetti bowl of IIAs looks more complicated and incomplete now than ever before. And recent developments in Chile and Colombia suggest that reform preferences may be subject to change in the short term. Moreover, the impacts of incremental reform on government regulation and, in particular, their ability to promote sustainable and inclusive development has yet to be understood. It is likely that they will not be known until further ISDS judgements are rendered. Governments continue to operate in an arena of high uncertainty, given that a significant degree of interpretative power remains in the hands of arbitrators in a system that continues to be decentralised and ad hoc and where governments lack powers of review. In this circumstance, ISDS cases will continue to deliver important information. However, the lessons governments draw from these opportunities will depend on who dominates reform debates and the beliefs they hold about the relationship between investment protection and sustainable development.

For now, PTA investment chapters present both challenges and opportunities for current reform efforts. On the one hand, PTA investment chapters have provided governments with the opportunity to update investment protection standards and procedures for resolving investment disputes. For weary governments favouring reform, replacing an existing BIT with a PTA investment chapter poses fewer reputational risks than terminating or renegotiating a standing treaty. On the other, investment chapters appear to be contributing to fragmentation in international investment law, which will increase the hurdles for governments in seeking to comply with their investment protection commitments. PTAs may also slow the pace of future reform since they are more difficult and cumbersome to renegotiate than BITs (or CFIAs) once they are put in place. PTA investment chapters, therefore, may generate new challenges for governments seeking to reform their investment protection commitments in the future.

REFERENCES

Allee, T. and C. Peinhardt 2014. "Evaluating Three Explanations for the Design of Bilateral Investment Treaties." *World Politics* 66(1): 47–87.

Alschner, W. 2018. "The Global Laboratory of Investment Law Reform Alternatives." *American Journal of International Law* 112: 237–243.

Alschner, W. and D. Skougarevskiy 2015. "Mapping the Universe of International Investment Agreements." *Journal of International Economic Law* 19(3): 561–588.

Alschner, W., M. Elsig and R. Polanco 2021. "Introducing the Electronic Database of Investment Treaties (EDIT): The Genesis of a New Database and Its Use." *World Trade Review* 20(1): 73–94.

Béland, D. 2009. "Ideas, Institutions, and Policy Change." *Journal of European Public Policy* 16(5): 701–718.

Berge, T. L. and T. St John 2021. Asymmetric Diffusion: World Bank 'Best Practice' and the Spread of Arbitration in National Investment Laws." *Review of International Political Economy* 28(3): 584–610.

Calvert, J. 2022. *The Politics of Investment Treaties in Latin America*. Oxford: Oxford University Press.

Calvert, J. and K. Tienhaara 2022. "Beyond 'Once BITten, Twice Shy': Defending the Legitimacy of Investor-State Dispute Settlement in Peru and Australia." *Review of International Political Economy*, online first.

Chang, H-J. 2004. "The Regulation of Foreign Direct Investment in Historical Perspective." European Journal of Development Research 16(3): 687–715.

El Tiempo 2020. "Colombia sí tendrá que devolver 19.1 millones de dólares a minera Glencore" [Colombia Must Return 19.1 million Dollars to Miner Glenore.] 24 September. www.eltiempo.com/justicia/cortes/colombia-tendra-que-devolver-dinero-a-glencore-por-sancion-de-contraloria-620619, accessed on 20 June 2023.

Elkins, Z., A. T. Guzman and B. A. Simmons 2006. "Competing for Capital: The Diffusion of Bilateral Investment Treaties, 1960–2000." *International Organisation* 60(4): 811–846.

Fermandois, J. 2011. "Pragmatism, Ideology, and Tradition in Chilean Foreign Policy Since 1990." In: G. L. Gardini and P. Lambert (Eds.), *Latin American Foreign Policies*. New York: Palgrave MacMillan, pp. 35–52.

Fiezzoni, S. K. 2011. "The Challenge of UNASUR Member Countries to Replace ICSID Arbitration." *Beijing Law Review* 2: 134–144.

Franck, S. 2005. "The Legitimacy Crisis in Investment Treaty Arbitration: Privatising Public International Law through Inconsistent Decisions." *Fordham Law Review* 73(4): 1521–1626.

2007. "Empirically Evaluating Claims about Investment Treaty Arbitration." *North Carolina Law Review* 86(1): 1–88.

Haftel, Y. Z. and A. Thompson 2018. "When Do States Renegotiate Investment Agreements? The Impact of Arbitration." *Review of International Organisations* 13(1): 25–48.

Kapeliuk, D. 2012. "Collegial Games: Analyzing the Effect of Panel Composition on Outcome in Investment Arbitration." *Review of Litigation* 31(2): 267–311.

Langford, M., D. Behn and O. K. Fauchald 2018. "Backlash and State Strategies in International Investment Law." In: T. Aalberts and T. Gammeltoft-Hansen (Eds.), *The Changing Practices of International Law*. Cambridge: Cambridge University Press, pp. 70–102.

Long, T., S. Bitar and G. Jiménez-Peña 2019. "Domestic Contestation and Presidential Prerogative in Colombian Foreign Policy." *Bulletin of Latin American Research* 39(4): 466-482.

Lozano, I. 2019. "Perú tuvo resultado adverso en solo 3 de 16 casos ante el CIADI "[Peru has lost in only three of sixteen cases before ICSID]. *La República*, 26 August 2019. https://larepublica.pe/economia/2019/08/26/economia-mef-peru-tuvo-resultado-adverso-en-solo-3-de-16-casos-ante-el-ciadi, accessed on 28 December 2024.

Moraes, C. H. and P. Cavalcante 2021. "The Brazil-India Investment Co-operation and Facilitation Treaty: Giving Concrete Meaning to the 'Right to Regulate' in Investment Treaty Making." *ICSID Review* 36(2): 1–15.

Nunnenkamp, P. 2017. "Biased Arbitrators and Tribunal Decisions against Developing Countries: Stylized Facts on Investor–State Dispute Settlement." *Journal of International Development* 29(6): 851–854.

Peacock, C., K. Milewicz and D. Snidal 2019. "Boilerplate in International Trade Agreements." *International Studies Quarterly* 63(4): 923–937.

Peinhardt, C. and R. L. Wellhausen. 2016. "Withdrawing from Investment Treaties but Protecting Investment." *Global Policy* 7(4): 571–576.

Peña, K. 2021. "Cancillería se defiende tras nuevo arbitraje ante el CIADI: "Chile tiene una trayectoria indiscutida como un país receptor de inversión extranjera."" Diario Financiero, 13 April 2021. https://www.df.cl/empresas/energia/cancilleria-se-defiende-tras-nuevo-arbitraje-ante-el-ciadi-chile-tiene

Polanco Lazo, R. 2016. "Two Worlds Apart: The Changing Features of International Investment Law in Latin America." In: A. Tanzi, A. Asteriti, R. Polanco Lazo and P. Turrini (Eds.), *International Investment Law in Latin America*. Leiden: Brill, pp. 68–97.

Pose, N. 2019. "Economic Ideas and North-South Preferential Trade Agreements in the Americas." *Latin American Journal of Trade Policy* 4: 34–53.

Poulsen, L. N. S. 2015. *Bounded Rationality and Economic Diplomacy: The Politics of Investment Treaties in Developing Countries*. Cambridge: Cambridge University Press.

Puig, S. and G. Shaffer 2018. "Imperfect Alternatives: Institutional Choice and the Reform of Investment Law." *American Journal of International Law* 112(3): 361–409.

Putnam, R. D. 1988. "Diplomacy and Domestic Politics: The Logics of Two-Level Games." *International Organisation* 42: 427–460.

Rivas, J. A. 2013. "Colombia." In: C. Brown (Ed.), *Commentaries on Selected Model Investment Treaties*. Oxford: Oxford University Press.

Roberts, A. 2018. "Incremental, Systemic, and Paradigmatic Reform of Investor–State Arbitration." *American Journal of International Law* 112(3): 410–432.

Sattorova, M. 2018. *The Impact of Investment Treaty Law on Host States: Enabling Good Governance?* Oxford: Hart Publishing.

Schill, S. W. 2017. "Reforming Investor–State Dispute Settlement: A (Comparative and International) Constitutional Framework." *Journal of International Economic Law* 20(3): 649–672.

Schwebel, S. 2011. "The United States 2004 Model Bilateral Investment Treaty: An Exercise in the Regressive Development of International Law." In: S. Schwebel (Ed.), *Justice in International Law: Further Selected Writings*. Cambridge: Cambridge University Press.

Simmons, B. A. 2014. “Bargaining over BITs, Arbitrating Awards: The Regime for Protection and Promotion of International Investment.” *World Politics* 66(1): 12–46.

Sornarajah, M. 2008. “A Coming Crisis: Expansionary Trends in Investment Treaty Arbitration.” In: K. P. Sauvant and M. Chiswick-Patterson (Eds.). *Appeals Mechanism in International Investment Disputes*. New York: Oxford University Press.

Spears, S. A. 2010. “The Quest for Policy Space in a New Generation of International Investment Agreements.” *Journal of International Economic Law* 13(4): 1037–1075.

Suárez Ricuarte, F. 2019. “Judgement C-252 of 2019 Constitutional Court of Colombia: Change of Precedent on the Control of BITs.” Investment Treaty News, 19 September. www.iisd.org/itn/en/2019/09/19/judgment-c-252-of-2019-of-the-constitutional-court-of-colombia-change-of-precedent-on-the-control-of-bits-federico-suarez-ricaurte/, accessed on 28 June 2023.

Thakur, T. 2021. “Reforming the Investor–State Dispute Settlement Mechanism and the Host State’s Right to Regulate: A Critical Assessment.” *Indian Journal of International Law* 59(1–4): 173–208.

Tienhaara, K. 2018. “Regulatory Chill in a Warming World: The Threat to Climate Policy Posed by Investor–State Dispute Settlement.” *Transnational Environmental Law* 7(2): 229–250.

UNCTAD 2005. *South-South Cooperation in International Investment Agreements*. UNCTAD: New York and Geneva.

2012. *Investment Policy Framework for Sustainable Development*. https://unctad.org/publication/investment-policy-framework-sustainable-development-2012-edition, accessed 6 March 2023.

2022a. *Investment Dispute Settlement Navigator*. https://investmentpolicy.unctad.org/investment-dispute-settlement accessed 6 March 2023.

2022b. International Investment Agreements Navigator. https://investmentpolicy.unctad.org/international-investment-agreements/countries/165/peru?type = bits accessed 6 March 2023.

Usynin, M. and S. Gáspár-Szilágyi 2018. “The Growing Tendency of Including Investment Chapters in PTAs.” In: F. Amtenbrink, D. Prévost, and R. Wessel (Eds.) *Netherlands Yearbook of International Law vol 48*. The Hague: Asser Press, pp. 267–304.

VidigalG. and B. Stevens 2018. “Brazil’s New Model of Dispute Settlement for Investment: Return to the Past or Alternative for the Future?” *Journal of World Investment & Trade* 19: 475–512.

Villaveces-Niño, M. and C. Caballero-Argáez 2020. “Technocracy, Decision Making and Economic Policy in Colombia.” In: P. Sanabria-Pulido and N. Rubaii (Eds.), *Policy Analysis in Colombia*. Bristol: Bristol University Press, pp. 203–222.

Waincymer, J. 2009. “Balancing Property Rights and Human Rights in Expropriation.” In: P.-M. Dupuy, E.-U. Petersmann and F. Francioni (Eds.), *Human Rights in International Investment Law and Arbitration*. Oxford: Oxford University Press, pp. 275–309.

Yazbek, N. 2010. “Bilateral Investment Treaties: The Foreclosure of Domestic Policy Space.” *South African Journal of International Affairs* 17(1): 103–120.

12

Trade Protectionism and Integration in Latin America

The Cases of Brazil and Mexico

Nicolas Albertoni and Carol Wise

12.1 INTRODUCTION

This chapter concentrates on two country case studies in the Latin American region: Brazil and Mexico. Together, these two emerging economies (EEs) represent over half of the total regional trade (exports + imports) (World Bank 2020b). As Mukherjee (2016, 23) states, 'a contextual comparison of individual cases … ensures that the generalisations made from the large-N analysis are not too sweeping'. Our insights on these two case studies also derive from large-N quantitative work undertaken by Albertoni (2023), but full coverage of this quantitative data lies beyond the scope of this chapter. Hence, although our analysis is qualitative in nature, our arguments are rooted in a mixed-methods approach. As different studies on policymaking have shown, case analysis helps us ascertain causal mechanisms in more detail than can be gleaned from large-N projects (King et al. 2021).

Our analytical baseline begins with the 2008–2009 global financial crisis (GFC), which hit EEs on the trade account, rather than the huge financial shocks felt in the developed countries. Some prominent economists were quick to congratulate EE policymakers for resisting protectionist temptations (Rodrik 2009; Boffa and Olarreaga 2012). Our data suggests that such accolades were premature. It is true that Latin America showed remarkable resilience when faced with the GFC and Brazil, one of the two countries at hand, had rebounded by 2010–2011 (Wise et al. 2015). However, drawing on data from the Global Trade Alert (GTA 2020), we found an explosion of protectionism throughout the world economy during the GFC, most of it in the form of non-tariff measures (NTMs). As the World Trade Organization (WTO) (2016: para 11) reported, 'of the 2,835 trade-restrictive measures, including trade remedies, recorded for WTO members since 2008 … only 708, or 25%, had been removed by mid-May 2016'.

From a theoretical standpoint, the latest studies and political debates on recent trade dynamics have focused on the US, China, the European Union (EU), and Japan. Otherwise, the political economy literature has paid little attention to how these protectionist global dynamics have interacted with emerging regions since the GFC. In line with the research questions laid out by the editors of this volume, our focus is on the preferential trade agreements (PTAs) that govern Mexico's trade under the US-Mexico-Canada Free Trade Agreement (USMCA, previously the North American Free Trade Agreement, or NAFTA), and Brazil's trade in the context of the Southern Cone Common Market (MERCOSUR). For purposes of clarity, and following Hofmann et al. (2019), the term 'PTA' includes free trade agreements, customs unions, and partial free trade agreements, which can take bilateral (e.g. two countries), plurilateral (e.g. many countries), plurilateral with a third country (e.g. EU-Australia Trade Agreement), or region-region (e.g. EU-MERCOSUR Trade Agreement) forms.

Both PTAs came into being in the early 1990s, as both states sought to institutionalise recently implemented trade and investment liberalisation programmes. The political economy literature at the time heralded these schemes as pathways to promote growth, forge healthy interdependence, and lock-in market reforms (Hufbauer et al. 1994; Lawrence 1996). Stepping back from the veracity of these claims, our research on these two PTAs in the decade following the GFC shows a rise in NTMs *within* these schemes despite conditions of high economic interdependence.

Our punchline here is that PTAs, long considered as key trade and investment-creating conduits, are also emerging as venues within which NTMs are simultaneously increasing. That is, members within the same scheme are deploying NTMs against each other. This is what Baldwin and Evenett (2009) refer to as 'murky protectionism:' the increased resort to non-transparent interventions, including everything from import bans and licensing requirements to controls on safety standards on manufactured goods, *within* these two Western Hemispheric PTAs. The good news is that membership in these PTAs has mitigated some intra-bloc protectionism, albeit against a backdrop of rising NTMs within these PTAs, nonetheless.

Another wild card that emerges from our analysis is the effects of the rapid entry of China into the Latin American region since joining the WTO in 2001. Once unthinkable, China has displaced the US as South America's top trade partner; in North America, China bumped Mexico down a notch in the rankings of US trade partners in 2003 (Wise 2020, 209). Whereas Brazil maintained a trade surplus with China from 2008 to 2018, Mexico has traded at a deficit with China over this same decade (Statista 2022). In 2018, Mexico's US$76.13 billion trade deficit with China accounted for the bulk of the region's overall commercial deficit with the People's Republic of China (PRC) (Wise 2020, 85). The declaration of a trade war on China by the first Trump administration in 2018 enabled Mexico to recapture its ranking as the top US partner for trade in goods (USTR 2024). However, as China has increased its export of manufactured intermediate goods to Mexico to circumvent high US tariffs, Mexico's trade deficit with China has expanded from the equivalent of US$65 billion in 2015 to over $110 billion at the start of 2024 (Ezrati 2024).

While China is obviously not a member of either PTA under study here, we find that the rise of trade competition from China beginning in the early twenty-first century has strongly influenced the choice of domestic trade policies in Brazil and

Mexico. In Brazil, policymakers, political leaders, and producers have complained that the export of raw materials to China and the import of intermediate manufactures and finished consumer goods back from China have triggered a process of 'premature de-industrialization' (Rodrik 2015). Castillo and Martins Neto (2016, 12) define deindustrialisation as 'a falling share of manufacturing employment and value-added in total employment and GDP . . . and a rising specialization in primary goods'. This phenomenon has been coined 'premature' in Brazil because, in contrast to other EEs, it is occurring at low levels of per capita income and shifting employment into low value-added services. Moreover, although it has become routine to blame China for this downward mobility, this transition has been underway in Brazil since the early 1990s.

In the case of Mexico, where Chinese-manufactured exports compete head-to-head in Mexico's home market and with Mexican-manufactured exports to the US market (Dussel and Gallagher 2013), domestic producers have pushed unsuccessfully for policies that would bolster those manufacturing sub-sectors experiencing deep losses both at home and abroad (Moreno-Brid 2013). Prior to joining Canada and the US as an official member of NAFTA in 1994, Mexican policymakers halted all state support in the realm of industrial policy; instead, these tasks were relegated to the market, that is, to (mainly private US) companies and other foreign direct investors flooding into the Mexican economy. With the rise of China in Mexican markets, rather than reinstate public policies to foster the restructuring and strengthening of industrial firms in the face of stiff Chinese competition, Mexican policymakers extracted hefty protectionist side payments from Beijing in exchange for Mexico's vote for the PRC's accession to the WTO. Although exceptionally high tariffs against hundreds of Chinese goods prevailed until 2011 (Hernández 2012, 83–84), their removal showed how little progress Mexican companies had made in the way of restructuring.

In both countries, ineffective policy responses towards external trade competition were super-imposed on domestic macro- and micro-economic policy frameworks that were insufficient to meet the competitive pressures at hand. This reform backlog became readily apparent when the decade-long commodity price boom, driven by heavy Chinese demand, petered out in 2014 (Gallagher 2016). Brazil fell into a deep recession, which has lasted nearly a decade with no end in sight. Although the commodity price boom had bypassed Mexico, government coffers benefitted indirectly from historically high oil prices. Nevertheless, the doldrums that hit both countries after the end of the 'China boom' confirm the extent to which China's rapid recovery and hence the quick rebound of commodity prices in 2010 saved them from the worst of the GFC. In Mexico's case, further economic pain was self-inflicted, as policymakers chose to raise interest rates in response to the GFC and to withhold any counter-cyclical fiscal stimulus for a year.

Subsequently, the advent of the US-China trade war in mid-2018, as well as the outbreak of the Covid-19 global pandemic in early 2020, has deepened the recession in both countries and further hampered growth. From a trade angle, the overriding themes of this chapter are economic underperformance, opportunities lost, and paths not taken. The chapter proceeds in four parts. In Section 12.2, we review prominent trends in the rise of murky protection from the angle of the global setting since the GFC. In Section 12.2, we offer a brief analysis of the political economy of trade in the Latin American region with a focus on our two country case studies. In this section, we define these respective PTAs, chart the rise of extra- and intra-bloc protectionism, and speak to their efficacy over time. In Section 12.4, we offer some final reflections and insights on the path forward for trade policy in Brazil and Mexico.

In 2018, the Trump Administration insisted on the renegotiation of NAFTA along more mercantilist lines and renamed it the 'US-Mexico-Canada Free Trade Agreement', or USMCA-FTA. Because this relaunching of NAFTA in June 2020 coincides with the advent of the US-China trade war and the pandemic-induced global recession, we limit our analysis to the 2008–2018 period. This decade alone offers sufficient evidence to support our argument.

12.2 THE GLOBAL CONTEXT

In the seventy-eight years since the end of World War II, we have seen a profound restructuring of the international political economy. We refer, first, to the repositioning of states in the international system and, second, to the ability of Bretton Woods institutions like the General Agreement on Tariffs and Trade (GATT) to accommodate the rise of EEs and other developing countries as part of this process. Within this context of upward mobility, the path to growth and economic prominence had been distinct for each country. Through the 1980s and 1990s, a second phase of globalisation took off, the first having occurred roughly from the 1890s up to the onset of World War I in 1914 (Bordo et al. 1999, 56–58). By the turn of the new millennium, barriers to trade, investment, and people flows had been significantly lowered. With new internet technologies driving data transmission and cross-border information, countries in East Asia, Latin America, and the former Soviet bloc took advantage of increased opportunities for international trade and investment.

The 1990s were a turning point of sorts, in terms of both trade liberalisation and growing signs of protectionist backlash. On the former was the signing of the Maastricht Treaty and formalisation of the EU in 1992, the launching of NAFTA and the completion of the Uruguay Round in 1994, and the 1995 incorporation of the GATT into a newly created WTO. Together, the WTO's members account for about 98 per cent of world trade; of its 166 members, two-thirds of which are developing countries (WTO 2024). Yet, on our latter point, the disastrous 1999 WTO Ministerial Meeting in Seattle, Washington, where environmental and labour activists successfully rallied a global coalition to protest the deleterious impacts of free trade, set an ominous tone for the GATT/WTO's next round of multilateral trade negotiations.

Nevertheless, at the insistence of the George W. Bush administration, the WTO launched the Doha Development Round in the immediate wake of the 9/11/01 terrorist attacks on the US. Not surprisingly, Doha turned out to be a losing proposition. This trade round signalled how multilateral negotiations had become more heterogeneous, conflictual, and removed from the kinds of consensual decision-making that characterised earlier multilateral negotiations under the GATT. Although the negotiations were already limping in the wake of the 2008–2009 GFC, it was not until the 2015 WTO Ministerial Meeting in Nairobi that trade ministers from 160 member countries failed to agree to keep the negotiations going. The common narrative held that it was 'new' issues on the trade agenda championed by the Organisation for Economic Cooperation and Development (OECD) bloc – the liberalisation of trade-related services and investment and the protection of intellectual property rights (IPRs), which clashed repeatedly with those of powerful EEs like Brazil and India (Vickers 2012). The latter, in contrast, were most adamant about increased market access and the liberalisation of 'old' sectors like agriculture and manufacturing in developed country markets. This is true, up to a point.

The newly formed Group of Twenty (G-20) developing countries at the WTO (Maswood 2007),[1] led by Brazil and India, insisted that their increasing international trade integration and importance to global growth warranted fresh thinking given a transforming multilateral order in which developing countries now comprised the majority. After all, since the late 1990s, developing countries as a group – led by China and secondarily India – had become the drivers of world growth, surpassing average US growth rates by about 3.5 per cent annually between 2000 and 2007 (Subramanian and Kessler 2013, 3). Tellingly, much of the post-mortem analysis on Doha sided with the G-20. For instance, as Stiglitz and Charlton (2005, 2) noted, 'the expectations of the developing country members had been tempered by negative experiences from previous rounds of trade negotiations ... they had not been fully aware of the cost of the obligations they had agreed to' in the Uruguay Round. Two World Bank economists, Finger and Nogues (2001, 15), went further, characterising the Uruguay Round as the 'politics of imperialism ... the concessions the North gained (the South gave) in new areas were entirely unrequited'.

After touting the Doha Round as an opportunity for developing countries to realise considerable gains at the negotiating table, the OECD bloc – led largely by the US, the EU, and Canada – did little to help bring these gains about. Perhaps most notable was the more mercantilist stance of the US at the Doha Round (Finger and Nogues 2001). Susan Schwab, former US Trade Representative from 2006 to

[1] The original members of the G-20 within the Doha Round were Argentina, Bolivia, Brazil, Chile, China, Colombia, Costa Rica, Cuba, Ecuador, Egypt, El Salvador, Guatemala, India, Mexico, Pakistan, Paraguay, Peru, the Philippines, South Africa, Thailand, and Venezuela. See: G-20, the developing-country coalition.

2009, observed that concerned parties had spent too much time negotiating over the rules that would guide the Doha negotiations and not enough on the substance of the proposals that had been tabled. Schwab (2011, 10) reported that a 'framework of rigid formulas and ill-defined, largely nonnegotiable flexibilities put all the negotiators in a defensive posture from the outset'. This, plus Doha's mandate for a single undertaking – no final deal until all parties agreed – meant that the slowest reformers and weakest performers (e.g. Bolivia, Egypt, and the Philippines) could hold out unrealistically for greater gains from the developed country bloc (Vickers 2012).

Simultaneous with the conclusion of the Uruguay round was an explosion of PTAs that encompassed both North and South (Tussie 2009). The WTO database on regional trade agreements reports that there were around fifty in effect in the 1990s, but by 2018, there were close to 500 (WTO 2023a). In contrast with earlier trade schemes, this new wave of PTAs was as much about trade creation as it was about investment (Lawrence 1996). Under Article 24 of the GATT, PTAs were allowed if the parties at hand notified the GATT/WTO of their intentions to negotiate such an agreement. Three other contingencies must also be met (WTO 2023b): the agreement must seek to cover substantially all trade, tariffs could not be higher than they were prior to forming the agreement, and the agreement must be open to new members. It was against this backdrop that non-transparent protectionist measures began to proliferate, with a marked escalation in the period following the GFC.

As can be seen in Table 12.1, the number of protectionist measures has outpaced the number of liberalising trade measures in all six regions depicted in the table. Table 12.2 identifies and defines the main protectionist measures that have been deployed, while Table 12.3 distinguishes between the levels of transparency that surround those protectionist NTMs currently at play. Of special interest in Table 12.1 is that Pacific East Asia, the EU, and North America – in this order – registered the highest use of non-transparent protectionist tariffs during the period under study. We note that these rising non-transparent NTMs coincided with the final phases of the Doha Round negotiations, adding an additional deterrent to its completion.

12.3 THE POLITICAL ECONOMY OF LATIN AMERICAN TRADE, 2009–2018

From a regional perspective, Latin America is an interesting 'median' case with regard to protectionist and liberalising trade policy measures. As Figure 12.1 shows, Latin America stands between Asia and Africa in terms of both the total number of protectionist and liberalising measures implemented between 2008 and 2018 (left axis) and the share of exports from the rest of the world (RoW) to the region affected by protectionist measures (right axis). It was once one of the most protectionist developing regions; Table 12.4 reflects the heroic efforts and success of Latin American trade

TABLE 12.1 *Mapping trade policy dynamics by region, 2009–2018*

Trade Policy Information	Sub-Saharan Africa	North America	Middle East & North Africa	Latin Am. and the Caribbean	European Union	East Asia Pacific
Number of protectionist measures implemented	613	2,619	1,015	2,151	2,701	4,842
Number of liberalising measures implemented	398	348	494	1,366	423	2,657
Share of protectionist interventions that use non-transparent ('murky') instruments	40%	77%	51%	44%	87%	83%
Region's percentage of exports affected by RoW's protectionism (average 2009–2018)	29%	30%	27%	36%	22%	39%
RoW's exports to the region affected by the region's protectionism (average 2009–2018)	25%	40%	10%	19%	23%	21%
Region's most used protectionist measures affecting RoW's exports	Finance measures that affect trade	Subsidies	Tariff measures	Tariff measures and non-automatic licensing	Subsidies	Subsidies and non-automatic licensing
Region's most affected sector by RoW's protectionism	– Motor vehicles, trailers (CPC 491) – Machinery for mining (CPC 444)	– Products of iron or steel (CPC 412) – Fabricated metal products (CPC 429)	– Products of iron or steel (CPC 412) – Basic organic chemicals (CPC 341)	– Products of iron or steel (CPC 412) – Fabricated metal products (CPC 429)	– Motor vehicles, trailers (CPC 491) – Products of iron or steel (CPC 412)	– Products of iron or steel (CPC 412) – Basic organic chemicals (CPC 341)

Source: Authors' creation based on Global Trade Alert ().

Notes: RoW (Rest of the World), Sub-Saharan Africa consists of forty-seven countries, North America of three countries, the Middle East and North Africa of twenty countries, Latin Am. and the Caribbean thirty-nine countries (Mexico included), THE European Union twenty-eight countries, and East Asia Pacific thirty-seven countries (China included).

TABLE 12.2 *Examples of NTMs listed under UNCTAD's MAST classification and GTA datasets*

Name	Description and examples
Sanitary and phytosanitary measures	Measures that are applied to protect human or animal life from risks arising from additives, contaminants, toxins, or disease-causing organisms in food. A requirement limiting the use of hormones and antibiotics in the production of meat. A sample test on imported oranges to check for the residue level of pesticides.
Technical barriers to trade	Measures referring to technical regulations, and procedures for assessment of conformity with technical regulations and standards. Restrictions on toxins in children's toys. Refrigerators need to carry a label indicating their size, weight, and electricity consumption level.
Contingent trade-protective measures	Measures implemented to counteract particular adverse effects of imports in the market of the importing country contingent upon the fulfilment of certain procedural and substantive requirements. Country A imposes an anti-dumping duty on imports of biodiesel products from country B, to offset an injurious dumping by country B found to exist via an investigation. Country A imposes a countervailing duty on imports of semiconductors from country B, to offset the subsidies granted by country B on the production of semiconductors found to exist via an investigation.
Non-automatic licensing, quotas, prohibitions, & quantity-control	Control measures generally aimed at restraining the quantity of goods that are imported. Only hotels and restaurants are allowed to import alcoholic drinks. A quota of 100 tons of tuna fish can be imported at any time of the year.
Pre-shipment inspection and other formalities	Live animals need to be cleared at a designated customs office for inspection. Requirement that goods must be shipped directly from the country of origin, without stopping at a third country.
Price-control measures	Measures implemented to control or affect the prices of imported goods. A minimum import price is established for fabric and apparel. Imports of fresh blueberries may enter free of duty between 1 January and 31 May, while in other months, seasonal duties apply.
Export-related measures	Export-related measures are measures applied by the government of the exporting country on exported goods. Exports of processed seafood products must be inspected for sanitary conditions. Exports of cultural heritage objects – sculptures or other precious works – are prohibited.

Source: UNCTAD, Classification of NTMs, https://unctad.org/en/Pages/DITC/Trade-Analysis/Non-Tariff-Measures/NTMs-Classification.aspx.

TABLE 12.3 *Interventions and their level of transparency*

Transparent	Non-Transparent
Import tariff	Consumption subsidy
Sanitary and phytosanitary measures	Capital injection and equity stakes
Technical barrier to trade	Financial assistance in a foreign market
Anti-circumvention	Financial grant
Anti-dumping	Import incentive
Anti-subsidy	In-kind grant
Import monitoring	Interest payment subsidy
Safeguard	Loan guarantee
Special safeguard	Price stabilisation
Import quota	Production subsidy
Import tariff quota	State aid
Instrument unclear	State loan
Export quota	Tax or social insurance relief
Export tariff quota	Import ban and licensing requirement
Export tax	Internal taxation of imports
	Local labour, operations, and sourcing
	Localisation incentive
	Trade balancing measure
	Intellectual property protection
	Control on personal and commercial transactions, and investments
	Controls on credit operations
	Repatriation & surrender requirements
	Entry and ownership rule
	Financial incentive
	Treatment and operations
	Competitive devaluation
	Trade payment measure
	Import-related non-tariff measure
	Public procurement access
	Public procurement localisation and preference margin
	Public procurement
	Labour market access
	Post-migration treatment
	Export ban, licensing requirement, subsidy
	Export-related non-tariff measure
	Foreign customer limit
	Tax-based export incentive
	Trade finance

Source: Global Trade Alert (2020).

TABLE 12.4 *Weighted mean tariff rate applied to all products (%)*

Country	Mid-1980s	Late 1980s	Mid-1990s	2000–2007	2008–2019
Latin America	50	34	12	8	5
Argentina	28	44	14	8	7
Bolivia	20	19	10	7	5
Brazil	80	51	13	9	8
Chile	36	15	11	5	3
Colombia	83	48	11	10	6
Costa Rica	53	n/a	12	4	2
Ecuador	50	40	11	9	6
El Salvador	23	n/a	9	6	3
Guatemala	50	n/a	11	6	2
Honduras	n/a	42	18	7	6
Mexico	34	11	14	8	3
Nicaragua	54	n/a	17	4	2
Panama	n/a	33	n/a	7	8
Paraguay	71	19	9.4	7	4
Peru	64	68	16	9	2
Uruguay	32	27	10	5	5
Venezuela	30	33	12	13	10

Source: Data from IADB and World Bank, https://data.iadb.org/ and https://data.iadb.org/.

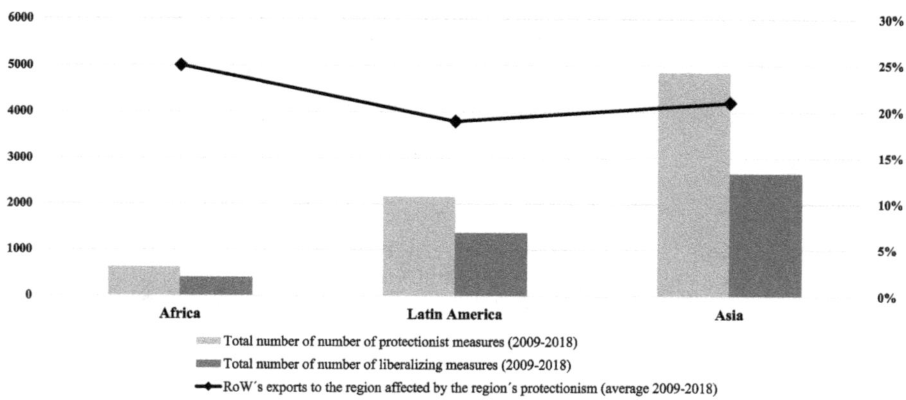

FIGURE 12.1 Latin America as a median case among the EEs in terms of protectionist measures.
Source: Global Trade Alert (2020).

reform since the 1980s. Even 'resource curse' states like Ecuador and Venezuela, where policymakers have resisted undertaking other structural reforms, have performed respectably on their respective levels of tariff reductions and trade openness.

Historically, the widespread and prolonged reliance on an import-substitution-industrialisation (ISI) development model, which originated in Latin America in the late 1950s, was a main drag on these economies. ISI 'represents a shift away from the outward orientation to export promotion, to an inward-looking orientation. ISI was designated to replace imports with domestic production under the guiding hand of the state. Governments used activist industrial, fiscal, and monetary policy to achieve growth' (Franko 2018, 615). ISI measures wreaked havoc on regional fiscal accounts and induced periodic balance-of-payments crises, especially given the general lack of macroeconomic acumen in the 1960s and 1970s. Former Panamanian President Nicolás Ardito Barletta (Ardito Barletta, 1994, 183–184) summarises the resulting inflation, and losses in terms of savings, investment, and productivity:

> Exchange rates were fixed relative to several of the main hard currencies. Import controls were part of the import substitution policies. Reserves were normally kept low and were not built up with favourable movements in the terms of trade. Fiscal policy consisted in deciding how much of the government deficit would be financed domestically because this would determine the increase in the quantity of money and inflation. Monetary policy was used mainly to keep interest rates low, producing excess demand for credit to priority sectors, which they [policy makers] defined.

Through the debt-riddled lost decade of the 1980s, to the Washington Consensus reforms of the 1990s, Latin America as a whole has become increasingly trade-oriented (see Figure 12.2). Even today, trade policy is subject to fierce lobbying on the part of those groups and sectors that stand to suffer the biggest losses from trade liberalisation. Moreira et al. (2019, 118) remind us that when 'trade is liberalized, there is no guarantee that it will remain liberalized.' These authors distinguish between two types of policy trajectories since the liberalisation of trade in the 1990s: 'Chile, Colombia, Costa Rica, and Mexico, have continued to reduce trade barriers, signed preferential trade agreements with an increasing number of regional and extra-regional partners, and persisted in maintaining and deepening open

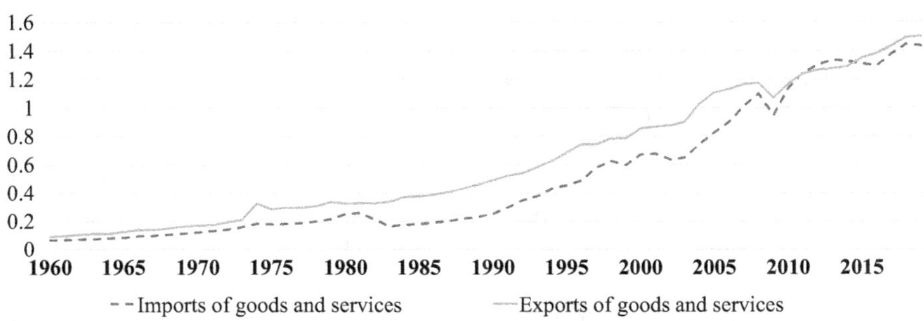

FIGURE 12.2 Latin America exports and imports (1960–2019) in US$ trillions.
Note: Exports of goods and services (constant 2010 US$), trillion dollars.
Source: World Bank national accounts data, and OECD National Accounts data files.

TABLE 12.5 *Main trade characteristics of Latin America (2019)*

Trade patterns	Data
Top 3 export destinations	US (43%), China (12%), Canada (3%)
Top 3 import origins	US (31%), China (18%), Brazil (5%)
Exports by product groups	Raw materials (30%) Intermediate goods (19%) Consumer goods (22%) Capital goods (23%)
Imports by product groups	Raw materials (7%) Intermediate goods (22%) Consumer goods (31%) Capital goods (37%)
Main products exported	Vehicles (13%) Mineral fuels (11%) Machinery (9%)
Main products imported	Electrical machinery (14%) Machinery (13%) Mineral fuels (12%)

Source: World Bank-World Integrated Trade Solutions (WITS), https://wits.worldbank.org/countrysnapshot/en/LCN.

trade ... Argentina, Brazil, and Venezuela, have resurrected some trade barriers or come up with new ones'.

In Table 12.5 we see that the US and China are Latin America's top trade partners. Moreover, raw materials account for 30 per cent of the region's exports, whereas intermediate, capital, and consumer goods make up the remainder. In Table 12.6, we can see that Brazil and Mexico sit on opposite ends of the export continuum: Brazil's main exports are raw materials (soybeans, crude petroleum, and iron ore), and Mexico's are manufactured goods (cars, vehicle parts, and trucks). In terms of both aggregate and per capita growth, the following case studies show that neither side of this continuum has resulted in the kinds of dynamic returns that each country is capable of delivering. Nor has the respective PTA to which each country belongs proved to be a springboard for upward convergence and prosperity.

12.3.1 *Mexico, Brazil, and Their Respective PTAs*

The two countries at hand represent an interesting mix in terms of their main economic and trade indicators. On the eve of the GFC in 2008, Mexico's economic openness was second only to that of Chile and Peru within the Latin American region. Conversely, after Venezuela, Brazil had the region's least open economy at the outset of the GFC (WTO 2017b). When the average growth of GDP between 2008 and 2018 is considered (see Table 12.6), both Mexico and Brazil's average annual GDP growth rates were 10 per cent over the decade, ranking them 143 and 144, respectively, out of 196 countries in the development indicators (World Bank

TABLE 12.6 *Main economic and trade characteristics of Brazil and Mexico*

	Brazil	Mexico
Economic figures		
GDP growth (Av. 2008–2018)	10% (Ranking 143 of 196)	10% (Ranking 144 of 196)
GDP PC	US$8,921 (Ranking 82 of 196)	US$9,673 (Ranking 79 of 196)
GDP PC growth (Av. 2008–2018)	1.02% (Ranking 141 of 196)	-3.43% (Ranking 159 of 196)
Trade figures		
Main export destinations	China: 26% US: 12% Argentina: 6%	US: 70% Canada: 4% Germany: 2%
Main import origins	China: 20% US: 17% Germany: 6%	US: 57% China: 13% Germany: 4%
Main exporting sectors	Soybeans: 14% Crude petroleum: 10% Iron ore: 8%	Cars: 11% Vehicles parts: 7% Trucks: 6%
Main importing sectors	Refined petroleum: 7% Vehicles parts: 4% Crude petroleum: 3%	Refined petroleum: 8% Vehicles parts: 7% Office machine Pts: 4%

Source: Authors' calculation of country rankings based on The Observatory of Economic Complexity, 2018, https://oec.world/en/profile/country.

2020a). In terms of average annual growth of GDP per capita. Brazil's per capita GDP growth was 1 per cent over this same period, ranked it at 144; Mexico, with an average annual per capita GDP growth rate of -3.43 per cent, ranked at 159 in the 196-country sample.

For separate reasons and in distinct ways, each has underperformed over the past two decades. In the case of Brazil, its anaemic growth rates in terms of aggregate and per capita GDP reflect the severe economic depression that ensued in 2014 when global commodity prices crashed; Mexico's disastrous record of GDP per capita growth reflects the self-inflicted fallout from the government's failure to respond effectively to the GFC. Unlike all of the other Latin America and the Caribbean (LAC) EEs (Argentina, Brazil, Chile, Colombia, Peru), Mexico's Central Bank raised interest rates, and the government rejected proposals for a fiscal stimulus until 2010. This downward compression on per capita income further exacerbated a long-time trend in Mexico whereby policymakers have consistently shifted the adjustment burden onto those who can least afford it (Pastor and Wise 1997).

These mediocre results have coincided in Brazil and Mexico within the context of two different institutional settings. In the case of Mexico, trade liberalisation was a unilateral endeavour in the late 1980s, and the nature of its participation in NAFTA is heavily weighted towards the bilateral relationship between Mexico and the US. NAFTA is a free trade agreement, meaning that its three members are free to maintain separate trade policies toward RoW. The roots of NAFTA are primarily economic, as powerful private intra- and inter-industry producers operating on both sides of the US-Mexico border lobbied hard for the reduction of barriers to cross-border production, and eventually won (Pastor and Wise 1994). Notably, between 1990 and 2019, Mexico negotiated fourteen PTAs with over fifty countries representing 60 per cent of world product. As of 2023, NAFTA/USMCA included a population of 442.4 million and a combined GDP of more than US$20 trillion, rendering it the second-largest PTA in the world. Along with side agreements on labour and the environment, the NAFTA accord promoted the free flow of goods, investment, and services within the North American bloc over a fifteen-year timeline.

In line with WTO rules, most barriers came down in the first ten years of the agreement. Tariffs and non-tariff barriers were eliminated on 65 per cent of North American goods by the five-year point; tariff reductions on automobiles occurred over a ten-year period, with the rules-of-origin stipulation that such vehicles must meet a 62.5 per cent local content requirement to qualify for free movement within the bloc. In the agricultural sector, sensitive products were allotted a fifteen-year liberalisation schedule that ended in 2009. By 2009, NAFTA had been fully implemented. If judged according to its own narrowly defined goals of spurring growth based on higher levels of trade and investment, NAFTA has been a measured success (Wise 2009).

In the case of Brazil, MERCOSUR, established in 1991 by Argentina, Brazil, Paraguay, and Uruguay, has been the institutional setting for trade policy and regional integration. In contrast with NAFTA's bilateralism based on Mexico's strong dependence on the US market, MERCOSUR is a plurilateral arrangement. MERCOSUR comprises more than 285 million people, has a combined GDP of around US$3 trillion, and ranks as the world's sixth-largest economic bloc. Created in the wake of democratic transitions in both Argentina and Brazil, these long-time rivals sought to improve relations via the launching of a common market. MERCOSUR's main goal was to establish this common market by 31 December 1994 involving 'the free movement of goods, services and factors of production between countries through … the elimination of customs duties and non-tariff restrictions on the movement of goods, and any other equivalent measures' (OAS-SICE 2023). Yet, more than thirty years since its founding, the formation of a common market has eluded bloc members.

This is why MERCOSUR is referred to as an 'imperfect customs union' (Vaillant 2005, Albertoni 2023). In comparison with the economically oriented debates and strategies that led to the negotiation of NAFTA, MERCOSUR's origins are decidedly more political. To date, the members have agreed to eliminate some customs duties, to implement a common external tariff (CET) on certain products originating outside of MERCOSUR, and to adopt a common trade policy toward outside countries and blocs (Felter et al. 2019). Despite the failure to form a common market, MERCOSUR's four core members are not permitted to negotiate external PTAs or maintain an individual trade policy towards RoW. Unlike NAFTA, which violates the spirit of inclusiveness that underpins Article XXIV of the GATT 1994 (WTO 2023b) with regard to welcoming new members, MERCOSUR has been quite open to expansion. Venezuela, for instance, became a full member in July 2012 (but was suspended in late 2016 when an authoritarian regime took control); Chile, Colombia, Ecuador, and Peru have become associate members, and Bolivia has been in the process of becoming a full member since 2012.

After sluggish progress in the 1990s, MERCOSUR's Common Market Council (CMC) passed Decision 32/00 in 2000 – a renewed effort to deepen economic integration and bolster compliance between MERCOSUR members. Known as the 'Re-launching Agenda of MERCOSUR' (CMC decisions 22/00 to 32/00), the strategy sought to identify MERCOSUR's bottlenecks and generate proposals to resolve them. But more than two decades later, MERCOSUR remains trapped by its own structural barriers (Rodríguez 2021). We quote from a US Department of Commerce industry report on MERCOSUR's complicated tariffs and numerous exceptions (Exports.gov 2023):

> A MERCOSUR Common External Tariff (CET) on imports from non-member countries entered effect in 1995. MERCOSUR´s general rule is to apply a higher CET on higher-value-added imports. There are numerous sectoral and national exceptions to MERCOSUR's CET. Sectoral exceptions apply to capital, information technology, and telecommunication goods. At a national level, each MERCOSUR member is also allowed to exempt a certain number of goods from the CET. These exceptions, and the number of special import regimes in member countries, have greatly eroded the bloc's CET. MERCOSUR also lacks other mechanisms to become an effective customs union, such as a mechanism to distribute tariff revenues.

Furthermore, there are steep asymmetries between Brazil and Argentina, on the one hand, and Paraguay and Uruguay, on the other hand. The general notion that Brazil and Argentina are 'carrying the team' is troublesome, given the readiness of both countries to flaunt MERCOSUR rules at the drop of a hat. Such was the case in 2011, for example, when Brazil applied NTMs to car imports, no matter that 50 per cent of such imports come from Argentina (Bachega 2011).

Despite the many challenges MERCOSUR still faces, as a bloc, it has negotiated trade agreements with twelve individual countries, the South African Customs Union, and the EU (UN Comtrade 2019). About 60 per cent of MERCOSUR's total exports go to countries that have negotiated PTAs with the bloc. Although EU-MERCOSUR negotiations were concluded in 2019, social and environmental concerns stalled the final approval of this accord on the EU side. The 2022 energy crisis triggered by Russia's invasion of Ukraine has revived interest in MERCOSUR within the EU, as Argentina and Brazil are abundant in oil and natural gas; Bolivia has natural gas and lithium; and Argentina and Chile are also rich in lithium. Chile alone currently supplies the EU with 78 per cent of its lithium imports (Nolte 2023).

This jump-started another round of EU-MERCOSUR negotiations, with both sides inking a revised PTA in December 2024. This new version awaits approval by national legislatures in the four core MERCOSUR nations, Argentina, Brazil, Paraguay and Uruguay. On the EU side, passage of the EU-MERCOSUR agreement must reach a "qualified majority" based on two conditions: 55 percent of EU nation states (or 15 of the 27 EU members) must vote in favour and these member states must represent 65 percent of the EU population (European Commission 2024). Both sides claim to have overcome differences on a range of measures that held up the passage of the 2019 agreement, including climate change (deforestation) and protection of labour rights. Should this 2024 text come to pass, it would mean sizable tariff reductions on both sides for autos, machinery, chemicals, pharmaceuticals, dairy, spirits, and wine. Government procurement, a sustainability commitment in the extraction of critical raw materials, and some minor access to EU agriculture are other highlights of the draft PTA. After 24 years of start and stop negotiations for an EU-MERCOSUR PTA, this is the closest both sides have come to bringing one to fruition.

12.3.2 *Mexico: Bilateralism and Protectionism*

After following the general Latin American pattern of import substitution industrialisation (ISI) up through the 1970s, Mexico launched an East-Asian-style manufacturing export-led development model. The differences with this East Asian strategy were Mexico's dependence on volatile oil revenues to finance the state budget, its cancellation of all industrial policy in 1992, and the country's heavy reliance on US foreign direct investment (FDI) to advance its industrialisation drive. As a prelude to NAFTA entry, Mexican policymakers signed on to Washington Consensus policies based on liberalisation, privatisation, and deregulation (Williamson 1990). Mexico's entry into NAFTA in 1994 has propelled manufactured exports and integrated Mexico into some powerful global value chains (GVCs). However, the current development model is that of a neoliberal export manufacturer, where policymakers remain committed to a hands-off trade strategy and a tight macro-prudent monetary policy that has hampered long-term growth.

Hindsight shows that Mexican policymakers mistook NAFTA as a development strategy in and of itself. Cast by its designers in the jargon of economic integration theory, NAFTA was projected to trigger a growth boom that would benefit all three member countries, but especially Mexico, as the least developed of the three. The ongoing narrative was that the elimination of barriers at the border would promote scale economies related to greater specialisation, increased technological capabilities, and more efficient deployment of those factors for which Mexico has a comparative advantage (Hufbauer et al. 1994). It was also argued that the blending of Mexico's abundant factors with the capital, technology, and know-how that the US brought to the table would trigger a dynamic pattern of economic convergence among the three members. According to this narrative, Mexico would readily advance up the industrial and technological learning curve and substantially increase its per capita income. On this last claim, the data confirm that nothing could be further from the truth.

Keep in mind that at the time of NAFTA's launching in 1994, China was a mere speck on the economic horizon. It was unimaginable that China could bump Mexico down a notch in its ranking as a US trade partner, and virtually no one envisioned that China would go on to become a de facto player in NAFTA – now one of the overriding characteristics of the North American market. NAFTA's golden age was the period between 1994 and 2000, when the average annual growth rate of total US trade with North America was around 17.7 per cent, and the average annual growth rate of North American FDI in this sub-region was about 24.2 per cent. However, by 2003, Chinese exports were burrowing through the more sophisticated sub-sectors of the US electronics market (computer peripherals, sound and television equipment, telecoms), which Mexico had once claimed as its own.

Between 2000 and 2005, Mexico increased its share of US imports by 25 per cent, while China's share of US imports grew by 143 per cent. By 2011, 31 per cent of all US imports from Mexico were deemed to be under direct threat from Chinese competition in the US market, and some 46 per cent of Mexico's manufacturing exports to the US were classified in this same category (Dussel and Gallagher 2013). A key difference between China and Mexico is that the technological strengths within Mexico's manufacturing sector stem from intermediate inputs that are developed in the advanced economies, processed in Mexico, and shipped back out. China's technological capabilities are the result of assertive public policies and generous state funding in the development of intermediate goods for export (Kroeber 2016). At first glance, the data depict Mexico as flourishing within GVCs (see Figure 12.2). Yet, Figure 12.3 tells a different story, which is highlighted in a recent study by *The Economist* (2020, 1). The study cautions that Mexico will remain at the end of the 'factory line' (see Figure 12.4) without a more targeted and proactive industrial policy: 'Mexico seems best placed to increase its position in the U.S. supply chain, but there are issues here too. … More fundamentally, Mexico will struggle without government policy to actively promote supply chain shifts, and without policy that attracts investment more broadly'.

Foot-dragging on essential domestic reforms (e.g. competition policy, tax policy, energy, and financial services) has rendered Mexico a sophisticated contract assembler, at best. Especially fatal has been the lack of technical support and credit access for those small and medium-sized firms that provide the bulk of Mexican employment. In the bigger picture, China's lower costs on utility inputs for industrial production, more favourable corporate tax rates and its blitzkrieg educational investment in the higher-skilled professions confirm that Mexico's laissez-faire manufactured export strategy is simply missing the mark. The rapid rise of China in the NAFTA economic bloc has made urgent the deployment of public policy in the expansion, upgrading, and infusion of technology into Mexico's manufacturing sector (WTO 2017a).

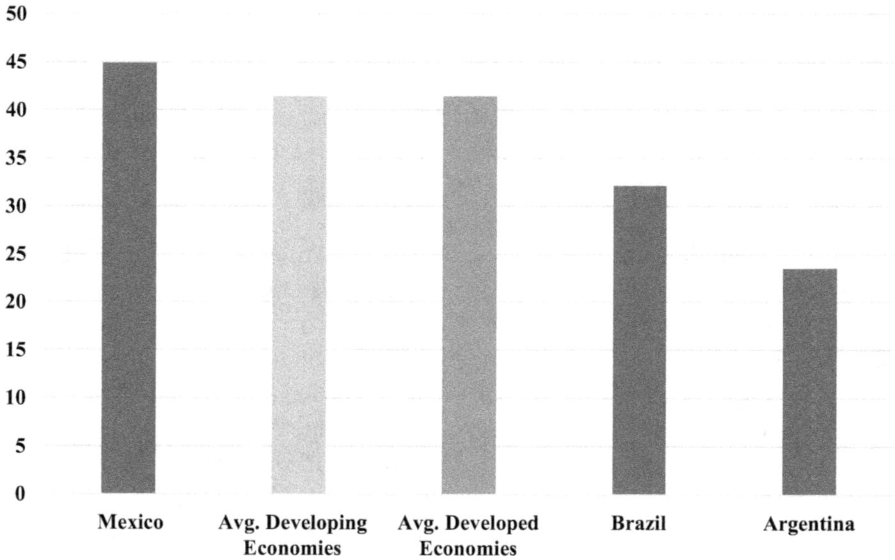

FIGURE 12.3 The GVC participation index (% share in total gross exports, in 2015).
Source: WTO, Trade in Value Added and Global Value Chains, www.wto.org/english/res_e/statis_e/miwi_e/countryprofiles_e.htm.
Note: The last publicly available data by country is for 2015.

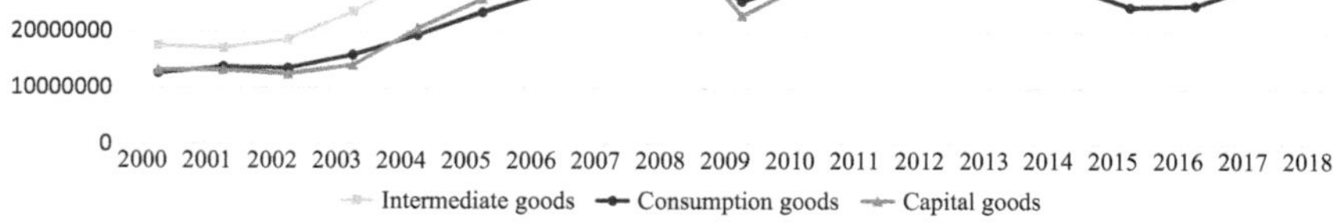

FIGURE 12.4 Mexico's export of intermediate, consumer capital goods between 2000 and 2018 (in thousands of dollars).
Source: Authors' creation based on World Bank-World Integrated Trade Solutions (WITS), https://wits.worldbank.org/countrysnapshot/en/LCN

Turning to the rise of protectionism in Mexico post-GFC, just as a wave of liberalisation in the early 1990s occurred as a result of Mexico's strong political and economic ties with the US and its eagerness to join NAFTA, current protectionist responses are partially a reaction to rising US protectionism (Campbell and Webber 2017, 13). As Table 12.7 shows, NAFTA has seemingly cemented Mexico's

TABLE 12.7 *Top destinations of intermediate, consumption, and capital goods (average share in Mexico's total exports between 2008 and 2018)*

Consumption goods	% in total exports	Intermediate goods	% in total exports	Capital goods	% in total exports
US	79	US	65	US	87
Canada	3	Canada	3	Canada	3
Germany	3	China	2	China	1
Colombia	2	UK	2	Brazil	1
Brazil	2	Colombia	3	Germany	1
China	1	Belgium	2	Netherlands	1
Chile	1	Brazil	3	Colombia	1
Argentina	1	Guatemala	1	France	1
Guatemala	1	Switzerland	2	Japan	0.5
Panama	1	Spain	1	UK	0.4

Source: Authors' creation based on World Bank-World Integrated Trade Solutions (WITS), https://wits.worldbank.org/countrysnapshot/en/LCN.

intense dependence on the US market, despite policymakers' periodic declarations about their intentions to diversify Mexican trade towards Asia. The Trump administration's insistence on renegotiating NAFTA and the resulting USMCA marked the first time the US has raised trade barriers in the context of a PTA (Albertoni and Wise 2021). In Mexico, an explicit 'anti-trade' narrative that had been directed mainly towards China, broadened after the GFC; with the advent of Trump-style protectionism and the travesty of USMCA's higher content requirements that favour the US market, the data show that Mexico has been quite responsive to protectionist measures.

In the decade following the GFC, Mexico's share of exports has been consistently more impacted by those countries with whom Mexico has no PTA. On average, between 2009 and 2019, 14 per cent of Mexico's exports were affected by close trading partners and 21 per cent by those countries with no trade agreement with Mexico. In Figure 12.6, we probe deeper and count the number of protectionist measures leveraged towards Mexico on the part of its close vs not close trading partners; in Figure 12.7, we count the number of protectionist measures that Mexico has initiated towards the exports of close vs not close trading partners. Since 2014, countries with no trade agreements with Mexico have been consistently more impacted by Mexico's protectionism than those participating in a PTA with Mexico.

It is worth noting that GVCs do not seem to restrain protectionism along the same lines as PTAs. Here, we follow Gaulier et al. (2019, 1), who measure intermediate goods traded between two countries as a proxy for the GVC link between them. More concisely, a World Bank report (2020c, 5) defines GVCs as follows: 'a global value chain breaks up the production process across countries. Firms specialise in a specific task and do not produce the whole product'. In Figure 12.8, we probe the

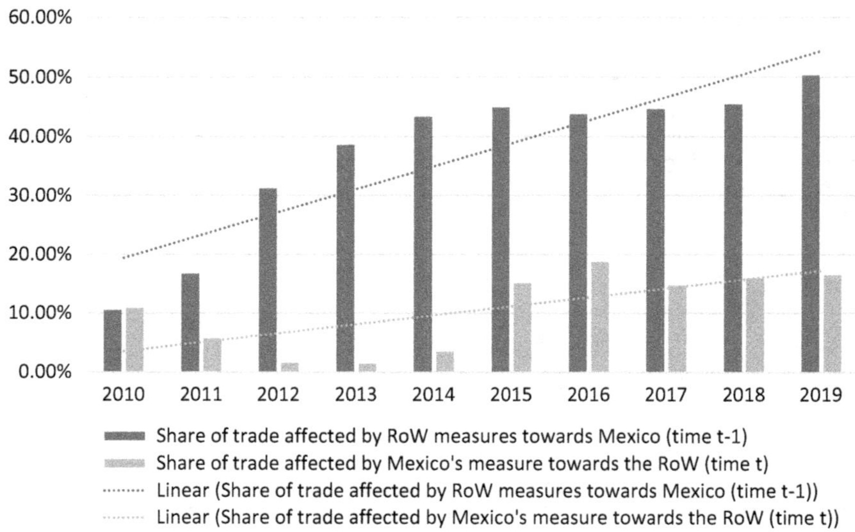

FIGURE 12.5 Share of Mexico's total exports affected by protectionism measures vs RoW exports to Mexico affected by protectionism measures (average 2009–2019).
Source: Authors' creation based on the Global Trade Alert (2020).

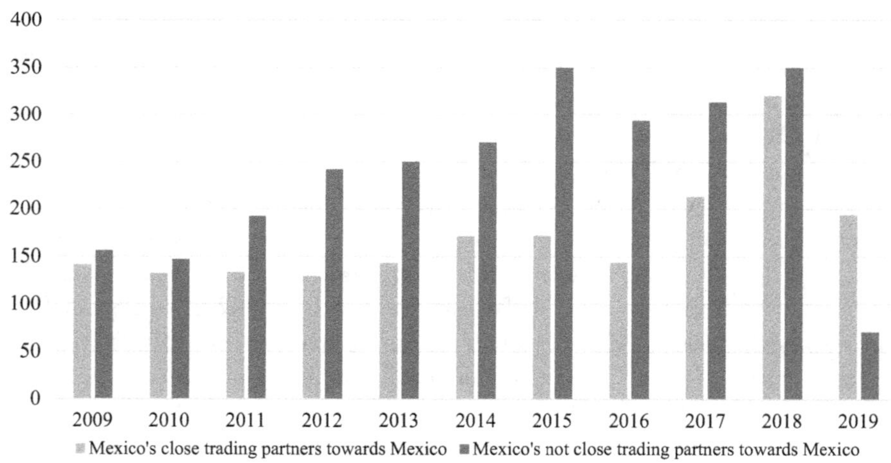

FIGURE 12.6 Number of protectionist measures towards Mexico by close and not close trading partners.
Source: Authors' creation based on Global Trade Alert (2020).

level of protectionism Mexico has faced from close trading partners through potential GVC ties (e.g. the US, Canada, China, Colombia, and Brazil). Interestingly, between 2009 and 2019, 36 per cent of Mexico's exports have been affected by close trading partners linked to Mexico through GVCs and 21 per cent by those countries that have no PTA with Mexico.

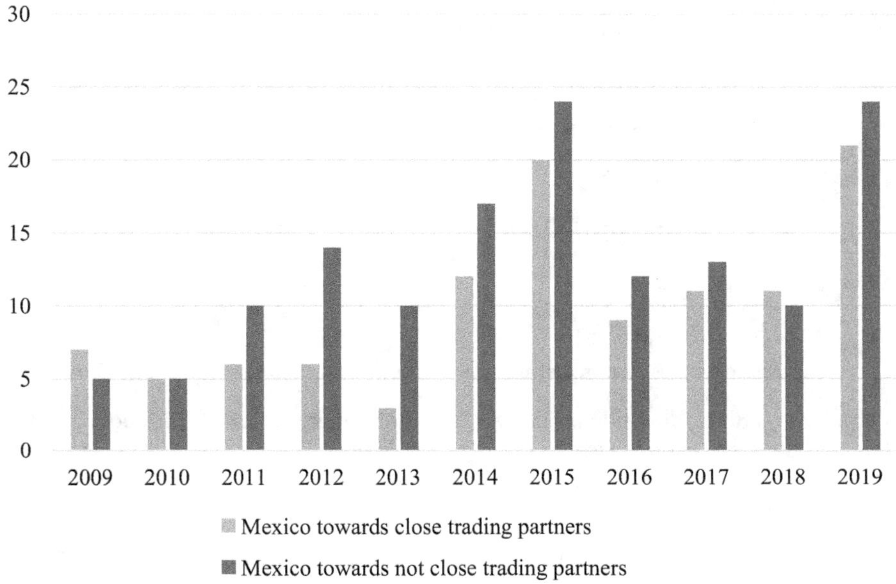

FIGURE 12.7 Number of protectionist measures implemented by Mexico towards close and not close trading partners
Source: Authors' creation based on Global Trade Alert (2020).

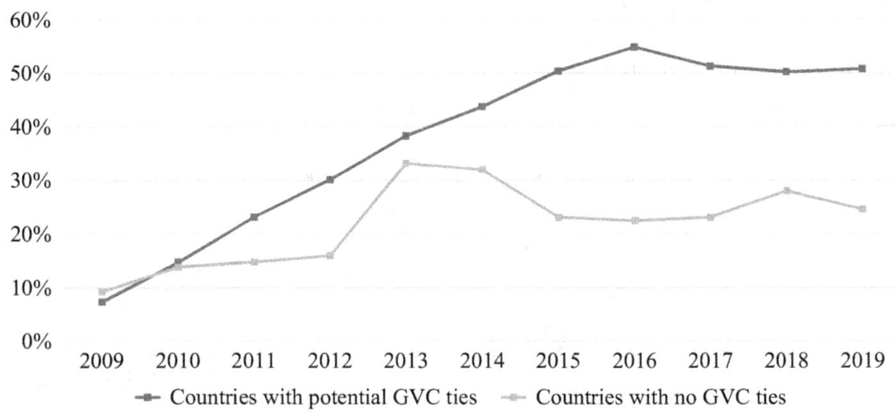

FIGURE 12.8 Share of Mexico's exports impacted by GVC ties vs no GVCs ties.
Source: Authors' creation based on Global Trade Alert (2020).

There is one additional twist to this story. Although we have found that protectionism is higher on the part of RoW towards Mexico, and that Mexico's protectionism toward its non-close trading partners is somewhat higher than with its PTA trade partners, Figure 12.9 shows that the level of non-transparent protectionist interventions used by Mexico towards close trading partners is much higher. On average,

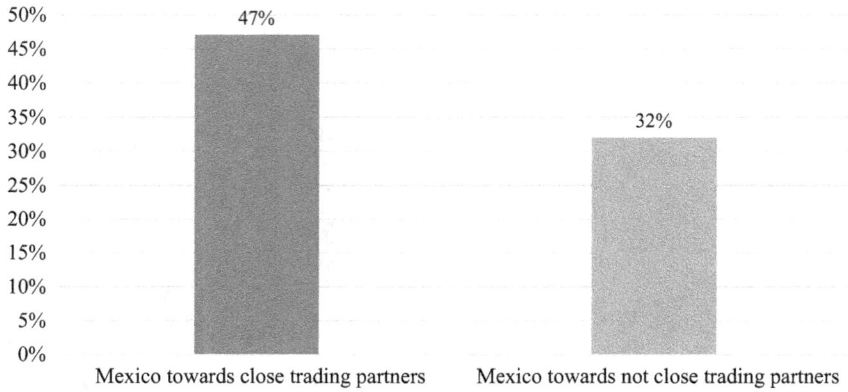

FIGURE 12.9 Share of non-transparent protectionist interventions by Mexico towards close and not close trading partners (average 2009–2019).
Source: Authors' creation based on Global Trade Alert (2020).

from 2009 to 2019, 47 per cent of Mexico's protectionist measures towards close partners were non-transparent, whereas 32 per cent of its protectionist measures towards countries that have no PTA with Mexico were non-transparent. Furthermore, the share of non-transparent protectionist interventions towards Mexico by close trading partners (82 per cent) is slightly higher than by countries with which it has no trade agreements (80 per cent).

Given Mexico's inordinately high level of dependence on the US market for trade and FDI, and the fact that much of this trade-related cross-border investment is carried out within North American GVCs, it seems safe to conclude that Mexico is bearing a heavy brunt of US protectionism (Pérez Arguello and Albertoni 2019). As can be seen in Table 12.8, those sectors that are most affected by protectionism against Mexico are the very products that form the backbone of the NAFTA market.

12.3.3 *Brazilian Protectionism (in Comparison with Mexico)*

From the 1930s to the late 1960s, the Brazilian economy adhered to an ISI model. Under ISI, Brazilian policymakers deployed sweeping industrial policies (import barriers, subsidies, and generous state sponsorship) and successfully established the domestic production of automobiles, steel, and a capital goods sector. However, after fifty years of these protectionist policies, Brazil's role in global trade was disproportionately low compared with the top ten EEs (Wise et al. 2015). The country's historic lack of exposure to global trade has been costly in terms of growth, inflation, and overall competitiveness. Despite succumbing to the 1982 debt shocks and embracing Washington Consensus policies of trade liberalisation and privatisation, those sectors built up under ISI have retained preferential treatment, regardless of Brazil's membership in MERCOSUR. Given this continued preferential treatment, Brazil's industrial

TABLE 12.8 *Sectors most affected in and by Mexico (2009–2019)*

Sectors most affected in Mexico (by main trading partners' protectionism)	Sectors most affected by Mexico's protectionism (towards main trading partners)
By close trading partners	
Products of iron or steel	Products of iron or steel
Other fabricated metal products	Cereals
Basic iron and steel	Sugar and molasses
Motor vehicles, trailers and semi-trailers	Food products
Prepared and preserved fruits and nuts	Wearing apparel, except fur apparel
By countries with no trade agreements with Mexico	
Motor vehicles, trailers and semi-trailers	Products of iron or steel
Computing machinery and parts	Other fabricated metal products
Electric motors, generators and transformers	Cereals
	Basic iron and steel
Electricity distribution and control apparatus	Wearing apparel, except fur apparel
Pharmaceutical products	

Source: Authors' creation based on Global Trade Alert (2020).

sectors have been a magnet for incoming FDI, although little of this FDI has resulted in the incorporation of Brazil into GVCs outside of MERCOSUR.

Apart from the previously mentioned differences between NAFTA and MERCOSUR, a broader comparison of the institutional context for trade policy in Mexico and Brazil reveals two contrasting patterns. Given that Mexico was controlled by a single-ruling party from 1929 to 2000, the country's entry into NAFTA in 1994 was a highly autocratic affair. Domestic debates over NAFTA were tightly circumscribed, and any quantitative estimates on the future effects of NAFTA on the Mexican economy were withheld from the Mexican people (Pastor and Wise 1994). To this day, the neoliberal policy preferences of domestic elites have held sway over Mexico and the nature of its participation in NAFTA. In Brazil, the launching of MERCOSUR was preceded by an authoritarian military regime that ruled from 1964 to 1985. As Argentina had sent its own military regime back to the barracks in 1983, a commitment to democracy and civilian rule prompted the cross-border olive branch that led to the 1991 establishment of MERCOSUR. For both countries, the long delay in the formation of a customs union and CET suggests that these goals were secondary.

Mexican and US business elites had been engaged in cross-border production since the 1960s, and the acute recession of the 1980s weakened those producers that relied on selling to the domestic market. Having successfully secured protectionist policies throughout the post-war period, this latter contingent was marginalised. Suddenly, within the confines of an autocratic government structure, NAFTA entry was framed as the next logistical step for Mexican development. Conversely, the

Brazilian state had long coddled domestic producers across sectors, and the 1980s crisis did little to diminish their fervour for a protectionist trade model. Under the tutelage of the World Bank and other multilateral institutions, both Mexico and Brazil proceeded with the unilateral reduction of tariffs and non-tariff barriers in the late 1980s. But unlike Mexico, trade liberalisation in Brazil was swept up in the transition to democracy and the heightened mobilisation of civil society, including powerful leaders in the business sector.

In Mexico, there was far too little domestic input on trade liberalisation and NAFTA entry; in Brazil, a significant institutional restructuring post-1985 gave greater influence to the industrial sector and civil society in Brazilian trade policy-making (Albertoni 2023). In Brazil, the general clamour for greater social input on trade policy led to new consultation and coordination mechanisms, even though some of the proposed measures ran counter to what was agreed on within MERCOSUR. Whereas NAFTA was rubber-stamped by the Mexican Congress, in Brazil, the Congress was able to closely scrutinise the MERCOSUR treaty, and its ultimate ratification resulted in loopholes that favoured powerful domestic actors. In short, Mexico has offered too little support for producers struggling to survive within the country's neoliberal manufacturing export-led development model, while Brazil's protectionist policies have spared producers from having to fully compete within the global economy (Oliveira et al. 2018).

12.3.4 *What's China Got to Do with It?*

In Figure 12.3, we saw that in 2015 Mexico's participation in GVCs (as a per cent of exports) was around 10 per cent higher than Brazil's. And yet, Mexico's GVC participation is linked overwhelmingly to the US market, and capital goods (the end of the assembly line) are its dominant exports (Figure 12.3). In comparison, Brazil has succeeded in diversifying its trade partners, including the US, Argentina, and the Netherlands (see Table 12.9), and intermediate exports are double the amount of consumer and capital goods exports (see Figure 12.10). Although China has been Brazil's top trade partner since 2009, it accounted for just 9 per cent of Brazil's intermediate exports in our designated time period. From 2001 to 2017, 66 per cent of Brazil's exports to China were primary products (soybeans and ores), while 50 per cent of its imports from China were electrical machinery and equipment, nuclear reactors, boilers, and other machinery (Wise 2020, 82).

Between 2008 and 2018, Brazil ran a hefty trade surplus with China, while Mexico traded with China at a steep deficit. From 2001 to 2017, 34 per cent of Mexico's imports from China were identical to Brazil's imports from China (Wise 2020, 85). Intermediate and capital goods accounted for just 3 per cent of exports from Mexico to China, while intermediate goods accounted for 9 per cent of exports from Brazil to China (see Tables 12.7 and 12.9). In this period, 19 per cent of Mexico's exports to China consisted of vehicles (other than rail or tramway). Interestingly, in 2017, total

TABLE 12.9 *Top destinations of intermediate, consumption, and capital goods (average share in Brazil's total exports between 2008 and 2018)*

Consumption goods	% in total consumption goods' exports	Intermediate goods	% in total intermediate goods' exports	Capital goods	% in total capital goods' exports
Argentina	20	US	15	US	23
US	14	Netherlands	9	Argentina	13
Netherlands	7	China	9	Netherlands	12
Paraguay	4	Argentina	7	Mexico	6
Mexico	3	Germany	3	Singapore	4
Belgium	3	Italy	3	Chile	4
Singapore	3	UK	3	Panama	4
Uruguay	3	Canada	3	Germany	4
Chile	3	India	2	Colombia	2
Colombia	2	Korea	2	Paraguay	2

Source: Authors' creation based on World Bank-World Integrated Trade Solutions (WITS), https://wits.worldbank.org/countrysnapshot/en/LCN.

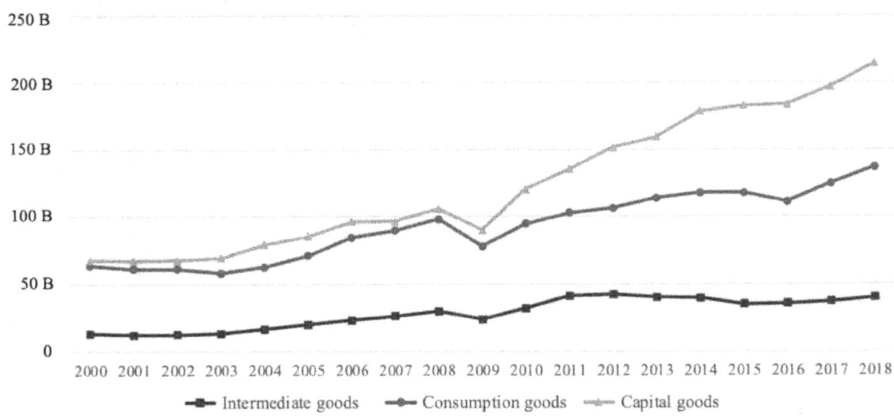

FIGURE 12.10 Brazil's export of intermediate, consumer, and capital goods between 2000 and 2018 (in thousand US$).
Source: Authors' creation based on World Bank-World Integrated Trade Solutions (WITS), https://wits.worldbank.org/countrysnapshot/en/LCN.

trade between Mexico and China was US$80.9 billion, whereas Brazil's total trade with China was US$74.8. When seen together, these figures raise two related questions: why, given that Brazil has built up significant exports of intermediate and capital goods, do so few of these goods go to its top trade partner, China? Why, given Mexico's success in diversifying away from a trade model led by primary exports, does it export so few intermediate and capital goods to RoW? The answers lie, first, in the shortcomings of domestic trade policy and, second, in each country's PTA membership.

Regarding domestic trade policy, protectionism has been the overriding response to the rapid entry of China in both countries since 2002. Earlier in the chapter, we noted the eleven-year protectionist side payment that Mexico extracted from China as a quid pro quo for Mexico's vote in favour of China's 2001 accession to the WTO. Otherwise, Argentina and Brazil have led the region in the filing of anti-dumping complaints against China at the WTO, although Mexico has periodically followed suit. As noted by the International Bar Association (IBA 2010, 5): 'Manufactured goods generally feature prominently on the list of Chinese products usually targeted by Latin American AD action, with metallurgical products often occupying second place. In Brazil, Argentina and Mexico, petrochemicals and minerals amount for an important share as well'.

Furthermore, between 2008 and 2018, both countries adhered to a strict macro-prudential policy framework, based on high-interest rates, primary budget surpluses, and capital account liberalisation. As we mentioned earlier, Mexico was so wed to this approach that it raised interest rates as an anti-inflation precaution when the GFC struck. Brazilian policymakers launched a successful counter-cyclical response to the GFC, all the while maintaining some of the world's highest interest rates and an overvalued exchange rate. Flush with cash during the commodity price boom from 2003 to 2013 (Gallagher 2016), these prices did not correct until the post-boom crash in 2014.

In both cases, a shift away from tight macro-prudence and a well-designed industrial policy could have helped to boost manufactured exports to RoW and perhaps to China. Between 2003 and 2011, the Brazilian government announced a mandate to export, innovate, and internationalise, and channelled generous support to companies through Brazil's National Development Bank (BNDES). This helped to attract about US$60 billion in Chinese FDI from 2000 to 2021 (Dussel 2022, 7); nevertheless, the pull of commodity prices was so strong that the bulk of the designated funds (and Chinese FDI) went to energy and oil sector development (Hochstetler and Montero 2013, 1490–1491). Remarkably, in Mexico, policymakers implemented an industrial policy in 2012 that favoured selected industries with high FDI inflows that were already thriving on competitive advantage (Wise 2020, 211). In other words, foreign companies and well-established North American high-tech sectors in Mexico are being rewarded, while most domestic companies are not included in this programme. Mexico has attracted about 10 per cent of the Chinese FDI that has poured into Brazil and made little effort to attract more.

What do these respective PTAs have to do with the deficiencies and asymmetries that mark each country's trade and investment relationship with China? In the case of MERCOSUR, Figure 12.3 shows that the difference in GVC participation

TABLE 12.10 *Most affected sectors in and by Brazil (2009–2019)*

Most affected sectors in Brazil (by main trading partners' protectionism)	Most affected sectors by Brazil's protectionism (towards main trading partners)
Close trading partners	
Sugar and molasses	Electric motors, generators and transformers
Motor vehicles, trailers and semi-trailers	Basic organic chemicals
Products of iron or steel	Motor vehicles, trailers, and semi-trailers
Pumps, compressors, pneumatics and engines	Electrical energy
Other general-purpose machinery and parts	Other fabricated metal products
Not close trading partners	
Products of iron or steel	Basic organic chemicals
Basic iron and steel	Machinery for mining & construction
Other fabricated metal products	Electric motors, generators, & transformers
Motor vehicles, trailers and semi-trailers	Other fabricated metal products
Aircraft and spacecraft	Motor vehicles, trailers, & semi-trailers

Source: Authors' creation based on Global Trade Alert (2020).

between Brazil and Argentina is about 10 per cent; moreover, Brazil exports about 40 per cent of its consumer, intermediate and capital goods to Argentina. Although Brazil exports another 52 per cent of goods in these three categories to the US market, this trade is conducted outside of North American GVCs (Albertoni and Rebolledo 2018). Brazil's GVC participation consists mainly of intra-industry trade with Argentina in the auto sector. Table 12.10, however, suggests that even this may be an exaggeration, as motor vehicles, trailers and non-trailers are the targets of two-way protectionism (Bachega 2011, Oliveira et al. 2018) – by Brazil and against Brazil on the part of close and not close trading partners alike.

The embedding of Brazilian protectionism within MERCOSUR has been costly to the country's industrial sector. At about 9 per cent, MERCOSUR's CET is second only to Venezuela's 10 per cent weighted mean tariff rate (see Table 12.4); moreover, MERCOSUR's higher tariffs – applied to information technology, telecom, and capital goods – are simply counter-productive (Exports.gov 2023). At its peak in 2005, Brazil carried a trade surplus of US$8 billion in manufactured goods, but by 2012 this had turned into a US$90 billion deficit (Jenkins 2015, 50–52). Some of this deficit can be blamed on the overvaluation of the Brazilian currency during most of the 2003–2013 commodity price boom, but about 29 per cent can be attributed to displacement by Chinese manufactured imports.

Whereas path dependence governs Brazil's trade relationship with China, which has always followed a pattern of old-fashioned comparative advantage, Mexico sank into a similar pattern after once accounting for about 11 per cent of China's manufactured imports (Wise 2020, 85). However, as China's own manufactured exports began to flood the North American market, and Mexico found itself trading at a deficit with China by 1993, it shifted towards the same traditional trade profile that characterises Brazil-China trade. By the 2010s, ores, slag, and agriculture accounted for 24 per cent of Mexican exports to China (Wise 2020, 85). One telling lesson from the US-China trade war is the agility with which China has been able to diversify its supplier base of intermediate imports and re-engineer its GVCs (Baldwin and Evenett 2020; Albertoni and Wise 2021, 20–22).

Mexico is a potential winner on this front, as a flood of private Chinese companies producing electronic components, construction equipment, and installing warehouse and factory grids are now setting up operations in Mexico to supply US producers and consumers with goods hit by high US tariffs (Goodman 2023). There are two contradictions here: first, it took a drastic US-China trade war to bring Mexico's potential strengths to life; and second, since the PRC's 2001 accession to the WTO, the spectre of Chinese inputs entering the US market stamped 'made in Mexico' has haunted US producers and policymakers. The US has the first Trump administration to thank for bringing this scenario to life (Puyana 2018; Noland 2020).

12.3.5 *Brazil and MERCOSUR: An 'Imperfect Customs Union'*

Turning more specifically to Brazil's trade policies, we saw in Table 12.9 that, apart from Brazil's trade with Argentina, its exports to the remaining MERCOSUR partners (Paraguay and Uruguay) consist of a small share of consumer durables. Figure 12.11 shows that a rise in Brazil's protectionist responses towards RoW coincided with the end of the commodity price boom in 2014. Figure 12.12 shows that Brazil has consistently implemented more protectionist measures against countries with which it has no trade agreements than towards close trading partners,

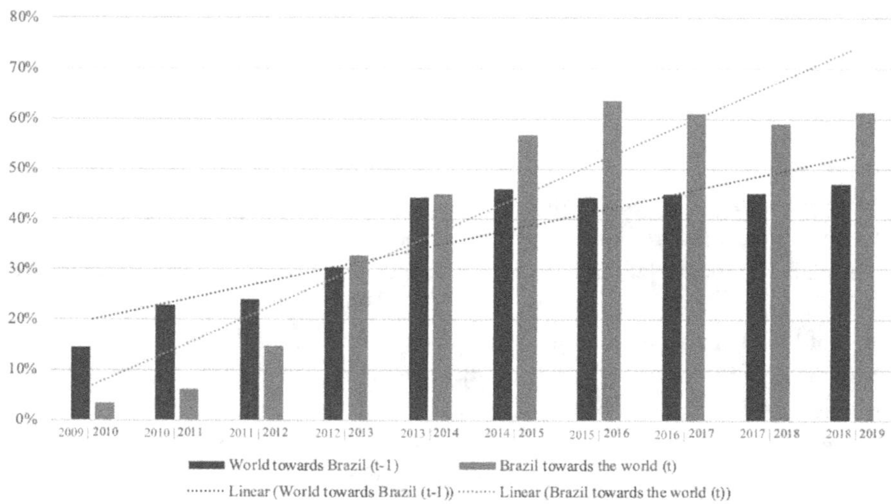

FIGURE 12.11 Share of Brazil's total exports affected vs world exports to Brazil affected by protectionist measures (average 2009–2019)
Source: Authors' creation based on the Global Trade Alert (2020).

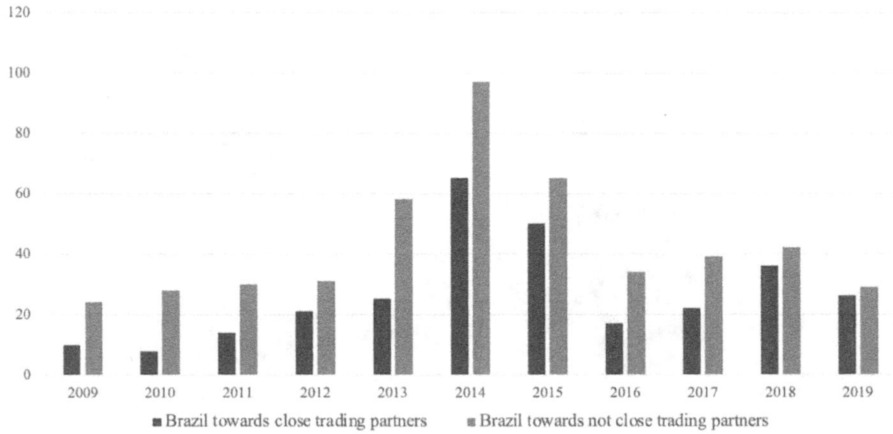

FIGURE 12.12 Brazil's number of protectionist measures implemented towards close and not close trading partners.
Source: Authors' creation based on Global Trade Alert (2020).

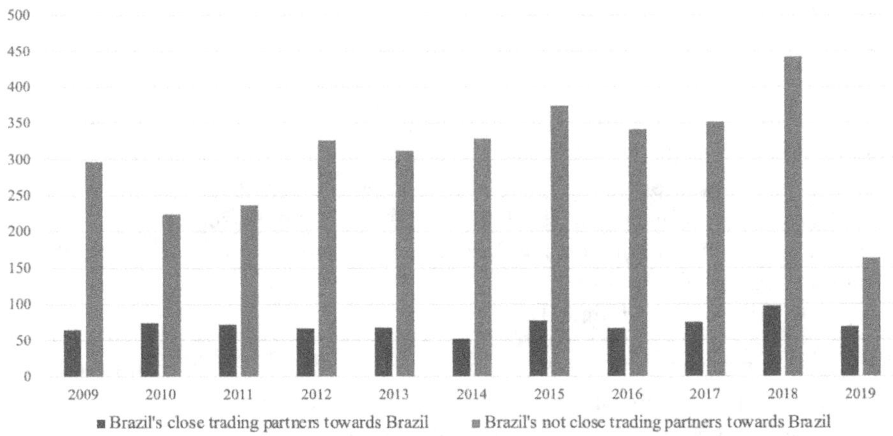

FIGURE 12.13 Number of protectionist measures towards Brazil by close and not close trading partners.
Source: Authors' creation based on Global Trade Alert (2020).

while Figure 12.13 reflects that those protectionist measures that have most affected Brazil are from countries with which it has no trade agreements. This last figure captures the protectionism of key non-PTA trade partners (China and the US) towards Brazil. It appears that Brazil has been caught in some of the crossfire related to the US-China trade war (Evenett and Fritz 2018).

Regarding the level of transparency in trade measures, Figure 12.14 shows that the share of protectionist non-transparent instruments used by Brazil towards close trading partners is much higher (an average of 74 per cent between 2009 and 2019) than with countries with which it has no trade agreements (56 per cent).

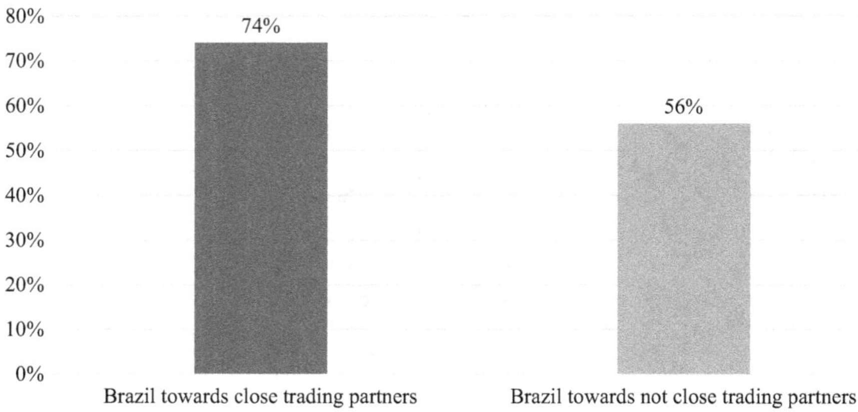

FIGURE 12.14 Share of protectionist interventions that use non-transparent measures by Brazil (MERCOSUR) towards close and not close trading partners (average 2009–2019).
Source: Authors' creation based on Global Trade Alert (2020).

This mimics Mexico's pattern. In the case of Brazil, we quote from Nicolas Albertoni's interview with Tatiana Palermo, former Brazilian Vice-Minister of Agriculture and chief agricultural trade negotiator:

> MERCOSUR is a good example for your argument. Although the countries do not apply tariffs among them (with some exceptions), there are numerous non-tariff and other barriers (like, for example, extremely complex rules of origin, and different sanitary and phytosanitary requirements that make agricultural trade within the bloc very difficult). Non-tariff barriers in Brazil are usually not directed towards specific countries. At the same time, it is usually more difficult for the Brazilian government to justify such barriers within MERCOSUR.

When interpreting the comments of Brazil's former chief agricultural trade negotiator, keep in mind that the country's top trade partners are China, the US, and Argentina. In Figure 12.15, we see that Brazil's close trading partners are less likely to deploy non-transparent measures towards Brazil, but that 85 per cent of such measures stem from its non-close trading partners. Although this former trade negotiator cautions that 'it is usually more difficult for the Brazilian government to justify such barriers within MERCOSUR', this does not mean that Brazil has refrained from leveraging non-transparent protectionist measures against its fellow PTA members. Together, the data in Figures 12.11–12.15 confirm the extent to which Brazil has painted itself into a messy protectionist corner.

12.4 FINAL REFLECTIONS

The Nobel Laureate Douglass North has consistently reminded us that development need not be 'a story of inevitability in which the past neatly predicts the future'

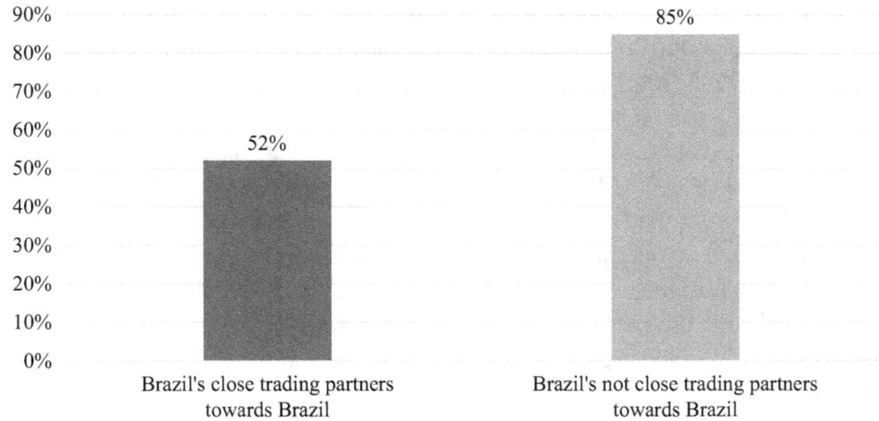

FIGURE 12.15 Share of protectionist interventions that use non-transparent measures towards Brazil (MERCOSUR) by close and not close trading partners (average 2009–2019).
Source: Authors' creation based on Global Trade Alert (2020).

(North 1990, 98–99). And yet, for over thirty years, Brazil and Mexico have slogged away at trade policies that guarantee the tedious repetition of sub-par outcomes. In the best of all worlds, Brazil would open its market to RoW, continue to diversify its trade and investment partners, and test the waters outside of MERCOSUR. Uruguayan policymakers have done just this, stating that the pursuit of a PTA with China has become their main goal (Elliott 2022). With its rich factor endowments and solid industrial base, Brazil has the potential to realise much higher gains from trade. Mexico is another story. There, political and economic elites have kicked away Ha-Joon Chang's (2003) ladder of state support and settled for a hands-off manufactured export-led development strategy that has delivered anaemic growth and *negative* per capita income returns.

Both Brazil and Mexico continue to struggle with low growth related cumulatively to the 2014 crash in commodity and oil prices, the pandemic, and erratic policy interventions. Mexico, in particular, is still reeling from some of the trade war tariffs imposed by the US regardless of NAFTA/USMCA. Amid tensions over the Russo-Ukrainian war, Brazil is straddling the need to maintain its strong bond with China. Since the early 2000s, Brazil is the Latin American country that has benefitted most from its trade and investment relationship with China. During the 2000s, Chinese FDI in Brazil started in the extractive sector, shifted to infrastructure, and is now moving into manufacturing. In 2022, for example, China's Great Wall Motor Company purchased a Daimler auto manufacturing plant in Brazil, with plans to develop electric vehicles (EV) and batteries; Chinese electric automaker BYD also announced its intention to invest in factories in Brazil that process lithium and iron phosphate for EV batteries (Albright et al. 2023, 15–16). Brazil will have the opportunity to engage in emergent GVCs around EVs and green energy. That is, *if* policymakers get this right and streamline MERCOSUR's excessive tariffs and NTMs.

In the case of Mexico, despite the numerous PTAs it has signed with RoW, policymakers have done little to diversify away from the country's dependence on the US market. Remarkably, the Biden administration maintained some of the first Trump administration's trade war tariffs to the detriment of China, Mexico and RoW. With the November 2024 election of Trump to a second term, even higher tariffs are being threatened (Colvin and Gillies 2024). Paradoxically, however, misguided US trade policies have opened trade and investment opportunities that Mexican policymakers should seize on. The relocation of Chinese manufacturers to Mexico and the PRC's sourcing of Mexican intermediate inputs in lieu of US ones (Albertoni and Wise 2021) has shed light on the potential relationship that Mexico could enjoy with China. Although unpredictable market forces have brought about this favourable turn of events, they will not sustain them. Rather, it is incumbent upon Mexican policymakers to deploy proactive public policies to nourish, deepen, and extend these promising ties with China. In the absence of a concerted strategy towards China and RoW, Mexico has little chance of becoming more than an upscale contract assembler, reaping lower value-added gains at the end of the 'factory line' (*The Economist* 2020, 1).

REFERENCES

Albertoni, N. 2023. *The Murky Rise of Trade Protectionism in an Interconnected and Uncertain Global Economy*. New York: Routledge.

Albertoni, N. and A. Rebolledo 2018. "Trade, Economic and Political Integration in Latin America: The Cases of the Southern Common Market (Mercosur) and the Pacific Alliance." In: Sauvé, P. et al. (Eds.), *The Pacific Alliance in a World of Preferential Trade Agreements*.Cham: Springer.

Albertoni, N. and C. Wise 2021. "International Trade Norms in the Age of Covid-19 Nationalism on the Rise?" *Fudan Journal of the Humanities and Social Sciences* 14(1): 41–66.

Albright, Z., R. Ray and Y. Liu 2023. *China-Latin America and the Caribbean Economic Bulletin*. Boston, MA: Global Development Policy Center, Boston University.

Ardito-Barletta, N."Managing Development and Transition: Fifty Years After Bretton Woods,". In Kenen, P. (Ed.), Managing the World Economy, The Peterson Institute for International Economics, Washington D.C., 1994.

Bachega, H. 2011. "Brazil to Slap Barriers on Car Imports." *Reuters*, 12 May 2011, www.reuters.com/article/us-brazil-imports-barriers/brazil-to-slap-barriers-on-car-imports-idUSTRE74C15020110513 (accessed 22 April 2023).

Baldwin, R. and S. Evenett 2009. *The Collapse of Global Trade, Murky Protectionism, and the Crisis: Recommendations for the G20*. London: Centre for Economic Policy Research (CEPR).

Baldwin, R. and S. Evenett 2020. *COVID-19 and Trade Policy: Why Turning Inward Won't Work*. London: Centre for Economic Policy Research (CEPR).

Barletta, N. A. 1994. "Managing Development and Transition." In: P. B. Kenen (Ed.), *Managing the World Economy: Fifty Years after Bretton Woods*.Washington, DC: Institute for International Economics.

Boffa, M. and M. Olarreaga 2012. "Protectionism During the Crisis: Tit-for-tat or Chicken-Games?" *Economics Letters* 117(3): 746–749.

Bordo, M., B. Eichengreen and D. Irwin 1999. "Is Globalization Today Really Different than Globalization a Hundred Years Ago?" NBER Working Paper 7195, Cambridge, MA.

Campbell. P. and J. Webber 2017. "Trump to Give Mexican Car Trade a Bumpy Ride." *Financial Times*, 5 January.

Castillo, M. and A. Martins Neto 2016. "Premature Deindustrialization in Latin America." ECLAC Productive Development Series no. 205, Santiago, Chile.

Chang, H. 2003. *Kicking Away the Ladder: Development Strategy in Historical Perspective*. London: Anthem Press.

Colvin, J. and R. Gillies 2024. "Trump threatens to impose sweeping new tariffs on Mexico, Canada and China on first day in office." OA online 26 Nov 2024, www.oaoa.com/local-news/trump-threatens-to-impose-sweeping-new-tariffs-on-mexico-canada-and-china-on-first-day-in-office/ (accessed 23 January 2025).

Dussel, E. 2022. "Monitor of Chinese OFDI in Latin America and the Caribbean 2022." www.redalcchina.org/monitor/images/pdfs/menuprincipal/DusselPeters_MonitorOFDI_2022_Eng.pdf (accessed 16 April 2023).

Dussel, E. and K.P. Gallagher 2013. "NAFTA's Uninvited Guest: China and the Disintegration of North American Trade." *CEPAL Review* 110: 83–108.

Elliott, L. 2022. "Uruguay's Global Ambitions Shake up Latin America's Mercosur Trade Bloc." 26 December 2022, www.ft.com/content/1d8834b4-b531-4263-b435-6354128a1a9d (accessed 24 April 2023).

Ezrati, M. 2024. "Mexico Also Wants to Decouple from China", *Forbes* 26 October 2024, www.forbes.com/sites/miltonezrati/2024/10/26/mexico-also-wants-to-decouple-from-china (accessed 24 December 2024).

European Commission. 2024. Questions and Answers on the EU-Mercosur Partnership Agreement, ec.europa.eu/commission/presscorner/detail/en/qanda_24_6245 (accessed 24 December 2024).

Evenett, S. and J. Fritz 2018. "Brazen Unilateralism: The US-China Tariff War in Perspective." Global Trade Alert Report 23. CEPR Press, www.globaltradealert.org (accessed 23 April 2023).

Exports.gov.2023. "International Trade Administration, US Department of Commerce." www.trade.gov/export-solutions (accessed 10 April 2023).

Felter, C., D. Renwick and A. Chatzky 2019. "Mercosur: South America's Fractious Trade Bloc." *Council on Foreign Relations*, July, www.cfr.org/backgrounder/mercosur-south-americas-fractious-trade-bloc (accessed 16 October 2019).

Finger, M. and J. Nogues 2001. "The Unbalanced Uruguay Round Outcome: The New Areas in Future WTO Negotiations." Policy Research Working Paper 2732, World Bank Development Research Group.

Franko, P. 2018. *The Puzzle of Latin American Economic Development*. Oxford: Rowman & Littlefield Publishers.

Gallagher, K. P. 2016. *The China Triangle: Latin America's China Boom and the Fate of the Washington Consensus*.New York: Oxford University Press.

Gaulier, G., A. Sztulman and D. Ünal 2019. "Are Global Value Chains Receding? The Jury is Still Out. Key Findings from the Analysis of Deflated World Trade in Parts and Components." *International Economics* 161(1): 219–236.

Global Trade Alert (GTA). 2020. Database Handbook. www.globaltradealert.org (accessed 14 February 2020).

Goodman, P.S. 2023. "Why Chinese Companies are Investing Billions in Mexico." *New York Times*, 7 March. www.nytimes.com/2023/02/03/business/china-mexico-trade.html (accessed on 18 April 2023).

Hernández, R. 2012. "Economic Liberalization and Trade Relations between Mexico and China." *Journal of Current Chinese Affairs* 41(1): 49–96

Hochstetler, K. and A. Montero 2013. "The Renewed Developmental State: The National Development Bank and the Brazil Model." *Journal of Development Studies* 49(11): 1484–1499.

Hofmann, C., Osnago, A. and M. Ruta 2019. "The Content of Preferential Trade Agreements." *World Trade Review* 18(3): 365–398.

Hufbauer, G., Schott, J. and D. Clark 1994. *Western Hemisphere Economic Integration*. Washington, DC: Institute for International Economics.

International Bar Association (IBA). 2010. "Anti-Dumping Investigations against China in Latin America." IBA, 2010, 5–6, www.ibanet.org/ENews_Archive/IBA_Jan_2010_ENews_AntiDumping_investigations_against_China.aspx (accessed 16 April 2023).

Jenkins, R. 2015. "Is Chinese Competition Causing Deindustrialization in Brazil?" *Latin American Perspectives* 42(6): 42–63.

King, G., R. O. Keohane and S. Verba 2021. *Designing Social Inquiry. Scientific Inference in Qualitative Research*. Princeton: Princeton University Press.

Kroeber, A. R. 2016. *China's Economy: What Everyone Needs to Know*. New York: Oxford University Press.

Lawrence, R. 1996. *Regionalism, Multilateralism and Deep Integration*. Washington, DC: Brookings Institution Press.

Maswood, J. 2007. "Punching Above Its Weight? The G20 and the Doha Trade Negotiations." Woodrow Wilson Center. www.wilsoncenter.org/event/punching-above-its-weight-the-g20-and-the-doha-trade-negotiations (accessed 20 April 2023).

Moreira, M., E. Stein, K. Li, F. Merchán, C. Martincus, J. Blyde, D. Trachtenberg, J. Cornick, J. Frieden and M. R. Chatruc 2019. *Trading Promises for Results: What Global Integration Can Do for Latin America and the Caribbean*. Washington, DC: Inter-American Development Bank.

Moreno-Brid, J.C. 2013. "Industrial Policy: A Missing Link in Mexico's Quest for Export-led Growth." *Latin American Policy* 4(2): 216–237.

Mukherjee, B. 2016. *Democracy and Trade Policy in Developing Countries*. Chicago, IL: University of Chicago Press.

Noland, M. 2020. "Protectionism under Trump: The China Shock, Deplorables, and the First White President." *Asian Economic Policy Review* 15(1): 31–50.

Nolte, D. 2023. "A Last Chance at an EU-Mercosur Agreement." *International Politics and Society*. 6 February 2023. www.ips-journal.eu/topics/economy-and-ecology/a-last-chance-at-an-eu-mercosur-agreement-6489/ (accessed 27 March 2023).

North, D. 1990. *Institutions, Institutional Change, and Economic Performance*. New York: Cambridge University Press.

OAS-SICE. 2023. *Treaty Establishing a Common Market between the Argentine, Brazil, Paraguay and Uruguay*. www.sice.oas.org/trade/mrcsr/treatyasun_e.asp (accessed 12 April 2023).

Office of The US Trade Representative (USTR). 2024. "Mexico: Trade and Investment Summary". ustr.gov/countries-regions/americas/mexico (accessed 23 December 2024).

Oliveira, I., P. da Motta Veiga, S. Polónia Rios and F. Ribeiro 2018. "The Political Economy of Trade Policy in Brazil." Working Paper CINDES/IPEA. www.ipea.gov.br/portal/index.php?option = com_content&view = article&id = 35017&Itemid = 432 (accessed 24 April 2023).

Pastor, M. and C. Wise 1994. "The Origins and Sustainability of Mexico's Free Trade Policy." *International Organization* 48(3): 459–489.

2021. Marcelo Elizondo: "Los resultados hoy están mostrando un Mercosur que se achica." *Perfil*, 31 March. www.perfil.com/noticias/economia/marcelo-elizondo-las-decisiones-que-hay-que-tomar-hay-sobre-el-mercosur-son-politicas.phtml (accessed 21 April 2023).

Rodrik, D. 2009. "The Myth of Rising Protectionism." *Project Syndicate Blog*, 12 October 2019. www.project-syndicate.org/commentary/the-myth-of-rising-protectionism?barrier = accesspaylog (accessed 13 October 2012).

Rodrik, D. 2015. "Premature Industrialization." NBER Working Paper no. 20932, Cambridge, MA.

Schwab, S. 2011. "After Doha: Why the Negotiations are Doomed and What We Should Do about It." *Foreign Affairs* 90(3): 104–117

Statista. 2022. Data available at www.statista.com/statistics/1105881/mexico-trade-value-china/, (accessed 22 November 2022).

Stiglitz, J. and A. Charlton 2005. *Fair Trade for All.*New York: Oxford University Press.

Subramanian, A. and M. Kessler 2013. "The Hyperglobalization of Trade and Its Future." Working Paper 13-16. Washington: Peterson Institute for International Economics.

The Economist. 2020. "Will Latin America Take Advantage of Supply Chain Shifts? *The Economist Intelligence Unit.*www.eiu.com/n/campaigns/will-latin-america-take-advantage-of-supply-chain-shifts/ (accessed 26 March 2023).

Tussie, D. 2009. "Latin America: Contrasting Motivations for Regional Projects." *Review of International Studies* 35(1): 169–188.

UN ComTrade. 2019. ComTrade Database, comtradeplus.un.org/ (accessed 24 December 2024).

Vaillant, M. 2005. "Mercosur Southern Cone Integration under Construction." *Internationale Politik Gesellschaft* 2: 52–17.

Vickers, B. 2012. "The Role of the BRICs in the WTO." In: M. Daunton, A. Narlikar and R. Stern (Eds.), *The Oxford Handbook on the WTO*. Oxford: Oxford University Press.

Williamson, J. 1990. "What Washington Means by Policy Reform." In: J. Williamson (Ed.), *Latin American Adjustment: How Much Has Happened.* Washington, D.C.: Institute for International Economics.

Wise, C. 2009. "The North American Free Trade Agreement." *New Political Economy* 14(1): 133–148.

Wise, C. 2020. *Dragonomics. How Latin America is Maximizing (or Missing Out on) China's International Development Strategy*. New Haven: Yale University Press.

Wise, C., Armijo, L. and S. Katada (Eds.) 2015. *Unexpected Outcomes. How Emerging Economies Survived the Global Financial Crisis*. Washington, DC: Brookings Institution Press.

World Bank 2020a. World Development Indicators. https://data.worldbank.org/indicator/NE.TRD.GNFS.ZS?locations=ZJ-BR-MX (accessed 15 January 2023).

World Bank 2020b. Global Economic Prospects. A *World Bank Group Flagship Report.* http://pubdocs.worldbank.org/en/267761588788282656/Global-Economic-Prospects-June-2020-Highlights-Chapter-1.pdf.

World Bank. 2020c. *World Development Report 2020: Trading for Development in the Age of Global Value Chains*. Washington, DC: World Bank.

WTO. 2016. "Report to the TPRB from the Director-General on Trade-Related Developments." *World Trade Organization*, 4 July 2016. www.wto.org/english/news_e/news16_e/trdev_22jul16_e.htm (accessed 23 April 2023).

WTO. 2017a. Trade Policy Review Mexico. WTO Secretariat WT/TPR/S/352. www.wto.org/english/tratop_e/tpr_e/tp452_e.htm (accessed 23 April 2023).

WTO. 2017b. Trade Policy Review Brazil. WTO Secretariat WT/TPR/S/358. www.wto.org/english/tratop_e/tpr_e/tp458_e.htm (accessed 23 April 2023).

WTO. 2020. What We Do. www.wto.org/english/thewto_e/thewto_e.htm (accessed 13 July 2020).

WTO. 2023a. Regional Trade Agreements Database. https://rtais.wto.org/UI/charts.aspx (accessed 15 February 2023).

WTO. 2023b. Understanding on the Interpretation of Article XXIV of the General Agreement on Tariffs and Trade 1994. www.wto.org/english/tratop_e/region_e/region_art24_e.htm (accessed 12 April 2023).

WTO. 2024. Understanding the World Trade Organisation: Developing Countries, www.wto.org/english/thewto_e/whatis_e/tif_e/dev1_e.htm#:~:text=About%20two%20thirds%20of%20the,Also%20in%20this%20section (accessed 24 December 2024).

13

Anti-China Sentiment and the Politics of Brazilian Agribusiness

Daniela Campello and Francisco Urdínez

13.1 INTRODUCTION

> An environment of 'geopolitical suspicion' toward China aggravated by the pandemic of the new coronavirus (Covid-19) should affect the 5G supply chain, bringing impacts on the strategy and competition in Brazil. At a time when we need to make a quantitative and qualitative leap in technology, it would be interesting to let the competition work: Chinese fighting with Americans, with Nordics, to see who serves us better. [But] at this time when we should take this plunge, this 'cloud of suspicion' comes and creates a geopolitical problem in something that was strictly economic.

This diagnosis appeared in an interview by Mr. Paulo Guedes – Jair Bolsonaro's Finance minister – granted to CNN Brazil, in July 2020. In the conversation, Mr. Guedes unabashedly suggested that, despite the advantages of competition, the suspicion that China was to blame for the pandemic of Covid-19 could create unexpected costs for countries adopting Chinese technology. The minister further claimed that, for geopolitical reasons, China could possibly decide to "turn off the buttons" and interrupt communication and security services and declared that "from a geopolitical perspective we are on Trump's side."

Brazil ended up never banning Huawei from selling to 5G suppliers, thanks to enormous pressure from local companies and from the Chinese government, but these declarations illustrate the animosity the Bolsonaro government maintained toward China throughout its four years in office. This confrontational, often aggressive tone included public declarations by government officials, as the one quoted above, tweets, and even jokes – like the one made by the then Minister of

The empirical analysis presented in this chapter was originally published in the article "Voter and Legislator Responses to Localized Trade Shocks from China in Brazil" (*Comparative Political Studies*, Vol. 54, Issue 7, 2021).

Education, and later Executive Director of Brazil at the World Bank Abraham Weintraub – about the Chinese accent speaking Portuguese.[1]

The animosity described precedes the pandemic of Covid-19 but worsened after it. During the crisis, the president, his sons, and other government officials frequently associated the country with the virus and actively helped spread fake news suggesting the virus was created purposefully by China to increase its international standing.[2] These comments raised concerns among Chinese officials and ultimately led to an unusually harsh response from the Chinese Ambassador to Eduardo Bolsonaro, the president's son and then president of the Foreign Relations Commission of Brazil's Lower Chamber. There were also speculations that delays in the export of inputs for the production of vaccines were a quiet response to the attacks.

Irrespective of the president and his family's personal views about China, from an international relations perspective the confrontational tone that permeated relations with the country during the Bolsonaro administration is intriguing, to say the least. Even considering the enormous effect Chinese growth had on world markets in the past two decades, the Brazilian case still stands out as a country transformed – not only economically but also politically – by the expansion of Chinese markets.

Still, it can always be argued that the president's behavior toward trading partners is the result of multiple pressures, including those exerted by those harmed by Chinese competition.

The indifference of winners from trade with China to those attacks, however, poses a puzzle to international political economists. Why did groups that benefited so much from the expansion of Chinese markets not publicly stand up to defend the country from the government's attacks? The indifference of winners from Chinese trade to the anti-China stance that characterized the Bolsonaro years is the object of this article. Before moving forward, however, it is important to identify winners and losers from the boom in Chinese-Brazilian trade observed since the early 2000s.

13.2 ESTABLISHING WINNERS AND LOSERS IN BRAZIL-CHINA TRADE

Since China's accession to the World Trade Organization (WTO), bilateral trade has grown exponentially between the two countries (Figure 13.1a). In less than ten years, China went from Brazil's twelfth major export destination to becoming the country's main trade partner. In 2000, Brazil received 2.3 percent of its imports and sent 2.0 percent of its exports to China (by value); in 2021, these numbers had risen

1 https://g1.globo.com/politica/noticia/2020/04/06/weintraub-publica-post-com-insinuacoes-contra-a-china-depois-apaga-embaixada-repudia.ghtml

2 https://oglobo.globo.com/saude/vacina/queimando-as-pontes-diplomaticas-com-china-veja-como-governo-bolsonaro-agiu-24848598

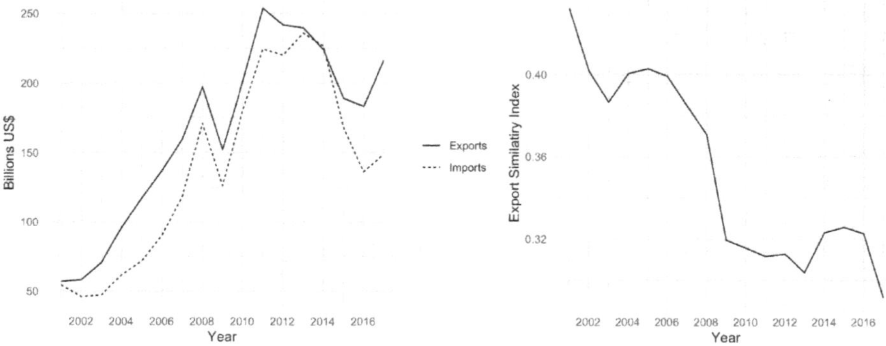

FIGURE 13.1 Brazil-China trade indicators. (a) Brazilian exports to and imports from China. (b) Export similarity index.
Note: (a) Presents trends in Brazilian imports and exports to China, and (b) displays the export similarity index [source: UN Comtrade]. The export similarity index captures the competition between China and Brazil in the world market. It is calculated as $S(bc, w) = \Sigma_i \text{Min}[X_i(bw), X_i(cw)] * 100$, where $X_i(bw)$ is the share of product i in the exports of Brazil to the world, and $X_i(cw)$ is the share of product i in the exports of China to the world.
Source: Own elaboration based on data from UN Comtrade.

to 21.7 percent and 31.3 percent, respectively. Thanks to a substantial expansion of Chinese trade (Figure 13.1a), Brazil experienced an unprecedented boom in trade and fiscal revenues and an acceleration of economic growth rates in the past decade (Jenkins 2015).

As Figure 13.1b shows, Brazil and China developed a commodity-for-manufacture pattern of trade. Thanks to this pattern, Chinese trade produced a remarkably positive shock in Brazil's agro-exporting areas, and hurt industrial sectors like textiles, electronics, and machinery (Jenkins 2015; Paz 2018).

Chinese demand for commodities has produced an unprecedented shock in agro-exporting areas (Costa et al. 2016). To cope with the fast-growing soy market and its subproducts, the agricultural frontier has advanced toward the states of Mato Grosso, Goiás, and Mato Grosso do Sul, at the expense of South America's largest savanna, the so-called Cerrado (Oliveira and Schneider 2016; Spring 2018). Traditional agro-exporting states, such as Rio Grande do Sul and Paraná, also gradually replaced other crops (cotton, corn, rice, and tobacco) with soybeans.

As both agribusiness and industry are clustered geographically in Brazil, the income shocks associated with Chinese trade were not limited to citizens working in the tradable sectors. As most affected municipalities become wealthier/poorer, residents working in services also experience the impact of these "localized" shocks (Figure 13.2).

It would be natural to expect, thus, that as much as it makes sense for losers from Chinese trade to share and even exacerbate the government's anti-China sentiment,

FIGURE 13.2 Chinese import (left) and export (right) shocks per worker by Brazilian microregions.
Note: Variables are expressed in deciles (Costa et al. 2016).
Source: Own elaboration.

those benefited by booming exports to China should actively oppose the confrontation of their main market.

Students of the politics of international trade have long investigated economic determinants of trade attitudes (Kaltenthaler et al. 2004; Mansfield and Mutz 2009; Milner and Tingley 2011). Most of this work evolved within the Open Economy Politics (OEP) paradigm and assumes that these attitudes reflect individual self-interest derived from well-established economic models.

The Stolper-Samuelson – or factor-endowment – model assumes costless intersectoral mobility of factors of production and posits that trade benefits (harms) individuals who own relatively abundant (scarce) factors. The Ricardo-Viner – or specific-sectors – model relaxes the assumption of full-factor mobility and postulates that trade favors individuals who are employed in the export-oriented sectors (intensive in abundant resources) and hurts those who are employed in import-competing sectors (intensive in scarce resources). It follows that pro- and anti-trade preferences should form along factoral and sectoral lines, respectively, depending on the level of factor mobility observed in a given economy (Rogowski 1989; Hiscox 2002).

Empirical work on the determinants of trade preferences at the individual level has mostly focused on the developed world. These studies are hardly conclusive, but several of them found a consistent association between high skills (abundant factor) and support for free trade in Organisation for Economic Co-operation and

Development (OECD) countries, and interpreted this as evidence in support of the factor-endowment model (Scheve and Slaughter 2001; Kaltenthaler et al. 2004; Mayda and Rodrik 2005).[3]

Recent research has challenged this interpretation, though, questioning the centrality of material interests and moving toward examining the impact of ideas, values, and attitudes on the understanding of trade views (Hiscox 2002; Hainmueller and Hiscox 2006; Mansfield and Mutz 2009; Lü et al. 2012; Ardanaz et al. 2013; Sabet 2016; Rho and Tomz 2017).[4]

Another strand of this literature, however, argues that weak empirical evidence of the relevance of self-interest stems from its overly strict definition, derived directly from individual factor-ownership or employment in tradable sectors. Mansfield and Mutz (2009), for example, argue that strictly defined self-interest rarely shapes policy preferences because people do not understand the connection between personal well-being and public policies. Rather, they maintain that trade preferences are sociotropic and are formed based on how people *believe* policies affect their community.

Survey experiments indicate that sociotropic preferences should not be seen as automatic replacements for individual-level information, as both seem to interact depending on the context. Yet, it emerges that individuals typically do not respond to positive country-level information by increasing their approval rates for trade; instead, they tend to react by lowering their approval rates when presented with negative information. For instance, when given negative information about their own sector, individuals may become concerned about the potential loss of their own jobs (Schaffer and Spilker 2019).

Other authors draw from the economic voting literature to advocate for more realistic meso-level theories of interest formation, rather than narrow self-interest (Fordham and Kleinberg 2012; Ansolabehere et al. 2014). They assert that local economic conditions influence individuals' perception of government's management of the economy and that it is very difficult to separate individual from group interests. People may know little about trade, but they learn from family, friends, neighbors, coworkers, business leaders, and organized groups; individuals living near one another are likely to share interests and experience economic booms and crises. Negative characterizations of partner countries resonate with those that are harmed by trade, such as business leaders and their employees, but also with a whole network of secondary economic beneficiaries of activities in these sectors (Kleinberg and Fordham 2010; Colantone and Stanig 2018a).

Along these lines, several studies have turned their focus to the political impact of localized shocks associated to trade (Margalit 2012; Ardanaz et al. 2013; Jensen et al.

[3] Some studies have also found evidence consistent with the sector-specific model but only in the case of import-competing sectors (Mayda and Rodrik 2005).

[4] See Hafner-Burton et al. (2017) for a review of this literature.

2017). Those studies posit that, when trade shocks hit a specific region, income effects are not restricted to those working in affected sectors but are broadly felt by residents in that region.

More directly and related to this chapter, scholars have found that localized income shocks from trade with China cause a higher vote share for the Democrats (Che et al. 2022) and push voters to political extremes (Autor et al. 2016) in the United States. In Europe, import shocks from trade with China are associated with an increase in support for nationalist and isolationist parties (Colantone and Stanig 2018b), and to a general shift to the right among the electorate (Broz et al. 2021).

Below, we report the results of a national survey conducted in Brazil, which investigates how localized income shocks related to trade with China affect individuals' perception of integration with the country as posing an opportunity or a risk to Brazil.

13.2.1 *The Survey: Trade and Brazilians' Perceptions of China*

Do trade shocks from China affect Brazilians' perceptions of its main trade partner? To answer this question, we conducted a stratified survey in Brazilian municipalities that experienced strong income shocks associated with import and export from trade with China, as calculated by Costa et al. (2016), and also in a control group of residents in areas unaffected by Chinese trade.

Costa et al. retrieved data from the Brazilian Institute of Geography and Statistics to determine changes in labor market outcomes of regions producing manufacturing goods affected by rising Chinese import supply and localities specializing in raw materials demanded by China, for four decades: 1980s, 1990s, 2000s, and 2010s. Our analysis uses the 2010 estimates, which are the closest to the survey. The calculation of export and import shocks is described in detail in the Appendix.

With these data in hands, an online survey company[5] conducted a survey of perceptions of economic integration with China, fielded in September 2018. To capture variation in trade shocks, localities were classified into three strata, according to whether they experienced large import shocks, large export shocks, or neither.

Overall, 15 percent of the national population lives in municipalities that suffered export shocks larger than US$1,190 per worker, and 23 percent of the national population lives in municipalities that suffered import shocks larger than US$880 per worker. The resulting stratified national sample of 1,352 cases was selected to be

[5] We hired the company Netquest, which is certified by ISO 26362 standards for online access panels and carries out the questionnaires online. For more information, see www.netquest .com.

representative of these proportions at a subnational scale, and it is described in Table 13.A.1 in the Appendix.

Each respondent was asked the question "How much do you agree with the sentence: stronger ties with China will bring more risk than opportunities to Brazil," with answers varying along an ordinal scale ranging from "strongly disagree," to "strongly agree," our main dependent variable [RISKOPPORTUNITY].[6]

The survey gathered additional relevant information on individuals' educational level [EDUCATION] and income [INCOME], which according to the factor-endowment model, should have a negative impact on views about trade in developing nations.[7] Information was also gathered concerning self-reported ideology [IDEOLOGY], a self-reported scale ranging from 1 to 10, where 1 represents extreme left-wing beliefs and 10 indicates extreme right-wing beliefs, age of the respondent [AGE], and sector of employment (agriculture/extractivism, manufacturing, and services) [EMPLOYMENT].

The main model of interest can be defined as follows:

$$RiskOpportunity_i = \beta_{...}Threshold + \beta IS_l + \beta XD_l + \beta_{...k}Individual_i$$

where INDIVIDUAL denotes individual characteristics, l represents locality and i represents one individual.

13.2.2 *Results*

The models presented below test the hypotheses that individuals' perception of China as predominantly a risk (rather than opportunity) should increase/decrease with the magnitude of the import/export shock suffered by her locality. We used ordered logit models as they preserve the maximum amount of the information in the dependent variable without imposing linearity on the underlying relationship between the explanatory variables and the five-point scale on which individual responses are calibrated (Mayda and Rodrik 2005).

Model 1 includes only individual characteristics as explanatory variables (See Table 13.1). Model 2 adds the main variables of interest, that is, import and export shocks to the respondent's locality. Model 3 adds sector of employment together

[6] Questions about trade or investment were intentionally avoided since the goal was to capture individuals' appraisals of China as a partner to Brazil.

[7] Our sample is, on average, more educated than the Brazilian average – by design, because we stratified the sample to guarantee variation in our main variable of interest, that is trade shocks. We do not find this problematic, though, because here our interest is on the Sample Average treatment Effects (SATE), and not with the Population Average Treatment Effect (PATE); that is, we are not using our sample to estimate a parameter in the Brazilian population but rather to estimate the association between quantities in our sample. For this, the main requisite is that we have adequate variation in these quantities in each group, which we do (see Miratrix et al. 2018).

TABLE 13.1 *Respondents' assessments of ties with China*

	Model 1 RISK-OPPORTUNITY	Model 2 RISK-OPPORTUNITY	Model 3 RISK-OPPORTUNITY	Model 4 RISK-OPPORTUNITY
Gender	0.255	0.252	0.261	0.263
	(0.143)	(0.143)	(0.144)	(0.143)
Age	−0.0151*	−0.0151*	−0.0147*	−0.0147*
	(0.00700)	(0.00704)	(0.00712)	(0.00713)
Income	0.00311*	0.00318*	0.00330*	0.00331*
	(0.00153)	(0.00155)	(0.00159)	(0.00159)
Education	−0.0933**	−0.0936**	−0.0905**	−0.0919**
	(0.0313)	(0.0313)	(0.0315)	(0.0317)
Ideology	0.0239	0.0220	0.0232	0.0233
	(0.0191)	(0.0194)	(0.0198)	(0.0196)
Import shock per capita		0.456***	0.450***	0.416**
		(0.126)	(0.130)	(0.141)
Export shock per capita		0.0810	0.0957	0.0932
		(0.0677)	(0.0764)	(0.0756)
Works in manufacturing			0.234	−0.00938
			(0.172)	(0.272)
Works in agro-extractive activities			−0.744	−0.866
			(0.928)	(1.361)
Works in manufacturing × Import shock				0.308
				(0.206)
Works in agro-extractive × Export shock				0.0825
				(0.477)
Cut 1	−2.992***	−.917***	−.873***	−2.882***
	(0.310)	(0.317)	(0.329)	(0.325)
Cut 2	−1.278***	−1.200***	−1.153***	−1.161***
	(0.313)	(0.321)	(0.333)	(0.330)
Cut 3	0.716*	0.799*	0.848*	0.842*
	(0.311)	(0.319)	(0.333)	(0.330)
Cut 4	2.743***	2.828***	2.878***	2.872***
	(0.348)	(0.357)	(0.371)	(0.368)
Observations	1,352	1,352	1,352	1,352
AIC	3,630.1	3,629.2	3,630.1	3,633.1

Note: The dependent variable RISKOPPORTUNITY is "Stronger ties with China will bring more risk than opportunities to Brazil." All models are estimated through ordered logit. In parentheses, standard errors clustered at a microregional level. Statistical significance: * $p < 0.05$, ** $p < 0.01$, *** $p < 0.001$.

with trade shocks, and model 4 contemplates an interaction of sector of employment and trade shocks. The rationale is that those employed in the manufacturing industry should be more sensitive to import shocks, while those employed in agriculture should be more responsive to export shocks.

The interactive effects of Model 4 are not significant, meaning that at an individual level, there are no differences in the import shock for those working in manufacturing and in export shocks for those working in agro-extractive sectors. This implies that within a specific area, being employed in a sector that experiences losses or gains does not significantly impact views of China compared to other residents. These findings strengthen the argument that when trade shocks are localized, their income effects extend beyond employees in the directly affected industry, encompassing those working in non-tradable sectors within the same locality. In other words, the impact of trade shocks on attitudes toward China is not limited to those directly employed in the affected sector but also affects individuals working in other industries in the same geographical area.

Among various individual attributes, education emerges as the most crucial factor. Brazilians with higher levels of education are less inclined to perceive relations with China as risky. This observation is particularly noteworthy, given the scarcity of high-skill labor in the country. It suggests that education likely influences attitudes such as cosmopolitanism or exposure to free-trade ideas, rather than being solely determined by economic factors (Hainmueller and Hiscox 2006; Ardanaz et al. 2013). Furthermore, the research findings align with existing literature, indicating that men and older citizens tend to view integration with China more favorably. On the other hand, although income shows statistical significance, its practical relevance in shaping attitudes appears to be minimal.

Most importantly, results reveal that the residents of municipalities hit by import shocks are more likely to perceive integration with China as a risk to Brazil. This finding is robust across model specifications. Export shocks produce no equivalent effect, though; residents in areas that benefited from export shocks do not find ties with China any more as an opportunity than those living in unaffected localities.

When expressed as average marginal effects, we observe that a unit increase in import shocks per worker increases the chances that an individual views China more as a risk than as an opportunity. The probability of strongly agreeing or agreeing that China is a risk rather than an opportunity is 18 percent when the shock per worker is US$ 266, the national average, and grows to 25 percent when the impact is US$ 1,220, the top decile, and 33 percent when the impact is US$ 2,140, the maximum observed in the sample. Equivalent average marginal effects for export shocks do not present statistically significant effects (Figure 13.3). Figure 13.A.2 in the Appendix expresses findings as predicted probabilities from the logistic models.

These results highlight an asymmetry in the responses to China among residents in regions that have either benefited or been adversely affected by Chinese trade. We posit that these divergent reactions are likely influenced by the information disseminated by individuals working directly in sectors exposed to Chinese markets and competition. Our hypothesis is that individuals employed in companies directly impacted by Chinese competition are cognizant of China's role in their losses,

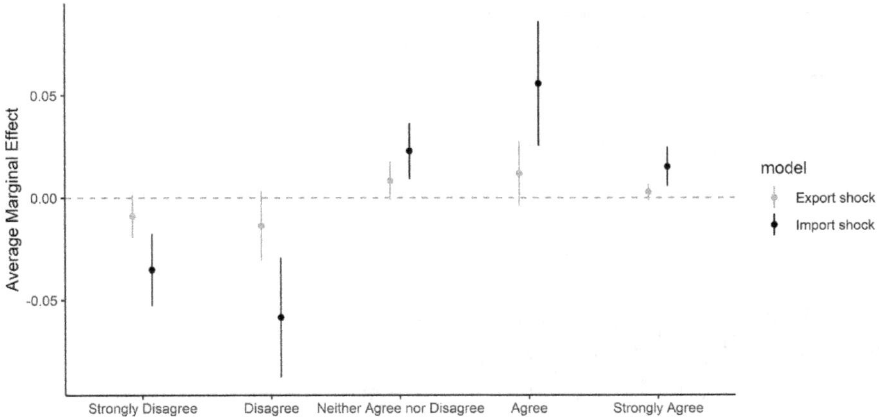

FIGURE 13.3 Average marginal effect of one-unit increase in import shock and export shock on the probability of seeing China as a risk.

whereas those working in businesses benefiting from Chinese imports may not readily associate those benefits with China.

One way to test this hypothesis is by examining how business associations that represent companies that are winners and losers from Chinese trade refer to China. The National Industry Confederation (CNI) and the National Confederation of Agriculture offer an interesting illustration of the same asymmetries observed among residents of localities benefited and harmed by Chinese trade.

Articles posted on the CNI website, in reference to China, frequently mention Chinese protectionism, complain about the low value added of Brazilian exports to China, defend subsidies for Chinese products, and point to Chinese unfair competition in Latin America, among other negative topics. Many suggest that Brazil should not recognize China as a market economy (Urdinez and Masiero 2015). The website of the National Confederation of Agriculture (CNA), conversely, often refers to China altogether along with other Asian markets, and rarely credits the boom experienced by Brazilian agribusiness to the country, but to the "competitiveness of Brazilian producers."

We can also observe those different responses to China in local news. It is easy to find newspaper articles citing industries hurt by what is often depicted as Chinese "unfair competition." "Ball made in China thrashes in price and knocks down competition in Brazil,"[8] "Chinese competition swallows markets for Brazilian products,"[9] "Fashion pole, Prado neighborhood, suffers from Chinese competition,"[10] "Competition with garlic from China affects income of 12,000 producer

8 "Bola feita na China goleia no preço e derruba concorrência no Brasil Estado de Minas" – Economia – 5/19/2014.

9 "Concorrência chinesa engole mercados de produtos brasileiros," G1 – Economia – 2/3/2011.

10 "Polo de moda, bairro Prado sofre com concorrência chinesa," Brasil 247 – 7/19/2012.

families,"[11] "Invasion of Chinese products closes industries in Brazil,"[12] "Chinese competition worries the Capixaban printing industry."[13]

These examples suggest that residents of localities heavily affected by Chinese competition have elements to blame the country for their economic decay. We found no equivalent of such news associating the success of commodity producers to China.

13.3 WHY ARE WINNERS APPARENTLY INDIFFERENT TO CHINA?

The asymmetry of responses between winners and losers from trade is not new to the literature. Studies on lobbying traditionally assume that special interest groups (SIGs) who spend the most effort on lobbying and other political activities should be the ones to get the most government support. This contrasts, however, with the so-called losers' paradox – the disproportionate support losing industries receive relative to winning ones (Hufbauer and Rosen 1986; Hufbauer et al. 1986; Ray 1991). After all, lobbying to reverse losses and lobbying to secure new gains should be equally attractive to interest groups.

Baldwin and Robert-Nicoud (2007, 1064) suggest that the explanation for this puzzle relies on the so-called NIMBY (not in my backyard) syndrome. Consistent with prospect theory's claim that losses loom larger than equivalent gains (Kahneman and Tversky 1979; Jervis 1992), special interest groups seem to fight harder to avoid losses than they do to achieve benefits from government in trade-related activities.

Mayda and Rodrik (2005) note this same asymmetry in individual support for protectionism. Based on large-N survey data from several developed and developing countries, they conclude that individuals employed in import-competing industries are more likely to favor trade restrictions, compared to those that work in non-trade sectors. Individuals employed in export-oriented sectors, however, are not significantly less predisposed to trade restrictions.

The tendency to blame competitors for negative import shocks while ignoring the role of trade partners in fostering favorable export shocks is also in line with what psychologists label the "self-serving bias" – the human tendency to blame others for losses, while taking credit for gains (Shepperd et al. 2008; Larsen 2021).

It should not be surprising, thus, that individuals are more sensitive to the losses caused by Chinese competition – business closures, neighbors, and family job losses – than to the benefits brought by the expansion of the Chinese market. We should not be surprised, either, that losers blame China for their losses, whereas

[11] "Concorrência com alho da China afeta renda de 12 mil famílias de Produtores," *Canal Rural* – 4/25/2019.

[12] "Invasão de produtos chineses fecha indústrias no Brasil" – *Revista Exame* 9/18/2011.

[13] "Concorrência chinesa preocupa Indústria gráfica brasileira" – *Folha de Londrina – Economia*, 6/23/2013.

winners fail to recognize the relevance of the expansion of Chinese markets to the prosperity they have enjoyed since the early 2000s.

In addition to self-serving bias and the asymmetric effects of losses relative to gains, some characteristics of the Brazilian commodity market help explain players' indifference toward China. Brazilian exports of agribusiness goods amount to US$84.9 billion, with the Chinese market representing 34 percent. This share reaches 79 percent in the case of soybeans, almost twice the share of chemical wood pulp (39 percent) and meat of bovine animals (47 percent) (Li et al. 2022). Specialists estimate there are 243,000 soy producers in Brazil, and that the soy supply chain generated around 1.4 million jobs.

Given the significant dependence of soy exports on the Chinese market, one might reasonably anticipate that soy producers would be among China's most fervent advocates in Brazil. Interestingly, we find no evidence in support of that. There are hardly any references to China on the websites of any of the APROSOJAs (the Brazilian state and national associations of soy producers), and none of these associations publicly repudiated anti-China declarations from the Bolsonaro administration.

On the contrary, the APROSOJAs frequently aligned with producers of other grains, predominantly corn, and beef, in support of Bolsonaro, seemingly unconcerned about his adversarial stance toward China. During the presidential campaign of 2022, the state of Minas Gerais branch of APROSOJA (APROSOJA-MG) released an open letter in support of the re-election of President Bolsonaro. The letter invited farmers, ranchers, and rural workers, that is, the entire *productive* sector, to work together "day and night" to support the re-election of President Bolsonaro, in their words a president "aligned with the wishes of the productive sector."

We conjecture that the low levels of vertical integration in the soybean market help explain this paradox. Brazilian producers sell their grains to storage units, which can be cooperatives and state and public companies. They also sell to industrial companies, which will produce soybean meal, crude, and refined oil, or directly to big trading companies such as the American multinationals ADM, Bunge and Cargill, the Chinese Cofco, or the Brazilian Amaggi, among others. As in any commodities market, prices are set internationally.

This structure implies that producers are distant from their end markets, having poor information about the impact of Chinese markets on prices and, therefore, their performance. Many producers do not even know that China is their main consumer market or has an office in the country. It was only in 2020 that the Brazilian Ministry of Agriculture opened a Chinese division. It is not surprising, thus, that soy-producing associations ignored when the Foreign Relations Minister Ernesto Araujo attributed the responsibility for the coronavirus pandemic to China and compared Chinese lockdowns to Nazi camps.

In fact, the only public defense of Brazil-China relations came from Mr. Blairo Maggi – dubbed "the soy king" – a former Minister of Agriculture, senator, and governor of the State of Mato Grosso, whose family owns Amaggi. Different from other soy producers, Amaggi operates in all stages of the agribusiness supply chain, including logistics and exports of agricultural commodities like soy and corn. The company owns soybean crushing and fertilizer blending factories, manages small hydropower plants (SHPs), and invests in photovoltaic power plants to harness solar energy in its main farms and warehouses. As such, unlike other companies that distribute their soy through intermediaries, Amaggi directly engages with importing markets. Consequently, its management, and most probably its employees, possesses a deep understanding of the pivotal role that the Chinese market plays within the Brazilian commodity sector.

We devise a few strategies to test the hypothesis that lack of vertical integration is what prevents employees in soy-producing firms – and, ultimately, residents of soy-producing municipalities – from realizing the benefits they accrue from Chinese markets. The first strategy is by comparing differences in approaches to China among associations that represent soy producers, such as the APROSOJAs, vis-à-vis associations that represent the soy industry, more exposed to end markets. An example would be the Brazilian Association of Vegetable Oil Industries (ABIOVE).

An alternative test of this hypothesis could be to compare the APROSOJAs with associations that represent more vertically integrated sectors like meat, such as the Brazilian Association of the Brazilian Association of Animal Protein (ABPA). We plan to explore this hypothesis in future research.

13.4 CONCLUSION

This chapter examined whether localized import and export shocks associated with growing trade with China affect Brazilians' views about economic integration with the country. The analyses presented leveraged a recently published dataset that calculates import and export shocks from China, per worker, at the municipal level in Brazil (Costa et al. 2016). Thanks to a commodity-for-manufacture pattern of trade between the two countries, along with the fact that both industry and agribusiness activities are geographically concentrated in Brazil, the distribution of trade shocks is highly skewed in the country. This implies that few localities experience strong shocks, whereas the majority are unaffected.

The main argument advanced in the study was that when trade shocks are localized, attitudes about trade and trade partners should respond to income shocks that occur at the local level. As such, responses to these shocks should not be restricted to those employed in losing industries but rather spread to other *residents* working in the service sector in the same locality.

The chapter presented the results of a national survey aimed to test whether income shocks related to international trade influenced residents' views of Brazilian ties with China. It tested the hypothesis that those who live in localities hit by import (export) shocks should see ties with China as posing predominantly a risk (opportunity) to Brazil.

Results offered support for these hypotheses but only among losers from Chinese trade; import shocks affected residents' assessments of China, while export shocks did not. Sectors of employment did not affect responses under any specification, either independently or as a moderator of the impact of shocks.

We discussed how the results align with prospect theory's idea that losses have a stronger impact than equivalent gains (Kahneman and Tversky 1979; Jervis 1992). Additionally, we highlighted previous research indicating that special interest groups are more motivated to avoid losses rather than pursue benefits in government-related trade activities.

We also suggested that the structure of the Brazilian commodity sector can help explain why winners of Chinese trade seemed indifferent to their main market. Taking soy as an example, we argued that limited vertical integration separates producers from their end markets, leaving them unaware of the influence of the Chinese markets on prices and their own performance.

Ultimately, these findings extend the research on losers of globalization beyond the developed world, which so far received most of the attention in the literature. They suggest that, in countries where mechanisms of compensation are known to be scarce, asymmetric responses to losses from trade may be a potential driver of the backlash against globalization.

REFERENCES

Ansolabehere, S., M. Meredith and E. Snowberg 2014. "Mecro-Economic Voting: Local Information and Micro-Perceptions of the Macro-Economy." *Economics and Politics* 26(3): 380–410.

Ardanaz, M., M. V. Murillo and P. M. Pinto 2013. "Sensitivity to Issue Framing on Trade Policy Preferences: Evidence from a Survey Experiment." *International Organization* 67(2): 411–437.

Autor, D. H., D. Dorn and G. H. Hanson 2016. "The China Shock: Learning from Labor-market Adjustment to Large Changes in Trade." *Annual Review of Economics* 8: 205–240.

Baldwin, R. E. and F. Robert-Nicoud 2007. "Entry and Asymmetric Lobbying: Why Governments Pick Losers." *Journal of the European Economic Association* 5(5): 1064–1093.

Broz, J. L., J. Frieden and S. Weymouth 2021. "Populism in Place: The Economic Geography of the Globalization Backlash." *International Organization* 75(2): 464–494.

Che, Y., Y. Lu, J. R. Pierce, P. K. Schott and Z. Tao 2022. Did trade liberalization with China influence US elections? *Journal of International Economics* 139: 103652.

Colantone, I. and P. Stanig 2018a. "Global Competition and Brexit." *American Political Science Review* 112(2): 201–218.

2018b. "The Trade Origins of Economic Nationalism: Import Competition and Voting Behavior in Western Europe." *American Journal of Political Science* 62(4): 936–953.

Costa, F., J. Garred and J. P. Pessoa 2016. "Winners and Losers from a Commodities-for-manufactures Trade Boom." *Journal of International Economics* 102: 50–69.

Cruz, J. E., G. d. S. Medina, and J. R. d. O. Júnior 2022. Brazil's Agribusiness Economic Miracle: Exploring Food Supply Chain Transformations for Promoting Win–Win Investments. *Logistics* 2022, 6(23): 23–42. https://doi.org/10.3390/logistics6010023

Fordham, B. O. and K. B. Kleinberg 2012. "How Can Economic Interests Influence Support for Free Trade?" *International Organization* 66(2): 311–328.

Hafner-Burton, E. M., B. L. LeVeck and D. Victor 2017. "No False Promises: How the Prospect of Non-Compliance Affects Elite Preferences for International Cooperation." *International Studies Quarterly* 61(1): 136–149.

Hainmueller, J. and M. J. Hiscox 2006. "Learning to Love Globalization: Education and Individual Attitudes toward International Trade." *International Organization* 60(2): 469–498.

Hiscox, M. J. 2002. "Commerce, Coalitions, and Factor Mobility: Evidence from Congressional Votes on Trade Legislation." *American Political Science Review* 96(3): 593–608.

Hufbauer, G. and H. Rosen 1986. *Trade Policy for Troubled Industries. Policy Analyses in International Economics*. Washington DC: Institute for International Economics.

Hufbauer, G., Berliner, D. and K. Elliot 1986. *Trade Protection in the United States: 31 Case Studies*. Washington DC: Institute for International Economics.

Jenkins, R. 2015. "Is Chinese Competition Causing Deindustrialization in Brazil?" *Latin American Perspectives* 42(6): 42–63.

Jensen, J. B., D. P. Quinn and S. Weymouth 2017. "Winners and Losers in International Trade: The Effects on US Presidential Voting." *International Organization* 71(3): 423–457.

Jervis, R. 1992. "Political Implications of Loss Aversion." *Political Psychology* 13(2): 187–204.

Kahneman, D. and A. Tversky 1979. "Prospect Theory: An Analysis of Decision under Risk." *Econometrica* 47(2): 263–292.

Kaltenthaler, K., R. Gelleny and S. Ceccoli 2004. "Explaining Citizen Support for Trade Liberalization." *International Studies Quarterly* 48(4): 829–851.

Kleinberg, K. B. and B. O. Fordham 2010. "Trade and Foreign Policy Attitudes." *Journal of Conflict Resolution* 54(5): 687–714.

Larsen, M. V. 2021. "How Do Voters Hold Politicians Accountable for Personal Welfare? Evidence of a Self-Serving Bias." *The Journal of Politics* 83(2): 740–752.

Li, W., M. Zhou, C. Kou C, M. J. Nonnemberg, U. M. Lima, S. Q. A. Bispo, M. Araújo and F. Pedrosa 2022. "China-Brazil Agricultural Trade Research." Technical Note No 7 – Department of International Political and Economic Relations, Institute of Applied Economics (IPEA).

Lü, X., K. Scheve and M. J. Slaughter 2012. "Inequity Aversion and the International Distribution of Trade Protection. *American Journal of Political Science* 56(3): 638–654.

Mansfield, E. D. and D. C. Mutz 2009. "Support for Free Trade: Self-interest, Sociotropic Politics, and Out-group Anxiety." *International Organization* 63(3): 425–457.

Margalit, Y. 2012. "Lost in Globalization: International Economic Integration and the Sources of Popular Discontent." *International Studies Quarterly* 56(3): 484–500.

Mayda, A. M. and D. Rodrik 2005. "Why Are Some People (and Countries) more Protectionist than Others? *European Economic Review* 49(6): 1393–1430.

Milner, H. V. and D. H. Tingley 2011. "Who Supports Global Economic Engagement? The Sources of Preferences in American Foreign Economic Policy." *International Organization* 65(1): 37–68.

Oliveira, G. d. L. T. and M. Schneider 2016. "The Politics of Flexing Soybeans: China, Brazil and Global Agroindustrial Restructuring, *The Journal of Peasant Studies* 43(1): 167–194.

Paz, L. S. 2018. "The Effect of Import Competition on Brazil's Manufacturing Labor Market in the 2000s: Are Imports from China Different?" *The International Trade Journal* 32(1): 76–99.

Ray, E. 1991. "Protection of Manufactures in the US." In: D. Greenaway (Ed.), *Global Protectionism: Is the US Playing on a Level Field?* London: Macmillan.
Rho, S. and M. Tomz 2017. "Why Don't Trade Preferences Reflect Economic Self-Interest?" *International Organization* 71(S1): S85–S108.
Rogowski, R. 1989. *Commerce and Coalitions: How Trade Affects Domestic Political Alignments*. Princeton: Princeton University Press.
Sabet, S. 2016. *Feelings First: Non-material Factors as Moderators of Economic Self-interest Effects on Trade Preferences*. Unpublished manuscript, Cambridge, MA.: Harvard University.
Schaffer, L. M. and G. Spilker 2019. "Self-Interest versus Sociotropic Considerations: An Information-based Perspective to Understanding Individuals' Trade Preferences." *Review of International Political Economy* 26(6): 1266–1292.
Scheve, K. F. and M. J. Slaughter 2001. "What Determines Individual Trade-Policy Preferences?" *Journal of International Economics* 54(2): 267–292.
Shepperd, J., Malone, W. and K. Sweeny 2008. "Exploring Causes of the Self-Serving Bias." *Social and Personality Psychology Compass* 2(2): 895–908.
Spring, J. 2018. "Soy Boom Devours Brazil's Tropical Savanna." *Reuters*. www.reuters.com/investigates/special-report/brazil-deforestation/, accessed on 28 August 2018.
Urdinez, F. and G. Masiero 2015. "China and the WTO: Will the Market Economy Status Make any Difference after 2016?" *Chinese Economy* 48(2): 155–172.

Appendix

13.A.1 CALCULATION OF EXPORT AND IMPORT SHOCKS

The criteria to define these three groups were based on a conservative rule: municipalities in the top quartile of the import shock (above US$ 880 per worker) and municipalities in the top quartile of the export shock (above US$ 1190 per worker). Municipalities below the threshold in both serve as our control group (Figure 13.A.1).

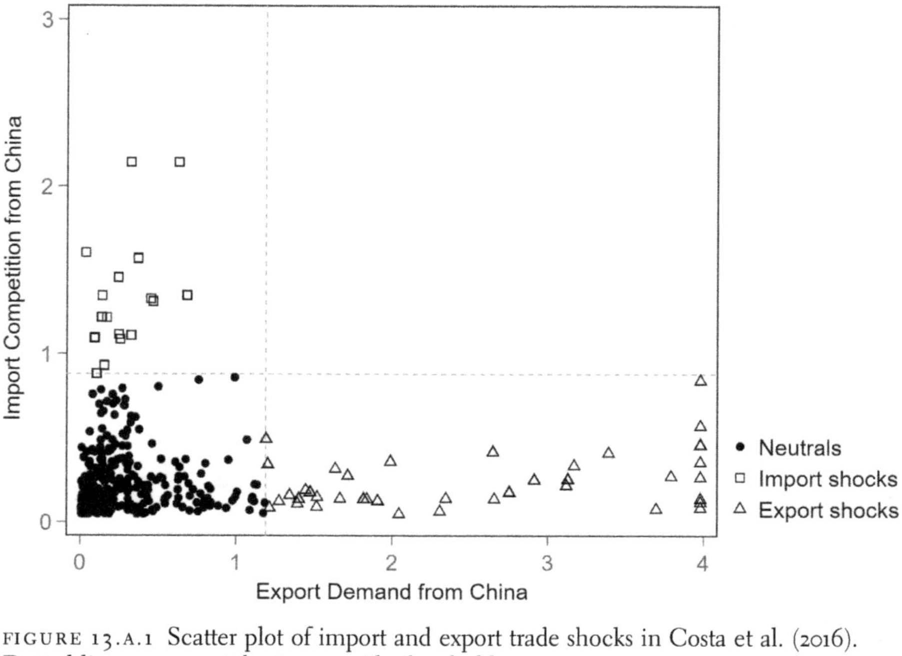

FIGURE 13.A.1 Scatter plot of import and export trade shocks in Costa et al. (2016). Dotted lines represent the top quartile threshold.
Source: Authors' own elaboration.

The shocks are calculated with data from the IBGE to calculate the impact of imports and exports for four decades: 1980s, 1990s, 2000s, and 2010s. The shocks are calculated using eighty-two traded goods sectors, including twenty-four agricultural sectors, eight extractive sectors, and fifty manufacturing sectors. We restrict our analysis to the 2010 estimate, as it is the closest to our study. For each microregion (m), they estimate export shocks (*XD*) using data on trade with China for each sector (*j*), as follows:

$$XD_m = \sum_j \frac{L_{mj,}}{L_{Bj,}L_{m,}} \Delta X_j$$

The variable $L_{mj,}$ is defined as the size of the workforce in sector j within microregion m, while $L_{Bj,}$ and $L_{m,}$ are the Brazil-wide workforce in sector j and the total workforce in microregion m, respectively. ΔX_j represents change in the value of exports from Brazil to China between 2000 and 2010. Similarly, for each microregion m, they estimate import shocks (*IS*), using data on trade with China for each sector j, as follows:

$$IS_m = \sum_j \frac{L_{mj,}}{L_{Bj,}L_{m,}} \Delta I_j$$

where ΔI_j represents change in imports of Brazil from China in the same period (Costa et al. 2016, 55). Shocks are measured in thousands of 2010 US dollars per worker. The data reveal that between 2000 and 2010, the average Brazilian microregion received an import competition shock from China of US$260 per worker and an export demand shock of US$466 per worker. Both variables are highly skewed to the right, implying that a low percentage of microregions suffered large export or import shocks from China.

TABLE 13.A.1 *Survey sample composition by municipality*

Municipality	Microregion code	State	Region	Cases
Ag. Urbana de São Luis	21002	Maranhão	North-East	49
Aracajú	28011	Sergipe	North-East	4
Araraquara	35024	São Paulo	South-East	8
Araxá	31023	Minas Gerais	South-East	8
Assis	35039	São Paulo	South-East	10
Barreiras	29001	Bahia	North-East	4
Belém	15007	Pará	North	79
Belo Horizonte	31030	Minas Gerais	South-East	182
Blumenau	42012	Santa Catarina	South	11
Bragança Paulista	35048	São Paulo	South-East	8
Brasília	53001	Distrito Federal	Center-West	14
Campo Grande	50902	Mato Grosso do Sul	Center-West	10
Cuiabá	51901	Mato Grosso	Center-West	15
Curitiba	41037	Paraná	South	49

(*continued*)

TABLE 13.A.1 (*continued*)

Municipality	Microregion code	State	Region	Cases
Divinopolis	31043	Minas Gerais	South-East	8
Florianópolis	42016	Santa Catarina	South	5
Formiga	31044	Minas Gerais	South-East	2
Fortaleza	23909	Ceará	North-East	20
Franco da Rocha	35058	São Paulo	South-East	7
Goiânia	52010	Goiás	Center-West	12
Guarapari	32010	Espírito Santo	South-East	7
Guarulhos	35059	São Paulo	South-East	21
Ipatinga	31039	Minas Gerais	South-East	8
Itaguaí	33017	Rio de Janeiro	South-East	4
Itapecerica da Serra	35060	São Paulo	South-East	15
João Pessoa	25022	Paraíba	North-East	5
Joinville	42008	Santa Catarina	South	14
Jundiaí	35047	São Paulo	South-East	10
Limeira	35027	São Paulo	South-East	9
Macaé	33901	Rio de Janeiro	South-East	28
Maceió	27011	Alagoas	North-East	6
Manaus	13901	Amazonas	North	41
Marilia	35901	São Paulo	South-East	49
Maringá	41009	Paraná	South	9
Mogi das Cruzes	35062	São Paulo	South-East	20
Natal	24018	Rio Grande do Norte	North-East	6
Osasco	35057	São Paulo	South-East	28
Palmas	41918	Paraná	South	12
Paracatu	31002	Minas Gerais	South-East	4
Paranavaí	41917	Paraná	South	3
Passos	31047	Minas Gerais	South-East	8
Pato Branco	41027	Paraná	South	6
Pelotas	43901	Rio Grande do Sul	South	53
Piracicaba	35028	São Paulo	South-East	9
Poços de Caldas	31051	Minas Gerais	South-East	13
Porto Velho	11901	Rondônia	North	8
Recife	26901	Pernambuco	North-East	20
Ribeirão Preto	35014	São Paulo	South-East	6
Rio de Janeiro	33018	Rio de Janeiro	South-East	61
Salvador	29021	Bahia	North-East	19
Santos	35063	São Paulo	South-East	8
São Jose dos Campos	35050	São Paulo	South-East	22
São Paulo	35061	São Paulo	South-East	220
Senhor do Bomfim	29917	Bahia	North-East	5
Sorocaba	35046	São Paulo	South-East	21
Uberlandia	31018	Minas Gerais	South-East	4
Valença	29907	Bahia	North-East	4
Vitoria	32009	Espírito Santo	South-East	59

13.A.2 COMPOSITION OF THE STRATIFIED NATIONAL SAMPLE

13.A.3 PREDICTED PROBABILITY OF CONSIDERING CHINA A RISK OR AN OPPORTUNITY

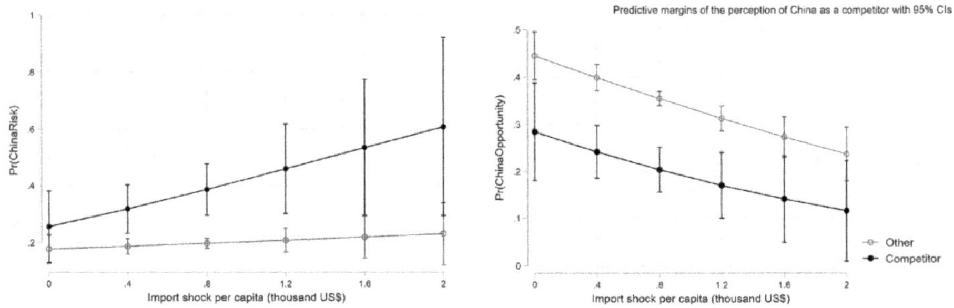

FIGURE 13.A.2 Predicted probabilities for ChinaRisk and ChinaOpp from logistic models for import trade shocks conditioned on an individual's perception of China as a competitor.
Source: Authors' own elaboration.

Index

Note that page numbers in bold represent tables, while those in *italics* represent figures.

For EU product safety concerns, contact us at Calle de José Abascal, 56–1°,
28003 Madrid, Spain or eugpsr@cambridge.org.

www.ingramcontent.com/pod-product-compliance
Lightning Source LLC
LaVergne TN
LVHW011704200926
848484LV00004B/1068
* 9 7 8 1 0 0 9 5 6 8 0 8 1 *